Norumbega Reconsidered:
Mawooshen
and the
Wawenoc Diaspora

The Indigenous Communities of the Central Maine Coast in Protohistory: 1535 – 1620

**Questions, Controversies, Paradigms, and Uncertainties
Maps and Annotated Bibliography**

H. G. Brack

Davistown Museum Publication Series Volume 4

ISBN 0-9769153-2-4

Third Edition

Copyright © 2006, 2008, 2010 by Harold G. Brack
Davistown Museum
ISBN 0-9769153-2-4
ISBN13 978-0-9769153-2-4

Cover photos:
Top: Marcus Lescarbot, (1609). *Histoire de la Nouvelle France*. Paris: Chez Jean Milot. Map inserted between pages 480 and 481. Map title: Figure de la Terre Neuve Grande Riviere de Canada et Cotes de l'Ocean en la Nouvelle France. Via Archives of Canada
http://www.canadiana.org/ECO/PageView?id=901e3bd4d1&display=36652+0539
(This is the map reprinted in Bourque, 2001, pg. 114).

Bottom: Section of map by Jean Boisseau, 1643, Engraving, hand colored, 35.0 x 55.0 cm. This map is a reproduction of Champlain's 1632 map in his *Les Voyages*. Courtesy Osher Map Library.

Cover design by Cory R. Courtois
Pages Plus (www.pagesplusme.com)

Ordering information

This publication may be ordered from or purchased at any of the following locations:
Online at
www.davistownmuseum.org

The Davistown Museum, 58 Main Street, Liberty, ME 04949 (207) 589-4900
Davistown Museum Office, PO Box 144, Hulls Cove, ME 04644 (207) 288-5126
The Liberty Tool Co., Main Street, PO Box 346, Liberty, ME 04949 (207) 589-4771
Captain Tinkham's Emporium, 34 Main Street, PO Box 321, Searsport, ME 04974
Hulls Cove Tool Barn, 17 Breakneck Road, Bar Harbor, ME 04609 (207) 288-5126
Maine Artists Guild Bookshop, Main Street, PO Box 346, Liberty, ME 04949

Copies will also be available at many Maine bookshops and local museum shops.

Pennywheel Press
P.O. Box 144
Hulls Cove, ME 04644

Norumbega:
What was it? Where was it?
Who lived there, and where did they go?

Section of map by Samuel de Champlain, *Carte geographique de la nouvelle franse en son vray meridian*, in his *Les Voyages,* 1613.

This publication is dedicated to Maine archaeologist James S. Petersen, who was murdered in Brazil in 2005.

Published by
The Davistown Museum
Liberty, Maine

Pennywheel Press
P.O Box 144
Hulls Cove, Maine 04644

Assistant Editors: Beth Sundberg, Kerry Hardy, Chuck Marecic

Many thanks to Judith Bradshaw Brown for editorial suggestions and to Keith Goodrich for assistance with the bibliographies.

Acknowledgements

This publication was made possible by a grant from MBNA, a donation from the Barker Steel Co. LLC, and research support from the Jonesport Wood Co., Inc.

We would also like to thank:
Merryspring Park, Camden, ME
College of Atlantic Thorndike Library
Liberty Tool Company
Osher Map Library
Penobscot Marine Museum
Maine State Library
Ne-Do-Ba: Abenaki in Western Maine website: www.avcnet.org
Pennacook Nation website: www.cowasuck.org
Abenaki History website: tolatsga.org

Author's note

The current edition includes a variety of new citations, essays, maps, and a guest essay by Kerry Hardy, director of Merryspring Park, in Camden, Maine. Readers of this revised edition please note that our website version is regularly updated and will contain new information, opinions, research publication citations, and corrections as received at the museum office in Hulls Cove.

Norumbega Reconsidered: Mawooshen and the Wawenoc Diaspora

OYSTER BEDS, DAMARISCOTTA RIVER, LINCOLN COUNTY, MAINE.

Figure 1 Rufus King Sewall, 1895, Ancient voyages to the western continent: Three phases of history on the coast of Maine, pg. 24.

Table of Contents
Main Text

Appendices

Annotated Bibliographies

Preface
The Wawenoc Diaspora: A Lost Chapter in Maine History

I have always been drawn to history, curious about what happened in the places I've lived and visited in the centuries before I got there. For the past thirty six years, my attention has focused on New England's maritime and industrial history, a natural outgrowth of my business of seeking, buying and selling old woodworking tools. More recently, I founded and am curator of The Davistown Museum, a regional tool, art, and history museum in Liberty, Maine. Sources that both piqued and satisfied my interests include the many history books I discovered in the stacks at the Maine Historical Society, the historically significant sites I found on my tool-buying journeys along the back roads of coastal Maine and New England, the stories told by old timers selling their tools, the content of local and regional history texts that I salvaged from attics and barns, and the Native American tools, artifacts, and hoards that I found in New England tool chests and collections, and, more recently, the Internet. In my reading and conversations, I frequently came across mention of the Wawenocs, pre- and protohistoric Native American residents of the coastal New England region that I traversed on my tool picking trips between Boston and West Jonesport, and later Hulls Cove. I began to study their history, which posed some compelling questions that I researched and present in *Norumbega Reconsidered*.

I began my research in 1975, when I became a lifetime member of the Maine Historical Society and spent hours in the stacks and reading room, immersing myself in historical society publications, town histories, and Williamson's (1832) *History of the State of Maine*. I found frequent reference to the Wawenoc Indians as the principal indigenous community of the central Maine coast. While navigating the peninsulas of coastal Maine, I frequently encountered place names such as Pemaquid, Pentagoet, Medomak, Muscongus, and Narramissic, footprints left by the Native American communities, including the Wawenocs, who populated the area in previous centuries. I had long been intrigued by the phenomena of colonial roads following ancient Indian pathways throughout New England, such as the Old Connecticut Path to the west of Boston, near where I grew up. I observed similar patterns in Maine.

When I read Snow's (1980) *The Archaeology of New England*, I was startled by his casual dismissal of the Wawenoc community: *"Wawenoc Indians, who appear in many later documents, were simply residents of the coastal drainages between the Kennebec and Penobscot that I have chosen to lump with the Kennebec"* (my italics) (Snow, 1980, pg. 61). By the late 1980s and early 90s, I noted that a completely new view of Maine's ethnohistory had developed, purportedly based on "new research" and "French sources," that extended Snow's dismissal of the Wawenoc community by deleting all reference to the traditional Abenaki communities described by Williamson and many other writers. Major Maine and maritime peninsula historians Bourque (1989), Baker et al. (1994), Judd and Churchill (1995), and Prins (1996) eliminated mention of the Wawenoc community. I became intrigued by this rapidly changing interpretation of Maine's ethnohistory and began notes for writing what would become *Norumbega Reconsidered* to examine what happened to the Wawenocs and why.

In 1999, I opened The Davistown Museum in Liberty, Maine, to exhibit my growing collection of historically significant tools and art. A major museum mission involves the recovery, study, and exhibition of hand tools that document regional, state, and local history, particularly the maritime culture of coastal New England until the end of the wooden ship-building era. That mission led me to research and write about the history of the area in which the museum is located. I continued to encounter evidence of indigenous communities, who lived in Maine and New England prior to European settlement, in my research and on the back roads I traveled while acquiring tools. I found trips down the old Mast Trail (Route 220) from Montville and Liberty (Davistown Plantation) to Route 1 in Waldoboro and then south past Salt Bay and the Damariscotta shell middens to be particularly evocative of that Native American presence.

My concern about where the Wawenocs had gone in pre- and protohistoric Maine and in history books since 1980 climaxed in 2001 with the publication of Bourque's (2001) important history, *Twelve Thousand Years: American Indians in Maine.* He firmly established what I now refer to as the Bourquian paradigm, which dismisses English accounts that refer to the Wawenocs and other Abenaki communities in favor of French accounts that do not. In 2003, I began to write a revised edition of *Norumbega Reconsidered*, tracing accounts, both English and French, of coastal Maine and New England Native American communities.

My research and my personal experiences lead me to conclude that the traditional English narrations of Maine's ethnohistoric past are surprisingly consistent with French sources and that the Wawenocs should be recognized as an important component of the Native American confederacy of Mawooshen. *Norumbega Reconsidered* explores the contemporary ethnohistoric eradication of the tribal identity of the Wawenoc Indians and the literature that preceded it and reconsiders the narratives and journals of French explorers and observers, including Samuel de Champlain and Father Pierre Biard. Many of their observations undermine contemporary arguments for eliminating reference to the Abenaki communities of coastal Maine, including the Wawenocs. I hope that a reconsideration of Norumbega, Mawooshen, and the Wawenoc diaspora will reinstate the Wawenocs and other extinct Abenaki communities to their deserved place in the narrative of Maine's protohistoric and historic past.

Introduction

Norumbega Reconsidered explores the questions, controversies, and uncertainties about the ethnic identity and historical significance of the Wawenoc Indians of the central Maine coast, their residence in the Norumbega bioregion and their participation in the Native American trading confederacy of Mawooshen. The presence of the Wawenoc community living on the central Maine coast prior to 1620 has been noted by writers and historians for almost 300 years. In 1989, Maine's state archaeologist, Bruce Bourque, suggested (*Ethnicity on the Maritime Peninsula 1600 - 1759*) an alternative to traditional narrations about Maine's historic past. He claimed that Etchemins of Maliseet/Passamaquoddy descent were the inhabitants of the central Maine coast at the time of European contact. Bourque and others cite Marc Lescarbot's 1609 map and selected commentary by Champlain and Biard in their journals as supporting the new paradigm. As a result of the widespread circulation of publications such as *American Beginnings* (Baker, 1994) and *Twelve Thousand Years* (Bourque, 2001), the new "Bourquian" paradigm of the ethnicity of the indigenous communities of the central Maine coast has gained wide acceptance. Concurrently, narrations or descriptions of the robust communities living on the Maine coast at the time of European contact (1535 – 1620) have been minimal in comparison to archaeological documentation of indigenous communities in prehistory or historical descriptions of events and warfare after 1620.

This study asks and attempts to answer the following questions. Who were the Wawenocs? Where did they live, and why did they disappear from our landscape and our history books? What do older historians have to say about this community? How do contemporary revisionists' interpretations differ from traditional commentary? I conclude that denoting Wawenocs as "Etchemin" (the French term for Native Americans of New Brunswick and Eastern Maine) obscures, submerges, and excludes the role of the Wawenocs in Maine's protohistory. No Wawenocs survived to defend their language, traditions, or historical significance. The contemporary renaming of their communities and culture as "Etchemin" eliminates an important chapter in Maine history. A review of French sources such as Champlain, Lescarbot, and Biard suggests that the Wawenocs were "Almouchiquois" (Eastern Abenaki), and not "Etchemin" (Maliseet/Passamaquoddy), as shown on Lescarbot's map of 1609 and as Bourque and others have repeatedly asserted since 1989.

Numerous French and English historians and observers and the Native Americans captured by George Waymouth and interviewed in England (Purchas, 1626) attest to a vigorous, highly populated and socially, politically, and militarily active network of indigenous communities living on the Maine coast at the time of European contact (1525 – 1620). The rich ecology of the Gulf of Maine in protohistory further supports these observations. Uncertainties about the ethnicity and intercommunity relations of these earlier inhabitants of Maine, especially of those living between the Kennebec and Penobscot rivers, have nevertheless characterized recent writings on this topic.

Use of the generic term "Etchemin" to describe this network of villages, formerly known as the territory of the Wawenoc Indians, obscures and submerges their ethnic identity, complex social hierarchy, intercommunity relationships, historical significance, and the impact of their encounter with European traders and settlers. The new paradigm of "Etchemins" as the indigenous residents living along the central Maine coast at the time of contact with Europeans raises questions that are examined in the following text.

What was the ethnicity of the "Etchemins" denoted on Marc Lescarbot's 1609 map? Were they of Passamaquoddy/Maliseet descent, as alleged by several noted contemporary ethnohistorians? Or did these communities, formerly considered one of four important Abenaki (Abenaque) communities in Maine by English settlers and writers (e.g. Williamson, 1832) and more recently denoted as "Eastern Abenaki," constitute a distinct ethnic entity, which later came to be known as the Wawenoc Nation? Are French sources such as Champlain, Lescarbot, and Biard consistent in their description of an "Etchemin" community living along the central Maine coast at the time of contact? What is the significance of the Champlain map of 1632 showing "Almouchiquois" (Eastern Abenaki), not "Etchemins" living on the central Maine coast? What links, if any, exist between these settlements on the central Maine coast, described in the narration of the Land of Mawooshen (Purchas, 1625) as a confederacy of indigenous trading communities lying between the Saco River and Schoodic Point, and the meaning and significance of Norumbega, the geographical area on either side of the Penobscot River, noted on many early maps (Baker, 1994)? What are the implications of the uncanny overlapping of the confederacy of Mawooshen with the land of Norumbega? *Norumbega Reconsidered* presents my commentary on the context and substance of this ethnohistoric conundrum, followed by a guest essay by avocational historian Kerry Hardy and an annotated bibliographic citations giving voice to the wide range of viewpoints about Maine's ethnohistoric past.

After studying many primary and secondary sources, I have reached a number of conclusions, which I present and support in *Norumbega Reconsidered*. My first conclusion is that French sources, such as Champlain, Lescarbot, and Biard can, ironically, be interpreted as supporting the traditional English interpretation of Maine's ethnohistory as consisting of Abenaque, later denoted as Eastern Abenaki, communities living in the area between the Saco River to the west and the Penobscot River to the east at the time of European settlement. Lescarbot's map of 1609 was a tentative protohistoric rendition of the geography and ethnicity of the Maine coast and may have been influenced by the recent victory of the Micmac and Maliseet/Passamaquoddy over the "Almouchiquois" (Abenaki communities of coastal Maine) in the battle of Saco in 1607. Ironically, Lescarbot's poem (Appendix D) describing this attack of Etchemins on the Eastern Abenaki of the central Maine coast clearly contradicts his 1609 map. Two decades of additional French contact with the indigenous communities of the Maritime Peninsula resulted in Champlain's map of 1632, which radically redrew Lescarbot's 1609 map. Champlain's 1632 map, though well known, is not cited by advocates of the new Bourquian paradigm. The Champlain map clearly denotes "Almouchiquois" as the inhabitants of Mawooshen and the central Maine coast.

Secondly, my research leads me to conclude that the Wawenocs of the central Maine coast are an especially notable example of an extinct Eastern Abenaki community whose history has been "submerged" (Quinn, 1990, pg. 12) by the appearance of a subsequent culture which conquered, acculturated and/or exterminated its predecessors.

Third, I contend that the Native American confederacy of Mawooshen was an interrelated network of indigenous communities in a bioregion rich in marine resources long known as Norumbega and that the Wawenocs were an important community in this confederacy.

Finally, I observe that the use of the generic terms "Etchemin" and "Wabanaki" obscure and submerge the ethnicity, complex social organization, intertribal relationships, and historical significance of the Wawenocs and other ethnic groups, such as the Androscoggins and the Canibas, who are no longer represented by surviving tribal nations. Also submerged or eliminated is the community specific impact of their encounter with European traders and settlers and the pathogens that accompanied them.

The revision of the traditional understanding of the ethnicity of the indigenous communities of Maine's past has squelched acknowledgement of the vibrancy, complexity, and diversity of the Native American communities in a regional confederacy (Mawooshen) and in a bioregion (Norumbega) that flourished in protohistory. The Bourquian paradigm of an oversimplified, streamlined protohistoric "French description" of ethnic communities during the critical years of first contact, 1534 – 1620, is inaccurate and an unacceptable component of this process. The Bourquian paradigm ignores how closely French sources often correlate with traditional English narratives in their description of the indigenous communities of Maine's protohistoric past. The process of Euro-American ethnohistoric "naming," or rather renaming, the indigenous communities of the central Maine coast eliminates one of the most interesting chapters in Maine history. My intention is to restore that chapter to its rightful place.

Protohistory and the Phenomenon of Naming

Protohistory is the interface of history with prehistory, expressed in the phenomena of literate cultures making written observations about non-literate societies of the same era. *The description of the countrey of Mawooshen,* published by Samuel Purchas in 1625 and derived from interviews with Native Americans kidnapped by George Waymouth near Pemaquid in 1605 is an example of this interface; the Abenaki communities described are "protohistoric." Likewise, the Lescarbot map of 1609 noting Etchemins as the inhabitants of the central Maine coast is protohistoric. The fundamental disagreement among late 20th century writers pertaining to the ethnicity of these communities prior to the tumultuous years of European contact and the great pandemic that followed is about the cultural affiliation, ancestral homelands, and historical significance of these indigenous peoples. The fact that ethnocentric historians of European descent renamed these indigenous communities only complicates the puzzles of protohistory. The Etchemins of Lescarbot's 1609 map did not call themselves by that name.

Our traditional description of "Wawenoc" as the cultural community living on the central Maine coast in prehistory may also be derived from a later renaming of these residents, who may have described themselves with obscure Algonquin names that have been lost to us (Hardy, 2006). Williamson's (1832) description of the Wawenocs as one of the principal Abenaki tribes of Maine may have arisen after their seventeenth century migration to St. Francis and then to Bécancour in Canada. No reference to the word "Wawenoc" can be dated prior to this diaspora (Hardy, 2006). Gordon Day (1998) provides an incisive analysis of the confusion between the Androscoggin community that lived along the river of that name circa 1600 and the later Arasagunticooks of the St. Francis refugee community in Canada, which evolved during and after the French and Indian wars and was an ethnic composite of Androscoggins, Rockameka, Amaseconti, and other small inland dwelling New England Abenaki communities. After 400 years of European settlement and history writing, conflicting opinions about the ethnicity of Maine's indigenous communities remain unresolved.

Bourque's *Twelve Thousand Years* (2001) is among the most important, comprehensive, and thorough texts published on Native Americans in any part of North America in any decade. There is only one minor problem in this text: Bourque presents a radically revised interpretation of the identity and historical significance of the indigenous communities living on the central Maine coast between the Penobscot and Kennebec rivers at the time of European contact. Insofar as 20th century observers can understand and reconstruct the cultural history of indigenous peoples and not erase their presence with oversimplified maps and ethnohistoric generalizations, some questions still lie unanswered. Who were the Wawenocs? Was this the name they used to describe themselves in protohistory? What was their ethnicity? What is their historical significance and their relationship to Norumbega and the land of Mawooshen? Why not reconsider the meaning of Norumbega and attempt to understand and acknowledge the indigenous communities that once lived between the Penobscot and Kennebec rivers but left no descendents to defend their existence, traditions, or the significance of their ancestral homelands?

In the preface to *Twelve Thousand Years*, Bourque writes: "What's in a name? Sometimes a great deal - for both ethnic groups and the larger society - the parties who, in a sense, negotiate ethnic identity through names" (Bourque, 2001, pg. 9). He continues: "The English generally employed group names strictly to place of residence... We have often chosen French terminology over English because it is generally less geographically determined and reflects a greater intimacy with the region's nature populations" (Bourque, 2001, pg. 12).

Herein lies the key to the Wawenoc diaspora. Who is it that "negotiate(s) ethnic identity through names"? Are not names such as Canibas, Penobscot, Pigwacket, Maliseet, and Passamaquoddy derived from the indigenous communities who were identifying themselves, not "negotiating" their ethnic identity? And if the name Wawenoc was not the term that the indigenous communities of the central Maine coast used to identify themselves in protohistory, then who were the residents of the central Maine coast at this time and what did they call themselves? Who is now negotiating the ethnic identity of the Wawenoc community, if not the late 20th century ethnohistorians writing texts that use names like "Etchemin," a term that neither the Wawenocs nor any other indigenous community used to describe themselves, let alone "negotiate" their ethnic identity?

And who had the greater intimacy with the Wawenoc and other Abenaki communities on the central Maine coast west of the Penobscot River, specifically between 1602 and 1675? How many thousands of English interacted with this indigenous population? How many dozens of French observers? How many hundreds of raiding Micmac fighters, and why?

Where, in fact, are the ethnohistorians who will provide an "accurate and balanced portrayal" (Bourque, 2001, pg. 104) of the indigenous residents of the central Maine coast at the time of European contact? Why not let all the voices of the past and present, of whatever ethnicity, including Native Americans, French, English, et al, provide those "fragments of historic information" for that rhythmic reconstruction, deconstruction, and reconstruction of the stories of ethnohistory?

In the postmodern era now littered with the scalps of deconstructed historians of every description, the bad news is that ethnocentricity is a given. The good news is that, in the age of post-deconstruction, storytelling is okay again. We now recognize that a single scientifically verifiable definition of protohistoric culture of the past is not possible. This opens the door for students of Maine history to listen to a wide range of opinions expressed by a diversity of voices: contemporary commentators, Native American descendents of the indigenous communities of the past (although, in the case of the Wawenocs, none survived), and antiquarian writers and historians. Individual students can then arrive at their own conclusions about the prehistory, protohistory, and history of Maine and its indigenous inhabitants. Many questions may never be satisfactorily answered. How boring would a definitive study of 12,000 years of Native Americans in Maine be if there were not at least one controversial question to prompt a reconsideration of Maine's fascinating ethnohistoric past?

The Wawenoc Diaspora

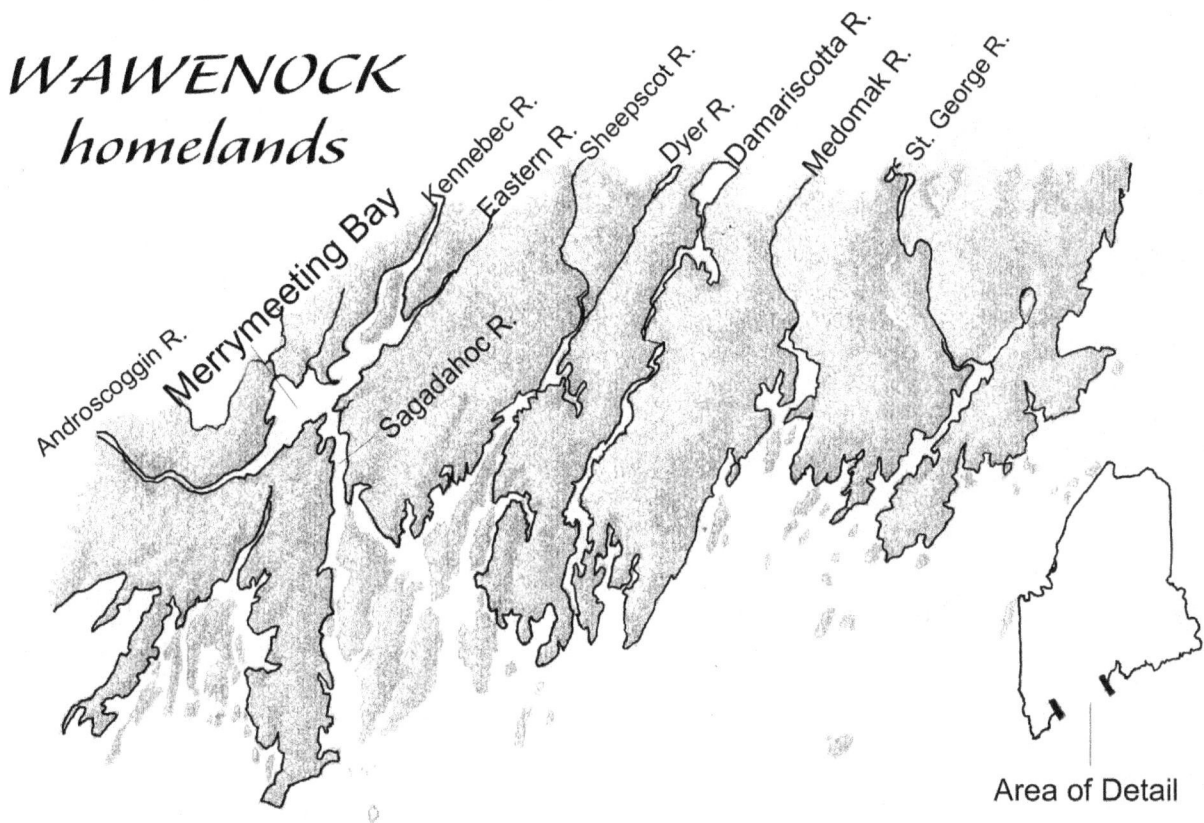

Drawn by Kerry Hardy, Merryspring Nature Center

Figure 2 Wawenock homelands courtesy of Kerry Hardy.

The Wawenoc diaspora was a component of the dispersal of the populations of a series of tidewater villages along the central Maine coast, including Canibas villages to the west of the Wawenoc homelands and Penobscot communities to the east, during the tumultuous years of contact with European visitors, 1602 - 1620. Exact boundaries between these cultural groups may never be known and may never have existed. The names by which these communities called themselves in prehistory are also unknown to us. Traditional community boundary lines used by Euro-Americans were not part of the political and social milieu of indigenous communities. This lack of historical data explains, in part, the wide variety of often contentious opinions about the ethnicity these communities in pre- and protohistory.

Until the late 20th century, the English oral and written history of Maine included the Wawenoc Indians as one of four Abenaque (later Eastern Abenaki, now Wabanaki) communities living west of the Penobscot River at the time of European contact and settlement. The term "Etchemin" had been traditionally used by most ethnohistorians to denote indigenous Algonquin communities living north and east of the Penobscot River, including the Passamaquoddys and Maliseets (also now called Wabanaki). The Penobscot community has been denoted both as Etchemin (Williamson, 1832; Bourque, 2001) and as Eastern Abenaki (Snow, 1980; Russell, 1980). The English version of Maine's ethnohistory records the Wawenocs as living between the Penobscot and Kennebec Rivers and includes such important historical figures as Samoset and at least one Bashebas (head chieftain or regional leader) of the land of Mawooshen. Canibas (Kennebecs), Androscoggins, Pigwackets, and Massachusetts, all called Almouchiquois by the French, lived along the rivers to the west of the ancestral homelands of the Wawenocs. Wawenoc communities were located on the Sheepscot, Damariscotta, Medomak, and St. Georges rivers to the east of the Kennebec River.

The Wawenoc diaspora began with the destruction of a large part of the Wawenoc community during the intertribal fur trade wars, also called the beaver wars, and was followed by massive casualties in the great pandemic of 1617 – 1619. A small component of the Wawenoc community survived to participate in the French and Indian wars and relocated to Bécancour Canada, after the fall of Norridgewock (1724.)

It is impossible to date the beginning of warfare over the control of fur trapping and trading in New England, but such conflicts in the St. Lawrence River valley began in the mid-16th century. Long-standing conflicts between indigenous communities of eastern Canada and corn-growing Iroquois were centuries old (Parkman, 1983). Micmacs, called Souriquois by the French, and living outside of Maine in Nova Scotia and northern New Brunswick, raided cornfields in the lower Kennebec region prior to Champlain's 1605 visit (Champlain, 1912). Supplied with firearms by French traders, Micmacs and Etchemins attacked the "Almouchiquois" at Chouacouet, the Abenaki horticultural community at Saco in 1607, in a dispute over trade goods, including beaver pelts. This attack killed the Saco River sagamore, Olmechin. Soon after, the English killed the Bashebas superchief whom Champlain had previously met in the Penobscot River in 1604 and who was fighting alongside Olmechin (Biard, 1611, in Thwaites, 1898). Lescarbot's French poem recounting this attack and describing the sagamores and superchiefs who participated in it is reprinted in Appendix D. These attacks were later extended to include the Kennebec (Canibas) and Wawenoc communities on the central Maine coast. A second round of warfare in 1615-1617 killed another Mawooshen Bashebas, probably the Penobscot Asticou.

The intertribal warfare among the indigenous communities in the Gulf of Maine bioregion culminated in the great pandemic of 1617-1619, which killed as much as 95%

12

of the coastal population of Native Americans living between Cape Cod Bay and Schoodic Point to the east of Mount Desert Island. The combination of the unraveling of the confederacy of Mawooshen and the death of a large portion of the population of indigenous communities of the central Maine coast provided an opportunity for both surviving Penobscots from the north and Etchemins from the east to extend their influence and control of the Maine coast westward during these years of upheaval and turmoil. Penobscots and Etchemins were soon joined by a swirl of refugees from southern and central New England, who were fleeing English settlers, smallpox, and, after the beginning of King Philips War (1675), the near certainty of annihilation by well-armed colonists seeking to clear the land of indigenous inhabitants. The relative stability of ethnic communities of the late 16th century along the Maine coast soon evolved into a confusing composite of survivors from the cataclysmic encounter with European settlers and the virgin soil epidemics that accompanied them. The Wawenocs were only one among many indigenous communities first cleared from the land and then erased from our history books.

A more gradual dispersion of Wawenoc remnants occurred as they migrated up the Kennebec River, first to Norridgewock and then, after the beginning of the King Philip's War (1675) and the destruction of Norridgewock (1724), to their final destination at Bécancour in Quebec.

Frank Speck (1928) interviewed the last speaker of the Wawenoc dialect, Francis Neptune, at Bécancour in the early 20th century. The physical destruction and scattering of the Wawenoc community during the period from 1600 to 1763 (Treaty of Paris; demise of New France) has been followed by a modern ethnohistoric diaspora in the late 20th century by the deletion of most or all reference to this community by contemporary historians such as Snow, Bourque, Prins, Churchill, Baker, Salisbury, Morey, and others.

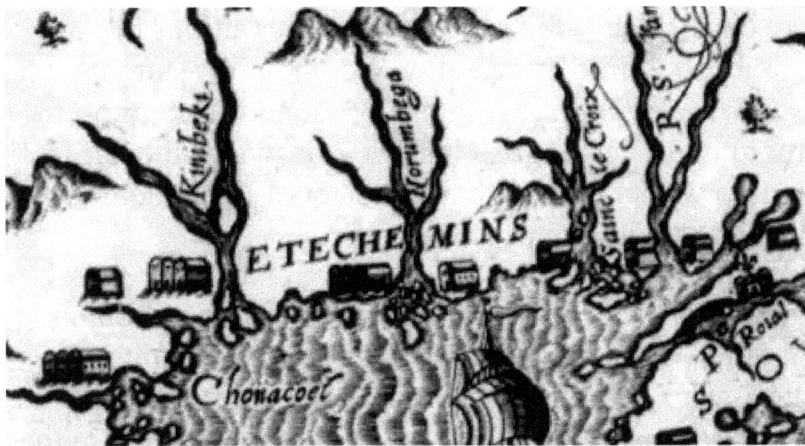

Figure 3 An enlargement of the center of the Lescarbot map on the cover (Lescarbot, 1609c).

Contemporary writers, led by Maine archaeologist Bruce Bourque, cite French sources, especially Champlain, Lescarbot, and Biard, and Micmac (Mi'kmaq) informants to postulate an Etchemin hegemony at the time of European contact stretching from their ancestral homelands in New Brunswick and far eastern Maine west along the entire Maine coast to the Kennebec and Saco rivers.

13

Bourque's revised ethnohistory of the central Maine coast uses French maps of the period, specifically Lescarbot's 1609 map and several observations made in Champlain's journals and denotes "Etchemins" as occupying the areas formerly known as the ancestral homelands of the Eastern Abenaki, including the Androscoggins, Canibas, and Wawenocs. Advocates of the Bourquian paradigm ignore Champlain's definitive map of 1632 that clearly depicts Almouchiquois living on the central Maine coast and numerous conflicting observations in Champlain and Biard's journals.

The current focus on French explorers and observers as the definitive source of information about Maine's ethnohistoric past has been influenced by lingering and justified Native American resentment about the "English [who] viewed and treated Native societies as sub-beings. [Whereas] ...The French were delicate in their dealings with the Wabanaki people." (Soctomah, 2005, pg. 30). The irony of the benign treatment of indigenous communities by the French, in contrast to the cruelty of the English, is that the ascendancy of a politically correct French version of Maine's ethnohistoric past inadvertently erases the memory of and respect for the now extinct indigenous communities of the central Maine coast.

The recent tendency to delete reference to ethnic communities such as the Canibas and Wawenocs occurs in the context of a recent revival of interest in the narrative of the land of Mawooshen. This narrative was derived from interviews of the five Native Americans kidnapped by George Waymouth in his 1605 expedition to the central Maine coast and the Penobscot River. Ferdinando Gorges and others interviewed these captives, recorded their description of Mawooshen, and gave it to Richard Hakluyt (d. 1616), that indefatigable narrator of English voyages to North America. Samuel Purchas published it in 1625. This narrative was recorded and published by English, rather than by French, observers as was Rosier's *A True Relation*, which describes Waymouth's encounter with large numbers of well-organized, well-armed Native Americans living west of the Penobscot River. Both narrations are consistent with later English observations of the Wawenoc community living in the area at the time of and after Waymouth's visit. A recent annotated version of Rosier's *A True Relation* (Morey, 2005) identifies Samoset, long identified as a Wawenoc sagamore in earlier English histories, as one of the natives kidnapped by Waymouth. This assertion will certainly be the subject of lively debate in any future reconsideration of the identity of Waymouth's captives.

The Penobscot Marine Museum in Searsport, Maine used the Lescarbot map of 1609 in a 2005 exhibition at that celebrated George Waymouth's 1605 voyage up the Penobscot and presented the story of Mawooshen, as told in Purchas. Ironically, this exhibition told the story of Mawooshen as recounted in English sources, while using the French map that labels residents living between the Penobscot and Kennebec rivers as Etchemins, not Abenakis. "Marc Lescarbot visited Acadia in 1606, returning to France the following year. A product of his trip was a history of New France. It reports on the knowledge of

14

the Natives collected by the French. His map shows the inhabitants of coastal Maine called themselves Etchemins" (Penobscot Maritime Museum, 2005).

The lingering controversy of the meaning and location of Norumbega, with its uncanny resemblance to the land of Mawooshen and the ancestral homeland of the Wawenocs, provides an additional context for a reconsideration of the English version of Maine's ethnohistory. Although the French lost the Battle of Quebec in 1759 and, thus, control of the North American continent, a contemporary interpretation of an alleged "French version" of Maine's ethnohistory reigns supreme in the late 20th century. Ironically, many French observations and the updated Champlain map of New France in 1632 are consistent with the English version of the ethnicity of Maine's indigenous communities, despite its being criticized as both "ethnocentric" and "geographically" determined (Bourque, 2001). I know of no contemporary Native American commentary on the significance and fate of the Wawenocs as an Eastern Abenaki community.

The English Version of Maine's Ethnohistoric Past

Maine historians writing up until 1950 note the Wawenocs as one of a group of Maine Indian communities, most of which are familiar to Maine residents today. Pigwackets, Androscoggins, Kennebecs, Penobscots, Passamaquoddys, and Maliseets are all an indelible part of Maine's historic past. In 1832, William Williamson, Maine's most eminent 19th century historian, recapitulated 250 years of the oral and written history of Maine's Abenaki Indians and included the Wawenocs as one of Maine's principal indigenous communities. His description of Maine's Indian tribes, both Abenaki and Etchemin, dominated the popular understanding of Maine's ethnohistory until the revisionists of the late 20th century replaced regional names of ethnic units such as Canibas (Kennebec Indians) with generic terms such as "Eastern Abenaki," soon followed by "Wabanaki" and most recently "Etchemins," reviving Lescarbot's anomalous 1609 denotation. Most later 19th and early 20th century historians also utilized Williamson's ethnic descriptions of Maine's indigenous communities, which were based on the collective experience of thousands of English settlers in the Maine midcoast who came here to live after 1607. Williamson frequently cites the numerous earlier observers and historians (Smith, Hubbard, Hutchinson, Sullivan, Belknap, Gookin, Prince) who retell and recall oral and written histories of the many English who had intimate contact with the Wawenoc community, both before the diaspora and with its few survivors, such as Samoset and his father (?), Mentaurmet, of Indiantown Island, Boothbay.

Williamson provides the standard nineteenth century description of the coastal tribes of Maine who lived west of the Penobscot River: "The tribes of the Abenaques were four, 1. the Sokokis, or Sockhigones; 2. the Anasagunticooks; 3. the Canibas, or Kenabes; and 4. the Wawenocks" (Williamson, 1832, pg. 465).

Williamson made the error of describing the Saco River community as Sokokis, a long standing misnomer finally corrected by Day (1998), well over a century later. The Sokokis were the longtime residents of the Connecticut River Valley at and above Greenfield, MA; their earlier presence on the Saco River has never been documented. While the Pigwackets of the Presumpscot River occupied areas of the upper drainage of the Saco River, Day (1998) and other observers note that the actual tribal identity of the Saco River Indians has been lost. Snow (1980) and others now use the term "Massachusetts" to denote this community. The Saco River clearly marks the northern extent of the Massachusetts Indians with their wooden dugouts. To the east, the spruce-root/birch-bark technology of the Eastern Abenaki and a different Algonquin language dialect are clearly indicative of another culture.

Williamson (1832) quotes the following pertinent information from Gorges (1658) about the Tarentine (Etchemin and Micmac) attack on the Wawenocs and their political importance as leaders of the confederacy of Mawooshen at the time of Captain John Smith's 1614 observations:

> …the latter [Taratine] began the war. ...Gorges says, 'his [sagamore's] chief abode was not far from Pemaquid.' His place of immediate residence was probably between that river and Penobscot Bay. ...his political dominions included, at least, all the Indians upon the Kennebec, the Androscoggin, and probably the Saco. Capt. Smith further states... 'they hold the Bashaba to be chief, and the greatest among them.' (Williamson, 1832, pg. 214)

Gorges (1658) goes on to describe the final attack on the Bashebas and his "1,500 bowmen," which signaled the end of the confederacy of Mawooshen and the decline of the Wawenoc community.

Contemporary historians now equate Tarentines with Micmac; earlier historians such as Williamson (1832) included both Etchemins and Penobscots in their definition of Tarentine. The relationship of the Penobscots to either the aggressive Micmacs or the more peaceful Wawenocs during the Indian wars of the early 17th century remains unclear. Early historical narratives, including Lescarbot (1609b), agree that Micmacs and Etchemins (Passamaquoddy and Maliseet) swept down the Maine coast in 1607 to attack the more sedentary villages of the Massachusetts, the indigenous community on the Saco River, and their Abenaki allies from the east, the Androscoggins and Canibas, all called

Figure 4 Boisseau's copy of Champlain's 1632 map. Jean Boisseau, *Description de la Novvelle France*. 1634, Paris. Osher Collection.

"Almouchiquois" by Champlain. In his poem describing this attack, Lescarbot (1609) makes it explicitly clear that the Etchemins, including the Maliseet sagamore Chkouden

(St. John River) and the Passamaquoddy sagamore Oagimont (St. Croix River) were allied with the Micmacs. The "Almouchiquois" they were attacking included the Androscoggin sagamore Marchin, the Canibas sagamore's son Sasanoa, who was killed, and an unidentified Bashebas (superchief), possibly Wawenoc, Canibas, or Penobscot. This poem constitutes a convincing description of an ethnic rivalry between Micmac and Etchemin communities of maritime Canada to the east and Eastern Abenaki communities to the west in coastal Maine. While Lescarbot's map of 1609 might express the political impact of the 1607 victory of the Souriquois and Etchemins at the Saco River, no migration of Etchemins to the central Maine coast followed the attack and victory at Saco. Instead, the Lescarbot map is contradicted by the descriptions in his poem, the contents of which are consistent with Champlain's 1632 map, which denotes Almouchiquois and the Pentagoet living west of Schoodic Point. Ironically, Lescarbot's poem (Appendix D) and other observations by Biard and Champlain validate traditional English commentary on the ethnicity of Maine's indigenous communities.

A probability remains that what was once a friendly relationship based on reciprocity and shared resources between the Wawenocs and the Penobscots became antagonistic when the hunting and trapping Penobscots became caught up in the fur trading conflicts with the aggressive and well-armed Micmac and Etchemin communities to the east of the Penobscot homelands, as the confederacy of Mawooshen began unraveling. Williamson (1832) notes that the French supplied the Penobscot and other Etchemins and Micmacs with firearms during the fur trade wars in Maine (1607 - 1617.) By the time Smith made his observations of a Tarentine front line at the Camden Hills (1614), traditional Penobscot friendship with the Abenaki communities to the west may have evolved into an alliance, if temporary, with the aggressive Micmacs and Etchemins to the east.

Among the most important of all accounts of the indigenous residents of the central Maine coast is Rosier's (1605) narration of the George Waymouth voyage in 1605. Waymouth arrived at Pentecost Harbor near Cushing in May of 1605. From May 30th to June 8th, Rosier describes a constant stream of Natives approaching his ship or its shallop, "a light horseman," attempting to trade and expecting to trade, making numerous references to their nearby superchief, the Bashebas. In his excellent annotated version of Rosier's *Relation,* Morey (2005) asserts that, while the Bashebas spent the summer in Wawenoc territory, he lived further up the Penobscot River, presumably near Indian Island. He also comments on the "social advancement" of these aggressive traders, their persistence, expectations and ability to pursue diplomacy (Morey, 2005, pg. 56-57).

Rosier's description of the encounter of a Waymouth crew member (Griffin) with local Wawenocs illustrates the large indigenous population of the area:

> Griffin at his returne reported, thay had there assembled together, as he numbred
> them, two hundred eighty three Saluages, euery one his bowe and arrowes, with

their dogges, and wolues which they keepe tame at command, and not anything to exchange at all; but would haue drawen vs further vp into a little narrow nooke of a riuer, for their Furres, as they pretended. (Morey, 2005, pg. 63-65)

Declining the invitation to trade, Waymouth then kidnapped the five natives taken back to England. Then followed the second invitation to trade with the Bashebas by another group of natives who, according to Morey (2005), were not aware of the five kidnapped victims imprisoned below the deck of Waymouth's ship, Archangel:

> This day, about one a clocke after noone, came from the Eastward two Canoas ... we vnderstood them by their speech and signes, that they came sent from the Bashabes, and that his desire was that we would bring vp our ship (which they call as their owne boats, a Quiden) to his house, being, as they pointed, vpon the main towards the East, from whence they came, and that he would exchange with vs for Furres and Tabacco. But because our Company was but small and now our desire was with speed to discouer vp the river, we let them vnderstand, that if their Bashabes would come to vs, he should be welcome but we would not remoue to him. (Morey, 2005, pg. 69-70)

Rosier (1605), Champlain (1605), Biard (1611) and Smith (1614) make one of the most interesting observations about Maine's indigenous central coast inhabitants, i.e., that their population numbers were large. Rosier was very clear in noting 283 armed males sailing out of what Morey (2005) identifies as the Gay Island Gut off Cushing's Pleasant Point. Morey suggests they had a winter village ("Penapske-ot") located two miles up the St. Georges River to the east. If all were residents of this village, there would have been a native population of at least 1,000 men, women, and children in just in one lower section of the St. Georges River. This is unlikely; the Natives Waymouth encountered probably came from many villages. Nonetheless, considering that the natives Waymouth kidnapped and many of those coming to trade came from the highly populated Pemaquid - Muscongus Island region to the west of Cushing, population levels for the coastal tidewater areas of Norumbega between the Penobscot and Kennebec rivers could have approached 10,000 residents at that time, well above that estimated by Snow (1980) in his classic *The Archaeology of New England.*

No such detailed narration as that of Rosier exists of the Popham settlers' 1607 encounter with the Wawenocs of the central Maine coast, but the *Relation of a Voyage to Sagadahoc* (Davies, 1880), describing the Popham settlement, includes observations of frequent contacts and constant trading with local Canibas and Wawenocs. Davies also includes descriptions of Captain Popham's encounters with Micmacs, both before and after the battle at the Saco River in 1607. They first encountered Micmac warriors off Cape Sable, coming from Le Heve, Nova Scotia on the way to the Saco River battle. The later meeting was on the Sheepscot River near or below Wiscasset, where the Micmacs noted that they had killed the Kennebec sagamore Sasanoa's son. The author of the

Relation, probably the navigator Davies, also notes "skidwares and Dehanada wear in this fight" (Burrage, 1914), another indication of the close relationship of the Wawenocs and the Almouchiquois, as both were well known Wawenoc tribesmen who had been kidnapped by Waymouth and had just returned to Mawooshen from England.

Smith helps document the disintegration of Mawooshen with his observation that the Camden Hills at Mecaddacut (Camden) constituted a fortress "against the *Tarrantines*" (Smith, 1837, pg. 13). Locke (1859) also noted this dividing line at Mount Battie, which reflects the growing turmoil afflicting the communities of Mawooshen at this time. In 1615 or shortly thereafter, the last Mawooshen Bashebas, possibly Asticou, was slain, and Mawooshen as a political entity ceased to exist.

John Smith's 1614 pre-pandemic narrative (1837) also includes observation of horticultural activity along the Kennebec River. Smith goes on to lament Thomas Hunt's kidnapping of 27 Native Americans to the west of the Sagadahoc, one of the many cruelties inflicted upon indigenous peoples by the English. Smith's detailed descriptions of the New England coast include observations of a vigorous, socially sophisticated network of trading communities along the central Maine coast, vestiges of which still existed after the arrival of English colonists. These earlier observations provide the basis for Williamson's 1832 commentary on the ethnicity of Maine's indigenous communities. Later historians, such as Sewall (1895) and Greene (1906), perpetuate the memory of these thriving communities.

Greene has this comment on the domain of the Wawenocs:

> The two great centers of Wawenock settlement were where the Damariscotta oyster shell deposit exists and about the lower Sheepscot waters, though there were many minor ones. Indications point to this Damariscotta locality as the Norumbegua or Arambec of the ancients, and also as being the residence of the Bashaba, more strongly than any other place. ... There are several reasons why this place is indicated as the chief point in old Mavooshen. It shows to have been the center and abode of a mighty horde of eaters, much greater in extent than any other in America, and one of the largest in the world; it was as nearly central in their territory as any place that could be selected; the quality of the food was better than any other section has shown, being oysters instead of clams, and the ruling element usually takes the best in either civilized or barbarian life; lastly, when the Popham and Gilbert colony was visited by a delegation from the Bashaba, consisting of his brother Skidwares and Nahanada, extending an invitation to visit him, a locality northerly from Pemaquid was indicated by them, and not the lower Sheepscot, where the next greatest aggregation of offal deposit exists. (Greene, 1906, pg. 39 - 40)

Throughout two centuries, Maine's sometimes florid historians make repeated reference to the central Maine coast between the Kennebec and Penobscot rivers as the nexus of trade, an area rich in natural resources, and the center of the confederacy of Mawooshen.

The Bourquian Model: A French Version of Maine's Ethnohistory

An extensive literature exists discussing the presence of Native American communities in New England and maritime Canada, including those along the central Maine coast. An abrupt dividing line separates the writings of some of Maine's contemporary historians and archaeologists from the traditional view expressed by Maine and New England's older historians. Contemporary writers express a range of opinions about the ethnicity of these communities. Prominent commentators, such as Bourque (1989, 2001) have recently adopted an ethnohistorical model of Maine's history, based on an interpretation of the writings and observations of French explorers, which postulate an Etchemin hegemony in the Maine central coast west of the Penobscot River, in contrast to traditional observations of the earlier English settlers and historians recounting a robust Wawenoc community in this area. The revisionists' model of Maine's late pre-historic past splits the confederacy of Mawooshen into three parts, with hunting and gathering Etchemins living as far west as either the Androscoggin or the Saco Rivers, isolated Abenakis in central western Maine, and the mysterious horticultural Almouchiquois living from the Saco River south and west to southern New England. A fourth undisputed component of this ethnohistoric paradigm is the robust, aggressive, trading community of Micmacs (Souriquois) living to the east of Maine in northern New Brunswick and Nova Scotia.

Brasser's chapter, "Early Indian European Contacts," in volume 15 of the *Handbook of North American Indians* (Trigger, 1978), provides a concise summary of the reigning paradigm of the ethnicity of Native American communities in Maine. Brasser must be one of the last writers to have used the currently politically incorrect "T word," tribes, and doesn't include family hunting territories as a factor in indigenous community organizations, ignoring the important contribution of Frank Speck in his study of the Penobscot.

- The local units in New England, Virginia, and North Carolina have been united into confederacies or 'tribes' since the earliest recorded European contacts. These alliances were brought about by the intermarriage of chiefly lineage and by conquest, and their duration depended upon the success achieved in stabilizing these relationships. (pg. 78)
- ...the Indians on the eastern margins of the boreal forest ... *lived by hunting and fishing only and were organized in small, seminomadic bands* [italics added]. (pg. 78)
- *From the Saco River southward the native economy was primarily based on horticulture,* [italics added] and semi-permanent villages were located near the gardens in the river valleys. Both the southern horticulturists and the northern hunters used to spend the better part of the summer along the seashore, where they

gathered and smoked large amounts of fish and shellfish. (Brasser in Trigger, 1978, pg. 78)

Brasser is among the first of the revisionist historians to describe semi-nomadic communities, soon to be called "Etchemins," living to the east of the Saco River in the ancestral homelands of the Eastern Abenaki. This inadvertent and seemingly innocuous description of Maine's indigenous residents transforms the highly populated resource-rich region of Maine's central coast into the homeland of a nomadic hunting and fishing community, erasing the cultural uniqueness of the Wawenoc community, the presence of their ancestral village sites, their participation in the complex trading network of the confederacy of Mawooshen, and their important role in American history. If the Wawenoc community never existed, we need no longer inquire about or document their fate.

Following what he calls "French sources," i.e. Champlain, Lescarbot, and Biard, Bourque (2001) elaborates the revisionist description of Native American communities in Maine at the time of European contact, which Brasser (1978) had first summarized in the *Handbook of the North American Indians*:

> The early French sources name four ethnic groups on the Maritime Peninsula. ... Eastward from the Gaspé and St. John River lived the Souriquois... West of the Souriquois, between the St. John and Kennebec Rivers, lived the Etchemins... By 1605 members of this group were also engaged in the fur trade and in providing guides to the French. In the late seventeenth century, the Etchemins came to be referred to by the French as the Maliseets (or Malicites) between the St. John and Penobscot Rivers and as the Canibas between the *Penobscot* [italics added] and the Kennebec Rivers. (Bourque, 2001, pg. 106)

> West of the Kennebec and as far to the southwest as Massachusetts lived a third people, whom the Souriquois referred as Almouchiquois -- literally 'dog people' -- with whom they had been at war. This group's territory began at the Androscoggin River, which John Smith later named the Almouchicoggin. They were linguistically and culturally distinct from their neighbors to the east, wearing different clothing and hairstyles, using some dugouts in addition to birch bark canoes, and practicing horticulture. (Bourque, 2001, pg. 106)

Bourque's description of the Almouchiquois, including the Androscoggins, often noted to be the Abenaki by other writers, contrasts their lifestyle with that of the mobile hunting bands of the Etchemins and closely resembles the description of the Wawenoc Indians in older English narratives and documents, except for the reference to the dugouts. Bourque and others do not note that the term "dog people" probably derived from the Abenaki habit of using dogs to deter marauding raccoons at corn harvesting season. Bourque then continues, noting Champlain's post-diaspora (1629) description of a robust horticultural community in the upper area of the Kennebec drainage.

Champlain later described a fourth group, the Abenakis, who lived eight days travel south of the newly founded settlement of Quebec at Norridgewock, on the Kennebec River. They lived in 'large villages and also houses in the country with many stretches of cleared land, in which they sow much Indian corn.' (Bourque, 2001, pg. 107)

Bourque's revised description of an inland-dwelling Abenaki population and coastal Etchemins contrasts sharply with the descriptions of most English writers, both antiquarian and contemporary, who classify the coastal populations of Canibas, Androscoggins, Pigwacket, and Wawenoc as Abenaki (later Eastern Abenaki.) Bourque, instead, splits the Eastern Abenaki into two parts: Pigwackets and Androscoggins as Almouchiquois and Canibas as Etchemin. He mentions neither the Wawenoc communities nor the Penobscots, one of the most important participants in the trading network of Mawooshen. That the Canibas lived along the Penobscot River is a most newsworthy assertion; which French narrators made this observation and what is its source?

Baker et al (1994) describe the Abenaki as synonymous with the French Almouchiquois. Snow (1980) describes an Abenaki presence along the entire Maine coast west of the Maliseet/Passamaquoddy homelands and includes the Penobscots as an Abenaki community. If the Bourquian model of Maine's ethnohistory is widely adopted, community and cultural distinctions between Maliseet, Passamaquoddy, Penobscot, and others also disappear, along with many interesting chapters in Maine history. The refugee community at Norridgewock was a coalition of Abenaki survivors. The gradual restriction of Abenaki tribal remnants to inland locations after the fur trade wars and the pandemic of 1617-1619 doesn't mean that they were culturally different from the earlier inhabitants of the Maine coast. Ironically, Bourque then reverts to traditional English designations not used by his French sources: "To the west of Abenaki territory lay a group associated primarily with the Merrimack Valley and known to the English as the Penacooks" (2001, pg. 107). Bourque avoids a discussion of early English narrations or of French observations that contradict his thesis. He does not mention George Waymouth, Mentaurmet, Mawooshen and its villages, the complexity of its trading networks, or the "dynamism" of contact period ethnic interactions.

Bourque only refers to Mawooshen indirectly when he summarizes early observations of the intertribal rivalry limited to only two ethnic groups, the Micmac of Nova Scotia and the Etchemins of coastal Maine:

> Early English explorers in the Gulf of Maine described a rivalry that reflects the
> emergence of European influence there during the late sixteenth and early
> seventeenth centuries. On one side was Bessabez, the supreme Etchemin sagamore
> whom English sources describe as the preeminent leader of a domain that extended

from Frenchman's Bay at least to Saco and possibly as far west as Lac Mégantic in Quebec. On the other side was a group that lived to the east of Bessabez. Known to the English as Tarentines and to the French as Souriquois, they were mainly the ancestors of those who would later be called Micmacs. (Bourque, 2001, pg. 119)

But just a few pages earlier, Bourque noted ethnic dividing lines at both the Kennebec and Androscoggin rivers, not the Saco River, as contended by Brasser and by this description. Bourque makes no mention of the network of trading communities that were the essence of the "domain" of Mawooshen, nor does he elaborate on the complex social hierarchy necessary to sustain this confederacy. Also, Bourque doesn't elaborate on the fact that the sagamores he notes characterize all the villages of Mawooshen, large and small, the identities of many of which are now lost. It was this network of community leaders that provided the basis for the power of a "supreme," "preeminent" superchief, of whatever residential location in Mawooshen. This new paradigm obscures, submerges, and then excludes the role of the Abenaki (Eastern Abenaki), including the Wawenocs, from the protohistory of the central Maine coast.

Bourque also clearly states the now widely accepted revisionist take on European visitors (or lack thereof) in the Gulf of Maine before 1600.

> Contrary to conventional historical opinion, European-Native encounters in the Gulf of Maine were minimal during the remainder of the sixteenth century. The private companies of fishers and whalers, well organized and focused on maximizing their catch during a short season, were not particularly interested in interacting with the Natives, nor in exploring areas beyond their fisheries in the Gulf of St. Lawrence. (Bourque, 2001, pg. 114-115)

Numerous observations litter our history books noting hundreds of fishing and trading vessels visiting St. Johns, Newfoundland, during the summers of the 16th century. The reductionist Bourquian paradigm insists that of the +/- 100,000 English, French, Basque, and Portuguese fishermen and traders who visited the new-found-lands between 1500 and 1600, none ever sailed southwest of Sable Island to explore the Gulf of Maine and the great French Bay (Bay of Fundy). (See also Bourque and Whitehead, 1985). Not mentioned in this description is the encounter of David Ingram (see Hakluyt, 1589) with French fur traders at St. John, NB, in 1569, where, after he hiked from Mexico to the Great Lakes and then to Maine (Burrage, 1887), he obtained passage to Europe with these trading fishermen.

The Confederacy of Mawooshen

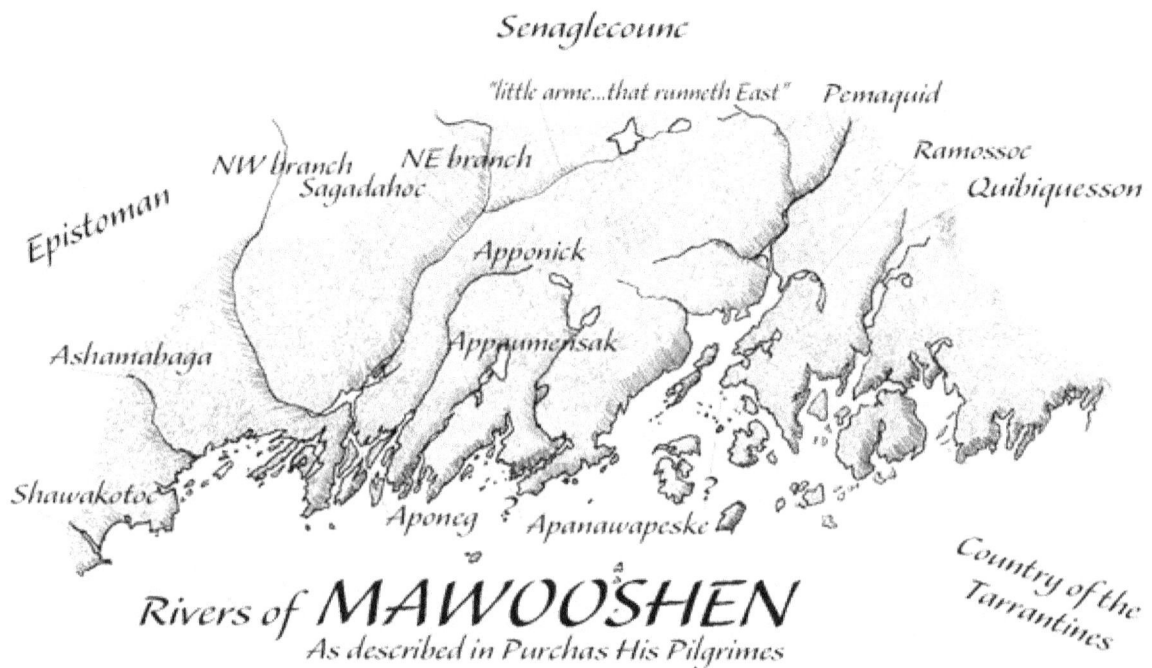

Figure 5 Coastline and rivers of Mawooshen, courtesy of Kerry Hardy.

I believe that the greatest and most enduring mystery of Maine's history is not when or where the Vikings, the Celts, or the Phoenicians landed, if they ever did, but how far and how long the Confederacy of Mawooshen extended in the space and time of Maine's pre- and protohistory? What was its relationship to "Norumbega," a geographical reference occurring frequently on maps issued before 1614? The early writers of New England's past and contemporary writers, such as Snow, make repeated references to the Confederacy of Mawooshen (Moasham, Moassom, Moasson) and to the semi-permanent or permanent villages that were the heart of this ancient dominion of Maine. Prins (1996) utilizes the politically safe generic term "Wabanaki" to describe Mawooshen:

> ...early seventeenth-century European records reveal that Wabanaki tribesmen inhabiting the Maine coast in that period referred to the region from Cape Neddick to Schoodic Point (the end) as Mawooshen. Under this name, they apparently understood an area 'fortie leagues in bredth, and fiftie in length, [comprising] nine rivers, [namely the] Quibiquesson, Pemaquid, Ramassoc, Apanawapeske, Apaumensek, Aponeg, Sagadehoc, Ashamahaga, Shawokotec. [Popham, 1857 and Purchas, 1617] (Prins, 1996, pg. 110)

(For a complete copy of Samuel Purchas' description see the Transcript of Samuel Purchas' Description of Mawooshen in Appendix F.)

While Prins fails to follow up on Purchas' quote and elaborate on the ethnicity, complexity, and fate of Mawooshen, the echoes of Mawooshen can be heard in the writings of Maine historians and explorers all the way back to the first mention of Norumbega. Rufus King Sewall, that stubborn, romantic, florid, and not always accurate Wiscasset historian, is particularly detailed in his description of Mawooshen, both in his *Ancient Dominions of Maine* (Sewall, 1859) and his article on Mavooshen (Sewall, 1896) in the *Lincoln County News*. It is important that Mawooshen was a confederacy of many Maine tribes and may have extended as far as the Massachusetts Indians to the southwest; to the Union River, Mount Desert Island, and Schoodic Point to the east; and far inland to the upper reaches of the Kennebec River watershed. Bourque (2001), Prins (1996), and others insist that this confederacy was Etchemin, ignoring the long tradition of describing Maine ethnic communities west of Schoodic Point as Abenaki, later Eastern Abenaki. Defining the Abenaki communities of Maine as Maliseet/Passamaquoddy in origin, as implied by Lescarbot's 1609 map, raises many questions about the history and culture of the indigenous communities of Mawooshen and how we interpret their interrelationship. Eliminating the Abenaki from the historical narration of Maine's pre and proto-history oversimplifies, obscures, and submerges the ethnicity, identity, and intercommunity dynamics of this unique alliance of Native American communities.

The alternative version of Maine's ethnohistory, repeated again and again in both old state and local histories and contemporary guides and encyclopedias, recapitulates the English version of a robust Abenaki community extending into the Penobscot River region. The confederacy of Mawooshen and its complex trading network was soon enlarged and expanded by contact with the European market economy after 1570 and its need for fish and furs, making Monhegan Island, Pemaquid, Damariscove Island, Boothbay, Pentagoet, and other Gulf of Maine locations such a hubbub of activity in the years just before and after the Plymouth colonists nearly starved to death.

The beginnings of the fur trade wars marked the end of the alliance between the Abenaki, including the Wawenocs, and the Penobscots and Etchemins to the east. The scattering of the Wawenocs coincides with the end of the alliance of the communities of Mawooshen and, uncannily, with the removal of the term Norumbega from maps that would soon say "New France," then "New England." Up until this moment, the Penobscots were part of the confederacy of Mawooshen and, with the Passamaquoddy and Maliseets to the east, participated in its trading networks until the cataclysmic advent of the Indian fur trade wars, which so dramatically altered Maine's ethnohistoric landscape. Until these wars, the Penobscot domain included the Blue Hill-Deer Isle peninsula, Castine, and the west shores of the Penobscot Bay above Camden. Once the fur trade wars started and the Wawenocs were attacked by the Micmacs and Etchemins, the Camden hills became a line of defense against the onslaught of more powerful neighbors to the east (Smith, 1614 [1837]; Locke, 1859). The fur trade wars had begun by the mid-16th century in the St. Lawrence River area. The formerly robust horticultural community noted by Cartier in 1535 at Hochalega (Montreal) was entirely abandoned when visited by Champlain in 1603, (Baxter, 1906) probably due to a combination of the first episodes of intertribal warfare over fur trapping and vending and the epidemics that accompanied contact with European culture. Parkman (1983) suggests that the horticulturalists were driven out by the hunting and trapping Montagnais, and Bourque (2001) notes the later conflicts between the Montagnais, who lived on the north side of the St. Lawrence River, and the Etchemins to the south during the mid-17th century.

After 1635, the turmoil of the fur trade wars, now called beaver wars, involved all of the Algonquin communities of northeastern America in a suicidal conflict with the Iroquoian community of New York and the lower St. Lawrence River valley. By the time of the fall of Quebec in 1759, most of these communities managed to destroy each other with the help of firearms supplied by both the British and the French. In this context, the Micmac attacks on the Massachusetts Indians and the cornfields of the Abenaki in central coastal Maine extend further back in time than Champlain's voyage in 1605 and were a direct result of attempts to control the fur trade in the hunting and trapping territories of the southern New England coast before the great pandemic and the depletion of the beaver population eliminated this region as a source of furs. That Massachusetts itself was once a source of furs and wampum helps explain these attacks. Aptucxet, at the head of Buzzards Bay, with its links to the Dutch trading community to the south, was a component of the florescence of late 16th century and early 17th century trading throughout the Gulf of Maine. That short portage from Aptucxet to Cape Cod Bay was only one link in this mammoth commodity trading network, which included all of Maine and extended down the St. Lawrence River valley to Todussac and Quebec. It was no accident that David Ingram, shipwrecked on the Mexican coast in 1568, could catch a French trading packet from St. John, New Brunswick, to Europe in 1569. He may have known where he was going before he arrived: Norumbega/Mawooshen.

In a recent publication on Mawooshen, Petersen, Blustain, and Bradley (2004) review and expand our understanding of Mawooshen, based on a reexamination of mortuary goods recovered by Warren Moorehead at Sandy Point (Stockton Springs) and Walker's Pond at Brooksville on the Eggemoggin Reach in the 1920's, a location also noted as Norumbega in the DeLorme Maine Atlas (1998). These mortuary goods, now at the Robert S. Peabody Museum of Archaeology, are scheduled for repatriation by NAGPRA, the federal law on repatriating to appropriate tribes mortuary-derived artifacts from old archaeological sites. Petersen et al don't mention the Wawenoc community, nor reference ancient Pemaquid as another Native American trading center, as was the Goddard site at Naskeag, but, nonetheless, they have made a major contribution to the re-evaluation of the role of Mawooshen in Maine's prehistory:

In fact, prehistoric and early historic leadership in Mawooshen was likely based, in part, on control of regional trade on some level. The Etchemin were certainly involved in regional trade during the earliest 1600s. At least one extraordinary prehistoric site, Goddard, would support local participation of the ancestral Etchemin (Maliseet-Passamaquoddy) in a far-reaching regional trade network long before the Contact period. Situated on Naskeag Point at the eastern end of Eggemoggin Reach, Goddard is closer to Blue Hill Bay and Mt. Desert Island than it is to Penobscot Bay proper. Nonetheless, Goddard is rather close to both Sandy Point and Walker's Pond, quite likely representing a direct socio-cultural link with both of them. Goddard was also the scene of a few Contact period burials, along with others in the local area. (Petersen, 2004, pg. 6)

Goddard is primarily attributable to the early-middle portion of the Late Woodland (Ceramic) period, dated about 300-600 years before Sandy Point and Walker's Pond, that is, primarily A. D. 1000-1300 for Goddard, with some earlier and scant later occupations. Goddard can be interpreted as the setting of an intensive prehistoric 'trade fair' and it is not obviously matched anywhere within the broad Gulf of Maine region. If this local trade fair nexus can be verified, then the Mawooshen confederacy had prehistoric roots long before Bashabes came upon the scene and this would be something rather different than most scholars recognize for Mawooshen. (Petersen, 2004, pg. 6)

Most writers on this period of Maine history agree that the Micmacs attacked the confederacy of Mawooshen and defeated them during the fur trade wars. Is Williamson incorrect in alleging that the Etchemins, including the Penobscots, armed by the French, also participated in this attack? Following Bourque, Petersen, et al. (2004) reaffirm the presence of the Etchemins to the east of Mawooshen, who are noted as the ancestors of today's Maliseet and Passamaquoddy communities. This paradigm again raises questions about the unresolved and often unmentioned roles of the Penobscots in these intertribal wars, their former membership in the confederacy of Mawooshen, and the nature of their relationship with the Wawenocs, Canibas, and other tribal communities to the west.

The most intriguing of all the unsolved puzzles of Mawooshen is its relationship to the "Norumbega" noted on the many European maps issued before John Smith relabeled Norumbega, in its broadest context, New England. Champlain called the Penobscot River the River of Norumbega; along with the Kennebec and the Androscoggin, it was a key river in the trading network of Mawooshen. The indigenous residents of the many villages from Indian Island to either shore of the lower reaches of Penobscot Bay were among the most important participants in this trading network. As a bioregion, Norumbega extends both to the east and to the west of the Penobscot River; it can be interpreted as uniformly and uncannily overlapping the land of Mawooshen. There appears to be a direct link between the meaning of "Mawooshen" as a meat, especially shellfish meat-eating culture, and Norumbega, as a geographical environment rich in natural resources. What is the meaning and significance of Norumbega?

The Myths of Norumbega

Visitors to New England, and especially to Maine, will frequently encounter the term Norumbega. *American Beginnings: Exploration, Culture, and Cartography in the Land of Norumbega* (Baker, 1994) provides many of Maine and New England's most respected historians (D'Abate, Quinn, Prins, Morrison, Bourque, Whitehead, Axtell, Churchill, Reid, Baker, etc.) with a forum for a detailed exploration of the meaning of Norumbega, its location, and the identity of the Native Americans who lived here prior to English settlement. Most of the writers in *American Beginnings* follow the lead of Morison (1971), who debunks the 19th century assertion of Norumbega as a Viking name in the introductory chapter of his *The European Discovery of America: The Northern Voyages* and is the foremost among many historians who assert that it is entirely a myth. "Norumbega, apart from the name, which means 'quiet place between two rapids' in Algonkin, was wholly created by European imagination" (Morison, 1971, pg. 464). Morison does, however, introduce a note of lingering doubt, as do the other writers in *American Beginnings*, with his comment on the possible Native American understanding of the meaning of Norumbega: "Nolumbeka in the Abnaki tongue means either a stretch of quiet water between two rapids, or a succession of rapids interspersed by still waters. This exactly fits the Penobscot River above Bangor" (Morison, 1971, pg. 488). This description also applies to many other locations on the central Maine coast. The myths pertaining to Norumbega can be divided into five groups:

- **Norumbega as a Viking outpost**

The most persistent of the Norumbega myths may be that which holds that Norumbega was once a Viking outpost. This myth had particular popularity in the late 19th century and was a subject of numerous articles, essays, and books. The most famous advocate of this theory was Eban Norton Horsford (1891), author of *The Defenses of Norumbega,* a copy of which is on display at The Davistown Museum. Horsford and his followers contended that Norumbega was a Viking settlement located on the Charles River at Auburndale (Newton, MA), with a main port further downstream near Watertown Square. Horsford's folio text includes interesting photographs of early stone work along the river and of an ancient amphitheater within the Mt. Auburn Cemetery. Unfortunately, Horsford provides no evidence that these sites were actually built or inhabited by Vikings.

- **Norumbega as a mythical Native American kingdom**

The earliest European explorers visiting New England first heard of Norumbega as a regional reference contiguous with what Captain John Smith later renamed New England. The name soon came to have unfortunate specific reference to a mythical city of gold and riches. The English sailor David Ingram, shipwrecked on the coast of Mexico, allegedly followed Indian trails all the way to New England before discovering "Arambec," supposedly at the present site of Bangor, Maine, ca. 1568-9. Ingram's infamous and exaggerated description of the wealth of Norumbega published by Hakluyt (1589), in *Principal Navigations,* but withdrawn from subsequent editions (Quinn, 1977) was probably an outgrowth of the previous European discoveries of gold in many of the Central and South American cities that the Spanish explored in the 16th century. After Champlain visited the Bangor site in 1604 and found only the remains of a small village at the junction of the Penobscot River and the Kenduskeag Stream, this version of the meaning of Norumbega was considered as bogus as its later variant, the mythical Viking settlement on the Charles River at Watertown and Newton, Massachusetts. D'Abate and the other contributors to *American Beginnings* (Baker, 1994) explore the linguistic, geographical, and cartographic components of this Norumbega myth in great detail. The name lives on in Maine in the form of inns, mountains, and companies, just as it lived on in Massachusetts in the form of the now defunct Norumbega Park.

- **Norumbega as the Penobscot River**

Champlain (1922), Biard (Thwaites, 1896), and other French sources frequently referred to the Penobscot River as the River of Norumbega. Biard makes this comment in *Jesuit Relations*:

> The Pentegoet is a very beautiful river, and may be compared to the Garonne in France. It flows into French Bay [the bay of Fundy] and has many islands and rocks at its mouth; so that if you do not go some distance up, you will take it for a great bay or arm of the sea, until you begin to see plainly the bed and course of a river. It is about three leagues wide and is forty-four and one half degrees from the Equator. We cannot imagine what the Norembega of our forefathers was, if it were not this river; for elsewhere both the others and I myself have made inquiries about this place, and have never been able to learn anything concerning it. (Thwaites, 1896, pg. 47)

Part of the mystery of Norumbega was its multiple uses, as a designation for New England, a turreted city, a river, and a section of the central Maine coast. Obviously, Biard, Champlain, and English explorers kept hearing the term, sometimes pronounced as Arambec; they just could not find it in a literal sense. European "left" brains were already scribbling their history; the maps they produced are all inscribed "Norumbega," but what and where was it?

- **Norumbega as a cartographic mistake**

When Baker, D'Abate, et al (1994) advanced the argument that the existence of Norumbega was an illusion, an expression of fantasized desires, in essence, a cartographic mistake, they also inadvertently created yet another myth: that Norumbega is only a linguistic sign and "does not represent reality so much as human thought about reality" (D'Abate, 1994, pg. 62). (See Champlain's 1607 map in Appendix A.) In this context Baker, D'Abate, et al conclude that the concept of Norumbega is the result of the European quest for riches, that whole complex of mercantile fantasies that propelled the search for the northwest passage and prompted the European exploration of the major rivers of Maine. The nonexistence of Norumbega is a third contemporary myth, based on the inability to verify, by 20th century historiographic standards, the pre- and protohistoric presence of a regional confederacy without its own written records or maps.

Figure 6 Samuel de Champlain's 1607 map showing Norumbegue as a place name illustrates the confusion about the meaning and location of Norumbega.

A Greenland with few trees, a Cape Cod in an ocean filled with codfish, or any other geographical description protohistorically grounded in an ecology rich in natural resources, oral history, legend, interrelated ethnic communities, metaphor, and local ambiance cannot be subject to scientific verification, according to the contemporary standards of modern Euro-American historians. Norumbega was and is this bioregion of tidewater bays, estuaries, and reversing falls, the archipelago that is the essence of the central Maine coast. Grasping the significance of Norumbega's meaning requires a leap of imagination in order to understand the ubiquitous historical longevity of a Native American metaphor (Norumbega) for a region, a Cape Cod of the People of the Dawn, that flourished for a thousand years before Europeans arrived. As with the other myths, the myth that the Native American region of Norumbega never existed is incorrect.

- **Norumbega as contiguous with Mawooshen**

Perhaps our observation that Norumbega is a bioregion, not a city or a subcontinent, constitutes a fifth myth. Or perhaps the following assertion gets to the core of the true meaning of Norumbega. In *American Beginnings*, at the end of his essay "On the Meaning of a Name: 'Norumbega' and the Representation of North America," D'Abate (1994) concedes that Norumbega may have yet another meaning, raising:

> ...the possibility that even before Europeans began to elaborate their ideas about America, the word 'Norumbega' had had an Indian meaning. To ask for this meaning, as suggested earlier, is to pursue a different line of inquiry, not because names function differently in the minds of Indians but because the history of the set of conceptual relations that 'norumbega' stood for in the minds of sixteenth-century natives cannot be followed as can that of the Europeans. (D'Abate, 1994, pg. 85-87)

D'Abate and other *American Beginnings* editors raise the possibility that Norumbega has a Native American, rather than a Euro-American origin, noting that Norumbega "is a piece of Wabanaki nomenclature of rivers" and carries a meaning similar to quiet waters (D'Abate, 1994, pg. 87). Quinn (1994) makes this comment about traditional conceptions of Mawooshen and Norumbega: "It is the region from Cape Elizabeth northward and northeastward just beyond Mount Desert that was the essential Maine of the maps that we do have and that was the core of the mysterious Norumbega" (pg. 39). This is the region that coincides with what the Native Americans whom George Waymouth kidnapped described as Mawooshen.

William Francis Ganong (1917) explores, in detail, the nuances of the meaning of Norumbega:

> It is easy to find the source of Champlain's Norembegue, for this form of the name, and the stories he controverts, occur in a popular book which ran through seven editions prior to 1605 -- about the time when Champlain was writing (Harrisse, 155), viz., Les Voyages avantureux du Capitaine Jan Alfonce. This work was founded on Alfonse's well-known Ms. Cosmographie of 1544, in which he describes a cape, river, and city of NOROMBEGUE in the region of the present Maine. (Ganong, 1917, pg. 109)

Alfonse was the famous French navigator, born in 1484 as Jean Fonteneau and later adopting the last name of his Portuguese wife, Valentine Alfonse. Alfonse began his navigational career in 1496 and accompanied the La Rocque de Roberval expedition to Canada in 1542, before dying in a battle at La Rochelle, France, in 1544. The fact that

Norumbega was a well-known and well-publicized location prior to David Ingram's walk from Vera Cruz, Mexico to St. John, NB, in 1568 or 1569, indicates that it would be mistaken to assume that the term Norumbega originated with David Ingram's exaggerated descriptions; its origins are far earlier than Ingram's visit or the written history that accompanied European contact after 1600.

Common sense dictates that Norumbega denotes the estuaries, bays, reversing falls, oyster and clam shell middens, and general ambiance of the region between the Kennebec River and Mount Desert Island, with the river of Norumbega (the Penobscot) at its center. The Abenaki Confederacy of Mawooshen thrived for centuries in peaceful coexistence with the neighboring horticultural tribes to the west and northwest of the Norumbega bioregion and with the hunting and gathering Etchemins to the east. That it was primarily a shellfish harvesting, rather than a horticultural community, precludes neither semi-permanent village sites nor horticultural activities in sheltered inland river bottomlands, e.g. at Alna, Damariscotta Lake, or at the Wawinak, that loop in the St. Georges River. Morey (2005) gives a particularly interesting interpretation of the meaning of the word Mawooshen as an Indian word denoting shellfish meat-eating community, which highlights its intimate relationship with Norumbega as a bioregion.

> ...it is a compound word of the Eastern Algonquian language family and Eastern Abenaki (so-called) dialect... Broken down, the first element... is 'to eat something noble.' The second... is the generic determinative of the meat (flesh) of beasts, whether mammal, molusk, fish, or fowl. It therefore describes a population of people who primarily subsist on meat, or as hunters. (Morey, 2005, pg. 20)

The land of Mawooshen included the Kennebecs (Canibas), Androscoggins, Pigwackets, Massachusetts of the Saco River, and the neighboring Penobscots. Norumbega is contiguous with this florescence of Abenaki communities. In the pre-fur trade era, extensive, centuries-old trading relationships appear to have existed between the Abenaki communities to the west of Schoodic Point and the Etchemin and Micmac communities to the east of the Penobscot, Union, and Taunton river tidewaters. All the communities of Mawooshen shared a birch-bark, spruce-root technology which fostered the ironic combination of a highly mobile hunting and gathering (game-shellfish) culture and semi-permanent village locations. In the Abenaki confederacy of Mawooshen, horticultural activities were probably infrequent in areas east of the Penobscot River (e.g. Blue Hill–Deer Isle peninsula, Mount Desert Island, and the Taunton River watershed). A robust trading network exchanged maize, smoked oysters, and other foods from west of the Penobscot River for furs, moose hides, and lithics from the east. Inland and coastal canoe routes were the essential links facilitating the robust trading network of Norumbega.

Salisbury (1982) provides an eloquent summary of pre-contact tribal relationships, including the essential role that trading reciprocity played in maintaining a peaceful coexistence and the mutual sharing of abundant natural resources upon which it depended. Part of the essence of Norumbega as a resource-rich bioregion was that its environment was the key to the patterns of interaction in the trading economy of Mawooshen.

> The fruit of the Indian experience was an ethos in which relationships in the social, natural, and supernatural worlds were defined in terms of reciprocity rather than domination and submission. Developed centuries earlier when hunting and gathering were the primary modes of subsistence, this ethos had survived and continued to prevail as agriculture brought larger populations and more sedentary settlement patterns to the southern portion of New England. (Salisbury, 1982, pg. 10-11)

As Salisbury later makes clear, the gradual incursion by Europeans and their need for large quantities of furs caused radical changes in the lifestyles and tribal relationships of Native Americans from the 16th century onward. The fate of the Wawenoc community of the central Maine coast is but a footnote to the larger tragedy of European contact and the impact of its market economy on the trading economy of the indigenous communities of Norumbega. What was, at first, a physical extinction of the Wawenocs of Mawooshen by warfare and disease has now become an ethnohistoric cleansing of our contemporary history texts, as the memory of the history of a community without descendants dims and then is forgotten. No Wawenocs survive to defend their ancestral tribal homeland, perpetuate their language, or retell the traditions and history of that ancient dominion of Maine, Mawooshen, in the land of Norumbega. Euro-American beginnings; Native American endings.

The Current Paradigm

Not only have the Wawenocs and their confederacy of Mawooshen disappeared from Maine's landscape, they've also disappeared from Maine's history books, one of the most recent of which is *Maine, the Pine Tree State from Pre-history to the Present*, edited by Judd, Churchill, and Eastman (1995). Widely available in Maine bookstores, libraries, and classrooms, and the most comprehensive contemporary summary of Maine history, this popular text makes no mention either of the Wawenoc Indians or of the confederacy of Mawooshen. What new historiographic paradigm has evolved that would mandate that these and other contemporary historians now label all of Maine's indigenous First Nation Native Americans as either Wabanakis or Etchemins, thereby squelching the ethnic identities of Maine's indigenous communities? Would surviving Wawenocs or Kennebecs refer to themselves as "Etchemins"? Is the Penobscot community comfortable using this term to describe their ethnicity? Does the Passamaquoddy community utilize this label? "Etchemin" is a term that facilitates the loss of the identity and obscures the fate of Maine's pre-contact central coast inhabitants. The process of Euro-American ethnohistoric "naming," of, in fact, renaming indigenous communities eliminates one of the most interesting chapters in Maine history.

A closer look at Judd illustrates the extent of the impact of the current revisionist doctrine. *Maine: Pine Tree State from Prehistory to the Present* twice mentions the Samoset Hotel without recounting the tale of Samoset, a Wawenoc Indian from Muscongus Island, who greeted the Pilgrims at Plymouth in English in 1621. Judd et al make brief mention of Waymouth's sailing the Archangel up the St. Georges River (Morey, 2005, has made a convincing case that it was the Penobscot River) and kidnapping five Native Americans but fail to elaborate on who the English were encountering or even to note the existence of the Confederacy of Mawooshen. The tradition of a Native American confederacy of communities surrounding the homeland of the Wawenocs and noted as Norumbega on all maps before 1610 deserves acknowledgment and discussion among historians and students of Maine history as one of many versions of Maine's ethnohistoric past. What could be more interesting from the point of view of Maine's long tradition of humor than the observation that, during the confederacy of Mawooshen, prior to the intertribal fur trade wars and great pandemic, Massachusetts may have been a colony of Maine, an outlying district of a prospering series of Native American communities centered in the ancient dominion of the Wawenoc Indians?

Prins (Judd, 1995) uses traditional ethnic nomenclature to describe Maine's indigenous communities, although he omits the Wawenocs (pg. 98). Neither he nor Bourque clearly state why Native American tribal designations, such as Canibas (Kennebecs), while certainly geographic in nature, but also self-designated, are not "ethnic," whereas the now dominant term "Etchemin" is based on "ethnic or linguistic" criteria (Bourque, 2001).

Are Prins, Bourque, and others suggesting that words such as Pigwacket, Caniba, Wawenoc, and Penobscot are not indigenous in their origin but instead derive from a misguided English conception of geography? Prins inadvertently highlights the core issue about the loss of ethnic identity of the Wawenoc community with his ethnic definitions: "Etchemin (today's Maliseet and Passamaquoddy)... Armouchiquois (today's Abenaki)..." (pg. 98). Prins' use of ethnic labels differs significantly from those used by Bourque, representing a middle stage in eliminating the term "Abenaki" from contemporary ethnohistoric descriptions of the residents of the central Maine coast at the time of contact. Admittedly, the creation of education curricula or museum exhibitions is simplified by the use of the Lescarbot 1609 map labeled "Etchemins;" unraveling the convoluted and conflicting ethnic categories that characterize both older historical narratives, and the current reductionist view of Maine's ethnohistoric past is a confusing and complicated task, especially in classrooms where students have a short attention span.

It is interesting to note how closely Williamson (1832) follows the French description of the three major ethnic groups of the maritime peninsula in his ancient text. Williamson clearly used, from east to west, the Micmac-Etchemin-Abenaki model. The only significant difference in the Williamson (English) version and the Prins (Judd, 1995) (French version - stage one) of Maine's ethnohistory lies in the ethnic identity of the communities just west of the Penobscot River (the Wawenocs) and those living along the Kennebec River (the Kennebecs or Canibas) and the evaluation of their significance at the time of the first historically recorded contacts with Europeans (Champlain, 1604-5; Waymouth 1605). Bourque (2001) takes his interpretation of the "French version" of Maine's ethnohistory one step further than Prins by defining the Almouchiquois of the Saco River and the Androscoggins of the Androscoggin River *not* as Abenaki, but rather as Massachusetts Indians, another generic name for the series of horticultural communities stretching at least to Plymouth (Patuxet). The great pandemic of 1617 finished what the Micmac attacks of 1607 started: it eradicated these communities. Snow (1980) includes both the Massachusetts of the Saco River and the Pigwackets of the Presumpscot as members of the confederacy of Mawooshen. Were they culturally distinct from the Canibas and Wawenocs to the east, who also practiced horticulture in sheltered inland river valleys? A reconsideration of French sources suggests that all the communities of Mawooshen were Almouchiquois, i.e. Abenaki.

The French Sources: An Ambiguous Commentary

Samuel de Champlain, Marc Lescarbot, and Father Pierre Biard are the most important sources of information about the Native Americans encountered by the first European visitors along the central Maine coast. After arriving at St. Croix Island in 1604, Champlain explored the Penobscot River, encountering the Bashebas at or near the Kenduskeag Stream:

> I shall now leave this subject [the headwaters of the Penobscot River] in order to return to the Indians, who had conducted me to the falls of the Norumbega River, and who had gone to inform Bessabez their chief, and other Indians. They (in their turn) went to another little river to inform also their chief, whose name was Cabahis, and to notify him of our arrival... On the same day the above-mentioned Bessabez also came to see us with six canoes... Cabahis, the other chief, also arrived a little bit later... Afterwards each returned, Bessabez with his companions in their direction and we in ours, well pleased to make acquaintance with these people. (Champlain, 1922, pg. 293-294, 296)

Champlain's observations suggest that the Bashebas lived some distance from the Kenduskeag, where this meeting occurred, but in which direction is not made clear. In fact, Champlain was never able to pinpoint his residence. However, Ganong, one of the editors of Champlain's works, indicates in a footnote that Father Biard, who was not present at this meeting, calls the Bashebas "Sagamore of the Kadusquit, i.e. Kenduskeag" (Champlain, 1922, pg. 294). Nonetheless, there exists no evidence whatsoever that he lived at this location. It is interesting to note Champlain's mention of the sagamore Cabahis, who was also visiting with the Bashebas. The probable location for the residence of this sagamore was up the Narramissic River at Orland (a little river). This excerpt from Champlain further illustrates the complex network of indigenous communities, located on both major and minor rivers, which composed the confederacy of Mawooshen. In this and many other cases, the names by which indigenous communities would have identified themselves at their specific tidewater village locations have been lost, obscured, or forgotten.

After meeting with the Bashebas on the Penobscot River, Champlain continues:

> ...we set out for another river called Kennebec, distant from this place thirty-five leagues, and from Bedabedec [Owls Head] about twenty. The tribe of Indians at Kennebec is called Etechemins, like those of Norumbega. (Champlain, 1922, pg. 297)

This is the one and only direct reference to the Canibas as Etchemins in Champlain's journals. The key question is: who is applying this name to the Canibas, the Canibas themselves or Champlain's Micmac interpreters? On the basis of this single comment and the maps which Lescarbot then published in 1609, the English version of the ethnicity of Maine's indigenous central coast inhabitants has been discounted. Yet French observations can be interpreted as describing the same socially complex network of trading communities along the Maine coast noted by English sources. Both versions recall communities with different ethnicity (lifestyles, traditions, dress, social organization, material culture, and horticultural activities, or lack thereof) from the Etchemins of the Maliseet/Passamaquoddy community.

Champlain's first meeting with the Bashebas took place in the fall of 1604 on the Penobscot River. After attempting to proceed further west to the Kennebec River, Champlain encountered foul weather and fog, and, with Micmac guides unwilling to meet their adversaries up the Kennebec River, returned to spend a brutal winter at St. Croix Island. Champlain's next visit west of the Penobscot was in the summer of 1605. Describing his encounter with Mentaurmet, the sagamore of Indiantown Island, Champlain's journals note only the briefest of encounters, which took place on or near the Kennebec River rather than at a village site:

> As soon as we had anchored he came out to us in a canoe, separated a short
> distance from ten others in which were those who accompanied him. Drawing near
> our pinnace he made us a speech, in which he expressed his pleasure at seeing us,
> and said he desired an alliance with us, and through our mediation to make peace
> with their enemies. He added that the next day he would send word to two other
> Indian chiefs who were up country, one called Marchin, and the Sasinou, chief of
> the Kennebec river. (Champlain, 1922, pg. 316)

Marchin was an Androscoggin sagamore; this transcription illustrates the close relationship of these Abenaki communities. Champlain tells us nothing about the settlements in the Sheepscot River tidewater because he never visited any, providing no village descriptions or locations, population estimates, lifestyle analyses, or comments on dialect, armaments, artifacts, or modes of dress.

The next series of French encounters with natives of the central Maine coast living west of the Penobscot River occurred in October, 1611. Father Biard's description of his encounter in the Kennebec region with both the Almouchiquois and the Wawenoc Mentaurmet is much more detailed than Champlain's observations and undermines the assertion [Brasser (1978), Bourque (1989, 2001), et al.] that these natives were of the same ethnicity as the hunting and gathering residents of the St. John River drainage.

> Upon our return from this river Saint John, our route turned towards the country of
> the Armouchiquoys. Two principal causes led M. de Biancourt to take this route:
> first, in order to have news of the English, and to find out if it would be possible to
> obtain satisfaction from them; secondly, to buy some Armouchiquoys corn to help us

pass the winter, and not die of hunger in case we did not receive help from France. (Thwaites, 1896, pg. 30)

It is important to note that Biard is traveling up the Kennebec River, and not the Saco River, in his attempt to find corn in a region of the Maine coast that Bourque describes as occupied by Etchemins. Biard continues:

> We had already advanced three good leagues, and had dropped anchor in the middle of the river waiting for the tide, when we suddenly discovered Six Armouchiquois canoes coming towards us. There were twenty-four persons therein, all warriors. They went through a thousand maneuvers and ceremonies before accosting us... (Thwaites, 1896, pg. 34)

Biard then provides a very detailed narration of his overnight encounter with at first suspicious, but then singing and chanting, "Armouchiquois," probably either Canibas or Androscoggin from nearby areas of the Kennebec/Androscoggin tidewater.

> In the morning we continued our journey up the river. The Armouchiquois, who were accompanying us. told us that if we wanted any *piousquemin* (corn), it would be better and easier for us to turn to the *right* [italics added] and not, with great difficulty and risks to continue going up the river; that if we turned to the [page 37] right through the branch which was just at hand, in a few hours we would reach the great [Wawenoc] sagamore Meteourmite [Mentaurmet at Wiscasset] who would furnish us with all we wanted; that they would act as our guides, since they themselves were going to visit him. (Thwaites, 1896, pg. 36-37)

Then, when they entered Merrymeeting Bay, the "Armouchiquois" disappeared; Biard and de Baincourt, the shallop crew captain, thought that they were trapped and about to be attacked. When they were heading out of Merrymeeting Bay and downriver, Mentaurmet appeared and guided Biard to his village:

> When we arrived, Monsieur de Biancourt armed himself, and thus arrayed proceeded to pay a visit to Meteourmite. He found him in the royal apparel of Savage majesty, alone in a wigwam that was well matted above and below, and about forty powerful young men stationed around it like a body-guard, each one with his shield, his bow and arrows upon the ground in front of him. These people are by no means simpletons, and you may believe us when we say so. ...They led me to the largest wigwam of all; it Contained fully eighty people. (Thwaites, 1896, pg. 40)

Mentaurmet then informed Biard that the corn, which he was seeking to help sustain the new French colony at Port Royal through the winter, was unavailable. Biard provides much more detailed insight into the sophisticated social milieu of Mentaurmet's community, noting that the Wawenoc sagamore, though not the superchief of Mawooshen, is able to dictate to the "Armouchiquois" to the west an order to return

40

stolen goods and to arrange meetings with other sagamores (see above). Biard also makes clear that the French were on much more favorable terms with the inhabitants of the central Maine coast than were the British.

> Now Meteourmite had replied to Monsieur de Biancourt that as to the corn he did not have much, but he had some skins, if we were pleased to trade with him. ...When evening came and all had retired, Meteourmite sent some of his men to excuse the misconduct of the morning, protesting that all the disorder had originated not with him, but with the Armouchiquois; that they had even stolen a hatchet and a platter (a great wooden dish), which articles he herewith returned; that this theft had so displeased him that immediately after discovering it he had sent the Armouchiquois away from him; that, for his part, he was friendly toward us and knew very well that we neither killed; nor beat the Savages of those parts, but received them at our table and often made tabagie for them, and brought them a great many nice things from France, for which courtesies they loved us. These people are, I believe, the greatest speech-makers in the world; nothing can be done without speeches. ...Thence, as the season was advancing, it being already the 6th of November, we turned our ships towards Port Royal, stopping at Pentegoet, as we had promised the Savages. (Thwaites, 1896, pg. 42 - 46)

Biard then provides another interesting description of his encounter with the Penobscots to the east at Pentagoet (Castine):

> When we had advanced three leagues or more into the current of the river we encountered another beautiful river called Chiboctous [Bagaduce], which comes from the northeast to discharge its waters into the great Pentegoet.

> At the confluence of these two rivers there was the finest assemblage of Savages that I have yet seen. There were 80 canoes and a boat, 18 wigwams and about 300 people. The most prominent Sagamore was called Betsabes, a man of great discretion and prudence; and I confess we often see in these Savages natural and graceful qualities which will make anyone but a shameless person blush, when they compare them to the greater part of the French who come over here. (Thwaites, 1896, pg. 48)

Biard thus provides yet another characterization, in this case of the superchief of Mawooshen, which is at odds with the "French version" of the ethnicity of Maine's indigenous residents as hunting and gathering nomads. Biard also raises another issue in his description of the large number of natives encountered at Pentagoet. The high population levels noted at both the Kennebec and Penobscot River meetings and the sophistication, complex social hierarchy, and intimate intertribal relationships noted by Champlain and Biard at these encounters contradict descriptions of the "Etchemins" as impoverished, unsophisticated, and with a total population of only 1,000 persons scattered from the Saco River eastward through the St. John River drainage made by

Lescarbot (1609) elsewhere in the *Jesuit Relations*. The fact that Biard was visiting Mentaurmet, a Wawenoc sagamore, in his search for corn in 1611 raises fundamental questions about the current interpretation of the alleged "French version" of the ethnicity of Maine's central coast residents. Biard was visiting "Almouchiquois" on the Sheepscot River in his quest for corn, not "Etchemins" from the St. Croix region.

Ethnocentrism and the Problem of Samoset

Parkman (1983) helps us understand the context of map-making by French explorers and historians such as Champlain and Lescarbot, the latter of which made the first maps noting an Etchemin presence on the central Maine coast:

> From first to last, it was the policy of France in America to mingle in Indian politics, hold the balance of power between adverse tribes, and envelop in the network of her power and diplomacy the remotest hordes of the wilderness. (Parkman, 1983, pg. 250)

> In New France, spiritual and temporal interests were inseparably blended, and, as will hereafter appear, the conversion of the Indians was used as a means of commercial and political growth. (Parkman, 1983, pg. 283)

The inhabitants of the central Maine coast were, for all purposes, one of the "remotest hordes of the wilderness" (Parkman, 1983), since they lived so far south of the areas of most interest to the French in the St. Lawrence River and the Bay of Fundy to the north. The ethnocentrism with which Bourque (2001) charges Williamson also applies to Champlain, Lescarbot, Biard, and other French historians. The French were on a quest that combined religious conversion with the commercial domination of a whole continent. In a map drawn as early as 1609, there would be no earthly reason why French mapmakers would indicate that the central Maine coast was controlled by indigenous communities other than those such as the Etchemins so closely allied with the objectives of Champlain and his peripatetic fur traders and missionaries. It was for the purpose of obtaining the furs supplied by the Micmac traders and Etchemin trappers that French traders brought kettles, blankets, beads, firearms, and brandy. It was these trade goods and the predatory commercial milieu they represented that so effectively undermined the traditional lifestyles of these communities. Equally predatory English and Dutch traders soon followed, and, as Micmac middlemen lost control of the fur trade, intertribal competition and violence increased throughout the maritime peninsula, eventually involving Iroquois communities from the west by the third decade of the seventeenth century.

In the post-modern era, where all history writing and reading can be construed as ethnocentric storytelling, the suggestion that English sources are ethnocentric, but French sources are not is a most interesting assertion. The "pleasures of the text" indeed (Barthes, 1973). The French maps of the period, so dearly beloved by some contemporary historians and illustrating the Etchemin hegemony along the Maine coast at the time of contact with the first Europeans, also contain those annoying drawings of turreted castles at Norumbega on the Penobscot. Both the turreted castles and the inscribed designation of the Etchemin hegemony are on the same maps and cut from the same cloth. Here we have the confluence of prehistory with history, i.e. protohistory, that first period of written history, the initial scribbling. Why would the very first French map, later revised by Champlain with much more accurate geographical depictions, serve as the basis for a reinterpretation of Maine's ethnohistory?

Samuel Purchas published the description of the land of Mawooshen in 1625, long after Lescarbot drew his 1609 map that indicated "Etchemins" were the residents of the central Maine coast. While Champlain, accompanied by Lescarbot, made one exploratory visit up the Kennebec River to Wiscasset and Merrymeeting Bay before sailing south to visit Cape Ann and the Massachusetts coast, he never explored the estuaries and tidewater bays of the central Maine coast between the Penobscot and Kennebec rivers. Nor did any other French explorers, historians, or mapmakers visit and describe the resource rich homeland of the Wawenoc community. There were no French settlements in this area. Before the arrival of the English, the closest French settlement was the short lived St. Sauveur on Mount Desert Island (1613.) No French settlements are known to have been attempted between the Penobscot and Kennebec rivers, the alleged control of the area by the Etchemins not withstanding. The word Mawooshen never appears in Champlain's journals; he had almost no contact with the residents of the villages of Mawooshen. He never met the Wawenoc natives kidnapped by Waymouth, nor was he aware of the information that they provided to Fernando Gorges about the communities of the central Maine coast. Champlain also never encountered Samoset, one of the most important Native Americans in the annals of American history, a resident of the central Maine coast, a survivor of the great pandemic, and possibly one of the Native Americans kidnapped by George Waymouth in 1605 (Morey, 2005).

The oral and written traditions of the English version of Maine and New England history refer to and commemorate Samoset and the Wawenocs. There are, in fact, no French accounts of English settlements along the Maine and Massachusetts coasts. George Waymouth was not the only English explorer to have contact with the Wawenoc Samoset; Captain John Smith (1614), William Bradford (1908), and Captain Christopher Levett at Capemanwagom (Southport Island, 1623), whose account is cited in detail by Morey (2005, pg. 102-104), all testify to his helpfulness. Samoset visited the nearly starving Plymouth colony in March of 1621. Morison, in *Of Plymouth Plantation* (1963) cites Governor Bradford's account of Samoset's visit:

> But about the 16th of March [1621], a certain Indian came boldly amongst them
> and spoke to them in broken English, which they could well understand but
> marveled at it. At length they understood by discourse with him, that he was not of
> these parts, but belonged to the eastern parts where some English ships came to
> fish, with whom he was acquainted and could name sundry of them by their names,
> amongst whom he had got his language. He became profitable to them in
> acquainting them with many things concerning the state of the country in the east

parts where he lived, which was afterwards profitable unto them; as also of the people here, of their names, number and strength, of their situation and distance from this place, and who was chief amongst them. His name was Samoset. He told them also of another Indian whose name was Squanto, a native of this place [Plymouth - Patuxet], who had been in England and could speak better English than himself. (Morison, 1963, pg. 79)

Samoset's helpful information played a major role in alerting Governor Bradford to Monhegan Island as a possible source of lifesaving codfish, corn, and other staples, which Edward Winslow then obtained in the spring of 1622, just as the supplies of the Plymouth colonists were running out. Samoset was also instrumental in providing the colonists with important information about the availability of beaver pelts and other furs along the Maine coast, leading to the Plymouth colonists establishing their highly profitable trading posts at Cushnoc (Augusta) in 1628, Penobscot in 1630, and Machias in 1631 (Morris, 1976). Morison (1963) provides this footnote in the Bradford history:

Samoset was an Algonkian sagamore of Pemaquid Point, Maine, a region much frequented by English fishermen. He probably shipped with Capt. Dermer from Monhegan to Cape Cod shortly before the Pilgrims landed and worked his way overland to Plymouth. He conveyed 12,000 acres of Pemaquid Point to one John Brown in 1625, and lived until about 1653. (Morison, 1963, pg. 80)

Morison continues with this interesting comment, reflecting his understanding of the ethnicity of Maine's indigenous population:

Tarentine was the name then used for the Abnaki Indians, who occupied the shores of Maine from Casco Bay eastward and part of New Brunswick. They were the Vikings of New England, preferring to take corn from their neighbors than to grow it. (Morison, 1963, footnote, pg. 89)

This sounds like a description of Micmac raiding parties. Substitute "Etchemin" for Abenaki, and we have Bourque's "French version" of the ethnohistory of the central Maine coast. Neither Governor Bradford nor Morison provide any description of Samoset, an Algonquin Abenaki from the Wawenoc Nation, not a Penobscot or Maliseet, as one of those cornfield-raiding Viking types. Morison's humorous but hyperbolic footnote provides another example of the substitution of a generic label for a more accurate description of the ethnic complexity of Mawooshen, and this by one of New England's most famous historians.

Neither Morison (1963) nor Speck (1940) in *Penobscot Man* refer to the description of the land of Mawooshen printed by Samuel Purchas (1625) or acknowledge Samoset's residence within that confederacy, as Mawooshen is not listed in the index of Morison's history or in any other publication by Morison or Speck. Morison does, however, make another observation pertaining to the importance of the relationship between the Plymouth colonists and the Native Americans and European fisherman living along the Maine coast. Without the directions and assistance from Samoset and the fish and furs from the Maine coast, it was unlikely that the Plymouth colony would have survived beyond its first two years when more than half the colonists perished.

> Damariscove Island is off Boothbay, Maine; it is called Damerill's Isles on Capt. John Smith's map (1614) and was probably named after a fisherman who located there. The fishing along the Maine coast at this time was marvelous; 300 to 400 sail of various countries, of which 30 to 40 were English and some from Virginia, spent the early months of each year in Maine waters, returning to Europe in the summer. (Morison, 1963, footnote, pg. 99-100)

It was the rich natural resources of the Maine coast that attracted English fishermen and settlers, but Abenaki communities also used it for summer shellfish harvesting, wildfowl hunting, fishing, and trading. Morison describes the fisherman and the fishing, omitting a third important component in his sketch, i.e. the indigenous residents of the coast near Damariscove Island, who traded with the fisherman, providing them with both furs and corn, and who also aided them in careening their vessels to remove slops. (See below, *The Great Pandemic of 1617-1619*.)

Samoset's ancestral homeland was not far to the east of Damariscove Island, at Muscongus Island north of New Harbor. This was Wawenoc territory. There are no surviving Wawenocs to be included in contemporary lists of Wabanaki peoples, for example, as used in the American Friends Service Committee book title: *The Wabanakis of Maine & the Maritimes: A Resource Book by and about Penobscot, Passamaquoddy, Maliseet, Micmac and Abenaki Indians*. The only Abenaki communities listed by this text are those living at Bécancour, St. Francis, and Swanton, VT. The Wawenocs are listed as Bécancour Abenakis in this text (Maine Indian Program, 1989, pg. D-8 - D-9). What happened to the Abenaki of the central Maine coast, and where did they go?

Bradford and Morison are examples of the many writers and historians using English sources to provide important information about the historical context of the interaction of Maine's indigenous population with European fishermen, traders, and settlers. The story of Samoset and his encounter with the Plymouth colonists can be interpreted as ethnocentric romanticism: Anglo-Americans glorifying this encounter while exterminating, if inadvertently, his entire community and many others. The ethnocentrism of our tales about Samoset lie in the details we leave out of the stories we tell.

Reliance on only French sources (or English) for information about Maine's ethnohistoric past excludes a huge body of written history and oral traditions, which illustrate both the complexity of the relationships and the long history of contacts between the Native Americans in Maine and Europeans. Monhegan Island, Pemaquid, Damariscove Island, Boothbay, and the other tidewater areas of the central Maine coast were New England's most important nexus for the first encounters between Native Americans and Europeans, both French and English.

Revisionist's Paradigm Part I: The Conundrum

Figure 7 **New France in 1719.**

Traditional antiquarian writers such as Williamson (1832) describe a series of riverine centered communities, which formed the core of the English oral and written tradition about Native Americans in Maine. Williamson clearly differentiates the Abenaki, including the Wawenocs, from the Etchemins, among whom he includes the Penobscots.

Based on a reinterpretation of French sources, the Bourquian paradigm of a revised ethnohistory of coastal Maine highlights the many puzzles of late prehistory. The lack of written records and archaeological data necessitate reliance on the story-telling of a multiplicity of explorers, observers, narrators, and traders. We interpret and then reconstruct these stories at our pleasure. What, in fact, transpired at the time of European contact? Who were the indigenous participants, and how did they live and die? And what do Native Americans say about the ethnicity and cultural traditions of the tumultuous years of protohistory?

Late 20th century Native American commentators confirm the English version of a Wawenoc community along the central Maine coast. Their observations can be seen in the map *Indian Peoples of the Dawnland*, placed on the web by the Native American group Ne-Do-Ba: Abenaki in Western Maine. The Pennacook Nation website www.cowasuck.org has posted a detailed listing of the labyrinth of Abenaki communities and their geographic boundaries throughout New England. Included in their compilation of the names of indigenous communities are the Anasagunticook, Kennebec, and Wawenock. Their listing includes seven variations of the spelling of Wawenoc. The Abenaki History website (http://tolatsga.org/aben.html) has posted a similar description of the Abenaki Nation, its locations and populations, and estimates of the death rates in the pandemics of the 16th and 17th century. (See the chapter *The Great Pandemic of 1616-1619.*) This Native American website notes that:

> Extending across most of northern New England into the southern part of the Canadian Maritimes, the Abenaki called their homeland Ndakinna meaning 'our land.' The eastern Abenaki were concentrated in Maine east of New Hampshire's White Mountains, while the western Abenaki lived west of the mountains across Vermont and New Hampshire to the eastern shores of Lake Champlain. The southern boundaries of the Abenaki homeland were near the present northern border of Massachusetts excluding the Pennacook country along the Merrimack River of southern New Hampshire. The maritime Abenaki occupied the St. Croix and the St. John's River Valleys near the border between Maine and New Brunswick. New England settlement and war forced many of the Abenaki to retreat north into Quebec where two large communities formed at St. Francois and Bécancour near Trois-Rivieves. These have continued to the present-day. There are also three reservations in northern Maine (Penobscot, Passamaquoddy, and Maliseet) and seven Maliseet reserves located in New Brunswick and Quebec. Other groups of Abenaki, without reservations, are scattered across northern New Hampshire and Vermont. (http://tolatsga.org/aben.html)

The Pennacook Nation Cowasuck website defines the limit of the Abenaki homelands as extending to the boundaries of the Penobscot, Passamaquoddy, and Micmac communities to the east; the Abenaki History website includes these indigenous peoples as part of "maritime Abenaki." These differing descriptions of the geographical parameters of the Abenaki Nation help underscore why there is such a large variation of opinion about ethnicity in writings on this subject. For further discussion of the problem of the naming of various Abenaki communities, see the chapters "The Almouchiquois: Ethnicity Reconsidered" and "The Conundrum of Ethnohistory".

Unraveling the puzzles of the revisionist's paradigm means linking specific descriptions from various sources, both French and English, to reconstruct chapters in our ethnohistoric past that would otherwise be eliminated by the reductionism of the new paradigm of Maine's ethnohistory. For example, Morey (2005) helps link Champlain's and Biard's observations of a community west of the Penobscot at Wiscasset and the English narration of the ethnohistory of the central Maine coast. "Mentaurmet is described in the Mawooshen document of 1605 as the sagamore of Nebamocago (Indiantown Island, Boothbay)" (Morey, 2005, pg. 101). Morey goes on to contend that both Amoret (Samoset) and Tihanedo, two of the five natives kidnapped by Waymouth, were both sons of Mentaurmet, long known as a Wawenoc. French sources thus join

English in a contemporary documentation of an Abenaki community with no survivors to advocate its former significance.

Another puzzle of our ethnohistoric past is the identity of the indigenous communities living along the Saco River. Champlain (1922) first described the Saco River Indians as a sedentary horticultural community and as having an entirely different language and lifestyle from the communities in the Bay of Fundy near his settlements at St. Croix and Port Royal:

> Our Indian could understand only certain words, inasmuch as the language of the Almouchiquois, for so that nation is called, differs entirely from that of the Souriquois and Etechemins. ...They [Almouchiquois] till and cultivate the land; a practice we had not seen previously. (Champlain, 1922, pg. 325, 327)

Herein lies the fallacy of the excluded middle: Champlain made no contact with or observations of the Wawenoc community living midway between the Saco River and the St. Croix. He wasn't able to solve one of the puzzles of the Wabanaki: adjoining interrelated communities had subtle differences in dialect, material culture (e.g. styles of baskets), and ancestral traditions. In fact, there was no stark demarcation line between adjoining cultural communities (nations), who frequently traded with each other. Language differences appeared to be a function of both distance and the barrier of the Bay of Fundy, which promoted Algonquin dialect differentiation before the early modern era of commodity trading made the world of the indigenous communities of the maritime peninsula much smaller.

Bourque (2001) clearly contends that the Almouchiquois on the Saco River are not Abenaki, making a radical revision in the traditional understanding of the ethnicity of Maine's Native Americans by splitting communities once considered Eastern Abenaki into three separate ethnic identities based on their Algonquin dialect. The lack of an identity for the Saco River Indians (if not Abenaki, who were the Almouchiquois?) is an enduring ethnohistoric puzzle, now the subject of renewed attention under the spotlight of the revisionist paradigm of Maine's ethnohistory.

The Saco River is a long recognized cultural divide. Communities to the south had their own Algonquin dialect and more entrenched, uninterrupted horticulture and lacked the spruce-root/birch-bark technology that characterized the Eastern Abenaki. All other European observers also noted a large population of horticulturists living in semi-permanent villages west of the Saco. These communities all suffered a 90-100% death rate in the great pandemic of 1617-1619. Day (1998) notes that the 1726 census listed only four Saco River Indians as surviving after a century of contact with Europeans. Day and others indicate that, since so little is known about the Saco River Indians, no tribal name has survived other than the generic terms "Massachusetts" (the Saco River was the northernmost limit of the Massachusetts culture) or "Almouchiquois" (Snow, 1980).

The uncertainty of the ethnicity of the Saco River community persists, despite Lescarbot's 1607 narration of the attack by the Micmacs and Etchemins at the Saco River. Later, observations of the impact of the 1617 pandemic on the Saco River villages by European observers also failed to record their tribal identity. To the east, the lifestyle and ethnicity of the Androscoggins and the Canibas are better documented by both French and English observers. The archipelago of the interior tidewaters, estuaries, and bays of the central coast between the Kennebec and Penobscot rivers, the area occupied by the Wawenoc community, was also poorly documented, with few visitors or traders leaving any written observations before 1623. While the ancestral villages of the Penobscots above Bangor are well documented (Speck, 1940), the history and location of communities to the east of the Penobscot River and Schoodic Point are not. Nonetheless, precontact indigenous cultural activities and intercommunity contact centered on trade and exchange between many small villages. Rapid canoe travel was the key to an interlocking trading network. The confederacy of Mawooshen occupied the entire Maine coast between Schoodic Point and the Saco River; multiple indigenous subcultures acted in concordance. Neither French nor English observers and narrators of that era support the new paradigm of Mawooshen as split by warring factors on either side of the Androscoggin or Kennebec rivers.

The brief period of intense and widespread tribal warfare in the Maritime Provinces and in coastal Maine was only a few decades long. After the French arrived with firearms and helped Abenaki and Micmac communities destroy each other, intertribal warfare moved west, and 250 years of violence ensued. Before these events (the beaver wars) occurred, commodity exchange and the reciprocity of shared ceremony connected a centuries-old network of indigenous villages and tribal nations. This was the land of Mawooshen, prior to the incursion of a European market economy.

Many smaller rivers and bays such as the Presumpscot to the west, the Narramissic at Orland (that "little river" noted by Champlain), and Taunton River at Sullivan (Waukeag) had their own communities, sagamores, and traditions, and all played a role in this complex trading network. All of this changed with the advent of the intertribal fur trade wars and the Micmac attacks on the central Maine coast. Contact with European culture tended to force these communities into larger, more competitive, and possibly more warlike social units. Increasingly hierarchical cultural units characterized more well-organized trading networks. Intertribal competition also encouraged violence and warfare. It was during this period of rapid social change that the summer retreats of the Penobscots on Mount Desert Island were overrun by the invading Micmacs, supplied with French firearms. Prins (1996) notes a "Micmac stronghold on Mount Desert Island" as a component of the widening impact of the turmoil which resulted from the competition for the control of the European fur trade. Since there are few written records to document this turmoil, the reductionism of a revisionist ethnohistory further obscures and covers over the ethnohistory of the Abenakis of the central Maine coast and the violence and epidemics which accompanied European contact.

The revisionist concept of semi-nomadism helps us forget the presence and fate of a culture whose rhythmic annual visits to the seashore and inland hunting camps were recapitulated by the European settlers who replaced them. Summer fishing camps and fall hunting stations were compatible with the semi-permanent tidewater village sites described in Purchas (1625) and echo our own modern response to the fauna, flora, and climate of the maritime peninsula. The more nomadic Etchemins lived east and north of the Schoodic Peninsula. In fact, the concept of semi-nomadism may not apply to the Penobscot community and their sacred Indian Island, nor necessarily to any of the marine resource-dependent Native American communities in the maritime peninsula. The wealth of Gulf of Maine marine resources, high population levels west of Schoodic Point, and well-documented series of complex trading networks all speak against the new paradigm of semi-nomadism as the dominant lifestyle of Maine's central coastal Native communities, at least until the cataclysmic events of the early 17th century put an end to the confederacy of Mawooshen. Unraveling the puzzles of Maine's ethnohistoric past, highlighted by the new revisionist paradigm, means confronting the reality that Maine's network of indigenous communities were forced to reorganize themselves in larger social units with thousands of bowmen in a self-destructive attempt to incorporate European supplied firearms, alcohol, and trade goods in a new social order.

The virgin soil epidemics that soon followed European contact quickly ended the embryonic coalescence and growth of Maine's indigenous communities into a variation of European-style city states i.e. regional communities of significant political, economic, and military status, and influence. There is at least a hint of similarity between the social hierarchy of a Canibas, Wawenoc, or Penobscot nation ca. 1350 and that of Siena, Florence, or Corona as Italian city-states of the same era.

The rapid disappearance of these communities four centuries ago leaves a legacy of unanswered questions. The Bourquian revolution (1989 ff.) and the new paradigm of an alleged French version of the identity of these communities further complicate the unraveling of the conundrums of this disorderly history. What was the ethnicity of these indigenous communities, what dialects did they speak, what alliances did they form, what battles did they fight, who were their leaders and when were they killed? What was Mawooshen, and what was its relationship to the Norumbega of the maps of the first European visitors? These questions may never be answered.

Dean Snow: The Abenaki or the Etchemins?

In a landmark article in *Ethnohistory,* Snow (1976) makes the following assertions:

> Sources on the Eastern Abenaki dating to about 1600 are crucial in establishing the ethnohistorical baseline, the initial cultural state from which all subsequent historical changes occurred. ...original inhabitants of the Penobscot, Kennebec and adjacent river drainages were occupied by the Abenaki rather than by the Malecite-Passamaquoddy as some have stated. [Hoffman, 1955 and Morrison, 1978] (Snow, 1976, pg. 291) (See Hoffman's 1955 map in appendix A.)

Hoffman was a precursor of the Bourquian revolution, also utilizing French sources to advocate an Etchemin influence in the central Maine coast c. 1600. The illusion of the existence of a definitive ethnohistoric baseline now joins the ideal of *Penobscot Man* as a footnote in ethnohistoric writings. Nonetheless, Snow's more traditional description of Maine's indigenous residents in 1600 is the antithesis of that later expressed by Bourque (2001) in *Twelve Thousand Years.*

Snow continues his sketch of the "ethnohistorical baseline" with this assertion:

> In the 17th century, the Eastern Abenaki controlled an area that is almost entirely contained within the modern State of Maine. Their major divisions coincided with four major river drainages within the larger area. From west to east, those divisions were Pigwacket, Arosaguntacook, Kennebec, and Penobscot corresponding to the Presumpscot, Androscoggin, Kennebec and Penobscot drainages. Colonial period sources provide a staggering number of synonyms and misnomers for the Eastern Abenaki and their various subdivisions, but these four seem to be the common denominators. Only the Penobscot survive in place today. Descendants of the others can be found in the old Abenaki refugee colonies of St. Francis and Becancour, Quebec. (Snow, 1976, pg. 291)

The Wawenocs of the central Maine coast are missing from Snow's list. Earlier in this text, Snow makes this noteworthy and paradigmatic comment on the Wawenocs (See also the annotated comments in Appendix G.):

> Wawenoc Indians, who appear in many later documents, were simply residents of the coastal drainages between the Kennebec and Penobscot that I have chosen to lump with the Kennebec. (Snow, 1976, pg. 61)

When discussing the indigenous communities of Maine in the 17th century, there is a good reason to leave out the Wawenocs. By 1620, what was once a flourishing network of tidewater villages had ceased to exist. Historians deal with the written records of history, archaeologists with the artifacts of prehistory. The ethnicity of the Wawenoc community cannot be documented archaeologically. Likewise, the Wawenocs flourished in prehistory, leaving few documents for historians to interpret. They are, therefore, proto-historic, i.e. disappearing at the beginning of history, the subject of incipient, tentative, even inconveniently inaccurate documentation, easily forgotten or omitted. The existence of many other indigenous communities of the past, e.g. the Saco River Indians, the Waukeag of Taunton River, the unidentified residents of the Narraguagus River, and the mysterious Machias River communities are also caught in that grey area between the science of archaeology and the writing of the history of Maine, as experienced and lived by its English and French explorers and settlers. The French established trading posts in the latter three locations in the 17th century but left few written records to document these and other communities located east of the Union River. Their ethnic identity remains unresolved.

The disappearance of the Wawenoc Indians from Maine's history books can be traced back in part to Snow's act of ethnohistoric erasure that was then embraced by Bourque and other contemporary ethnohistorians. Snow was particularly influenced by the opinions of Frank Siebert, collector and expert on the material culture of the indigenous communities of the Maritime Peninsula. Snow notes Siebert's assertion of the nonexistence of a Wawenoc community (see Appendix G). Siebert also felt strongly that Mawooshen was a figment of the imagination of early Euro-American writers mistaking the Mousam River for a larger political entity (Fisher, 2005). Snow's integration of the Wawenocs with the Kennebecs can be understood in the broad context of writing about the archaeology of the New England region as a whole; by 1620 the Wawenocs had ceased to exist as an important community. They were, for Snow, a footnote in his narrative. In a more focused survey of Native Americans in Maine, deleting the Wawenocs from the narrative of the contact period is part of a larger cultural reluctance to confront and document the scope of the calamity that wiped out so many indigenous communities. This omission has its roots in the failure to acknowledge that the Native American communities still existing in 1640 or 1650, prior to the final catastrophe of the Indian Wars (1675 - 1759), were radically different from the population that George Waymouth and Champlain encountered in such great numbers on the coast of Maine in 1604 - 1605. The traumatic events of 1607-1619 were the culmination of a tsunami of social and ecological change that began in the early-16th century with the first contact with French fur traders and European fisherman. The indigenous population encountered by European settlers after 1620 had been greatly reduced. Formerly stable ethnic communities such as the Wawenocs had been scattered. As with the American or French revolutions or the Civil War, momentous events occurred in a short period of time. In the case of the Wawenocs, few survived into the 1620s other than Samoset and a small portion of the original community. The fate of the Wawenoc Nation echoes the fate of other Abenaki communities.

The fundamental question remains: is Bourque correct in deconstructing Snow's earlier description of the ethnicity of the eastern Abenaki community c. 1600? The basis for Snow's ethnic categories was a language-based interpretation of Maine's indigenous communities. The riverine geography of these settlements and territories was important but secondary. His interesting comments on the Maliseet/Passamaquoddy language are quoted in our chapter entitled *The Almouchiquois: Ethnicity Reconsidered*. Snow notes that the dialects of Maine and New England's indigenous inhabitants date back to at least 2000 B.P.:

> With the exception of the Mohawk, all of the people of the coastal drainages from Nova Scotia to North Carolina, spoke Algonquian languages... The Eastern Algonquain langauages were geographically separated from other Algonquian languages, by Iroquoian and the other languages to the interior. The northern Iroquoian languages, including the Mohawk, were particularly important insulators that formed a block through central Pennsylvania and New York, and then down the St. Lawrence River Valley to the St. Lawrence... cutting the Eastern Algonquian speakers off from their lingustic relatives to the west and north. (Snow, 1976, pg. 27)

Snow asserts that this may have occurred as early as 3500-3800 B.P., when northern Iroquois split from the Cherokee. This isolation of the eastern Algonquian languages is the foundation for the various dialects that evolved to provide an important part, but not the only component, of the differences in ethnicity between the various communities of the Eastern Abenaki. Snow's observations are particularly important in view of Bourque's revisionist ethnohistory, which essentially denies the existence of the Abenakis and their individual dialects. Snow noted:

> Eastern Abenaki was spoken throughout western and central Maine. The Penobscot dialect, which apparently had upstream and downstream subdialects, survived into modern times, becoming a language in its own right by default as the other Eastern Abenaki dialects became extinct. There was a distinct Caniba dialect in the Kennebec drainage, and probably at least two additional dialects in the Androscoggin and Presumpscot drainages, respectively. The latter survived only as recombined fragments in the historic Abenaki refuge communities at St. Franics and Becancour, Quebec.... Western Abenaki was spoken by the people of the upper Merrimack drainage. It may well also have been spoken by the Sokoki of the upper Connecticut drainage, and these people in turn may have occupied what is now Vermont as far as the shores of Lake Champlain. ...Southeastern New England was occupied by Indians who spoke a number of dialects that were similar enough to be considered a single language. The shattered communities and dialects of this area are known to us by a series of confusing local names that I have chosen to lump under the heading 'Massachusett.' (Snow, 1976)

Snow is explicit in noting that both the Maliseet/Passamaquoddy (Etchemins) and the Micmac had their own languages. It is, ultimately, the difference in language that separate the Abenaki of coastal Maine and the Penobscot drainage from the Maliseet/Passamaquoddy. French observers, such as Champlain and Biard, frequently commented on these language differences, which became very pronounced once the Massachusetts culture was encountered at and to the southwest of the Saco River. Sharing the spruce-root/birch-bark technology, rapid canoe travel, and seasonal exploitation of a resource rich marine environment were not sufficient to overcome language differences to unite all these communities into one ethnic group, i.e. the "Etchemins."

In fact, there were no Etchemins occupying the central Maine coast west of Schoodic Point at any time prior to 1620 and few, if any, after that date. The conceit of an Etchemin hegemony on the Maine coast circa 1600 not only helps to submerge the ethnic identity of the Wawenocs and their role in Maine's ethnohistory, but also obscures the importance of the Penobscot community, in ancient Mawooshen as well as in the tumultuous years after 1620 and during the French and Indian wars (1675-1759), when an Etchemin hegemony can have credibility only if the ethnicity of the Penobscot community is considered to be "Etchemin," as both Williamson (1832) and Bourque (2001) contend. It is unlikely that Penobscot Nation members share the Bourquian enthusiasm for the French version of their ethnicity, which implies that they are descendants of the Maliseet/Passamaquoddys to the east.

As Snow's analysis of the pandemic in maritime Canada makes clear, too few Etchemins survived in a sparsely populated region to dominate the ethnic mix that characterized coastal Maine and the Penobscot region after 1620. Lescarbot's map of 1609 implies a long term presence in Maine of "Etchemins," but this map was also a depiction of the land of Mawooshen. Who lived there, "Etchemins" or Abenakis?

Eastern Abenaki Villages at the Beginning of the Historic Era

The following list of the villages of the Native Americans living in coastal Maine at the time of Waymouth's voyages is reprinted from Snow (1980). Snow extracted his synopsis from the description provided by Purchas (1625), who printed the narration of the land of Mawooshen given to Fernando Gorges and possibly others by the five Native Americans kidnapped by George Waymouth in 1605. Gorges' transcriptions were passed on to Hakluyt, who died before publishing them. Purchas printed the narration in 1625. Until Snow republished them, they went unnoticed by historians as recently as Speck (1940), who does not mention Mawooshen in *Penobscot Man*. The narration of Mawooshen constitutes a much more detailed description of the coastal populations of central Maine in 1605 than any provided in Champlain's journals. Thousands of English settlers, traders, fishermen, and explorers supplement the description of Mawooshen as much more than just a wilderness populated by a wandering hunting and gathering community reminiscent of the Montagnais to the north of the St. Lawrence River. Williamson's early description of the Penobscots as Etchemin (Williamson, 1832) has been followed by a broad recognition of Penobscot as Eastern Abenaki by most 20th century sources writing prior to the publication of Bourque's revisionist ethnohistory. Most observers and historians acknowledge the climate driven reliance of the inland dwelling Penobscot community on hunting, fishing, and trading in contrast to the Abenaki to the west, such as the Pigwackets, Arosaguntacooks, Kennebecs, and Wawenocs, who lived in coastal regions more suitable for horticultural activities than the Penobscot River region north of Bangor.

A review of Snow reveals that, while he has retained the use of five tribal names (Penobscot, Kennebec, Arosaguntacook, Pigwackets, and Massachusett) in his chart of the coastal villages of Maine, he has designated at least seven Wawenoc villages as being Kennebec. There may now be other corrections to be made in Snow's 1980 chart, but, nonetheless, he performed a very important service for New England ethnohistorians and students of Native American history by focusing renewed attention on the importance of the description of Mawooshen printed by Samuel Purchas. The omission of the Wawenocs from the list of the major indigenous communities of coastal Maine highlights the conundrum posed by the Wawenoc diaspora.

Population Data Derived from Purchas (1625)[a] by Dean Snow

Rivers		Villages				
Purchas	**Modern**	**Purchas**	**Modern**	**Men**	**Houses**	**Sagamores**
			Penobscot			
Quibiquesson	Union	Precante	Ellsworth	150	50	Asticou
						Abermot
*Pemaquid	Penobscot	Upsegon	Bangor	250	60	+Bashabes
		Caiocama	Indian Island	(130)		Maiesquis
		Shasheokeing	Old Town	(130)		Bowant
Ramassoc	Orland	*Panobscot	Orland	80	50	Sibatahood
Apanawapeske	Bagaduce	*Mescombe	Camden	80	50	Aramasoga
		Chebegnadose	Castine	90	30	Skanke
			Kennebec			
Apanmensek	St. George	*(Nusconcus)	Muscongus	(130)		+(Cabahis)
Apponick	Damariscotta	Appisham	?	(130)		Abochigishic
		Mesaqueegamic	?	80	70	Amniquin
		Matammisconte	?	90	80	Narracommiqua
Aponeg	Sheepscot	Nebamocago	?	300	160	+Mentaurmet
		Asshamo	?	70	80	Hamerhaw
		Neredoshan	?	100	120	Sabenaw
*Sagadohoc	Kennebec	*Kenebeke	Augusta	100	80	Apombamen
		Ketangheanycko	Waterville	330	90	Octoworthe
		Naragooc	Norridgewock	150	50	Cocockohamas
*Sagadohoc	Eastern	Massakiga	Dresden	40	8	
			Arosaguntacook			
*Sagadohoc	Androscoggin	*Amereangan	Lisbon Falls	260	90	Sasnoa
						Scawes
		Namercante	Livermore	120	40	Octoworokin
		Buccawganecants	?	400	60	Baccatusshe
			Pequawket			
Ashamabaga	Presumpscot	Agnagebcoc	?	240	70	+Maurmet
						Casherokenit
			Massachusett[b]			
*Shawakotoc	Saco		?			+(Onemechin)

[a] Names preceded by an asterisk (*) are found in Arber and Bradley (1910:192-193). Names preceded by a plus (+) are found in Grant (1907:44-77). Names in parentheses are found in one of those sources but are missing from Purchas (1625). Numbers in parentheses are my estimates for villages for which Purchas provides no numbers. The table is divided into major ethnic subdivisions (see text and Snow 1976d).

The very heart of Mawooshen was the highly populated estuarine region surrounding the four river drainages that constitute the western portion of the Norumbega bioregion: the St. George, Medomak, Damariscotta, and Sheepscot. What these riverine environments lack in comparison to the Kennebec and Penobscot Rivers in terms of volume of flowing water or distance of navigable river is more than made up for by the wealth of natural resources that characterized these areas, especially prior to the later construction of European mills and dams and clear-cutting of tidewater forests, which so radically altered the ecology of the central Maine coast. The first seven villages noted by Purchas and listed as Kennebec by Snow are almost certainly Wawenoc villages. Snow's question marks on his chart illustrate how little we know about the cultural milieu of the Wawenocs. The village at Camden was also probably a Wawenoc settlement. Those at Orland, Ellsworth, and Castine were likely occupied by either Penobscot or smaller affiliated tribes with similar nearly permanent villages, possibly with some horticultural activities at sheltered inland valley locations. Not listed is the thriving community northwest of Mount Desert Island, the Waukeag of Taunton Bay, where corn, bean, and squash horticulture was unlikely (Hale, 1948).

Mawooshen, an ancient land, which, by oral tradition, had once been lead by a Wawenoc Bashebas, included Ellsworth, Orland, Camden, Castine, and all of the villages that Snow lists as Kennebec, Arosaguntacook, and Pequawket. Mawooshen is more complex than Bourque's French version allows; each community had a sagamore subservient to one supreme superchief, the Bashebas. But does Snow's list of sagamores or Bourque's (2001, pg. 115) list of five superchiefs mean to imply that each community only had one sagamore? Why wouldn't many communities have more than one leader over a number of decades? And were there multiple Bashebas, one a Wawenoc, another a Penobscot? Could Onemechin from the Saco River area have been a superchief of Mawooshen?

The Penobscot were the more mobile and less settled members of the population group documented by Rosier (1605) and Purchas (1625); the vast domain of much of interior Maine was their hunting grounds. Indian Island is an example of an ancestral permanent village site typical of those throughout Mawooshen that evolved after 1100 A.D., due in part to the development of the birch bark canoe, which fostered mobility through rapid canoe travel. Rapid canoe travel, in turn, allowed the development of a vast trading network (Snow, 1980). When the confederacy of Mawooshen disintegrated, did the Penobscots become allied with their Maliseet/Passamaquoddy neighbors to the east (Etchemins) when they were caught up in the cataclysm of the fur trade wars caused by the impact of the European demand for beaver hats and coats? What about the mysterious Machias River Indians to the east? What dialect did they speak? Were they Passamaquoddy or Penobscot, or did they identify themselves with another name that has been lost to us? How were they impacted by the fur trade wars and the great pandemic? Another missing community, another diaspora, another palimpsest.

"Wawinak," The Oval Island, as "Arambeck"

Snow (1978), also a contributor to Volume 15 of the *North American Indians*, has, as noted, played an important role in the deletion of references to the Wawenoc Indians. In his essay "Eastern Abenaki" he contends that "Wawinak" in Penobscot means round or oval island and "is a village name, not a tribal or dialectical division." This is a particularly important comment in view of the probable location of a major Wawenoc village, possibly "Arambec" (Arambeck), at the oval loop in the St. Georges River at Hart's Falls just north of the Route 90 bridge. Snow, who gives deserved prominence to the description of Mawooshen in the writings of Purchas (1625) as an important part of Maine's ethnohistory, is also notorious for his comment on "lumping in" (Snow, 1976, pg. 296) the Wawenocs with the Kennebecs. Snow expresses the irritation of many contemporary historians with the nearly inscrutable labyrinth of older ethnic and community labels: "I have avoided most of the confusing babble of names by which New England Indians were known in later times" (Snow, 1980, pg. 42). Snow's (1978) essay on "synonymy" illustrates some of these many disparities and disagreements among contemporary ethnohistorians relating to the identity of the Native American communities of coastal and interior Maine.

Snow leaves the critical question of what dialect was spoken by the Wawenocs unanswered. Was there some ancient observer present, but not noted by Snow, who could prove that the Canibas and Wawenocs shared the same dialect? The place names recorded by Rosier (1605), Davies (1880), and particularly John Smith (1614) prior to the great dying were not in the Penobscot dialect and especially not in the Maliseet-Passamaquoddy languages. Yet "wawinak," as Snow notes, is a Penobscot word for "a loop in the river." The Wawenocs clearly had close links with both the Penobscot and the Canibas. Lumping them with one or another Eastern Abenaki culture may be justified once they cease to exist as an indigenous community, but the Wawenoc community was once an important part of Maine's ethnohistoric past.

When David Ingram hiked the Indian trails from Vera Cruz, Mexico, to the Great Lakes area and then east to Maine and St. John, New Brunswick, in 1568-9 to catch a French packet back to Europe, he likely followed the ancient coastal trails through southern Maine to the central coast near Waldoboro. During this trek, he noted and exaggerated the fabled indigenous city of Norumbega (Arambeck). Did he then follow the Senebec trail up the St. Georges River to Searsmont and then north to Bangor? Or did he go from Searsmont to Ducktrap and head east with friendly Native Americans via the Fox Islands and Eggemoggin Reach? Was the Norumbega he observed - the ancient Arambeck - not at Bangor (disproved by Champlain in 1604), but at the Wawinak, that loop in the St. Georges River just north of Warren? And is the town near the river Norumbega mentioned by Champlain in the narration of his voyages in the following excerpt another reference to Arambeck?

> ...this river (the Penobscot) is the one which several pilots and historians call Norumbega... They also describe how there is a great town thickly populated with skilled and clever indians who use cotton thread. I am convinced that the majority of those who mention it never saw it... (Champlain, 1922, Vol. 1. pg. 285)

A century of local pot hunting, followed by Moorehead's famous hit-and-run archaeological excavations in the 1920s, marked the Harts Falls site on the St. Georges River, just east of the Damariscotta shell heaps and on the banks of one of Maine's most productive alewife runs, as the likely location of one of the most important of the semi-permanent villages of Mawooshen. Mitchell and Spiess have conducted an important archaeological survey of this location (Mitchell, 2002). Mitchell is continuing his surveys on a yearly basis; no outside perimeter of the "Wawinak" site has yet been determined (Hardy, 2006). As recently as 2005, pottery shards in amounts sufficient to fill small buckets have been collected downstream from this large archaeological site. Can any of the villages listed in Purchas (1625) be identified with this location, one of the largest archaeological sites in New England and one of the few sites undisturbed by later New England town, village, or mill construction? Was this the village where some of the 283 warriors encountered by George Waymouth in the lower St. Georges River in 1605 lived? Was this the site of the ancient Arambeck, later exaggerated by David Ingram as a city of gold and riches at Bangor?

Is this location, just a short portage from Penobscot Bay via the Weskeag River at Rockland, the often-referenced location of the Bashebas' residence in 1605? Did he later move east to the "Maine" of Penobscot River or even further east to the Norumbega of Brooksville's Walker Pond (See Maine Atlas and Gazetteer, 1998, map 15.)? What evidence shows that the Bashebas was, in fact, a Penobscot living on Indian Island at Old Town, well away from the abundant marine resources of the Norumbega archipelago? In the decades ahead, what stories of Mawooshen and Arambeck will be uncovered as archaeologists and students of Maine's ethnohistory discover and study the Harts Falls site, one of the most important landmarks of ancient Norumbega?

The Elusive Bashebas of Mawooshen

The narratives and observations of early English and French explorers are littered with multiple references to a superchief of Mawooshen, the Bashebas. At least two, and possibly more, led Mawooshen in its last days (1605-1617). The Bashebas whom Champlain met in the Penobscot River in 1604 could have been a Wawenoc living near Pemaquid or a Penobscot only summering near Pemaquid. Whitney (1887) notes a Canibas Bashebas living on the south end of Swan Island in the Kennebec River at Dresden, long known as the location of an ancestral Canibas (Kennebec) community. Lescarbot (1911) notes the death of a Bashebas at the hands of the English just after the battle of 1607 at the Saco River. Was he the Bashebas Champlain met in 1604 at the Kenduskeag? Was the Bashebas to whom Lescarbot refers a Penobscot, a Wawenoc, a Canibas, or was he from another community in Mawooshen? The Bashebas whom Lescarbot describes at the battle of the Saco River of 1607 was killed in 1608, possibly by the English. Canadian historian Harvey (2000) identifies Asticou, another Bashebas, as both an Almouchiquois and as Penobscot. Asticou's death, in 1615 or shortly thereafter, coincided with the collapse of Mawooshen as a confederacy of indigenous Native American communities. The European ethnic cleansing of the central Maine coast with firearms, alcohol, trade goods, and pathogens was well underway before the first permanent European settlers arrived in 1623.

The questions surrounding the ethnicity of the Bashebas of Maine in Mawooshen and the dialect he spoke remain unresolved. Was the Bashebas really an Etchemin of Maliseet/Passamaquoddy descent, or was he an Abenaki, as many other writers and observers noted? If he was an Etchemin, speaking a significantly different Algonquin dialect than the Eastern Abenakis, was he unable to understand the language of the Saco River community prior to the breakup of the confederacy of Mawooshen? If he was an Abenaki, living between the Etchemins to the east and the Saco River community of the Almouchiquois to the west, was the dialect he spoke also one that allowed communication with both, whereas the dialect of the Micmacs far to the east made communications with the "Almouchiquois" difficult or impossible?

The community affiliation and place of residence of the Bashebas is undetermined. English observers note "near Pemaquid." Champlain and Biard suggest Kenduskeag or on the lower Penobscot, e.g. near Brooksville or Castine. His obvious mobility and broad constituency make a permanent place of residence, if any, impossible to determine. The probability that there were at least two, and perhaps more, Bashebas holding power between 1605 and 1617 only complicates this puzzle.

According to English observers (Rosier, Gorges, Smith, et al), the residence of at least one Bashebas may have been in close proximity to the massive oyster shell middens at Damariscotta, possibly on the St. Georges River or slightly to the east, near Owls Head.

It is only a quick canoe ride to Thomaston from the Wawinak, that loop in the St. Georges River. The very short portage from Thomaston east to the Weskeag River, if any was required at that time, provided easy access to the entire Penobscot River just south of Owls Head. The beckoning of the Wawenocs to Waymouth's explorers and later (1607) to the Popham colonists to meet the nearby Bashebas pointed to the north and east, suggesting the west side of the Penobscot River below the Camden Hills as his likely residence. In contrast to the observations of Rosier, Smith, Davies, Gorges, and many others, the new paradigm of Maine's ethnohistory avoids all mention of the highly populated communities of the tidewater areas between the Kennebec and Penobscot rivers, the most likely residence of the Bashebas. It is unlikely he lived in one northern semi-permanent residence in the winter (Indian Island: Bourque; Kenduskeag: Biard) and another in the summer near the Camden Hills. The Penobscot communities at Old Town and Indian Island are well-known, well-documented ancestral homelands of the Penobscot. A Penobscot-Mawooshen superchief could have lived there. But, if the Bashebas and Samoset were Penobscot, why would their fame and presence not be a part of the oral traditions of the Penobscots? Why then would Speck (1940) not mention either in his study of the Penobscot community? There is no significant archaeological evidence that would place the Bashebas' residence at Bangor or above Bangor as Bourque insists. No French or English commentators note any specific indigenous reference to a Bashebas living at Indian Island in Old Town; all English observers noted he lived "near Pemaquid." The names of the natives kidnapped by Waymouth and the descriptions of the nearby communities listed by Smith (1614) ("*Mecaddacut* [Camden], *Segocket* [Owls Head]... *Nusconcus* [Muscongus, the home of Samoset]*, Pemmaquid,* and *Sagadahock*" pg. 14) are in the Abenaki dialect. These words reflect the presence of a Wawenoc interpreter and guide on his 1614 voyage. This guide is identified by Smith as "Dohnnida" (Smith, 1837, pg. 25); he was a Wawenoc, not a Penobscot or Maliseet/Passamaquoddy. The organization of the trading confederacy of Mawooshen with the Penobscot River at its center also suggests his residence could be anywhere east or west of the Penobscot River. No French or English observers, however, note his presence east of Castine, with the exception of Biard's reference to Asticou at St. Saveur (Mount Desert Island) in 1613. The number of reigning Bashebas, their ethnic identity (as Eastern Abenaki,), and their place of residence will be subjects of speculation as long as anyone cares to inquire about the ethnicity of the indigenous residents of protohistoric Maine.

The assertion by Bourque (2001), Prins (1996), and others that the Bashebas killed by the Micmacs in 1615 was a Penobscot ("Etchemin") superchief raises a very specific problem. The Fernando Gorges (1890) quote, which appears so often in almost every Maine history text, clearly describes the demise of the Bashebas and his community:

> [Bessabez] had under him many great Subjects... some fifteen hundred Bow-Men,
> some others lesse, these they call *Sagamores*... [He] had many enemies, especially

those to the East and North-East, whom they call *Tarrentines*... [H]is owne chief abode was not far from *Pemaquid*, but the Warre growing more and more violent between the *Bashaba* and the *Tarrentines*, who (as it seemed) presumed upon the hopes they had to be favored of the *French* who were seated in *Canada*[.] [T]heir next neighbors, the *Tarrentines* surprised the *Bashaba* and slew him and all his People near about him. (Gorges, 1890, 2, pg.74-76; reprinted in Bourque, 2001, pg. 119)

When John Smith sailed along the Maine coast in 1614, the turmoil of the intertribal conflicts of the fur trade wars was well underway. Both Smith (1837) in 1614 and later other historians (Williamson, 1832; Locke, 1859) clearly note that the Camden Hills were the line of defense between the attacking Tarentines coming from the north and east and the Abenaki communities to the west and south of Mecaddacut (Camden). If the chief residence of the last Bashebas was, in fact, Indian Island or another nearby Penobscot River location, what was he doing living behind enemy lines a year before he was killed? By 1614, the attacking Souriquois (Micmac) had already overrun much of the eastern section of Mawooshen. It was at this time that Prins (1996) notes that they had established a stronghold on Mount Desert Island. Other sources, such as Williamson (1832) are very clear that the attacking "Tarentines" also included "Etchemins" and possibly even Penobscots, whom Williamson indicates had been supplied with firearms by the French. Aside from raising the question of a temporary alliance between the Penobscots and the Micmacs, the reality of radically altered ethnic relationships in Maine during the pre-pandemic turmoil of 1614 - 1617 makes it difficult to argue that, in 1615, the Tarentines (Micmacs, etc.) were attacking and conquering a community, which they had already occupied for at least a year.

Is it possible that the Bashebas and his fifteen hundred bowmen were trapped at Indian Island, surrounded by Micmacs on the lower Penobscot River and Mount Desert Island? If this was the scenario, then why would the Bashebas have been the victim of a surprise attack? And then there is the reference to "the northeast" in the description of the attack on the Bashebas. The area to the northeast of Indian Island was, and is today, one of the most unpopulated areas of the eastern United States. There were no nearby communities of Etchemins; "northeast," in fact, refers to the Penobscot River itself in the temporary alliance of the Penobscots with the Micmacs and Etchemins to the east, which Williamson (1832) describes in his *History of Maine*. That is, the attack on the Bashebas and his bowmen came from the northeast from this location. Gorges' (1658) description only makes sense if the Bashebas was living at or west of Mecaddacut (Camden) as implied by many descriptions of his "nearby" presence in early narratives. It is unlikely that "Tarentines" attacking what Prins (1996) and Bourque (2001) call the "Etchemin superchief" at Indian Island were coming from a location to the northeast of Bangor or Indian Island. There is the possibility that further research will show that the attacking

Souriquois came down the Penobscot River from the north, but this remains an unlikely scenario, and does not match the traditional narrations provided by Gorges and others.

The issue of the identity of the Bashebas is further complicated by French sources, specifically Biard, in his description of the rout of the French settlement at Saint Sauveur (Mount Desert Island) by Captain Argall and the English in 1613. Hearing of the attack on the French at St. Sauveur, a number of natives came to Biard in the evening:

> ...offering us their canoes and their help to take us anywhere we wished to go. They also made the proposition, that if we wanted to live with them, there were three Captains -- Betsabes, Aguigueou and Asticou, each one of whom, for his share, would take ten of our band (since there were thirty of us left), and would take care of us until the following year, when the French ships would arrive upon the coast; and that in this way we should be able to go back to our own country without falling into the hands of the wicked Ingres, as they call the English. (Thwaites, 1898, pg. 71)

Biard's observation that Asticou was one of three captains, one of whom was also called Betsabes, raises the question of whether or not Asticou was an earlier successor of the Bashebas who succeeded Olmechin after Membertou's war of revenge in 1607. Canadian historian D.C. Harvey has earlier noted that Asticou was the "sagamore of the Armouchiquois (Penobscots) on the frontiers of Acadia; fl. 1608-16" (Harvey, 2000). Therefore, the identity and location of the residence of the last Bashebas of Mawooshen remains unresolved. There is no reason why Mawooshen didn't have Penobscot superchiefs. The issue in identifying the ethnicity of the multiple Bashebas of Mawooshen lies in conflicting historical descriptions and especially in the fact that the unraveling of Mawooshen was well underway when the last Bashebas was killed. Did this Bashebas and his 1,500 bowmen really live at Indian Island on the Penobscot? Or did his residence and his community lie to the west of the front line of the attack by the "Tarentines," so frequently noted as the Camden Hills at Mecaddacut?

Wawenoc Palimpsest

These conflicting Euro-American versions of Maine's ethnohistory and the description of the confederacy of Mawooshen (See Figures 19 and 20 in the Map Appendix A.) by Native Americans demand further exploration of another side to *American Beginnings* (Baker, 1994), i.e. Native American endings, the demise of the coastal populations of Native Americans that inhabited the New England coast before European settlement. More specifically, why did the Wawenoc Indians living along the estuaries and rivers to the south of Davistown Plantation disappear from the landscape of coastal Maine? The vestigial trails, burial grounds, and coastal middens of the Norumbega bioregion are an archeological fact, not a cartographic myth. Norumbega was not a city filled with gold, nor was it a cartographic mistake. The later intermingling of Wawenoc, Kennebec, Androscoggin, Pigwacket, and Massachusetts survivors with the Penobscots and the incursion of Etchemins from eastern and northern Maine to fill the void left by the devastating virgin soil epidemics of 1617 - 1619 resulted in European encounters with an amalgam of survivors from many tribes after 1620. This is the "ethnic composite" acknowledged by Speck (1940, pg. 301) in his later postscript to the publication of *Penobscot Man*. This diverse population of Native Americans from many decimated communities coalesced in Maine to continue the fight begun by southern New England Indians in the King Philip's War. While southern New England was quickly cleared of Native Americans after 1676, the deep forests, rich natural resources, and remote locations of surviving tribal remnants in central and northern New England, including backcountry areas of the Norumbega bioregion such as Davistown, allowed these surviving bands of Native Americans to continue sporadic attacks on European settlements until the fall of Quebec in 1759. Even after the fall of Quebec, indigenous survivors of the French and Indian Wars continued to play a role in regional politics through the medium of the Wabanaki Confederacy, which was organized by the Penobscots and other Native Americans in Maine in the late 18th century.

The principal Wawenocs villages were in tidewater locations, many at the head of the tide of the rivers originating in the watershed of the Davistown Plantation, now the towns of Liberty and Montville. These rivers are the Sheepscot, Medomak, and the St. Georges. The Davis Stream, which leads to Damariscotta Lake, originates just southwest of the Davistown Plantation boundary in Washington, Maine. The Davistown Plantation, part of the Norumbega backcountry, was a component of the inland hunting grounds of the Wawenocs and abutted the family hunting territories of the Penobscots to the northeast. Frye Mountain and the Passagassawakeag River watershed are the probable southern limits of the Penobscot family hunting territories. The Montville village called "The Kingdom," one of the earliest mill sites established in the Davistown Plantation, perpetuates the Algonquin word muskingum (elk's eyes, deer eyes) (Boyd, 1885) and, as in the case of many New England place names, can be considered a vestigial reference to these ancient hunting grounds. The Kingdom Falls location is particularly interesting, not only as an ideal out-of-the-wind winter campsite, but also as the probable age-old site of commodity exchange between the Wawenocs to the south, Penobscots to the north and east, and Canibas to the west, prior to European settlement and the beginning of the French and Indian Wars.

The Muskingum is one of many backcountry winter hunting grounds connected by ancient trails to the coastal villages of the Wawenocs and the extraordinary marine resources located in the riverine environments near Wiscasset, Damariscotta, Boothbay, and Pemaquid. The presence of the Wawenocs and other nearby indigenous communities, such as the Canibas and Penobscots, is recorded by archaeological sites, shell middens, vestigial pathways, crossroads, place names, oral and written histories, chronicles, and the observations of numerous French and English explorers and visitors before 1620. Medomak, Cushnoc, Sheepscot, Norumbega, and Senebec are a few among many echoes of the voices of the dislocated indigenous peoples whose ethnic identities and community affiliations have been gradually erased from many of the contemporary texts in the annotated citations which follow.

The seasonal migrations of the Wawenocs and nearby Penobscots are inscribed in the Davistown landscape and can be seen today in the labyrinth of back country roads which still follow the prehistoric Indian paths. The archaic and ceramic period cultures to which these trails give voice are also recorded by archeological remnants from 12,000 years of Maine history. The nearby Damariscotta and Medomak shell middens are a counterpart to the Muskingum and provide compelling testament to the existence, longevity, and abundant resources of these prehistoric Native American communities. The continuity of midden deposits, their huge size (The Damariscotta River whaleback oyster heap, now destroyed, was among the largest known in the world.), and the many trails leading from the back country to these coastal sites provide compelling evidence that the Wawenocs shared their extraordinary natural resources with neighboring communities (Canibas, Penobscot, etc.). The lingering trail systems and associated canoe routes of the Eastern Abenaki and the Penobscots, including the Wawenocs, abound throughout coastal Maine and converge on these marine resources (Cook, 1985.) The combination of the shell middens, early stone tools and other artifacts, burial grounds, ancient trails, and lingering place names constitute a voice from the past, which cannot be ignored in the documentation of Maine's state, regional, and local history.

The extensive network of archaeological sites in the Norumbega bioregion, especially along the coast adjacent to the Sheepscot, Damariscotta, Medomak, and St. Georges Rivers, and the chronicles of early explorers, such as Rosier, provide vivid evidence of the florescence of these Native American communities. Clearly designated on the many maps discussed in *American Beginnings* (1994), this region is contiguous with the confederacy of Mawooshen recounted by Samuel Purchas' *Purchas, his Pilgrimage*

68

HEART OF THE OYSTER-SHELL BED, DAMARISCOTTA
RIVER, LINCOLN COUNTY, MAINE.

Figure 8 A remarkable and rare photograph of the oyster shell midden at Damariscotta prior to its destruction. (Rufus King Sewall, 1895, *Ancient voyages to the western continent: Three phases of history on the coast of Maine,* pg. 26)

(1625). Recent analysis of growth patterns of shellfish remains from middens in the central coast indicates that these communities were nearly permanent (Spiess, 1983). The current paradigm that all Native Americans living east of the Kennebec River were wandering hunters and gatherers is contradicted by archaeological evidence consistent with both English and French chronicles of a tidewater network of Native village locations and the oral and written history of the confederacy of Mawooshen.

The combined processes of the physical eradication of Native American villages and landscapes and Euro-American construction of new villages, new communities, and new historical perspectives - the advent of a new culture - continues the pattern of the layering of one historical palimpsest upon another. Evidence of the former existence of the indigenous communities of coastal Maine has been obliterated in physical acts of destruction. In many locations, this palimpsest may be a layer of rubbish underlying the shady streets of numerous Maine villages. That the history of the prior existence of the now extinct Abenaki community of the Wawenocs has been squelched and then deleted from what Wiseman calls the White Man's version of the cultural history of Native Americans is an unacceptable chapter in the saga of the "disappearing Indians" (Wiseman, 2001).

Palimpsest: 1. a piece of writing material or manuscript on which the original writing has been erased to make room for other writing. 2. a place, etc., showing layers of history, etc. (*The Oxford Dictionary and Thesaurus*, 1996, pg. 1075)

Euro-American control of the writing, and now the nearly sectarian neoconservative rewriting, of the ethnohistory of the indigenous residents of the central Maine coast and other New England locations has gradually obliterated our memory of the many Native American communities which preceded us and are, in many cases, no longer represented by survivors who can defend and renew their ancestral heritage. The reconnoitering of history means peeling back contemporary revisionist theories of what we now think about Native American presence in coastal Maine before and during the first colonial dominion and re-evaluating the now debunked commentaries of the past. The most important corollary of this reconsideration is listening to Native Americans as they recount alternative non-European histories of their past. Are there yet any surviving Abenaki of Wawenoc descent to undertake this challenge?

The broad sweep of revisionist theory has erased from our recent written history acknowledgment of and respect for the Wawenoc community and their ancestral homelands of the central Maine coast, now considered too unimportant -- too much of a bother -- to document, to remember. Contemporary revisionist ethnohistoric reductionism ironically recapitulates our long inattention to the significance of the story of Mawooshen retold by Purchase, reinforcing our pattern of covering up and forgetting the past, obscuring the links between Mawooshen and Norumbega. Revisiting the narratives and tales of the older historians is the first step in reconsidering and remembering this past. This process of remembering discloses a culture that, in the case of the Wawenocs, commingled briefly with its European invaders before disappearing with no descendants. A reconsideration of the meaning of Norumbega and the Wawenoc diaspora involves taking a journey into the collective remembrances of the past, which must include not just those of our European ancestors or the traditions of the Penobscot, Passamaquoddy, and Maliseets of the historic era but also the communities of the eastern Abenaki (Pigwackets, Androscoggins, Kennebecs, Wawenocs) that did not survive the European conquest of North America. And what of the Penobscots, key members of the confederacy of Mawooshen; were they Eastern Abenaki (Snow, 1976b), Etchemins (Williamson, 1832, Bourque, 1989) or Maritime Abenaki (Abenaki History website)?

Peeling back the revisionist paradigm of Maine's ethnohistory means encountering, exploring, and groping through that inconvenient "babble" of disorderly history, all those ethnic voices clamoring to be heard. Can snippets of the narrations and conversations of earlier observers, indigenous and Euro-American, be woven together to reconstruct the story of the dislocated and then erased communities of the central Maine coast? And if we are going to reconsider the ethnicity and cultural significance of the inhabitants of the central Maine coast at the interface of prehistory and history, i.e. protohistory, what is the basis of their florescence? More specifically, what is the environmental basis for the evolution of the trading confederacy of Mawooshen in the bioregion of Norumbega?

The Ecology of the Central Maine Coast

Analysis of the ecology of the central Maine coast provides another viewpoint from which to consider the ethnohistoric controversy pertaining to the confederacy of Mawooshen and its relationship to Norumbega and the Wawenoc community. No reconsideration of the ethnohistory of the maritime peninsula can escape the geographical realities of the region. The Gulf of Maine bioregion is dominated by a series of southeasterly flowing rivers that begin with the trickle of the North River at Hanover and Marshfield, MA, and ends with the St. John and Petitcodiac rivers, and Moncton and Chignecto Bay at the head of the Bay of Fundy in New Brunswick. In between lay the major rivers of New England: Merrimack, Saco, Androscoggin, Kennebec, Penobscot, and St. Croix. Scattered all along this coast are smaller rivers, which have had large historical roles, both in prehistory and European settlement: Charles, Piscataqua, Presumpscot, Sheepscot, Medomak, St. Georges, Narramissic, Union, Skillings, and, east of Schoodic point, the Narraguagus, Pleasant, Machias, etc. These rivers are, in turn, components of distinct watersheds (Figure 9), which have a primordial relationship with the Native American communities of prehistory. The revisionist suggestion that these communities of the past were not riverine- centered, but rather nomadic, wandering, hunting, and gathering cultures is one of the most startling elements in the two cultures controversy. The intimate relationship of the Massachusetts, Pigwackets, Androscoggins, Kennebecs, Penobscots, Passamaquoddys, and Maliseets to specific river basins and watersheds is an incontrovertible part of the

Watersheds of Maine

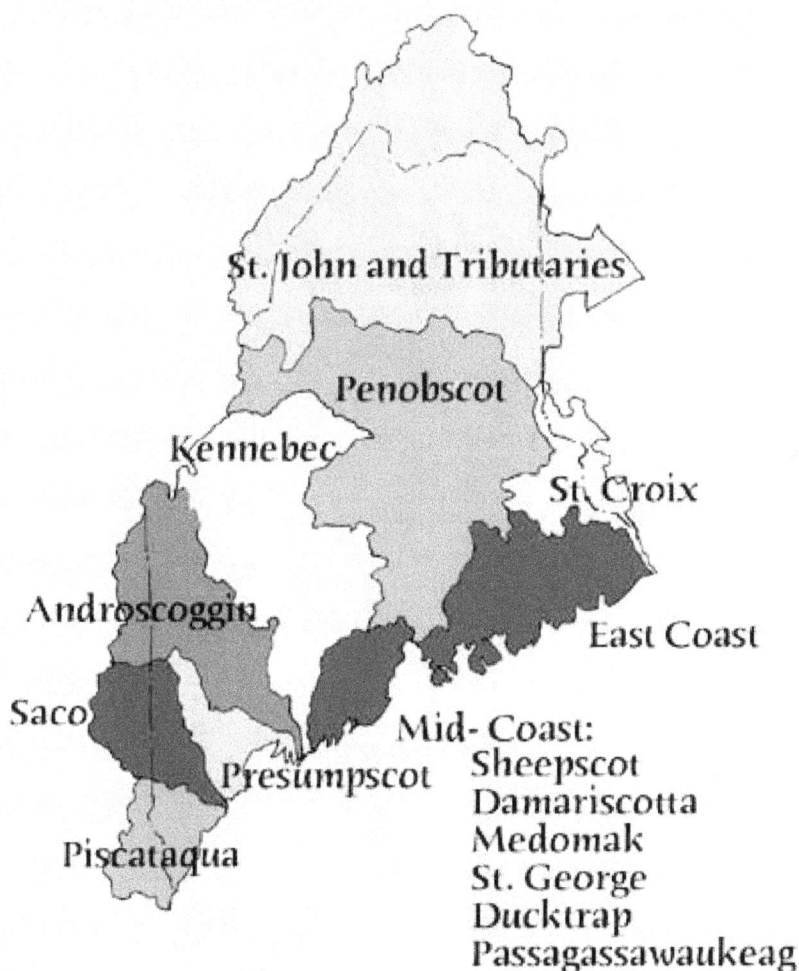

Figure 9 Courtesy of Kerry Hardy, Director of Merryspring Park, Camden, ME.

history of the maritime peninsula. That the Wawenoc community, whose ancestral homelands included four small rivers rather than one large one, is omitted from this

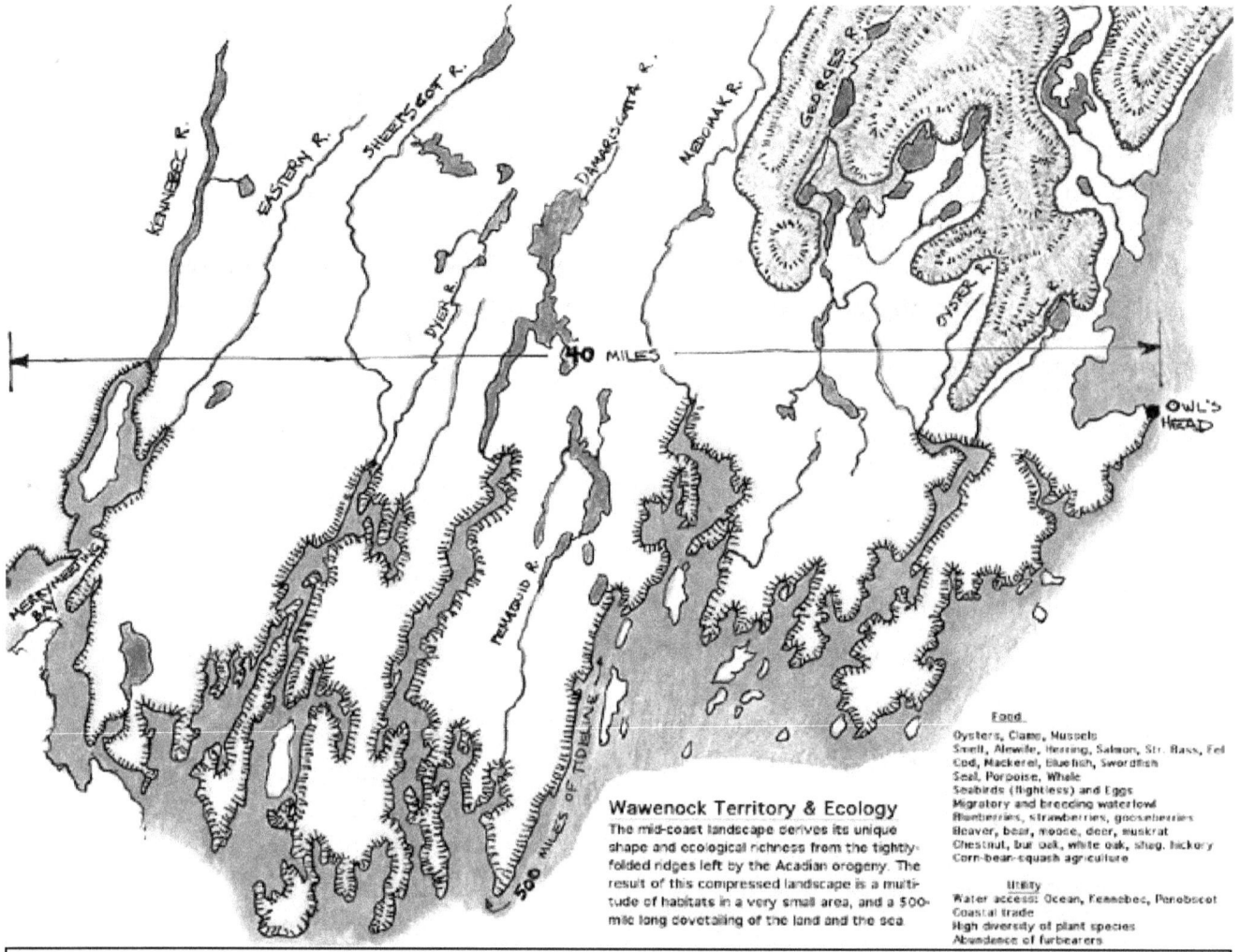

Wawenock Territory & Ecology
The mid-coast landscape derives its unique shape and ecological richness from the tightly-folded ridges left by the Acadian orogeny. The result of this compressed landscape is a multitude of habitats in a very small area, and a 500-mile long dovetailing of the land and the sea

Food
Oysters, Clams, Mussels
Smelt, Alewife, Herring, Salmon, Str. Bass, Eel
Cod, Mackerel, Bluefish, Swordfish
Seal, Porpoise, Whale
Seabirds (flightless) and Eggs
Migratory and breeding waterfowl
Blueberries, strawberries, gooseberries
Beaver, bear, moose, deer, muskrat
Chestnut, bur oak, white oak, shag. hickory
Corn-bean-squash agriculture

Utility
Water access: Ocean, Kennebec, Penobscot
Coastal trade
High diversity of plant species
Abundance of furbearers

Figure 10 Wawenoc Territory and Ecology. Courtesy of Kerry Hardy, Director of Merryspring Park, Camden, ME.

history only adds to this controversy.

A closer look at the watersheds of the central Maine coast between the Kennebec and Penobscot rivers, the heart of Norumbega and the confederacy of Mawooshen, and the homeland of the Wawenoc community, reveals a virtual archipelago of southeasterly running ridges and peninsulas separated by small rivers and bays. Though small in area compared with the vast reaches of the Penobscot drainage to the north and east, this bioregion has over 500 miles of shoreline. Its tidewater bays and inlets and its inshore and offshore fisheries constitute one of the world's richest marine ecosystems.

Hardy's (2006) listing of the major resources of this area recalls the work of Russell (1980) and establishes the parameters of this resource-rich environment. (See Figure 10 and the list of resources in the bottom corner.) One can then extend this listing to an overall inventory of the natural resources available to the indigenous communities of the past: fur-bearing animals, moose and deer, waterfowl, terrestrial birds, timber resources, native fruits, plants, and other flora and fauna listed in such detail by Russell. In fact, Russell's appendix of the trees, shrubs, and herbaceous plants of southern New England also applies in almost all cases to the ecology of the central Maine coast. Russell's appendix gives the common name, botanical designation, and use of the resource and covers everything from black and white ash (basketry, bows, arrows, medicine) to pussy willow (hoops and handles), and witch hazel (bows, medicine). Russell notes that his listing of over 150 trees, shrubs, and plants is in no way complete. However, it does suggest the diversity of natural resources available to residents of the central Maine coast in the era before European settlement. The maps of edible nut trees for Maine and its central coast compiled by Hardy provide one example of the rich non-marine resources of this area (Figure 11.)

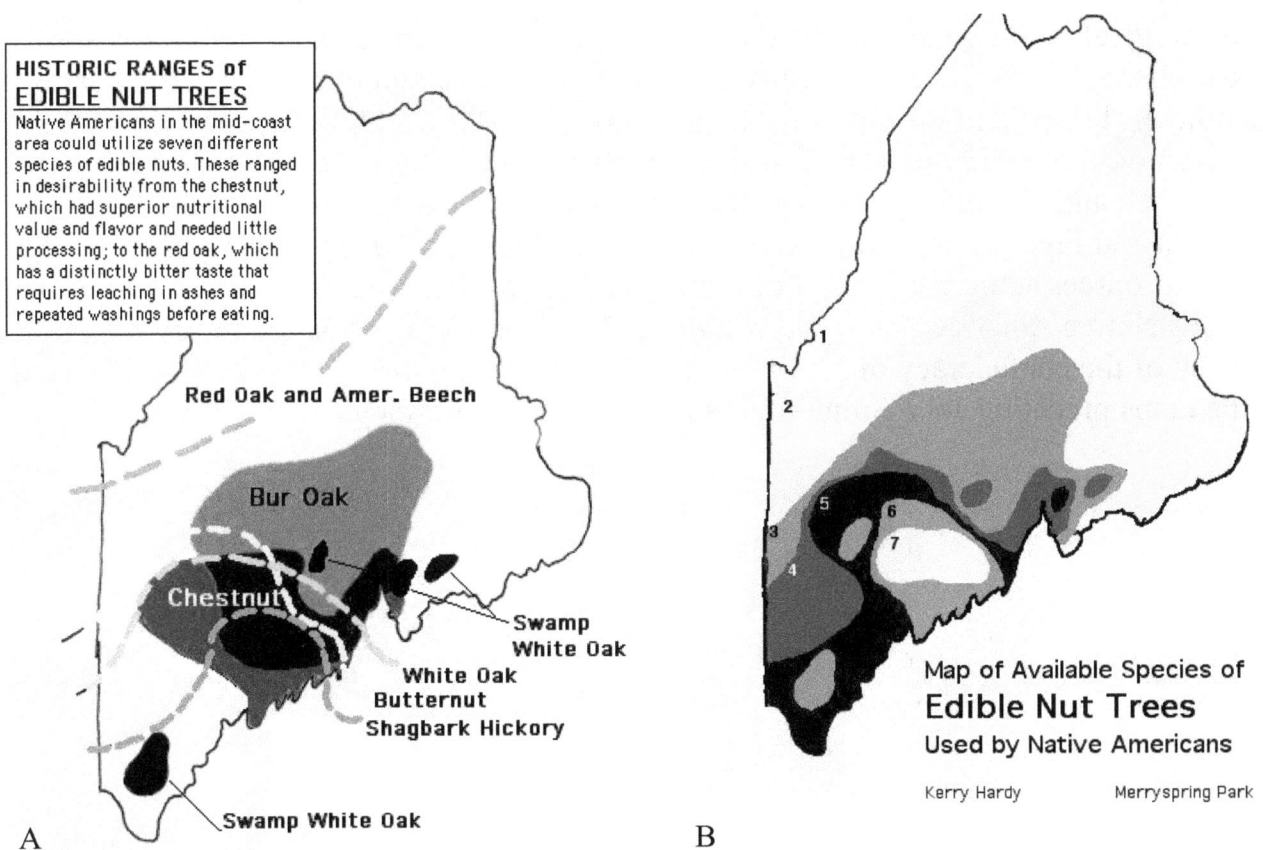

HISTORIC RANGES of EDIBLE NUT TREES
Native Americans in the mid-coast area could utilize seven different species of edible nuts. These ranged in desirability from the chestnut, which had superior nutritional value and flavor and needed little processing; to the red oak, which has a distinctly bitter taste that requires leaching in ashes and repeated washings before eating.

Red Oak and Amer. Beech

Bur Oak

Chestnut

Swamp White Oak

White Oak
Butternut
Shagbark Hickory

Swamp White Oak

A

Map of Available Species of **Edible Nut Trees** Used by Native Americans

Kerry Hardy   Merryspring Park

B

Figure 11 Courtesy of Kerry Hardy, Director of Merryspring Park, Camden, ME. Information for these maps is from A: Burns, Russell M. and Honkala, Barbara H. (1990). *Silvics of North America.* Agriculture Handbook 654. U.S. Department of Agriculture, Forest Service, Washington, DC. B: The American Chestnut Foundation, 469 Main St Suite 1, PO Box 4044, Bennington, Vermont 05201.

The synergistic combination of marine and terrestrial resources in combination with

Maine's unique geography formed a habitat capable of supporting a significant population of semi-permanent villages. Its history of occupation by indigenous peoples can be traced thousands of years into the past. In fact, the region between the Kennebec and Penobscot rivers is the component of the resource-rich Gulf of Maine bioregion that excelled over all others in its natural wealth and unique ecology. The existence of these resources provides the basis for the flourishing Native American communities who lived here before contact with the European settlers who undermined and then destroyed their culture.

The presence of these communities is confirmed by the archaeological evidence of their activities. The oyster shell middens of the Damariscotta River are among the largest in the world. Many smaller clam and oyster middens characterized every cove and tidewater bay in the region. Due to subsequent English settlement at many important tidewater locations between the Kennebec and Penobscot rivers, further archaeological research at critical head-of-tide village sites is impossible. In contrast, the most thorough archaeological investigations along the Maine coast have been carried out to the east of the Penobscot River by the Abbe Museum and its sponsors, and by Bourque, Petersen, and others. The Abbe Museum excavations (1920 - 1960) also document the florescence of indigenous communities east of the Penobscot River and the land of the Wawenocs. Mawooshen and Norumbega overlap and include the archipelagos of the Deer Island peninsula and Frenchman's Bay. The consistency of distribution and the wealth of the natural resources along the Maine coast are sufficient in and of themselves to suggest a vigorous Native American presence without reference to their ethnic identities, the oral tradition of the confederacy of Mawooshen, or the lingering inscription of Norumbega on all the maps predating John Smith's 1614 renaming of Norumbega as New England.

The Myth of the Limits of Horticulture

A vigorous, socially complex culture of Native American communities could have flourished along the central Maine coast without any horticultural activities. Such was the wealth of natural resources in this region that no bean-maize-squash agriculture was necessary to support these communities. However, this wealth of marine resources cannot be used to argue against horticultural activities. Nor can the assertion be made that, for climatological reasons, horticulture east of the Saco River was impossible. In fact, horticulture was widespread in the sheltered inland valleys of the central Maine coast, as evidenced by the hundreds of farms in the ancient Pemaquid region in Maine's first colonial dominion. The climate did not suddenly change in1623 when English farmers flooded the tidewater areas formerly inhabited by the Wawenocs and Kennebecs. Beginning with Champlain and Biard, French sources clearly document widespread maize cultivation in these sheltered locations. In *A dictionary of the Abenaki language in North America* (1722), the French missionary Rasle documents the extent of maize horticulture in the Kennebec River watershed with his multiple listings of numerous varieties of corn (red, white, yellow, black, multicolored, and "nenabiminar-- corn which comes quickly") (Hardy, 2006). The implication in Vol. 15 of the *Handbook of North American Indians* (1978) and in other contemporary sources that maize horticulture was restricted to areas west of the Saco River is incorrect.

The major climatic event of the millennium was the sudden cooling of the little ice age in the mid-14th century. This cooling was unabated in the 17th century, but was still not sufficient to inhibit horticultural activities in the area between the Kennebec and Penobscot rivers. Coastal fogs and onshore summer winds meant that horticultural activities had to and still must occur in the sheltered river valleys above the head of tide in areas of the central Maine coast west of Schoodic Point. The same frost limitations on beans-maize agriculture that deterred back-to-the-land immigrants of the late 20th century from farming in the northern and eastern locations would also have limited horticultural activities in pre- and protohistory. The traces of corn kernels found by Spiess (1980) at Pemaquid and dating to the 15th century were probably grown inland in sheltered river valleys and brought to Pemaquid as one commodity of the complex trading network that characterized not only the confederacy of Mawooshen but also all Native American communities on the maritime peninsula and to the west and south. Smoked oysters, blueberries, clams, wampum, birch bark, stone edge tools, moose hides, and other furs are only the most commonplace of trade goods that inevitably would have included sassafras, nuts, beans, corn, spruce gum, spruce root, sweet grass, and dozens of other natural renewable resources. The myth of the few wandering homeless nomads living on the central Maine coast prior to European settlement is just that, a myth. This myth, along with the nonexistence of Mawooshen, Norumbega, the Wawenocs, and other communities, is the vestige of an historic ethno-cleansing that is symbolized by the 400£

bounty on Native American scalps issued by the Colony of Massachusetts in the mid-18th century. That 95% of New England's mid-16th century coastal population east of Cape Cod were killed by epidemic (most) and warfare (a lesser percentage) by 1620 is testament to the potency of virgin soil epidemics and the efficiency of both French and English firearms, which played a major role in exterminating the indigenous populations of the maritime peninsula. That the florescence of Abenaki First Nation indigenous communities on the central Maine coast west of Schoodic Point has yet to be affirmed, to be given voice, by descendants of these communities, however few, is the contemporary challenge of this ethnohistoric controversy. The rich natural resources of the central Maine coast and the presence of horticultural activities in sheltered valley locations in the late ceramic period underscore the degree to which the ethnohistory of the indigenous communities of this area have been submerged and obscured.

Maritime Resources of Mawooshen

When the apple blossoms bloomed in that golden age before the European invasion of New England, the estuaries and streams of the central Maine coast came alive. Sturgeon ran up beyond the tidewater to spawn; smelt made their annual appearance during the six weeks before the solstice. Elvers, those nocturnal baby eels, 6,000 to the pound, made their midnight appearance. Frost fish were already gone, to return again in the fall. Alewives, those bony herring, were making a run to the ponds from the St. Georges to the Sheepscot to spawn. Cod was ubiquitous in inshore bays. Oysters, mussels, clams, and scallops were ready to hand to relieve the starving time. The lobster was so common that it was used as fertilizer for maize - bean horticulture in areas along the southern New England coast. In Maine, alewives and shad served the same purpose in areas beyond the head of the tide and the summer fog line. There was no end to the spawning season. Flounder came both in the spring and the fall. Mackerel, striped bass, and bluefish ran up the estuaries in the warm season, perhaps because the cold Labrador current of the Gulf of Maine drove them to these warmer environments; only sharks were deterred and stayed to the southward (July and August). The brook trout ran in all seasons. Whale hunting and swordfishing were millennia old, though the deep sea fishers may have disappeared before the era of Mawooshen. Only the Passamaquoddy are noted as a sea mammal hunting culture in the ceramic period (Erickson, 1978). What might be considered the romantic fantasy of a lost paradise was, in fact, one of the world's richest ecosystems: the Gulf of Maine and the archipelago of the central Maine coast. No such wealth of edible resources existed on the Penobscot River above Bangor or along the endless mudflats of the upper Bay of Fundy -- Etchemin territory.

In the fall, the eels returned full grown, 25% oil; they had been 5% oil in the spring. As with moose, deer, bear, pine marten, otter, and other mammals, eels and other fish were fattened by summer feeding, ready for the late fall and early winter harvest that preceded the starving time. These nocturnal eels came above the tidewater to hibernate in the winter mud of the spawning ponds, the same habitat used by the beaver. In Scotland, the huge schools of eels gyrating in their mating rituals were mistaken for Lock Ness monsters. In Maine, they were an important late winter food source. Colonists used wood barrels made with staves and shaped by heading knives to hold speared eels; in Mawooshen, lithic and bone spears filled birch-bark and spruce-root baskets, only later made with crooked knives and basket knives fashioned by European steel (Figure 12.) Cast iron cooking pots, steel edge tools, and firearms for hunting signaled the end of the era of annual rhythms of indigenous populations harvesting the natural resources of the ecosystems of the Gulf of Maine bioregion. When the Euro-Americans came, all the breeding beaver were slaughtered by the invading forces of a market economy that decimated the beaver population and introduced pathogens that caused a virgin soil epidemic that devastated the indigenous communities of Mawooshen. The Wawenoc community has disappeared and is forgotten; the depletion of the regions natural resources has taken longer. Tenacious lobster populations are among the last survivors of this earlier ecological florescence.

Ecology is Economy

The Native American communities living on the New England coastline had something in common with the Euro-American settlements that evolved after 1600: their economy was almost wholly dependent on the ecological characteristics of the bioregion. In the case of Euro-American settlers in New England, the combination of marine and timber resources were the key elements in the growth of a market economy that allowed successful settlement of what myth at least maintains was a wilderness. As Russell, (1980), Cronon (1983), and many other writers point out, when the first settlers arrived in New England, they found vast sections of open land formerly cultivated or burned for deer hunting by Native Americans who died in the great epidemic of 1617 - 1619. In fact, the land was not wilderness. The economies of these former communities were also intimately dependent on the same ecological and natural resources that sustained the later European settlers. The vital role that marine resources, such as shellfish, codfish, alewives, eels, and crabs, played in the Native American diet recurred in the dependence of the first European settlers on these food sources.

The vast forests of New England provided the habitat for the deer, moose, and other wildlife so essential to the economy of indigenous communities. With their steel edge

Figure 12 Basket knife, circa 1600 - 1700. This rare variation of the crooked knife was used for splitting the wood for ash baskets. This tool illustrates the use of cementation steel (blister steel - the blisters are clearly visible on the tool) for the production of steel edge tools and other trade items. This tool was almost certainly made in Europe and may have been specifically designed and produced to meet the needs of Native American basket makers during the early days of contact with European traders. By 1600, blister steel made by the cementation process was becoming widely available in northern Europe and in England, and helped to fill the rapidly growing need for steel for edge tools and weapons in the late Elizabethan era. Up until that date German steel made from the spathic ores of Carinthia (Austria) had been the primary source of high quality steel. For additional commentary on late medieval and early modern steel production strategies for the edge tools that made exploration of the New World possible, see The Davistown Museum publication *Hand Tools in History*. (Davistown Museum 011006T1)

tools, Euro-American settlers made more use of the timber resources of New England, vis-à-vis shipbuilding and the coasting and West Indies trade, than the Native American communities, but the link between ecology and economy is an essential characteristic of both cultures. Indigenous communities recognized the usefulness of edge tools made with steel and quickly adopted axes, hatchets, knives, and tomahawks for warfare, including scalping, and for hunting and canoe- and basket-making.

Perhaps the most interesting common link, and one that brought both cultures into intimate contact with each other, was the Native American reliance on fur-bearing mammals, such as beaver, otter, and moose, and the sudden demand in the European communities for many of these same furs, as the beaver populations of eastern, central, and northern Europe became depleted in the 16th century. The search for these furs brought European traders to all coastal regions of North America from the St. Lawrence River valley to the Chesapeake Bay region. Thwaites (1898) notes a well-established French fur trading network in place as far south as the Potomac River by 1578. Before beaver populations were depleted in New England by a predatory market economy that harvested all the breeding females, the Massachusetts and southern and central Maine coast were also a productive source of these pelts. For centuries, if not millennia, the beaver population provided essential clothing for Native American communities throughout New England. Hardy's (2005) depiction of the beaver habitat in the lower St. Georges River basin provides a microcosmic overview of a small slice of the Gulf of Maine bioregion, which was the heart of the confederacy of Mawooshen (Figure 13.)

Before Europeans came in search of beaver and other furs, thousands of Basque, Spanish, French, and English fishermen had made the journey across the North Atlantic to the rich fishing grounds off the coast of Newfoundland. These "newfound lands" also included areas to the southwest of the Grand Banks, i.e. the land mass of the maritime peninsula west of Georges Banks, including the Bay of Fundy and the Gulf of Maine. To what extent the tens of thousands of fishing expeditions, which came to the coast of Newfoundland between 1500 and 1600, also penetrated the rich bioregion to the southwest of Nova Scotia remains an ongoing controversy. Nonetheless, the intimate relationship between ecology and economy is repeated again and again in both Native American and Euro-American settlement patterns. These communities shared not only a mutual interest in the fur trade and fishing but also an uncanny similarity in where and why they established communities on the New England and Maine coast. The southeasterly flowing rivers that empty into the Gulf of Maine were the location of principal tidewater villages of Native Americans who lived in the confederacy of Mawooshen and the land of Norumbega. These tidewater and riverine village sites - Cushnoc, Pejepscot, Pemaquid, Machias, and St. John to the east, and many others - became the first points of contact between indigenous and European trappers, traders, and fishermen in the form of trucking stations and trading posts.

While the trade goods and the pathogens brought to the New World by the European traders and fishermen soon devastated the Native American communities of the Maine

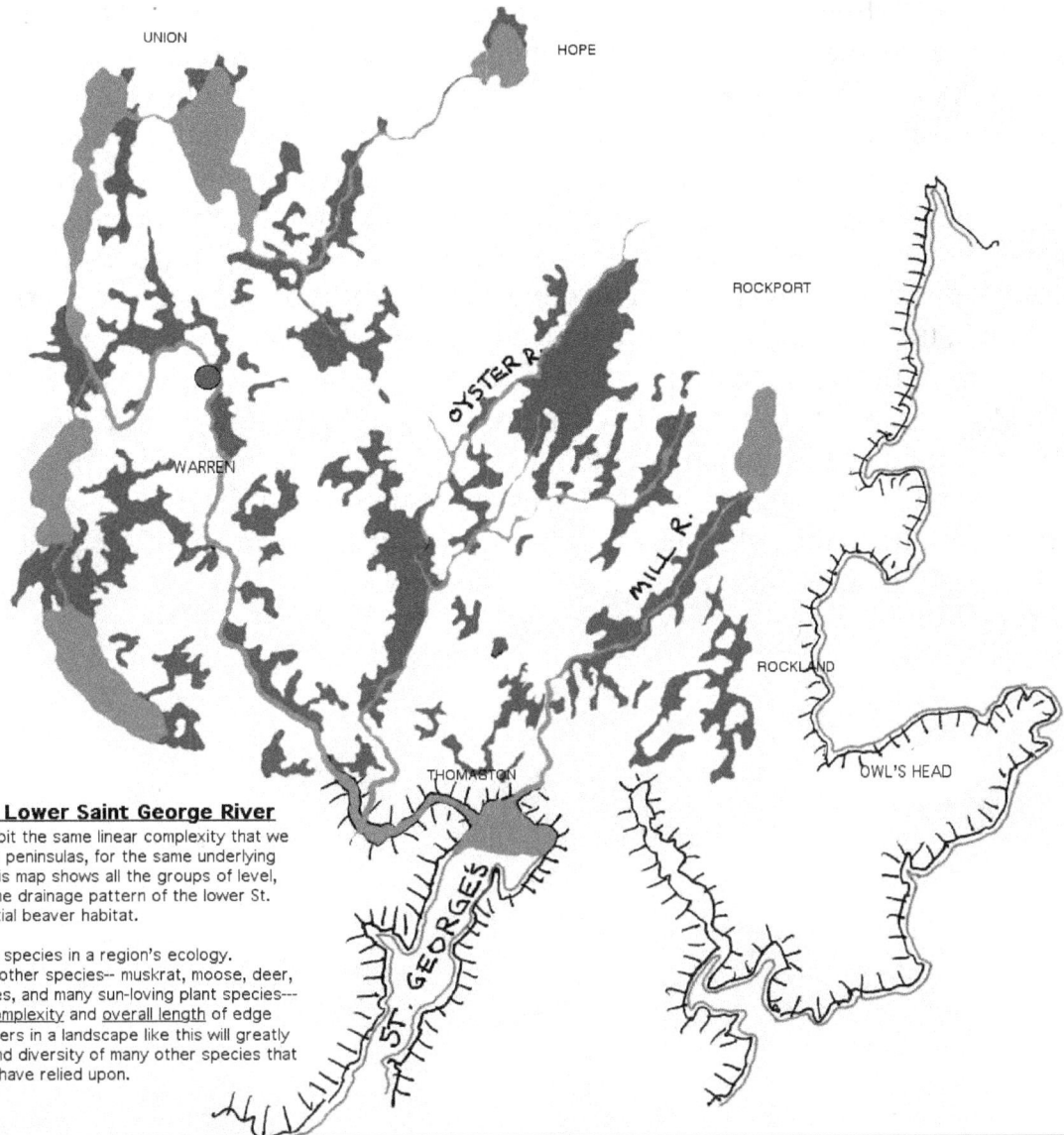

Beaver Habitat in Lower Saint George River

The mid-coast soils exhibit the same linear complexity that we see in the outlines of its peninsulas, for the same underlying geomorphic reasons. This map shows all the groups of level, poorly drained soils in the drainage pattern of the lower St. George River; i.e. potential beaver habitat.

Beavers are a keystone species in a region's ecology. Wherever they flourish, other species-- muskrat, moose, deer, waterfowl, painted turtles, and many sun-loving plant species--- will also prosper. The complexity and overall length of edge habitat created by beavers in a landscape like this will greatly increase the numbers and diversity of many other species that native Americans would have relied upon.

Figure 13 Courtesy of Kerry Hardy, Director of Merryspring Park, Camden, ME. This map is based on soil information from the USDA-SCS Soil Survey of Knox and Lincoln County, Maine.

coast, the economic activities of the new settlers recapitulated the older social patterns of the previous inhabitants of the Gulf of Maine bioregion. Europeans settled at the same head-of-the-tide locations so recently abandoned by the indigenous community after the great epidemic. They farmed many of the same open lands, which had been sites of Native American horticultural activities or where indigenous communities had created virtual parklands by burning undergrowth, allowing deer-browsing and harvesting. They went hunting in the fall when the caloric level of the game they were seeking was the highest, just as the indigenous communities had. They harvested the same clams, eels, alewives, codfish, and lobsters as Native communities. They were equally, if not more,

81

dependent on the vast timber resources of New England. The canoe routes used by Native Americans for thousands of years also became the essential riverine highways for 250 years of Maine shallops, rafts, dories, and small coasting vessels. The portages between canoe routes eventually became the ox paths and wagon roads of the later settlers. A look at Russell's (1980) map of the village sites and Indian trails of southern New England in 1600 illustrates how closely the settlement patterns and wagon trails of European settlers followed the old Indian trails and village sites of the recently departed indigenous communities of southern New England after the great epidemic.

Ecology determined economy. The tumultuous impact of contact with European explorers, traders, and settlers dramatically altered the ecology of the maritime peninsula. What was at first an increasing dependence on European trade goods soon became the systemic destruction of indigenous communities. The ecology of the virgin soil epidemic - that reoccurring phenomenon of the death of 90% of the population of all South, Central, and North American indigenous communities within 100 years of contact with Europeans due to the pathogens they brought - wiped out much of the population of the Gulf of Maine bioregion in the early 17th century.

The Great Pandemic of 1617-1619 and the Wawenoc Diaspora

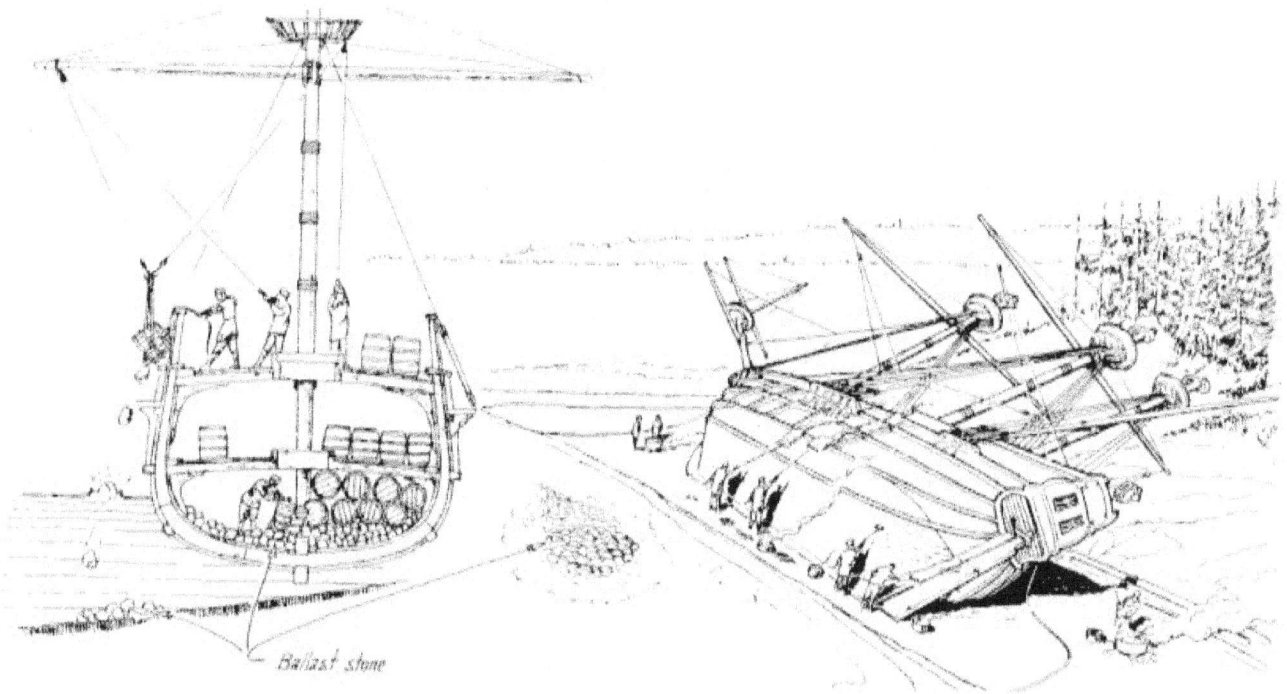

Seventeenth-century ship dumping ballast before careening and cleaning inside and out.
Drawing by S. F. Manning.

Figure 14 Use of Native Americans to help with careening and contaminated trade goods were the two most important sources of pathogens that caused the great virgin soil epidemic that swept the New England coast in 1617. Illustration from Jane Curtis, Will Curtis and Frank Lieberman. (1995). *Monhegan the Artists' Island.* Down East Books, Camden, ME, pg. 14.

The great pandemic of 1617 – 1619 in coastal New England and the Bay of Fundy was not the first virgin soil epidemic in the Gulf of Maine bioregion. Biard (Thwaites, 1896) recounts Membertou's recollection of an epidemic in Nova Scotia. Williamson (1832) notes an epidemic of an unknown cause in 1564 – 1570 and a typhus epidemic in 1586. Other pandemics may have swept the St. Lawrence River valley and played a role in the disappearance of the indigenous community at Hochalega (Montreal) between 1535 and 1603. The pandemic that swept the New England coast was, however, the first that was at least partially documented. The intertribal warfare over the fur trade that preceded the pandemic is also only partially documented, but enough is known about these conflicts, including the 1607 attack of the Micmacs and Etchemins on the Abenakis of the Saco River, to conclude that warfare played a major role in weakening the indigenous communities that lived along the New England coast. Contact with European traders and fishermen dramatically altered the Native American lifestyles by increasing the dependency on European trade goods. Cast iron cooking implements, firearms, knives, guns, and alcohol are all examples of trade goods contributing to the decline in the resilience of indigenous communities. Unfortunately, Native Americans had no resistance to the pathogens accompanying Europeans and their trade goods.

The etiology of the spread of the pandemic is the result of a number of factors, the following three of which are among the most important. First, contaminated trade goods, especially with the smallpox virus, have long been considered to be a major cause of epidemics that have periodically infected indigenous communities in the western hemisphere.

Secondly, the traditional necessity of careening ships to relieve them of accumulated slops after months at sea (see Figure 14 above) was an as yet unrecognized pathway for disease incubation. Native Americans were often utilized to help in this process. The higher tidal ranges of areas north of Cape Cod and into the Bay of Fundy coincide with locations often chosen for careening, and they are also the locations of the highest death rates of the pandemics that swept coastal New England. Additional impact from careening could have occurred by contamination of local shellfish habitat, etc. Snow (1980) has estimated the death rates from this pandemic and provides additional insight into the relationship between the pandemic and European visitors to the area after 1600:

> It is possible that there were serious epidemics throughout the 1500s and that the native population was larger by some substantial but unknown degree in 1500 than it was in 1600. ...the early voyages may well have involved crews too small to provide reservoirs for European diseases through the quarantine period imposed by long voyages. After A.D. 1600, expeditions were larger and crossings shorter. Champlain was accompanied by more than 100 men in 1604, and their crossing took less than a month (Grant 1907: 25-26). The incubation period for smallpox is 8 - 10 days, and the disease reservoir is always someone ill with or convalescing from the disease. The incubation period for measles in 8 - 21 days, and the reservoir consists solely of active cases of the disease. Both diseases are transmitted directly form one human to another, and it is not likely that either could survive a quarantine of a month and a half in a reservoir made up of a half-dozen fishermen. The odds increased dramatically that either or both diseases would survive the Atlantic crossing with the large and relatively fast-moving expeditions that came out of Europe in the first decade of the seventeenth century. (Snow, 1980, pg. 32 - 33)

Finally, more recent investigators such as Spiess and Spiess (1987) have suggested that viral hepatitis played a key role in the great pandemic. (See the special topic bibliography on the pandemic.) The consistency of the uniformity of virgin soil epidemics throughout the Americas were always the result of contact with Europeans who had built up a resistance to the diseases they transmitted. A number of observers note that the death rate throughout the Americas has averaged 90% in the first century after contact (Crosby,

1976). Maine, New England, and the maritime provinces were no exception to this phenomenon as Williamson (1832), Snow (1980), Spiess (1987), and many other commentators observe.

Williamson (1832) gives an early description of the plague that followed the Micmac attack on the Wawenocs:

> To these distresses succeeded a pestilence, which spread far and wide, and was exceedingly fatal. It has been called the plague. It raged in the years 1617 and 1618, and its wasting effects extended from the borders of the Tarantines, through the whole country, to the Narragansetts. (Williamson, 1832, pg. 216, citing Gorges, 1658)

While many historians note the pandemic rates from Cape Cod Bay to Schoodic Point, Snow's more comprehensive documentation makes clear that it was much more than just a coastal event. Snow provides the following estimates of the death rates for New England Native American "cultures" and those to the west as a result of the 1617 pandemic (Snow, 1980, pg. 34).

Aboriginal Cultures of New England[a]

Culture	Pre-epidemic population	Post-epidemic population	Mortality[b]
Maliseet-Passamaquoddy	7,600	2,500	67
Eastern Abenaki	11,900	3,000	75
Western Abenaki	10,000	250	98
Massachusett[c]	36,700	5,300	86
Monhegan-Pequot	13,300	3,000	77
Pocumtuck	15,200	800	95
Quiripi-Unquachog	24,700	1,200	95
Mahican	5,300	500	91
Mohawk	9,000-11,300	4,100-5,100	55
Munsee	24,300-51,300	4,500	81-91

[a] Pre-epidemic population estimates apply to the sixteenth century, whereas post-epidemic levels are those reached by the middle of the seventeenth century.
[b] In percentages.
[c] Includes Narragansett.

In some communities in Massachusetts the death rate was 100%. Most of the Massachusetts survivors were Narragansetts, many of whom later participated in the King Philip's War of 1675. Morison (1963) notes that Squanto, who may have been in England at the time of the epidemic, returned to Plymouth (Pauxtet) to find that all had perished. Many of the Eastern Abenaki survivors noted in Snow's death estimate may have been Penobscots, whose upriver isolation may have provided them some protection from the pandemic raging on the coast. Surviving Penobscots were later joined by Maliseets and Passamaquoddys from the east in the 18th century to regroup into the important indigenous community that they are in historic times.

Very little is known about the number of Wawenocs who survived the turmoil of 1607-1619 or their destination after the great pandemic. John Smith explored the New England coast in 1614, with the Wawenoc "*Dohannida*, [Tihanedo] one of their greatest Lords; who had long lived in *England*" (Smith, 1837, pg. 25). Tihanedo, Samoset's brother, was captured by Waymouth, interviewed in England by Gorges, helped retell the story of Mawooshen, guided John Smith along the coast of New England, and was still alive in 1623. Smith made his comment in 1614 just before the pandemic struck the New England coast. Tihanedo was one of the few Wawenocs known to have survived the pandemic that swept his community.

Samoset and his brother Tihanedo's survival of the great pandemic is an historical anomaly. Some Wawenoc survivors joined the Canibas on the Kennebec River and later at Norridgewock. Remnants of the Wawenocs, the Androscoggins, the Canibas, and the Pigwackets joined with other western Abenaki groups to form the core of what would later be called the St. Francis Indians after King Philip's War and the fall of Norridgewock in 1724. The few Wawenocs who survived the great pandemics and later cholera and smallpox outbreaks first went to St. Francis, then settled at Bécancour. Other Abenaki communities took refuge at St. Francis, where their descendents still live. Day (1965) provides detailed documentation of the evolution of the St. Francis community in Quebec following the Wawenoc diaspora.

In 1914, Speck (1928) interviewed the last surviving Wawenoc in Bécancour, Quebec. His interview with Francois Neptune, reprinted in *Wawenock myth texts from Maine,* along with the oral traditions and family histories recounted in *Penobscot Man*, are among the few indirect echoes of the voices of an earlier society recounting their own version of the history of their communities prior to the catastrophe of European contact. No known full-blooded Wawenoc descendants can now be identified in any location. The great pandemic and European firearms eliminated the Wawenoc Indians from New England's landscape. The physical disappearance of the Wawenocs has now been followed by the disappearance of their ethnic identity from contemporary history texts, especially after 1989 in the context of the hegemony of the new Bourquian paradigm. What can be "named" can be unnamed, i.e. - the pleasures of the text. This un-naming is a second regrettable diaspora that may yet be rectified. A more detailed consideration of the origins and evolution of Bourque's revisionist paradigm is necessary to understand the Wawenoc diaspora in the context of the ethnohistoric revisionism of the late 20th century.

Revisionist's Paradigm: Part II

Snow (1976) initiated the tradition of ethnohistoric revisionism that began the process of eliminating the ethnic and community identity of the Wawenoc Indians in contemporary history texts. Bourque then constructed a new paradigm of the ethnohistory of Maine in his landmark 1989 essay "Ethnicity on the Maritime Peninsula, 1600-1759," taking the elimination of the Wawenocs from the history of Maine one step further than Snow by emphasizing French rather than English sources:

> Beginning with Frank Speck, it has been widely held that aboriginal populations on the Maritime peninsula were organized in river-centered tribes ancestral to the modern St. Francis, Penobscot, Passamaquoddy, Maliseet, and Micmac. However, this view is at odds with the accounts of early-seventeenth-century French explorers who **"defined"** [bold added] non-river-centered groups named Abenaki, Etchemin, and Souriquois for the same region, and the difference of opinion has led to a protracted debate. (Bourque, 1989, pg. 257)

That debate might begin with a discussion of why the concept of "river-centered tribes" begins with Speck rather than with earlier historians, all of whom noted the river-centered presence of indigenous communities. Among those making this observation was Baird, quoted below. A tidewater and riverine pattern of community settlements throughout the maritime peninsula, including the central Maine coast, is implicit in the dependence of indigenous communities on maritime resources and the seasonal migration of anadromous species up the rivers of the Gulf of Maine. Bourque then proceeds to take issue with Snow's riverine model of ethnohistory:

> The notion that Native Americans on the Maritime peninsula were organized in river-centered tribes before contact with Europeans... first entered scholarly literature through nineteenth-century Anglo-American historical works such as Williamson (1832). ...the concept gained widespread acceptance through the writings of Frank G. Speck (1915, 1940), Speck and Eiseley (1942) and Speck and Hadlock (1946). Fifty years after Speck, Ernest Dodge (1957: 68) stated it most concisely: 'As a matter of fact, the entire tier of Algonquian tribes south of the St. Lawrence from the Mahican ...to the Micmac form a series of tribes centered on the large river valleys, each varying only slightly from its neighbors.' (Bourque, 1989, pg. 157-158)

But the riverine theory does not originate with Snow, Speck or Williamson, it originates in the memories of thousands of English settlers and travelers and even more fundamentally in the geographical reality that provided the abundant natural resources of the tidewater river valleys that later became the first choice of settlement by English colonists after the Native American diaspora.

There is also a "fly in the ointment" with respect to French explorers, who "defined" non-river centered cultures in the Maritime peninsula. Here is Biard's comment in chapter X, volume III in *Jesuits Relations:*

> These Sagamies divide up the country and are nearly always arranged according to bays or rivers. For example, for the Pentegoet River there is one Sagamore; another for the Ste. Croix; another for the St. John, etc. When they visit each other it is the duty of the host to welcome and to banquet his guests, as many days as he can, the guests making him some presents; but it is with the expectation that the host will reciprocate, when the guest comes to depart, if the guest is a Sagamore, otherwise not. (Thwaites, 1896, pg. 88)

There is another problem with the French process of "defining," i.e. French descriptions of the central Maine coast were limited to Champlain's coasting voyages in 1604-1605 and Biard's in 1611. None of Champlain's or Biard's explorations penetrated the ancestral homeland of the Wawenocs, with the exception of their visits to Wiscasset. Their observations don't contradict the English version of the ethnohistory of the central Maine coast.

Bourque continues to make his case against Snow's riverine model, repeating Snow's description of the long standing conventional version of the ethnicity of Maine's indigenous communities, which also inadvertently echoes Champlain's frequent riverine descriptions:

> Thirty years later, Dean R. Snow (1968: 1147-50; 1973) recast many of Speck's ideas into a more diachronic 'river drainage model' for the entire coastal Algonquian range. Snow (1976: 291-94) asserted that 'in the 17th century...' (Bourque, 1989, pg. 258)

Bourque then cites Snow's ethnohistoric synopsis already quoted in the chapter *Dean Snow: The Abenaki or the Etchemins?*

Bourque then presents his interpretation of the "French" ethnohistoric point of view, derived entirely from the journals of Champlain's voyages to Maine beginning in 1604, Lescarbot's observations, and Biard's memoirs published as the *Jesuits Relations* (Thwaites, 1898). The Bourquian interpretation of French sources has recently achieved what appears to be its final form in the definitive and influential publication *Twelve Thousand Years* (2001).

> Instead, the French described horticulturists named Almouchiquois west of the Kennebec and hunter-gatherers named Etchemin between the Kennebec and St. John, and Souriquois to the east of them. North of the western Etchemin and

Almouchiquois lived the Abenaki, another horticultural group. (Bourque, 1989, pg. 258-259)

Bourque doesn't mention one of the most interesting components of the French narration of Micmac and Etchemin descriptions of the Almouchiquois as "dog people." The indigenous peoples of protohistory had good reason to call the Almouchiquois "dog people," and not necessarily in derision, but more likely as a practical acknowledgement of the dogs kept by horticulturalists to prevent raccoons from destroying the precious maize crop, which was such an important trading commodity during the heyday of Mawooshen.

If one were to consult the Bicentennial Atlas, plates 1 and 2 of "Early Explorations in Maine" (Morris, 1976), one would note that, while Champlain's voyage of 1604 explored the Penobscot River to Bangor and the mouth of the St. Georges River (N.B. The Maine Atlas may be in error as Champlain did not go up the river itself) and visited Frenchman's Bay and Mount Desert Island, he then returned to winter at St. Croix Island, without further exploration of the coastal regions occupied by the Wawenoc Indians. On his next voyage in 1605, he bypassed the St. Georges River and went up the Kennebec River, taking the tortuous back river toWiscasset, where he met the Indiantown Island (Boothbay) sagamore Mentaurmet. Native Americans then guided Champlain through the Sassona River riptides back to the Kennebec and Merrymeeting Bay, which Champlain describes:

> Continuing our route we came to the lake [Merrymeeting Bay] ...which is three to four leagues in length. It contains several islands, and into it fall two rivers, the Kennebec, which flows from the north-north-east, and another from the north-west, down which Marchin and Sasinou were to come. Having waited for them all that day, and seeing they did not arrive... We therefore raised anchor and with our two Indians as guides left this lake, and came to anchor the same day at the mouth of the river... The channel by which we descended the said river is very much safer and better than that by which we had gone up. (Champlain, 1922, pg. 318-320)

After waiting in vain for Androscoggin and Kennebec sagamores to meet him, Champlain then makes this telling observation:

> The people live like those near our settlement; and they informed us that the Indians who cultivated Indian corn lived far inland, and had ceased to grow it on the coasts on account of the war they [the Souriquois, but before 1605]used to wage with others who came and seized it. That is what I was able to learn about this place, which I believe to be no better than the others. (Champlain, 1922, pg. 321)

Here Champlain clearly suggests that the inland dwelling horticulturalists had once lived near the coastal tidewaters but had moved inland due to intertribal conflicts that dated earlier than 1605. Champlain also expresses his unfamiliarity with these Almouchiquois and their culture, hardly a definitive new source of information to bolster the radical Bourquian transformation of the traditional understanding of the ethnicity of Maine's always riverine-centered indigenous communities.

At no time on his voyage did Champlain encounter the principal villages of the Wawenocs in such locations as Sawyer's Island, Southport Island, Newcastle, or the possible principal residence of the Bashebas up the St. Georges River, just north of the current site of the town of Warren. Bourque uses Champlain's non-encounter with the Wawenoc Indians as evidence that the Etchemins occupied the entire area between the upper Penobscot and the Kennebec at this early date (1605), just prior to the Wawenoc diaspora, conveniently ignoring the fact that Champlain met Native Americans at Wiscasset who fit the description of the Almouchiquois, not the Etchemins, and who had previously grown corn as a food source. When Champlain notes the community on the Sheepscot "lived like those near our settlement" on the St. Croix, he contradicts his own and Biard's later description of a more numerous and socially sophisticated population.

Bourque summarizes his interpretation of Champlain's viewpoint: "Furthermore, Champlain's Abenaki did not occupy what later became Penobscot territory, but rather the region northwest of it" (Bourque, 1989, pg. 159). Champlain, however, never observed any Wawenoc villages, nor those of the Kennebecs along the Kennebec River. It wasn't until after the Wawenoc diaspora, which was over by 1620, that the Etchemins (Maliseet, Passamaquoddy) and survivors from the pandemic to the west filtered into Mawooshen, supplementing the surviving Penobscot population. This ethnic mix from many locations became the principal inhabitants of the areas on both sides of the mouth of the Penobscot in historic times. Prior to this diaspora, the Penobscot Indians occupied the many village sites and summer trading stations from the east side of the Penobscot River all the way to the outer limits of Mawooshen at Schoodic Point.

In his essay on the ethnohistory of the Maritime Peninsula, Bourque continues with a description of tribal identities that helps clarify the confusing terminology in most history texts.

> The Souriquois of modern-day Nova Scotia and eastern New Brunswick apparently were named for a river that Champlain (1922-36, I: 169) called the Souricoa. ...Englishmen named these people Tarantines, ...both *Souriquois* and *Tarrentine* may have referred to these groups as middlemen in the fur trade between the Gulfs of Maine and St. Lawrence. (Bourque and Whitehead 1985)
>
> Both terms were later supplanted by *Micmac*. (Bourque, 1989, pg. 262)

Bourque then describes the horticulturists whom Champlain's informant observed living along the upper Kennebec River. Since Champlain did not observe the horticulturists who lived just east of Wiscasset, their presence, which early writers describe, is omitted from this description.

> Westerly along the coast lived a distinct horticultural people known as the Almouchiquois, ...Other horticulturists lived up the Kennebec. Champlain heard of them in 1604. ...In 1629 and Indian named Erouachy told Champlain (1922-36, 5: 313-17) that these 'Abenacquiouit' (Abenaki) lived seven or eight days south of Quebec in 'large villages and also houses in the country with many stretches of cleared land, in which they sow much Indian corn.' Champlain apparently regarded these people as distinct from those he had earlier met down river on 'the coast of the Etchemins,' who lived in sparse settlements and without agriculture. (Bourque, 1989, pg. 262)

By 1629, the fur trade wars in Maine and the great pandemic were over, and the incursion of English trappers, fishermen, traders, and settlers had taken its toll. Many of the remaining Native American residents of coastal Maine fled to more protected inland locations. In fact, a growing Abenaki nucleus around Norridgewock after 1620 was part of the pattern of withdrawal from vulnerable coastal village locations.

By the late 1620s, the Wawenoc diaspora was nearly complete, at least with respect to tidewater villages now occupied by English settlers, and the few surviving Wawenocs joined the Kennebecs (Canibas), who also suffered greatly in the pandemic of 1617-1619. Active trading by an ethnic mix of pandemic remnants continued after 1623. Thriving trading posts flourished at Pejepscot (Brunswick), Cushnoc (Augusta), and Taconic (Winslow). After the decline of the fur trade and the beginning of the Indian Wars in 1675, Father Rasle's mission at Norridgewock was the last Abenaki community in Maine. It was destroyed in 1724 by English and colonial forces seeking to end the periodic raids of the French and Indian wars.

By 1629, it was irrelevant that Champlain or any other visitors hadn't noted any Wawenoc horticulturists along the immediate Maine coast. Coastal Maine fog banks kept any horticulturist activity above the tidewater and well away from observations of coasting explorers. A period of three or four decades of disruption, dislocation, and chaos among the Native American inhabitants of the Maine coast west of Schoodic Point had already occurred. Confusing migrations, confederations, and trading patterns, combined with changes in subsistence patterns and the unfortunate French use of the word "Etchemin" to describe the residents of the central Maine coast, provide the basis for current confusion about cultural identity and ethnohistoric relationships in the 17th century.

Bourque gives his description of the pandemic, about which few historians disagree: "The New England pandemic of 1617-19 reached the Maritime peninsula (Dermer 1841: 350) and was soon followed by other epidemics" (Bourque, 1989, pg. 263). He then makes his new ethnohistoric paradigm explicit: "...the Souriquois killed the *Etchemin superchief Bashabes* [our italics added] and destroyed his alliance. By 1632, they were marauding as far south as Massachusetts" (Bourque, 1989, pg. 263). But Champlain's historian, Marc Lescarbot, had clearly described the Etchemin as allies with the Souriquois at the battle of Saco in 1607. (See Appendices D and E.) The Etchemin superchief noted by Bourque was at least the second Bashebas of Mawooshen killed in the fur trade wars. The Bashebas killed in 1617 may have been Asticou, probably a Penobscot and the last leader of the confederacy of Mawooshen.

The first Micmac attacks in Massachusetts predated European settlement, occurring even before Champlain's 1604 meeting on the Penobscot River with the Bashebas, who was seeking Champlain's assistance in warding off Micmac attacks (Prins, 1996). Not only were Micmacs raiding Massachusetts communities at or before 1604 during the period of warfare prior to the great pandemic, but also at least one Bashebas, probably a Wawenoc, and many sagamores were killed between 1607 and 1609 in the tumult of the earlier raids on the Saco, Androscoggin, and Kennebec Rivers by the Souriquois. Also of interest is that, by 1620, most Massachusetts Indians were casualties of the great pandemic. After 1620, there were few Massachusetts communities to attack. Raids on these communities started well before Champlain's 1605 visit to the Massachusetts coast.

The remainder of Bourque's essay describes the Etchemin presence in Maine in the 17th century:

> Primary references to the Almouchiquois ceased after Champlain's era. ...*Etchemin* was the term used for Indians of the Penobscot throughout most of the seventeenth century. ...The last specific reference to the Etchemin, dated 1694, refers to 'the river of Pentagoet otherwise of the Etchemins,' where 'the [Baron Vincent d'Abbadie] Sieur de St.-Castin [lived] with some valets. ...[H]e goes often [to trade furs] with the savages of whom the nation is very numerous.' (Bourque, 1989, pg. 263 - 264)

Unfortunately, "Etchemin" is also the term used by almost every New England historian to refer to Native Americans of Maliseet/Passamaquoddy descent (Prins, 1994). Williamson (1832) called the Penobscots "Etchemins," but their close alliance with the Wawenocs and the Canibas, their pivotal role in the confederacy of Mawooshen, and their unique Algonquin dialect clearly indicate a different ethnicity than that of the Passamaquoddy/Maliseets of that time.

Bourque then provides an explanation for the gradual elimination of reference to the tribal identities of the Native Americans who lived in Maine prior to 1607:

> As early as the mid-seventeenth century, however, the term *Abenaki* began to be used in reference to Indians throughout the Maritime peninsula. This usage probably originated in the missions of Quebec, where Abenaki from the upper Kennebec were the first visitors from Acadia. ...The extension of the term may also have been fostered by the prevalence of Abenaki as mission language. (Bourque, 1989, pg. 271)

This implies that Abenaki was a later name for the indigenous communities whose ancestors were the Maliseet/Passamaquoddy. Is this a modern ethnohistoric squelching of the centuries-old understanding that Abenakis lived west of the Penobscot River but not to the east in New Brunswick and Nova Scotia? Doesn't the term Abenaki as the designation of a specific indigenous culture originate with indigenous First Nation inhabitants of New England and not with the white historians who came later? Why is it necessary to reintroduce the term Etchemin, which the French last used in 1694, to describe the ethnicity of the residents of the central Maine coast?

Bourque goes on to summarize the new paradigm, which eliminates the traditional riverine description of the Native American inhabitants of Maine:

> This analysis has addressed the long-disputed issue of whether aboriginal populations on the Maritime peninsula were organized as riverine tribes, as proposed by Frank Speck, or in nonriverine groups, as described by French explorers. *Historical sources* [italics added] from the late seventeenth and early eighteenth centuries reveal that the ethnic divisions described by the early French were basically accurate. Champlain's labels, *Abenaki, Etchemin,* and *Souriquois,* remained current into the 1670s despite numerous epidemics and internecine warfare; only the term *Almouchiquois* was dropped almost immediately after Champlain left the Gulf of Maine. King Philip's War initiated several decades of geopolitical turbulence that ultimately transformed the ethnic composition of northern New England and the Maritime peninsula. (Bourque, 1989, pg. 273-274)

What are the historical sources, which Bourque cites above, and why didn't other New England historians recognize their significance prior to Bourque's discovery?

The confusion continues: were the Saco River Indians from the Massachusetts community and thus not Abenaki, who, it is now alleged, lived only to the north and the upper Kennebec River watershed? Were the Pigwacket Abenaki as most historians contend? Did they and other communities to the eastward have such a different Algonquin dialect that communities east of the Saco River could not understand those living on or west of the Saco River?

Most importantly, who were the Etchemins? Maliseets/Passamaquoddys as most historians describe them? Penobscots, in addition to the Maliseets/Passamaquoddys, as Williamson concluded in 1832? The ethnic identities of the indigenous communities of Maine's prehistory need further discussion, clarification, and documentation. Any educational curricula pertaining to the ethnohistory of the controversial years of first contact with Europeans must confront and identify the spectrum of viewpoints on this topic.

A Lost Chapter in Maine History

Bourque (1989) fails to mention that the geopolitical turbulence that transformed the ethnic composition of coastal Maine began long before King Philip's War in 1675 and, in fact, began long before the Souriquois (Micmac) attack on the Abenaki of the Saco River (1607). A French source in Biard's (Thwaites, 1896) memoirs notes that Membertou, the elderly Micmac chief who was an important informant for Champlain, recalled a virgin soil epidemic at and to the south of the Saco River long before Champlain's exploration of the area. This earlier pandemic apparently depleted a significant percentage of the population of the Saco River region; other early epidemics had occurred in the St. Lawrence River valley to the north in the 16th century (Parkman, 1983) and in the Penobscot River region in the late 16th century (Williamson, 1832, Petersen, 2004). Geopolitical turbulence resulting from contact with Europeans began with these earlier pandemics. The disruptive impact of firearms was enhanced by alcohol as a trade good; the great dying followed. Cultural dislocations can be dated at least to Cartier's observations of the cornfields at Hochalega (Montreal) in 1535. When Champlain visited in 1603, Hochalega had returned to wilderness. The European conquest of North America was well underway.

Prior to the settlement of the Maine coast by Euro-Americans, marauding English fisherman were known to have harassed and attacked individual Native Americans whom they encountered on fishing and trading expeditions. Additional incidents of assault also occurred during the construction and settlement of Fort Popham in 1607. However, most contemporary and antiquarian historians indicate that the relationships between the surviving Kennebec (Canibas) and Wawenoc Indians and most English colonists were peaceful, despite the conflicts arising out of their first contact with the English at Fort Popham. There were few incidents of violence after English settlers arrived at Arrowsic, settled the shores of the Kennebec and Sheepscot rivers, and began intensive trading with surviving Native Americans at Cushnoc, Pejepscot, and Pemaquid. In contrast to the Pequot wars of Connecticut (1635 f.), this peaceful coexistence lasted until the outbreak of the King Philip's War in southeastern New England, which then quickly spread to Maine. At that time, surviving remnants of a number of eastern Abenaki tribes joined the growing conflict (1675). By the early 18th century, the increasing casualties of the Indian Wars and the continued loss of economic (subsistence) opportunities forced the Kennebecs and remaining Wawenocs to join the Androscoggins and possibly the Pigwackets at Norridgewock, their last principal holdout in Maine.

The vestiges of an Abenaki (Almouchiquois) hegemony in central Maine are graphically illustrated by two French sources, Druillettes (Thwaites, 1896) and Rasles, French missionary and community leader at Norridgewock until its demise in 1724. Druillettes, the earlier source, visited numerous Androscoggin, Kennebec, and Sheepscot River villages in 1641 on his way to Boston. All are clearly Abenaki, as indicated by both the spelling and description of these communities. In 1641, they were but a surviving fragment of a much larger Abenaki or Almouchiquois population living before the beaver wars and great pandemic afflicted this region.

Father Rasles was the apparent narrator of the futile 1721 message sent to Gov. Shutes about getting rid of the numerous colonial forts on the Kennebec River (Ne-do-bah website http://www.avcnet.org/ne-do-ba/doc_1721.html). Three years after a flotilla of 90 canoes of Abenaki delivered their ultimatum to Capt. Penhollow at Arrowsic Island, Rasles and his missionary settlement at Norridgewock were wiped out. This was probably the last effort of organized Abenaki survivors to reassert some control over the lower Kennebec River and its encroaching colony of settlers and traders.

Rasles recorded the identity of the protesting Abenaki community and their allies. The list of protesters began with the Norridgewocks (1721). The following communities then signed the petition to Governor Shutes: the Penobscots, the Rockameka, and the Amasconti, the latter two eighteenth century survivors of earlier Canibas and Androscoggin communities (Hardy, 2006). That the Penobscots were still allied with the now inland dwelling Abenaki at this late date is indicative of the long association of the Penobscots with the Abenaki communities of the central Maine coast.

Bourque's revised ethnohistoric paradigm is dependent on only a few primary sources: the French explorer Champlain and his historian Lescarbot and the Jesuit priest, Father Biard. Neither Champlain, Lescarbot, or Biard ever entered the key river drainages of the central Maine coast east of Wiscasset during the voyages of 1604, 1605, and 1611. With their always river-centered observations, the same French sources continually confirm the riverine theory that was the dominant model in most commentary on Maine's ethnohistory beginning with Williamson (1832) and extending to all the major contemporary writers on New England's Native Americans, including Snow (1976), Russell (1980), Day (1998), Salisbury (1982), and others. Because they never traveled the rivers of Wawenoc territory east of Sheepscot Bay, the same French explorers cannot be reliable sources of information about the inland settlements of the Wawenoc community in the decades before or at the time of Champlain's 1604-5 visits to the central Maine coast. This lack of direct observation cannot provide information about the existence or nonexistence of indigenous horticultural activities or semi-permanent village sites usually located at the head of tide well inland from Champlain's coasting routes. The startling element in reevaluating French observations is their consistent reference to Native accounts of previous horticultural activities in tidewater regions west of the Penobscot River but east of the Kennebec River. Though horticulture played a minor role in the complex trading network of Mawooshen, the corn grown in the tidewater valleys of the Sagadahoc region sustained not only English fishermen salting their fish on the Maine coast but also the Plymouth colonists who were near starvation in the spring of 1622. There were no stark boundary lines separating regions with and without horticulture.

The conclusion that the Wawenocs of Damariscotta and the St. Georges River were Etchemins is one of the more bizarre developments of contemporary Maine ethnohistory. In fact, nothing in Champlain's journals contradicts the more or less obvious resource-based riverine thesis: all French encounters with Native Americans in Maine were within riverine environments - the Saco, Androscoggin, Kennebec, Sheepscot, and Penobscot. All indigenous communities were located in riverine environments, regardless of their ethnicity.

The identity of the indigenous residents of the tidewater villages between the Kennebec and the Penobscot Rivers in the decades preceding visits by Gosnold, Champlain, Waymouth, and others needs further discussion and investigation. The problem is obscured and complicated by the vague meaning of "Etchemin." Etchemin is a catch-all term, including at times Penobscot, Passamaquoddy, and Maliseet. Bourque now extends the term to include Wawenocs, Canibas, and Androscoggins. The term is now as misleading as "Tarentines," another generic term for "other" Indian communities used in the 19th century. Where in the writings of surviving descendants of western or eastern Abenaki communities is there any mention of "Etchemins" as ancestors or of ancestral homelands in the eastern maritime province with later migrations to the west?

Petersen (2004) supplies the most recent description of Etchemins as occupying the Wawenoc homeland. Also following Champlain and Bourque, he notes the Etchemin as the inhabitants of the maritime peninsula east of the Kennebec River. So the plot thickens: Etchemin as Abenaki/ Maliseet/Passamaquoddy/Micmac/Penobscot, Almouchiquois as Abenaki or not Abenaki, Abenaki as an isolated culture in northwest Maine, and Pigwackets, Androscoggins, Kennebecs, and Wawenocs as Etchemins, or as nonexistent? Here is White Man's history at its most brazen. If it is permissible to lump the Wawenocs with the Canibas, why not lump the Abenaki with the Etchemin or the Penobscot with either or both? If only Wabanaki lived in New England (or only Europeans in Europe), the grim details of harassment and conquest, of the impact of firearms and alcohol, the predatory commercial expectation, tendentious religious proselytizing, or the origins and spread of virgin soil epidemics would be obscured in generalized romantic and popular versions of First Nation Americans as the exotic other (Berkhofer, 1979).

Sanger (2000) makes the persuasive argument that archaeological data cannot be very useful in establishing ethnic identity. Nonetheless, when prehistory meets history, contentious issues of ethnicity can be avoided only by ignoring the rapid political and cultural upheavals that occurred in less than a century. These lost chapters in Maine history results from the confluence of our ignorance of actual events and indigenous communities with conflicting historical narrations and paradigms.

In this ethnohistoric confusion and obfuscation, the identity of individual indigenous communities is subsumed and then lost. The uncovering of the palimpsest of ethnohistory, a process of disclosure, even epiphany, implies a previous process of covering up, concealing, a historiographic erasing of the fate, the extinction, of those who came before us. This dynamic rhythm of covering over the hidden stories of history with one myth after another necessitates a reconsideration that is, in essence, a peeling back of the palimpsest of history. In the age of deconstruction and the "pleasures of the text," at least we recognize that our newest story may yet be another covering over of historical events that we ourselves do not understand.

George Waymouth's kidnapping of five Wawenoc Indians and Samoset's rendering of assistance to the Pilgrims are among the most important European encounters with Native Americans in the annals of American history. The emergence of these individuals and events from the shadows of prehistory marks a critical time in Maine's ethnohistory: the beginnings of the documentation of indigenous communities that would soon disappear, i.e. protohistory. Their lives, contributions, kidnappings, and communities were described and written about, if ever so briefly.

A revised ethnohistory now omits mentioning their presence, squelching the search for the nomenclature that they used to refer to their own communities, ancestral homelands, hunting and fishing territories, or trading networks. In view of Bourque's new ethnohistoric paradigm and its dominance in current descriptions of Maine history, it is appropriate to go back to Williamson's (1832), Speck's (1928) and Snow's (1976) traditional ethno-description, and reconsider the dynamic diversity of a series of closely related indigenous communities, which, nonetheless, were organized as distinct and differing cultural entities. In this lost chapter of Maine history, each community had its own ancestral village sites, traditions and variations in material culture. Though we are nearly powerless to document and reconstruct this milieu, renaming these communities as Etchemin without further documentation is unacceptable.

In his synopsis of Eastern Abenaki villages at the beginning of the historic era, extracted from Samuel Purchas, a primary historical source for information about Native Americans in Maine prior to 1607, Snow (1976) calls the villages of the central Maine coast Eastern Abenaki, not Etchemin. It is only in the writings of Bourque and a minority of other 20th century historians that the ethnic identity of the indigenous people of the central Maine coast is changed from Abenaki to Etchemin. Only one French map denotes Etchemins living on the central Maine coast; the observations of Champlain and Biard consistently describe an indigenous population distinctly different from the Maliseet/Passamaquoddy communities living east of Schoodic Point. Lescarbot's tentative 1609 map is clearly superceded by Champlain's more definitive 1632 rendering of the geography and ethnicity of the Maritime Peninsula. Therein lies the key to the current controversy over the ethnohistory of the central Maine coast and the meaning and significance of Mawooshen and its relationship to Norumbega -- two cultures, one on either side of the Kennebec River, or one confederacy (Mawooshen) of closely aligned Abenaki communities, in conflict with another culture to the east (Micmac allied with Maliseet/Passamaquoddy)?

Twelve thousand years of the history of Native Americans in Maine must include more information about the period between 1534, when Cartier first visited the St. Lawrence River where he over wintered, and 1619, the last year of the great pandemic. These years are currently a lost chapter in Maine's ethnohistory.

Mawooshen Reconsidered

The common theme in recent writings on Maine and Maritime ethnohistory is the splitting of the confederacy of Mawooshen into two distinct cultures with different lifestyles and dialects, i.e. the mysterious Almouchiquois west of the Kennebec River and the Etchemins to the east, the ancestors of the Passamaquoddy/Maliseet community.

Implicit in the social organization of the confederacy of Mawooshen, a vast region of semi-permanent tidewater village sites along the shore of the Gulf of Maine from Massachusetts Bay to Schoodic Point, is shared language, specifically the Abenaki dialect of the Algonquin language. There were differences between the Abenaki dialects of mid- coast Maine and the communities to the east in the maritime peninsula. The Micmacs of Nova Scotia could not understand the Massachusetts of the Saco River (Champlain, 1922). But the Bashebas could. The Micmac language had evolved, if ever so slightly, from its original Algonquin roots.

The Micmac community has its own interesting stories to tell, particularly with respect to possible early contact with Celtic culture and, later, a constant stream of Basque, then English and Nordic fishermen after 1500. When those European sailing ships appeared on the horizon, was the Micmac community already more sympathetic to the coming of a European-style market economy, more ready to be middlemen in the fur trade? And if there were two languages, two cultures on the maritime peninsula, could the dividing line be ecological, the wilderness (even now) of eastern Maine separating the sparsely populated hunting and fishing culture east of Schoodic Point ("the end," but the end of what?) from resource-rich Norumbega?

Rosier's *A True Relation* of George Waymouth's 1605 voyage to the St. Georges River (Penobscot River) and New Harbor (Cushing) (Morey, 2005) documents a vibrant and long established Native American community living and trading with European visitors near Pemaquid. When Davies narrated the *Relation of a Voyage to Sagadahoc in 1607 - 1608*, the presence of a Wawenoc Bashebas living near the Camden Hills was already a well-know fact:

> ...they ar three heigh mountains that Lye in upon the main Land near unto the ryver of penobskot in w[eh] ryver the bashabe makes his abod the cheeffe Comander of those pts and streatcheth unto the ryver of Sagadehock under his Comand. you shall see theise heigh mountains when yo shall not perseave the main Land under ytt they ar of shutch an exceedinge heygts. (Davies, 1880, pg. 405)

When John Smith sailed to the Penobscot Bay and westward along the coast in 1614, his descriptions of the communities and landmarks were derived from a Wawenoc observer, Dohnnida, who spoke an Abenaki dialect characteristic of the Wawenoc community, not an Etchemin dialect. Smith's observations document the presence of Mawooshen and its imminent demise:

> The most Northern part I was at, was the Bay of *Pennobscot*, ...the Riuer ranne farre vp into the Land, and was well inhabited with many people, but they were from their habitations, either fishing among the Iles, or hunting the Lakes and Woods, for Deer and Beuers. ...On the East of it, are the *Tarrantines*, their mortall enemies, where inhabit the *French*, as they report that liue with those people, as one nation or family. And Northwest of *Pennobscot* is *Mecaddacut*, [Camden] at the foot of a high mountaine, a kinde of fortresse against the *Tarrantines*, ...*Segocket* [Owls Head] is the next; then *Nusconcus* [Muscongus], *Pemmaquid*, and *Sagadahock*. Vp this Riuer where was the Westerne plantation are *Aumuckcawgen, Kinnebeck,* and diuers others, where there is planted some corne fields. (Smith, 1837, pg. 13-14)

At the time of Smith's voyage, the intertribal fur trade wars had already split Mawooshen into fragments, with the Camden Hills now being a demarcation line separating two opposing entities, i.e. the Almouchiquois to the west and the Souriquois (Etchemins and Micmacs, whom Smith and other English observers called Tarentines) to the east. The unresolved question of this demarcation line is: why and how long was the Penobscot community allied with the Micmacs? A second puzzle remains: if the Micmacs were allied with the Penobscots, why would they attack the Penobscot superchief and kill him (Baxter, 1884)?

Prior to the spread of the fur trade wars, local variations in dialect had not been sufficient to deter the evolution of a complex trading network throughout Mawooshen, the maritime peninsula and the great lakes to the west. Ancient Pemaquid was part of a network of long-established indigenous trading centers. Naskeag, at the entrance of the Eggemoggin Reach, typifies another well-documented location in Mawooshen (Petersen, 2004). In time, these trading centers became a component of a much more extensive trading network formed by the demands of European traders and consumers for beaver pelts. The firearms, steel tomahawks, kettles, beads, alcohol, blankets, and other goods that indigenous peoples received in return made trading centers, ranging from distant Tadoussac on the St. Lawrence River to Aptuxet at the head of Buzzards Bay, hubs for and of Native Americans anxious for trading opportunities. Between the northern ranges of French supplied trucking stations and southern New England trading posts were Gulf of Maine locations such as Pejepscot, Pemaquid, Pentagoet, Machias, St. John, and others.

The irony of the florescence of Mawooshen as a complex network of trading communities is that its success led to its destruction. The land of Mawooshen was center stage in this fur trade arena until the tensions, stress, and firearms of European commerce forever shattered the confederacy. A direct result of the impact of a predatory European intrusion into the Gulf of Maine bioregion, the Micmac and Etchemin invasion of

Mawooshen is best described by Williamson (1832) who cites Ferdinando Gorges' narration of the ethnohistory of the tumultuous years of the second decade of the 17th century:

> 'the *Bashaba* to be the chief and greatest among them,' ...His chief abode was not far from Pemaquid. ...His dominions, which were large, Gorges adds, were called by the general name of *Moasham*, or according to Belknap, *Mavooshen*; 'and he had under him many great Sagamores, some of whom had a thousand or fifteen hundred bowmen.' After his overthrow and death, he was never succeeded by another of equal rank or authority. (Williamson, 1832, pg. 464-465)

> The greatest aboriginal monarch of the east was entitled 'the *Bashaba*', previously mentioned, whose residence was with the Wawenock tribe. Besides his immediate dominions, extending probably from St. Georges to Kennebeck, the tribes westward to Agamenticus, and even farther, acknowledged him to be their paramount lord. His overthrow, in 1615 or 16, terminated the royal line and rank. (Williamson, 1832, pg. 494)

Gorges fails to note, and may not be consciously aware of, the critical role of Europeans and their firearms in the demise of Mawooshen and the death of the last Bashebas. Of particular interest is Williamson's use of the term "terminated the royal line," suggesting what is already obvious: multiple Bashebas led Mawooshen over a period of decades, rather than as a brief florescence of a trading culture stimulated by contact with Europeans.

French traders had supplied Micmac warriors with firearms before the Micmac attack on the Abenaki community on the Saco River in 1607, which is well documented. Prins (1996) provides the following description of this event (a more detailed description is excerpted in the annotated bibliography):

> Because Panoniac's killing could not be left unavenged, the old chief assembled a fighting force of about 40 Mi'kmaq and allied Maliseet warriors. Armed with spears, tomahawks, bows, and iron-tipped arrows and newly equipped with French muskets, the warriors boarded their shallops and sailed to Saco Bay, where they defeated the local Abenakis. They returned home knowing that sooner or later they would suffer an Abenaki counterattack. (Prins, 1996, pg. 109)

Of particular interest is Prins' assertion that forty warriors participated in the attack against the Saco River community. In the *Jesuit Relations,* Lescarbot (Thwaites, 1896) recounts his observations of Micmac, Maliseet, and Passamaquoddy warriors from many areas of the maritime provinces gathering at St. John and other locations in the Bay of Fundy before sailing down the coast to participate in the Saco River attack. Lescarbot implies that not forty, but several hundred or more Micmacs and Etchemins participated in this attack on the Almouchiquois of the central Maine coast. Sailing from England to

Maine, the Popham expedition encountered one group of Micmac warriors from the village of Le Heve on the east coast of Nova Scotia. These Micmac warriors later defeated their Abenaki opponents at the Saco River. The Popham expedition was eventually unsuccessful in its attempt to establish a permanent settlement at the mouth of the Kennebec River.

The most revealing description of the battle at Saco in 1607, one of the most important events in Maine history, is contained in Lescarbot's (1609b) *Les Muses de la Nouvelle-France*, a long poem in French that recounts the war in Saco in 1607. (See appendix D for a reprint of the original French edition of this work.) Lescarbot provides a panoramic view of this attack, which clearly pits Micmac and Maliseet against Abenaki. On one side were the attacking Souriquois, who include Membertou (a Micmac sagamore), Chkoudun (a Maliseet sagamore of the St. John River), and Oagimont (a Passamaquoddy sagamore of the St. Croix River). Lescarbot doesn't call them Etchemins; they are all Souriquois to him. On the opposite side are the Almouchiquois: Onemechin (the Saco sagamore), Marchin (an Androscoggin sagamore), and the superchief Bessabez. Both Onemechin and Marchin are killed along with two other Almouchiquois sagamores, one possibly a Kennebec, in a last minute attack by Membertou and Chkoudun, using French muskets. Lescarbot, a French, not an English source, here raises the issue of the true identity of the Almouchiquois: if the Bashebas is fighting with Onemechin and then supercedes him as leader of the Saco River community, or what is left of it, (Harvey, 2000), then a case can be made that the Almouchiquois were an integral component of the confederacy of Mawooshen. Therefore, it is probable that the Maine coastal region stretching east to the Penobscot River, including the Wawenoc settlements, was Almouchiquois (i.e. Eastern Abenaki) and not Etchemin, another culture and the antagonists, with the Micmacs, of these Abenaki communities.

Writing for the *Dictionary of Canadian Biography* in the 1930's, D. C. Harvey (2000), an important Canadian historian from Nova Scotia, offers the following description, which further confirms the possibility that Mawooshen was, in fact, an Abenaki (Almouchiquois) confederacy.

> ASTICOU, sagamo of the Armouchiquois (Penobscots) on the frontiers of Acadia; fl. 1608-16.

> According to Lescarbot he was the successor of Bessabes, who succeeded Onemechin (Olmechin) on the latter's death in Membertou's war of revenge (1607). The cause of this war against the Armouchiquois was their slaying of Panounias in revenge for previous slayings of Armouchiquois by Touaniscou, a Micmac. Bessabes in turn had been slain by the English because of the treachery of his followers in dealing with their abortive colony of Norumbega or Sagdahoc, planted by Sir John Popham and others in 1607 but withdrawn the following year. In Bessabes' place the Indians 'brought down from the backcountry a chief named

Asticou, a man grave, valorous and feared, who in the twinkling of an eye will gather together a thousand Indians.' He, in a statesmanlike manner, demanded that Angibault dit Champdoré, who had been sent by Du Gua de Monts in 1608 to pick up any furs gathered in the winter and to report on his colony, send him a representative of the Etchemins (Malecites) to treat with him. As a result Ouagimou was chosen and peace concluded with due ceremony between the Etchemins and the Armouchiquois at Chouacouët (Saco) in 1608. (Harvey, 2000)

This is a particularly interesting observation in that it pinpoints the reign of a second (?) superchief Bashebas as ending at the hands of the English, as indicated by Lescarbot. Even more significant is the identification of the Penobscots as Armouchiquois (Almouchiquois), further suggesting that the confederacy of Mawooshen was entirely Abenaki prior to its unraveling.

Prins (1996, pg. 109) gives 1615 as the date of the next Micmac attack on whom he calls Maliseets of the central Maine coast and also cites Gorges. Gorges comments on the death of the Bashebas after the surprise attack on his settlement. The Bashebas to whom he refers may be Asticou, who may have led the confederacy of Mawooshen from about 1608 to 1615. When he was killed, the confederacy of Mawooshen ceased to exist. Many other conflicts, attacks, and alliances probably occurred during the interval between these two documented incidents, but they were unrecorded by any European observers.

The impact of the rapid increase of the population of English settlers in southern New England restricted French control of the fur trade to areas east of Pemaquid by the third decade of the 17th century. Once the Puritan trading post was established on the Kennebec River (1623), Cushnoc superceded Pemaquid as one of the most successful trucking and trading stations in New England, at least until the beaver became virtually extinct in coastal Maine in the mid-17th century. The confederacy of Mawooshen was long gone, shattered by the gunfire of Etchemin and Micmac raiders supported by their hidden French backers and then further undermined by English settlers, whose failure at the Popham settlement in 1607 was accompanied by the successful alienation of the indigenous communities they also harassed.

Prior to the great dying, Mawooshen was an integrated series of semi-permanent tidewater communities intensively exploiting marine resources, but with the capacity and proclivity for maize, bean, squash, and tobacco horticulture in inland locations well away from Maine's cold ocean fogs. The inhabitants of Mawooshen went hunting in the early winter and harvested marine resources in the spring starving time and during the summer ambiance of ancient Norumbega. Contact with European traders before the great dying increased winter fur trapping and encouraged more extended summer coastal visits for trading with Europeans, who provided goods that served to undermine the social structure and community activities of the villages of ancient Mawooshen.

Lescarbot (1609) notes that the total population of the Etchemins was not more than 1,000. In another location Biard (Thwaites, 1896) puts the estimate at 3,500. Snow (1980) notes a much higher population before the pandemics of the early 17th century. In extending the Etchemin domain to include all of Maine west to the Saco River, Bourque (2001) fails to note the discrepancy in his own quotation from Gorges: "Fifteen hundred Bow-Men" implies a much larger population than that noted by Lescarbot or Biard, who were clearly describing the more sparsely populated areas to the east of Mawooshen. There is also an unresolved problem with respect to the residence of the Bashebas being "not far from Pemaquid" versus Indian Island at Old Town on the Penobscot River, which is quite far from Pemaquid. This raises the problem of reliance on one revisionist interpretation of the ethnohistory of the central Maine coast. Rosier, Smith, Davies, and Gorges are examples of English sources that cannot be left out of the debate about this absolutely fascinating chapter of Maine's history, i.e. Mawooshen. What was it and when did it flourish? Norumbega reconsidered.

Also not to be left out of this debate are the emerging Native American voices, who will be the most important component of any future debate about the ethnicity of Maine's indigenous communities in late prehistory. In the past, these voices were transmitted through the writings of Euro-American historians and anthropologists such as Frank Speck. Native American writers and historians, such as Wiseman (2001) and many others, are now emerging from Western Abenaki, Penobscot, Passamaquoddy, and other communities. Writers such as Donald Soctomah (2005) are up front about the central issue of Maine's ethnohistory: extermination. Implicit in the unidentified Micmac commentator's recounting of the origins of the People of the Dawn, which differs from Euro-American accounts and includes unfamiliar names, such as Amaseconti and Rocameca communities in southwestern Maine, is the disappearance or the invisibility of their few survivors.

A growing internet presence provides a new forum for Native Americans to counteract the submergence of Maine's Native American communities by the new revisionist ethnohistory, e.g. -The Abenaki Language (http://www.hmt.com/abenaki/language.htm); Cowasuck Band of the Pennacook-Abenaki People (http://www.cowasuck.org). The greatest challenge in reconsidering the squelched history of Native American communities in the Gulf of Maine bioregion and their thriving confederacy of Mawooshen is to locate, listen to, and make available the oral and written traditions that Native Americans, not Euro-Americans, wish to recount.

The Almouchiquois: Ethnicity Reconsidered

The meaning and significance of ethnic terms, such as Abenaki, Etchemin and Almouchiquois, is the most confusing element in the conflict between the French and English versions of Maine's ethnohistory. All the Native American communities of the maritime peninsula east of the domain of the Iroquois of New York and the St. Lawrence River valley (see map 13 in Appendix A) are Abenaki, including Maliseet, Passamaquoddy and Micmac, at least in the sense that the Abenaki culture is synonymous with the Algonquin language family. This common denominator gives rise to the modern term "Wabanaki," People of the Dawn, i.e. all the indigenous residents of the maritime peninsula. Wiseman articulates the broadest description of Abenaki culture:

> Each modern Abenaki citizen has over fifty million ancestors in A.D. 1350, more than the estimated population of North America at the time. The study of the evolution and divergence of our language also indicates that the widespread 'proto-Algonquins' of long ago are our linguistic ancestors. (Wiseman, 2001, pg. 3)

His map of what he calls the "Wobanakik" covers the entire maritime peninsula and Newfoundland and depicts the same culture and geographic area as "Wabanaki" (See map 13 in Appendix A). When Bourque (2001) reiterates the French version of Maine's ethnohistoric past as consisting of Souriquois, Etchemins and Almouchiquois, he is referring to subdivisions of the Abenaki (Wabanaki) culture.

Commentators such as Snow (1980), Day (1998), Salisbury (1982), Baker (1994), and many others subdivide the Abenaki into specific cultures. The map that Salisbury (1982) uses represents a broad consensus of New England historians about the ethnicity of New England's indigenous communities circa 1982, just before the beginning of the Bourquian era (1989). Salisbury's map shows the Iroquoian language family as occupying eastern New York and the St. Lawrence River Valley from Montreal north to just past Quebec on the St. Lawrence River. Salisbury notes: "Boundaries within St. Lawrence Iroquoians are insufficiently known today to be drawn with confidence" (Salisbury, 1982, pg. 15). Salisbury's map clearly illustrates Micmacs as occupying Nova Scotia and northern New Brunswick and the Maliseet/Passamaquoddy community extending down only to the Machias River, Eastern Abenaki from the Machias River to the Saco River, and the Massachusetts community south of the Saco River. Salisbury depicts Western Abenaki as living in New Hampshire and Vermont, Pocumtuck-Nipmuck as being in central Massachusetts, Narragansetts occupying Rhode Island and Mohegan, and Pequot as occupying eastern Connecticut.

The Algonquin community has historic roots both in the Delaware-Chesapeake Bay region and in the Ottawa, Canada, region. The Iroquois community was a virtual cultural island in an Algonquin sea that stretched west into Ohio. The introduction of French ethnic designations as the basis for a revised ethnohistory of Maine further confuses the already complicated ethnohistory of New England. As noted by Day (1998) and others, many of the names of indigenous communities, such as the Saco River Indians, were lost at the time of the great pandemic. The names of many other smaller communities, which were once components of the interlocking trading confederacy of Mawooshen, were also lost, when they were destroyed during the cataclysmic encounter with European civilization and its traders and settlers. This observation also applies to the Canibas, Wawenocs, and Penobscots, who may not have used these names to identify themselves five centuries ago. Here again is the palimpsest of history; in the layer of names, Etchemin now lies at the surface. Canibas and Penobscot lie closer to the surface than Wawenoc; the actual derivation of these names remains unclear and subject to debate.

Baker (1998) summarizes the uncertainty and unease of contemporary historians in their inability to understand clearly and to document the rapidly changing ethnic composition of Maine's western coastal communities at this time:

> So little is known about the Indians of southern Maine that they must be referred to generically as 'Wabanakis' since the names of their bands are not even known. (Baker, 1994, pg. 272)

In the context of the broader meaning of "culture" and "ethnicity," one could argue that, when Bourque is referring to Etchemins on the central Maine coast, he is talking about the same Eastern Abenaki communities referred to by their traditional names (e.g. Canibas, etc.) by other ethnohistorians. But commentators such as Snow (1980) and others are very clear that each of these individual communities is a component of important cultural subdivisions. In fact, Snow uses the term "cultures" to describe Eastern Abenaki, which include all the communities between the Penobscot and the Saco rivers, which he clearly differentiates from Maliseet/Passamaquoddy, Western Abenaki, Massachusetts, and other cultures. In this context, Bourque's designation of Abenakis as occupying only a small fragment of western Maine represents a radical revision of the ethnic descriptions of most ethnohistorians writing before the Bourquian era.

The decisive factor in differentiating one culture from another, including Abenaki from Etchemin, is language. At the time that he postulates his historic baseline analysis (1600), Snow makes a most important observation about language differentiation in the maritime peninsula.

> Maliseet-Passamaquoddy is a single language having two dialects that are still spoken in the St. John and St. Croix drainages, respectively. Goddard (1978a:70-71) discusses a language he calls 'Etchemin' that may have existed in this area around A.D. 1600, but the evidence is limited to a list of ten numbers copied down by Marc Lescarbot. At the time the list was made, Etchemin was being used to

refer to the Indians of New Brunswick and Maine in a very broad way (Snow 1978a), and I regard the linguistic evidence as too slight to be taken very seriously. It is conceivable that such a language could have been spoken in the St. Croix drainage. Goddard indicates that it resembles Eastern Abenaki, which was spoken in the adjacent Penobscot drainage. No more than a few hundred people would have lived in the St. Croix drainage in A.D. 1600, and the epidemics, which caused mortality rates to reach approximately 70%, could have reduced the population so much that survivors joined other communities and lost their linguistic distinctiveness. A later reoccupation of the St. Croix by Maliseet-Passamaquoddy speakers would explain why we get no clear reference to the Passamaquoddy as a separate tribe until 1727 (Gyles 1853) and why the Passamaquoddy dialect is so similar to Maliseet. However, this is all conjecture, for we cannot be sure that a distinct Etchemin language ever existed at all. (Snow, 1980, pg. 28-29)

In view of the widespread acceptance of Bourque's "French version" of Maine's ethnohistory and the broad dissemination of the map illustrating Etchemins as occupying midcoast Maine in 1600, as illustrated both in Bourque (2001) and at the Penobscot Maritime Museum's 2005 exhibition, one can see that a great deal has changed since 1980. Snow published his landmark essays and texts pertaining to the historic baseline in 1976 and 1980. Bourque followed with his nearly revolutionary French version of Maine's ethnohistory beginning with his 1989 essay *Ethnicity on the Maritime Peninsula*. When Baker and the other editors of *American Beginnings* published their text in 1994, the Bourquian model was already exercising a vast influence on how Maine's ethnohistory was interpreted. D'Abate and Konrad (Baker, 1994) provide this description in the general introduction to *American Beginnings:*

> The Indians of Norumbega -- whom the Europeans met, learned from, profited by, feared, and killed -- were the Wabanakis, the ancestors of the present-day Abenaki, Penobscot, Passamaquoddy, Maliseet, and Micmac tribes of Maine and the Canadian Maritimes.[10] (Baker, 1994, pg. xxxii)

This brief definition of ethnicity is followed by a footnote, which appears at the end of the text and provides the following, more detailed explanation for the use of the term Wabanaki in place of more specific ethnic designations:

[10]Bruce G. Trigger, ed., *Handbook of North American Indians* (Washington, D.C.: Smithsonian Institution, 1978), volume 15, labels the inhabitants of the predominant part of Maine as 'Eastern Abenaki.' A somewhat controversial terminology when first published in 1978, the term has been rejected by many scholars on the basis of subsequent research. Because of this debate, and because the terms tend to exclude the Micmac and the Etchemin (modern-day Maliseet and Passamaquoddy) groups, the labels 'Abenaki' and 'eastern Abenaki' are generally not used in this book. Instead, the term 'Wabanaki' is used as a general reference to

the native people of Maine and the Maritimes. Although the label 'Wabanaki' is less than ideal, it does not carry the degree of confusion currently associated with the terms 'Abenaki' or 'eastern Abenaki.' (Baker, 1994, pg. 316)

The editors of *American Beginnings* don't mention the many scholars who questioned the terms Abenaki and Eastern Abenaki, but Bourque is certainly the leading candidate. The "subsequent research" is, in reality, a reinterpretation of texts such as Champlain's journals (1912) and the *Jesuit Relations* (Thwaites, 1898), long available for scholarly research. Bourque's reinterpretation of these sources provides the basis for the widespread implementation of such terms as Wabanaki and Etchemin. However, there is a problem: further review of the French sources reveals ambiguous and conflicting descriptions of the ethnicity of Maine's coastal indigenous communities. The most important observation regarding the French sources is that they can be interpreted as indicating an "Almouchiquois" and not an "Etchemin" presence on the Maine coast prior to and at the time of Champlain and Biard's visits (1604, 1605, 1611). Biard makes these observations in the *Jesuit Relations*:

> All this New France is divided into different tribes, each one having its own separate language and country. They assemble in the Summer to trade with us, principally at the great river. To this place come, also several other tribes from afar off. They barter their skins of beaver, otter, deer, marten, seal, etc., for bread, peas, beans, prunes, tobacco, etc.; kettles, hatchets, iron arrow-points, awls, puncheons, cloaks, blankets, and all other such commodities as the French bring them. Certain tribes are now our implacable enemies, such as the Excomminquois, who inhabit the Northern coast of the great Gulf of St. Lawrence and do us a great deal of harm. This warfare was begun (as they say) when certain Basques tried to commit a wicked outrage... There are only three tribes which are on good terms of friendship with us, the Montaguets, the Souriquois, and the Eteminquois. I myself can witness to the friendship of the Etechemins and Souriquois, for I have lived among them, and for the Montaguets I have heard others speak. As to other tribes, no confidence can be placed in them. The French have nothing to do with them except to explore their coasts, and even then they are badly treated, although Champlain does not complain of these savages at all, in his latest explorations up the great river. (Thwaites, 1898, pg. 68-69)

Was that great river the Penobscot (Norumbega) or the St. Lawrence? It was at the junction of the Penobscot River and the Kenduskeag Stream at Bangor that Champlain first encountered one of the superchiefs of Mawooshen in 1604, and it was the coast of the Almouchiquois that Champlain explored in 1605. Champlain refers to the natives of the Penobscot and to those of the Kennebec region as Etchemins (Eteminquois) on at least one occasion in his journals. However, there are many other occasions where Biard and others express uncertainty about the ethnicity of the communities along the Maine coast:

These Irocois are known to the French chiefly for the perpetual warfare which they maintain against the Montagnais and Algonquins, allied and friendly tribes. To the South, however, the coast gradually advances up to the forty-third degree, where once more it is interrupted by a very large bay called French bay. This gulf, advancing far into the interiors and bending toward the North and the gulf of St. Lawrence, forms a sort of Isthmus; and this Isthmus is completed by the St. John, a very long river which, taking its rise almost at the very banks of the great Canadian river, empties into this French bay. This Isthmus has a circuit of fully five hundred leagues and is occupied by the Soriquois tribe. In this Isthmus is port royal, where we are now sojourning, lying on the parallel of 44° 40'. But this port (to obviate misunderstanding) is not on the Ocean lying eastward, but on that gulf which I have called French bay. To the West and north, from the river of St. John to the river Potugoet [Penobscot], and even to the river Rimbegui [Kennebec], live the Etheminqui. (Thwaites, 1898, pg. 67)

Here is another of the numerous ambiguous references to the identity of the indigenous communities lying between the Penobscot and Kennebec rivers. The "Etheminqui" (Etchemins) may or may not inhabit this area. Since no French explorers explored the smaller rivers to the east of the Kennebec, French sources cannot be used to validate the inscriptions on the Lescarbot map of 1609. The repeated identification of both Kennebecs and Androscoggins as Almouchiquois, those horticulturalists not supposed to have been growing corn east of the Saco River, further undermines the "subsequent research" i.e. reinterpretation of French sources.

From the Rimbegui river to the fortieth parallel the whole country is in the possession of the tribe called the Armouchiquois. Such is the distribution of the territory. The tribes amount to seven in number, differing from each other in language and character: the Excommunicated, the Algonquins, the Montagnais, the Irocois, the Soriquois, the Etheminqui and the Armouchiquois. *But of these neither the Excommunicated, nor the Irocois, nor the Armouchiquois are well known to the French.* [italics added] The remaining four tribes appear already to be united in firm friendship and intimacy with them. they stay over night among us; we rove about with them, and hunt with them and live among them without arms and without fear; and, as has thus far appeared, without danger. (Thwaites, 1898, pg. 67-68)

Here Biard is explicit in describing how little the French knew about the indigenous communities along the Maine coast west of Schoodic Point. In an obscure footnote in *A Memoir of Jacques Cartier,* Baxter notes a favorite method used by Native Americans to convey information using either sticks or pebbles:

Champlain, when he visited the Saco Indians, says that 'they placed six pebbles at equal distances apart, giving me to understand by this, that these marks were as many chiefs and tribes.' (Baxter, 1906, Footnote, pg. 229)

By any chance, would these be the six tribes of Mawooshen, i.e. the Saco River community, the Pigwackets, the Androscoggins, the Kennebecs, the Wawenocs, and the Penobscots? Or were these communities of the Massachusetts Indians to the southwest of the Saco River, including the Pennacooks?

The most significant of all contradictions and ambiguities in "French sources" lies in the radical difference between Lescarbot's initial, tentative, protohistoric map of 1609 and Champlain's more accurate map of 1632. Champlain's map is the first accurate geographical and ethnohistorical rendition of Nouvelle France and contradicts the Bourquian interpretation of the French version of Maine's ethnohistory.

Figure 15 Section of a map by Jean Boisseau, 1643, Engraving, hand colored, 35.0 x 55.0 cm.

Champlain's large map of 1632, later reduced in size for commercial distribution by Jean Boisseau in 1643, clearly shows "Almouchicois," not "Etechemins," as occupying the central Maine coast between the Penobscot and Kennebec rivers. To the east of "R. de Norembegue" is "Pemetegou," land of the Penobscots. Champlain's 1632 map clearly locates "Etechemins" in their ancestral homelands in the upper watershed of the St. Croix River. This map supercedes the Lescarbot map of 1609, illustrating a detailed understanding of the distribution of ethnic communities that came from almost three decades of preliminary and intermittent exploration and settlement in the maritime peninsula. It wasn't until 1633 that French settlement and Jesuit proselytizing became widespread in the Maritime Provinces. The fact that Champlain himself redrew the first map that showed Etchemins living in the central Maine coast and instead denoted Almouchiquois as living on the central Maine coast, raises a fundamental question: isn't the ethnicity of the Almouchiquois actually Eastern Abenaki, and weren't they the principal inhabitants of the confederacy of Mawooshen and the land of Norumbega, and not the Etchemins?

The Conundrum of Ethnohistory

Bourque and other archaeologists clearly document the changing technology and growing population of Native American communities on the coast of the maritime peninsula after the beginning of the ceramic period 2900 - 2700 BP. In particular, Bourque (2001) notes a growing lithic exchange network after 1000 BP, documented by extensive excavations at the Goddard site on Blue Hill Bay. (See also Petersen, 2004.) This trading network included other forms of commodity exchange including esoteric food products, such as smoked oysters, which have left no traces in the archaeological record except for the mammoth shell middens at Damariscotta. Corn was an important component of this trade network, though more difficult to document.

Bourque's text includes a detailed description of the ceramic technologies that appeared in Maine after 2700 BP. The wide variety of ceramic styles documented by Bourque implies a semi-sedentary lifestyle, not the nomadic hunting and gathering ways of a population who could not, as a practical matter, utilize ceramic containers. Bourque also discusses evidence of more complex social organization in native communities. Ironically, the evolution of semi-permanent village sites in coastal Maine after 1100 coincides with a debasement of pottery styles and skills at this time. Snow (1980) notes the importance of rapid canoe travel in the formation of these semi-permanent communities. The technology of spruce root and birch bark canoes and containers helped reduce dependency on fragile pottery vessels. The more sedentary lifestyles of either horticultural communities or mobile trading cultures with permanent village sites resulted in hierarchical status differentials. based not only on lineage and hunting territorial boundaries but also on control of trade, access to valuable local resources, favorable village locations on well-established trading routes. and the finesse of complex social organization leaders, who could negotiate, trade, communicate, initiate, and participate in ceremonial activities that enhanced the status of the community. The existence of this complex social milieu is consistent with the evolution of the confederacy of Mawooshen with its intricate trading network, which Bourque only references once in his description of the "Etchemin" superchief from Indian Island (Bourque, 2001).

During the era before the mass production of wampum with European-derived iron drills, the exchange of wampum belts as a significant act of leadership acknowledgment characterized the social interaction of indigenous communities throughout the northeast. The exchange of wampum symbolized the evolution of more complex, dynamic, interactive, indigenous communities. The late ceramic period included increasingly complex horticultural activity, i.e. the corn-beans-squash triad, extensive trading networks, increasing population density, growing diversity of resource use, and increasingly complex social organizations. These, in turn, imply the establishment of semi-permanent communities occupying the same village sites, winter hunting camps, and coastal trading and fishing stations over a period of generations. The introduction of European trade goods radically altered the evolution of Maine's indigenous population into a complex network of trading communities, which may or may not have included horticultural activities in the river bottomlands above the tidewater of the smaller rivers in the central coast. Sudden dependence on European-supplied kettles, blankets, food, and especially weapons brought a quick halt to the need for and the spread of horticulture in communities in the maritime peninsula now dependent on the fur trade for sustenance. Some commentators note that contact with European traders may have served to restrict existing horticultural activities in areas near beaver habitat, where trade goods undermined the need for growing corn and beans. Champlain described the impact of intertribal warfare on horticulture in the Sagadahoc, as noted. Obvious climatological restrictions on horticultural activities were only part of the reason why many European observers failed to note horticultural activities in coastal areas downstream from the sheltered river valleys where English settlers later grew corn.

The radical difference in opinion about the ethnic composition of the residents of the central Maine coast between the Penobscot and Kennebec rivers at the time of European contact and settlement raises questions about the accuracy of "White Man's ethnohistory." How truthful have we been about the cultural impact of European contact with indigenous populations of New England and elsewhere? There is obviously a vast literature on this subject, much of which is cited in the bibliographies that follow. Nonetheless, annoying, tendentious maps, both English and French, but especially the latter, provide an opportunity to perpetuate cultural bias and distorted history. It is difficult to illustrate rapidly changing ethnic alliances in one map. Charges of the reconstruction of historical events and the obfuscation of what actually transpired in the past can be made against any narrators, both French and English.

Bourque makes the following telling comments on the meaning of "ethnohistory" and past historians' long-recognized tendency to distort their accounts and aggrandize the role of their own culture in history.

- Only recently have scholars made deliberate attempts to write history with the Native perspective as a central focus. Many, both anthropologists and historians, refer to this research as ethnohistory, although some historians prefer the term 'new Indian history.' The goal of ethnohistory is to piece together fragments of historic information about Native peoples. (Bourque, 2001, pg. 103)
- Even in historical works where Indians are mentioned extensively, their perspective is rarely the central theme, and what is said about them is often badly distorted by ignorance and cultural bias. (Bourque, 2001, pg. 103-104)
- Nineteenth-century scholars were somewhat more objective but still prone to ethnocentrism--the tendency to place one's own ethnic group above others'. For example, while William D. Williamson's encyclopedic *History of Maine* attempts to

deal objectively with the region's Indian inhabitants, his New England perspective significantly distorts their story. (Bourque, 2001, pg. 104)

- The ethnohistorian must therefore apply the sensitivity of the anthropologist in using a variety of accounts written by people who lived in other places and at other times to construct an accurate and balanced portrayal of Native North Americans during the colonial era. Like the archaeological reconstructions presented earlier, the ethnohistorical hypotheses outlined below must be viewed as works in progress. However, as in archaeology, an encouraging amount of new data has appeared on the scene during the past two decades. (Bourque, 2001, pg. 104)

Bourque inadvertently delineates the key question for the reconsideration of the meaning and significance of Norumbega, Mawooshen, and the Wawenoc community. Exactly what is the bold new data that has emerged to discount the older, supposedly biased accounts of English observers and chroniclers of Maine's eastern Abenaki communities as they existed prior to the cataclysmic events of 1603 - 1619 and of their encounters with remnants of these communities after 1620? Specifically, how does Williamson's New England perspective distort his description of Maine's Native American communities written in 1832? What are some specific examples that would prove the nonexistence of the Wawenoc community, their ancestral homelands, and the complex hierarchy of social relationships implicit in a confederation of indigenous communities and trading networks in the land of Mawooshen? In fact, who represents the Wawenoc perspective? And how is it that no ethnohistoric bias exists in Champlain's, Lescarbot's, or Biard's description of the inhabitants of the central Maine coast well to the southwest of their Canadian maritime peninsula settlements? It is ironic that Champlain's and Biard's written accounts of visits to the communities on the Kennebec and the Sheepscot are not incompatible with the English accounts of Maine's Native American communities summarized by Williamson (1832). The late 20th century reinterpretation of Champlain's and Lescarbot's accounts by the new Bourquian model of Maine's ethnohistoric past splits Mawooshen/Norumbega into two cultures and eliminates the Wawenoc community from our contemporary history books.

116

White Man's History and the Scalping of English Historians

Both Axtell (1981) and Prins (1996) provide particularly interesting synopses of the evolution of commercial scalping in New England and the northeast, which earlier commentators once alleged was widely practiced in North America before European contact:

> The whorl of hair on the crown and especially male scalplocks, braided and decorated with jewelry, paint, and feathers, represented the person's 'soul' or living spirit. (Axtell, 1981, pg. 214)

> During the colonial wars in North America, Europeans began offering bounty for scalps, transforming the traditional trophy from a memento of valor into a commodity to be exchanged for cash or merchandise. Commercial scalping became common practice in the summer of 1689 when the Massachusetts government began recruiting Mohawk Indians from New York to take Wabanaki scalps (Baxter 6:491). In reaction, the French Crown offered payment for English scalps. (Prins, 1996, pg. 122)

> Nonetheless, from 1693 onward, Wabanaki warriors regularly 'brought in English Prisoners & Scalps,' for which the French colonial government paid them good cash (Calloway, 95-96). Soon, the gruesome practice became commonplace, and anyone -- Indian, French, or English - was eligible to scalp or be scalped. In other words, although Europeans did not introduce scalping to North America, they did institute its commercialization, turning tribal warriors into colonial mercenaries. (Prins, 1996, pg. 122)

Though many would now contend that scalping did originate with Euro-American mercenaries, a connection needs to be made between the barbarism encouraged by the French and English during their struggle for control of North America (1605 - 1763) and the objectives and intentions of European exploration and settlement of the new found lands. This brings us back again to the many French maps of Nova Francia, which tell us so much about the French ethnohistoric point of view and which contain those lingering notations about Norumbega, soon eliminated from English maps after John Smith renamed Norumbega "New England" in 1614.

In his own particular prejudiced, ethnocentric style, Parkman devoted much of his life to documenting and writing about the battle for North America and the failure of the French to maintain control over much of a continent they so successfully penetrated initially. The Lescarbot 1609 map is a most important chapter in the larger story of the French control of the Maritime Provinces and eastern Canada until the treaty of Quebec in 1763. The Lescarbot map reflects Champlain's success in establishing and then exploiting a friendly relationship with the Micmacs and Etchemins of Nova Scotia, New Brunswick, and the Montagnais to the north. That it was redrawn in 1632 to reflect a revised and expanded understanding of the ethnicity of the Maritime Peninsula only confirms

Champlain's need for an accurate understanding of the indigenous communities that he was attempting to control.

The thrust of French exploration and settlement in the St. Lawrence River basin (Todussac, Quebec) and the Bay of Fundy (St. Croix, Port Royal, St. John) was a combination of successful commercial enterprise, especially that of the fur trade, and the less successful attempt to facilitate religious conversion of the indigenous populations to the Catholic faith. The story of the attempt of the Jesuits to convert Native American populations begins with Father Biard's 1611 visit to Nova Scotia, New Brunswick, and New England. This was several years after Lescarbot published his 1609 map, but, already, the French clearly expressed their intention to control North America on the maps that they drew. These maps expressed French ethnohistoric viewpoints and prejudices as a matter of course. Having already met the principal Abenaki Bashebas on the Penobscot River in 1604 and made allies of the Micmacs, who attacked the Abenaki community at the Saco River in 1607, French mapmakers would have no reason whatsoever not to indicate an Etchemin hegemony in the small area of the central Maine coast between the Penobscot and Kennebec rivers, now virtually a forgotten chapter in Maine's ethnohistory. I noted earlier that the inscription "Etchemins" on the Lescarbot map accompanied the turreted towers of "Norumbega"; "cut from the same cloth" references the projection of European values and agendas expressed in maps or written history as new ethnohistoric paradigms. In this context, the Lescarbot map of 1609 inadvertently erased a previously existing indigenous community, i.e. the Wawenocs, not allied with the Franco-Europeans then making the maps and writing the history of a coastal region that they never actually explored or of the ethnic communities they never fully understood. Champlain later rectified the omissions in his 1632 map, a fact conveniently overlooked by those agreeing with the new Bourquian paradigm of Maine's protohistoric past. Can we yet peel back these new layers, these palimpsests, of White Man's history and allow the indigenous voices of pre-history to disclose themselves?

The spread of scalping is a symbol of the spreading influence of European commercial and religious values. In the period between Gosnold's visit in 1602 and the landing of the Pilgrims in 1620, the central Maine coast's ethnicity had been radically altered. The implication of the Lescarbot 1609 map that nomadic bands of wandering, hunting, and gathering Etchemins, whose ancestral homelands were to the east along the St. John's River, were long time residents of the central Maine coast and the first Native Americans, whom Waymouth and other European visitors encountered, represents "White Man's" rewriting of ethnohistory in its most blatant form. In the specific case of the central coast of Maine, the revisionist doctrine of the "Etchemin" hegemony and the disappearance of indigenous communities, such as the Wawenocs and the Penobscots, symbolizes the scalping of the English historians and squelching of Native American communities of the present. The implication of an Etchemin hegemony on the central Maine coast stretching into prehistory suggested by the Lescarbot map of 1609 is an ethnohistoric perversion equal to any myth ever spun by equally prejudiced English historians. Scalping as encouraged by both the French and English in their attempt to control, defeat, and then exterminate the indigenous populations of North America is a metaphor for both the English and French agendas of control and conquest and is one of the darker chapters in European settlement of this continent. Luckily, the Lescarbot map of 1609 isn't the only box of Cheesits in town.

The participation of Native American voices in the debate over the ethnicity of the central Maine coast is a necessary component of any reconsideration of the meaning and significance of Norumbega and Mawooshen. One can lament the metaphorical scalping of Maine's English historians who provided one version of the ethnicity of central Maine's coast. Most regrettable of all is that few, if any, Native Americans from the Wawenoc and Kennebec communities, and many others, survive to recount their ancestral traditions. Multiple versions of Maine's ethnohistoric past, including the ambiguous French narrations, and the English and Native American descriptions, must be a part of any attempt to construct educational curricula for the study of the history of Maine's indigenous communities. Ultimately, the substitution of the ethnic designation "Etchemin" for "Abenaki" creates unnecessary confusion about Maine's ethnohistoric past. The tragedy of that oversimplification is that many interesting chapters in Maine history are essentially erased from our history books. The scalping of the English historians is only one phase in the dynamic process of constructing, deconstructing, and reconstructing the lost chapters of Maine's ethnohistory.

Two hundred and fifty years later, there is at least the possibility that humor can leaven these gloomy images. An alleged "French version" of Maine's ethnohistory now reigns supreme. One might conclude a reconsideration of Norumbega and the Wawenoc diaspora with the following midsummer's night dream;

On the streets of Augusta in the dark of night, roams a figure in armor, carrying an Arquebus, that French-made firearm supplied to the Micmacs by French traders, and the head of a scalped Englishman at the end of his pike pole. This figure looks suspiciously like Samuel de Champlain, but look closely again. Could that be the ghost of one of our contemporary ethnohistorians carrying the scalp of Dean Snow? And isn't that the voice of Kate Smith singing "the last time I saw Hochalega," down the street from the local theater, featuring Ethyl Merman in "They threw out the baby with the babble?" And what of all these "Blue Paint burials" that have suddenly appeared in central coastal Maine, with their grave goods consisting of moldering history books and old letters of testimonials.

There lies William Williamson buried in a particularly bright blue paint grave at Wiscasset, Rufus King Sewall in a more purple colored grave on Indiantown Island at

Boothbay, Francis Greene buried at Newagen in a grave sprinkled with blue ochre, Frank Speck in a particularly large enclosure along Route 1 near the Damariscotta shell heaps, Cyrus Eaton with a gravestone painted blue along the Weskeag River in South Thomaston, and the torso of Dean Snow buried in the blue painted crypt in downtown Bangor at the Kenduskeag Stream. College students on Maine campuses are carefully reading the latest history *Eleven Thousand Nine Hundred and Fifteen Years of Native Americans in Maine.* Its author conveniently left out the 85 years between 1534 and 1619 pertaining to the destruction of Mawooshen, i.e. from Cartier's observation of Hochalega to the end of the pandemic, essays on inadvertent ethnohistoric cleansing not being in vogue. Students and scholars are also reading "The Eastern Abenaki, where did they go?" and "Simplicity and linearity on the central Maine coast from 1534 to 1619." One can hear background noise from a local student union at the end of a Monday night football game: Etchemin Super chiefs, 42, Wawenoc Patriots, 3. In the library, dedicated students of Maine history carefully outline their upcoming theses; "Norumbega Deconstructed," "Rusticators and the Myth of the Wawenoc Nation," "Lost Paradise of the Ancient Abenaki." Before awakening from this midsummer's night dream, finally recall the narration of William Bradford about the March 1621 visit of a Native American from Downeast greeting the Pilgrims in English and then providing critical information about fish, fur, and corn at Monhegan and on the Maine coast. There, in our dream, is Samoset, that Maliseet from Meductic, who saved the Plymouth colonists from starvation and whose domain included Indiantown Island (Boothbay), Louds Island (Muscongus Island), Damariscotta, and Arambeck, all eastern ancestral homelands of those wandering nomadic Maliseet/Passamaquoddys of the St. John River valley. But all dreams eventually end. Some are remembered; some are not. Our midsummer night's dream is a reminder of the diversity of opinions and unresolved issues pertaining to the identity and significance of the indigenous communities living at the interface of pre-history and history, i.e. protohistory.

Conclusion

Unfortunately, the story of the thriving protohistoric Wawenoc community and its subsequent scattering and dispersal is a lost chapter in Maine history, compounded by its current dismissal by contemporary historians. Allegedly based on "new research" and "French sources," the new Bourquian(1989) reinterpretation of Maine's ethnohistoric past submerges the history and fate of regional (eastern) Abenaki communities, including the Wawenocs, by the generic designation of "Etchemins" as residents of the central Maine coast. Revival of pre-1632 French terminology to describe the ethnicity of the indigenous population of Maine and the maritime peninsula at the time of the European settlement fails to provide an accurate portrayal of its diversity and changing ethnicity.

Any historical review of the identity, location, history, and significance of indigenous populations in Maine and the maritime peninsula must start with the Wabanaki ("Wobanakik," Wiseman, 2001) as the original centuries-old proto-Algonquin inhabitants. We must describe specific ethnic communities with the names that Native Americans used or would use to describe their own nations, e.g. Passamaquoddy, Maliseet, and Penobscot. We should extend this courtesy to those communities that did not survive contact with Europeans, e.g. Canibas, Androscoggins, Pigwackets, et al. The Wawenocs of the central Maine coast are a particularly notable example of an extinct Eastern Abenaki community whose identity, history, fate, and possibly even original name, has been "submerged" (Quinn, 1990) by the appearance of a subsequent culture which conquered, dominated, acculturated, and/or exterminated its predecessors.

The revision of the traditional understanding of the ethnicity of the indigenous communities of Maine's past has squelched acknowledgement of the vibrancy, complexity and diversity of the Native American communities in a regional confederacy (Mawooshen) and in a bioregion (Norumbega) that flourished in protohistory. The Bourquian paradigm of an oversimplified, streamlined protohistoric "French description" of ethnic communities from 1534 – 1620, the critical years of first contact, is inaccurate and an unacceptable component of this process. The Bourquian paradigm ignores how closely French sources often correlate with traditional English narratives in their description of the indigenous communities of Maine's protohistoric past. The process of Euro-American ethnohistoric "naming," or actually renaming, the indigenous central Maine coastal communities eliminates one of the most interesting chapters in Maine history.

Norumbega Reconsidered: Mawooshen and the Wawenoc Diaspora seeks to reinstate the Abanaki communities, including the Wawenocs, as an important part of Maine's ethnohistory. A reconsideration of the importance of the Native American confederacy of Mawooshen, the ecology of the Norumbega bioregion, and a receptiveness to Native American narrations about their history are essential components in uncovering and disclosing this lost chapter in Maine history. Hopefully, this book makes a start in so-doing.

Postscript to the Third Edition

Four important publications about Native Americans in Maine have appeared since the second edition of *Norumbega Reconsidered* was published in 2008. Kerry Hardy's (2009) eloquent commentary on the florescence of Abenaki culture on the central Maine coast and its ecological constituents (*Notes on a Lost Flute*) is a major contribution to our understanding of the complexity, vibrancy, and sustainability of indigenous communities in coastal Maine (see annotations in Bibliography J). The region between the Kennebec and Penobscot rivers, including the Sheepscot, Damariscotta, Medomak, and St. Georges rivers, was one of the richest ecological bioregions of the Atlantic coast. It is this region that is also referenced in the less eloquent National Park Service ethnographic overview and assessment of *Asticou's Island Domain* by Harald E. L. Prins and Bunny McBride (2007). To rename the indigenous Abenaki communities who lived as "semi-sedentary corn-growing villagers" (Prins 2007, 2) in this area as "Western Etchemins" and then describe them as foraging hunters and gatherers ranging the vast woodlands "east of the Kennebec Valley" eliminates a most important chapter in the history of Native Americans in Maine. This conflicting description of what was for two centuries known as the Wawenoc community as both hunting and gathering nomads and corn-growing Abenakis is present throughout the *Asticou's Island Domain* text and is made explicit in the map of Mawooshen (Prins 2007, 37) where the twenty tribal communities described in the text are illustrated by only thirteen community location markers. At no point does the Prins text indicate that the map of Mawooshen encompasses a highly populated (before 1600) ecologically rich region, which existed for several centuries or more as a vibrant smoked oyster and fur trading confederacy (Figure 1 on page 1). Omitted from the Prins map is the largest archaeological site in New England, the Harts Fall complex (Wawinak) on the St. Georges River (see page 61), the location of perhaps the largest and most important permanent tribal community of the confederacy of Mawooshen. Recent archaeological investigations indicate this site was permanently inhabited for thousands of years (Mitchell 2002).

The third new publication of interest, *Indians in Eden: Wabanakis and Rusticators on Maine's Mount Desert Island, 1840s-1920s* (McBride 2009), has been extracted from Prins and McBride (2007) and is a concise well written summary of Native Americans on Mount Desert Island after 1840. Thankfully, it uses the traditional descriptions of Native Americans in Maine (see annotations in Bibliography J,) avoiding the pitfalls of the Western/Eastern Etchemin quandary.

The fourth new publication is Loring's *In the Shadow of the Eagle* (2008). Appointed as the tribal representative of Native communities in Maine to the Maine State Legislature, Loring's narration recounts her experiences in a political world where Maine's indigenous communities, long isolated and marginalized, now at least have a partial voice in state affairs. Loring notes the lack of access of tribal students to the "ivy league" Maine colleges – Bates, Bowdoin, and Colby – in contrast to scholarships offered by the University of Maine System. Of particular note is the state law requiring the teaching of Maine Indian history in all public schools. Loring explores the many ambiguities of the Land

Figure 16 A highly decorated Native American crooked knife, c. 1998, found in Dexter, Maine. Photos courtesy of Rick Floyd.

Settlement Act, the casino referendums, and numerous other political and social issues of interest to indigenous communities in her narration of key day-to-day events in the legislature from January 2000 to the summer of 2002. Loring's focus is on the continuing unresolved issues of social equality and economic sustainability. Hopefully, the requirement to teach Maine's Native American history in public schools will include a broad survey of all the Abenaki and Etchemin communities living in or near Maine in prehistory, and not just the current paradigm of People of the Dawn where the narrative begins in the late afternoon of Native history (>1625).

This third edition of *Norumbega Reconsidered* includes an important map from Russell's *Indian New England Before the Mayflower* (1980), which was inadvertently left out of previous editions (see Appendix A Figure 35). One of the most important surveys of the indigenous Indians of New England before 1620, Russell's three decades old map is a reminder that eastern Abenaki communities, including the Wawenocs and "Sheepscots," members of the Wawenoc tribe, were the primary inhabitants of coastal and interior Maine west of Schoodic Point, the traditional easternmost geopolitical boundary line for the confederacy of Mawooshen. Prins and McBride, in *Asticou's Island Domain*, extend the eastern boundary of Mawooshen to the Narraguagus River. Providing some relief from the revisionism of the Bourquian paradigm, Prins and McBride frequently note Abenaki tribal communities as a component of the "Western Etchemins" living west of the Narraguagus River. In the annotations in Bibliography J for *Asticou's Island Domain* (Mount Desert Island), the latest descriptions of the confusing tribal alignments of the early 17th century are printed in bold. The relationship of the Native Americans living on or visiting Asticou's island domain with the Abenaki communities living between the Penobscot and Kennebec rivers is briefly referenced in the comprehensive historical survey that Prins and McBride present in this, as yet, unpublished text. That both Tahánedo, the sakom of Pemaquid, and Samoset are now considered wandering hunting and gathering "Western Etchemins" is a sad commentary on the disappearing history of one of New England's most important indigenous communities.

124

Norumbega Reconsidered
Short Bibliography

This short bibliography of sources cited in the text is followed by a more comprehensive series of annotated bibliographies pertaining to the indigenous communities of Maine in prehistory, protohistory and the historic period. Additional citations, comments and corrections are welcomed by the editor.

(1993). Special topic issue: Archaeology in Newfoundland and Labrador. *Newfoundland Studies*. 9.

Axtell, James. (1985). *The invasion within: The contest of cultures in colonial North America.* New York: Oxford University Press.

Baker, Emerson W., Churchill, Edwin A., D'Abate, Richard S., Jones, Kristine L., Konrad, Victor A. and Prins, Harald E.L., Eds. (1994). *American beginnings: Exploration, culture, and cartography in the land of Norumbega.* Lincoln, NB: University of Nebraska Press.

Barber, Russell J. (1983). *The Wheeler's site: A specialized shellfish processing station on the Merrimack River*. Peabody Museum Monographs 7. Cambridge, MA: Harvard University Press.

Barthes, Roland. (1973). *The pleasure of the text*. New York, NY: Hill and Wang.

Baxter, James Phinney, Ed. (1884). *Sir Ferdinando Gorges and his Province of Maine*. 3 vols. Portland, ME: Hoyt, Fogg, and Donham. Reprinted in 1890 by The Prince Society, Boston.

Baxter, James Phinney. (1906). *A memoir of Jacques Cartier: Sieur de Limoilou: His voyages to the St. Lawrence*. A Bibliography and a facsimile of the manuscript of 1534 with annotations, etc. New York: Dodd, Mead & Company.

Berkhofer, Robert. (1978). *White Man's Indian: Images of the American Indian from Columbus to the present*. New York: Alfred A. Knopf.

Bourque, Bruce J. (1989). Ethnicity on the Maritime Peninsula, 1600-1759. *Ethnohistory*. 36(3): 257-284.

Bourque, Bruce J. (2001). *Twelve thousand years: American Indians in Maine*. Lincoln, NE: University of Nebraska Press.

Boyd, Stephen G. (1885). *Indian local names with their interpretation*. York, PA: Self-published.

Bradford, William. (1908). *History of Plymouth Plantation, 1606-1646*. Davis, W.T., Ed. New York: Charles Scribner's and Sons. Republished in 1952 as *Of Plymouth Plantation, 1620-1647*. Samuel Eliot Morison, Ed. New York: Knopf.

Brasser, T.J. (1978). Early Indian European contacts. In: *Handbook of North American Indians*. Vol. 15. Trigger, Bruce G., Ed. Washington, D.C.: Smithsonian Institution.

Burrage, Henry S., Ed. (1887). *Rosier's relation of Weymouth's voyage to the coast of Maine, 1605*. Portland, ME: Gorges Society.

Burrage, Henry S. (1914). *The beginnings of colonial Maine 1602-1658*. Portland, ME: Marks Printing House for the State of Maine.

Cook, David S. (1985). *Indian canoe routes of Maine*. North Attleborough, MA: Covered Bridge Press.

Cronon, William. (1983). *Changes in the land: Indians, colonists, and the ecology of New England*. New York: Hill and Wang.

Crosby, A.W. (1976). Virgin soil epidemics as a factor in the aboriginal depopulation in America. *William and Mary Quarterly*. 23(2): 289-299.

Curtis, Jane, Curtis, Will, and Lieberman, Frank. (1995). *Monhegan the artists' island*. Camden, ME: Down East Books.

Davies, James. (1880). *Relation of a voyage to Sagadahoc, 1607 - 1608. American Journeys Collection*. Document No. AJ-042. Reprinted 2003 by Wisconsin Historical Society Digital Library and Archives. www.wisconsinhistory.org.

Day, Gordon M. (1965). The identity of the Sokokis. *Ethnohistory*. 12: 237-249.

Day, Gordon M. (1998). *In search of New England's Native past: Selected essays by Gordon M. Day*. Foster, Michael K. and Cowan, William, Eds. Amherst, MA: University of Massachusetts Press.

DeLorme. (1998). *Maine Atlas & Gazetteer*. Yarmouth, ME: DeLorme.

Erickson, Vincent O. (1978). Maliseet-Passamaquoddy. In: *Handbook of North American Indians: Northeast*. Vol 15. Trigger, Bruce G., Ed. Washington, D.C.: Smithsonian Institution.

Fisher, Carol Smith. (2005). Personal communication.

Ganong, William Francis. (1917). The origin of the place-names Acadia and Norumbega. *Proceedings and Transactions*. Ottawa, Canada: *Transactions of the Royal Society of Canada*, Series 3, Vol. 31, Sect. 2: 105-119.

Ganong, William Francis. (1933). Crucial Maps in the early cartography and place nomenclature of the Atlantic coast of Canada. V: The Compiled or Composite Maps of 1526-1600. Ottawa, Canada: *Transactions of the Royal Society of Canada*, Series 3, Vol. 27, Sect. 2: 149-195.

Gorges, Ferdinando. (1658). *A briefe narration of the originall undertakings of the advancement of plantations into the parts of America.* London, England: E. Brudenell for Nath. Brook.

Grant, W.L., Ed. (1907). *Voyages of Samuel de Champlain: 1604 - 1616.* New York: Charles Scribner's Sons.

Greene, Francis B. (1906). *History of Boothbay, Southport, and Boothbay Harbor, Maine 1623 - 1905 with family genealogies.* Portland, ME: Loring, Short and Harmon.

Hardy, Kerry. (2009). *Notes on a lost flute: A field guide to the Wabanaki.* Camden, ME: Down East Books.

Harp, Elmer, Jr. (1963). Evidence of boreal archaic culture in southern Labrador and Newfoundland. Paper no. 5. National Museum of Canada. Bulletin No. 193. *Contributions to Anthropology, 1961-62, Pt. 1.* Ottawa, Canada: Canada Department of Northern Affairs and National Resources.

Harvey, D. C. (2000). Asticou. *Dictionary of Canadian Biography Online* via http://www.biographi.ca/EN/ShowBio.asp?BioId=34150&query=Asticou.

Horsford, Eben Norton. (1891). *The defences of Norumbega and a review of the reconnaissances of Col. T. W. Higginson, Professor Henry W. Haynes, Dr. Justin Winsor, Dr. Francis Parkman, and Rev. Dr. Edmund F. Slafter.* NY: Houghton, Mifflin and Company.

Judd, Richard W., Churchill, Edwin A. and Eastman, Joel W., Eds. (1995). *Maine: The pine tree state from prehistory to the present.* Orono, ME: University of Maine Press.

Lescarbot, Marc. (1609a). *Nova Francia: A description of Acadia, 1606.* P. Erondelle, tr. London. Reprinted in 1928 by Routledge, London.

Lescarbot, Marc. (1609b). *Les Muses de la Nouvelle France: à Monseigneur le Chancellier.* Paris: Chez Jean Millot.

Lescarbot, Marcus. (1609c). *Histoire de la Nouvelle France.* Paris: Chez Jean Milot. Map inserted between pages 480 and 481. Map title: Figure de la Terre Neuve Grande Riviere de Canada et Cotes de l'Ocean en la Nouvelle France. Via Archives of Canada http://www.canadiana.org/ECO/PageView?id=901e3bd4d1&display=36652+0539

Levine, Mary Ann, Sassaman, Kenneth E. and Nassaney, Michael S. Eds. (2000). *The archaeological northeast.* Westport, CT: Bergin & Garvey.

Locke, John L. (1859). *Sketches of the history of the town of Camden, Maine; including incidental references to the neighboring places and adjacent waters.* Hallowell, ME: Masters, Smith and Co.

Loring, Donna M. (2008). *In the shadow of the eagle: A tribal representative in Maine*. Gardiner, ME: Tilbury House Publishers.

McBride, Bunny and Prins, Harald E. L. (2009). *Indians in Eden: Wabanakis and rusticators on Maine's Mount Desert Island, 1840s-1920s*. Camden, ME: Down East Books.

Mitchell, Harbour, III and Spiess, Arthur E. (Spring 2002). Early archaic bifurcate base point occupation in the St. George River valley. *Maine Archaeological Society Bulletin*. 42(1). pg. 15-24.

Morey, David C. (May 2005). *The voyage of Archangell: James Rosier's account of the Waymouth voyage of 1605 - A True Relation*. Gardiner, ME: Tilbury House, Publishers.

Morison, Samuel Eliot, Ed. (1963). *Of Plymouth Plantation: 1620 - 1647 by William Bradford: A new edition*. New York: Alfred A. Knopf.

Morison, Samuel Eliot. (1971). *The European discovery of America: The northern voyages A.D. 500-1600*. New York: Oxford University Press.

Morris, Gerald E., Ed. (1976). *Maine bicentennial atlas: An historical survey*. Portland, ME: The Maine Historical Society.

Parkman, Francis. (1983). *France and England in North America: Volume 1: Pioneers of France in the New World; The Jesuits in North America in the Seventeenth Century; La Salle and the Discovery of the Great West; The Old Regime in Canada*. New York, NY: The Library of America. Reprint of the first four volumes of what was originally an 8 volume set published in 1865.

Petersen, James B., Blustain, Malinda and Bradley, James W. (2004). "Mawooshen" revisited: Two Native American contact period sites on the central Maine coast. *Archaeology of Eastern North America*. 32: 1-71.

Prins, Harald. (1996). *The Mi'kmaq: Resistance, accommodation, and cultural survival*. Fort Worth, TX: Harcourt Brace College Publishers.

Prins, Harald E. L. and McBride, Bunny. (2007). *Asticou's island domain: Wabanaki peoples at Mount Desert Island 1500-2000*. Vols. 1 and 2. Bar Harbor, ME: Acadia National Park and The Abbe Museum.

Purchas, Samuel. (1625). The description of the countrey of Mawooshen, discovered by the English in the Yeere 1602.3.5.6.7.8. and 9. In: *Hakluytus posthumus or Purchas his pilgrims*. Vol 4. Henry Fetherston, London.

Quinn, David Beers. (1977). *North America from earliest discovery to first settlements: The Norse voyages to 1612*. NY, NY: Harper and Row.

Quinn, David Beers. (1990). *Explorers and colonies: America, 1500-1625*. London: Hambledon Press.

Quinn, David Beers. (1995). The early cartography of Maine in the setting of early European exploration of New England and the Maritimes. In: *American beginnings: Exploration, culture, and cartography in the land of Norumbega*. Baker Emerson W. et al. Eds. Lincoln, NB: University of Nebraska Press.

Rosier, James. (1605). A true relation of Captain George Weymouth his voyage. In: *A history of Maine: A collection of readings on the history of Maine 1600 – 1974*. Third Edition. Ronald F. Banks, Ed. (1969). Dubuque, IA: Kendall/Hunt Publishing Co.

Russell, Howard S. (1980). *Indian New England before the Mayflower*. Hanover, NH: University Press of New England.

Salisbury, Neal. (1982). *Manitou and Providence: Indians, Europeans, and the making of New England, 1500-1643*. New York: Oxford University Press.

Sanger, David. (Fall 2000). "Red Paint People" and other myths of Maine archaeology. *Maine History*. 39: 145-167.

Sewall, Rufus King. (1895). *Ancient voyages to the western continent: Three phases of history on the coast of Maine*. New York: The Knickerbocker Press.

Siebert, Frank T. Jr. (1973). The identity of the Tarrentines, with an etymology. *Studies in Linguistics*. 23: 69-76.

Smith, John. (1837). A description of New-England. *Collections of the Massachusetts Historical Society*. 3rd series, 6: 103-140.

Snow, Dean R. (1976a). *The archaeology of North America: American Indians and their origins*. London: Thames and Hudson.

Snow, Dean R. (1976b). The ethnohistoric baseline of the eastern Abenaki. *Ethnohistory*. 23(3): 291-306.

Snow, Dean R. (1978). Eastern Abenaki. In: *Northeast Handbook of North American Indians*. Vol. 15. Trigger, Bruce G. and Sturtevant, William C., Eds. Washington, DC: Smithsonian Institution.

Snow, Dean R. (1980). *The archaeology of New England*. New York: Academic Press.

Soctomah, Donald. (2005). A Wabanaki perspective. In: *A symposium to celebrate one land - two worlds: Maine Mawooshen 1605 - 2005: The 400th anniversary of George Waymouth's voyage to New England*. Rockland, ME: Island Institute.

Speck, Frank G. (1928). Wawenock myth texts from Maine. *Bureau of American Ethnology, 43rd Annual Report, 1925-1926.* Washington, DC. 169-197.

Speck, Frank G. (1940). *Penobscot man: The life history of a forest tribe in Maine.* University of Pennsylvania Press. Reprinted 1998: Orono, ME: University of Maine Press.

Spiess, Arthur E. and Cranmer, Leon. (Fall 2001). Native American occupations at Pemaquid: Review and results. *Maine Archaeological Society Bulletin.* 41(2): 1 - 25.

Spiess, Arthur, Sobolik,Kristin, Crader, Diana, Mosher, John and Wilson, Deborah. (2006). Cod, clams and deer: The food remains from Indiantown Island. *Archaeology of Eastern North America.* 34: 141-187.

Spiess, Arthur E. and Spiess, Bruce D. (1987). New England pandemic of 1616-1622: Cause and archaeological implication. *Man in the Northeast.* 34: 71-83.

Thwaites, Ruben G., Ed. (1896-1901). The Jesuit relations and allied documents: Travels and explorations of the Jesuit missionaries in New France, 1610-1791. 73 Vols. Cleveland, OH: Burrows Brothers.

Whitney, Seth Harding. (1887). *The Kennebec Valley: This work is devoted to the early history of the valley; also relating many incidents and adventures of the early settlers; including a brief sketch of the Kennebec Indian.* Augusta, ME: Sprague, Burleigh & Flynt, printers to the state.

Williamson, William D. (1832). *The history of the state of Maine; from its first discovery, A. D. 1602, to the separation, A. D. 1820, inclusive, Volume I and II.* Hallowell, ME: Glazier, Masters & Co.

Appendix A

A. Norumbega Reconsidered Maps

Table of Contents

Table of Figures

Introduction

Maps are an explicit expression of the ethnocentric process of "naming" or defining the geographical parameters of ethnic groups. The maps in the following appendix provide a variety of descriptions of boundaries of the indigenous populations of New England before, during and after contact with Europeans and European settlement. Most of the maps express a consensus of opinion about the presence of an Abenaki culture in the central coastal areas of Maine. One can argue ad infinitum about the exact meaning of Abenaki versus Wabanaki, Western and Eastern Abenaki, a Maritime Canadian Abenaki or none at all, etc. The boundaries drawn on maps three or four hundred years after the florescence of these cultures can only be a guess. We may never know the exact boundaries of various indigenous communities, just as we don't even know the names by which they called themselves four centuries ago. Some maps, such as that drawn by Frank Speck's son, illustrate exact family hunting ground boundaries, representing one extreme in our need to define, control, explicate and reach some kind of closure in solving the riddles of the ethnic boundaries of the indigenous communities of the past. Other maps are less specific, showing theoretical estimated community boundaries, which have obviously varied in time and space. With respect to the controversial protohistoric Lescarbot map of 1609, we have a map with minimal geographical accuracy but one that has had a major impact on recent speculations about ethnic boundaries in the maritime peninsula at the time of contact with Europeans. Champlain soon revised this map into a much more accurate depiction of New France in the third decade of the 17th century. The Hoffman map of 1955 is the first hint of the revisionist doctrines, which using selective French sources, have recently challenged the longstanding consensus of Abenaki communities living along the central coast of Maine at the time of contact with Europeans. These maps, along with the wide variety of historical narrations, which accompany them, can only be interpreted by individuals making their own educated conclusions about who lived where and when. In the age of post-modernism and post-deconstruction, the idea that some final definitive understanding of ethnicity and ethnic boundaries can be retrieved from the many stories of disorderly history is another myth that can be added to the list of those we have already constructed.

The last three maps are included in this publication for those who are not familiar with the landscape and towns of the central Maine coast. Of particular interest to the Davistown Museum is the very last map (c. 1930), which illustrates the surviving vestiges of a prehistoric Indian trading route, which went from Ducktrap, near Northport on the coast, west to Searsmont, West Appleton, South Liberty and thence down to Somerville where, following the present day route 105, it terminated at Augusta, called Cushnoc in the 17th century. This Indian trail, the shortest route from the coast to the Kennebec River for Native Americans traveling down from Nova Scotia, later became an important colonial road. Only part of this road can still be driven; the section between Searsmont and South Liberty has sunken into swamplands in some locations. The old county road from South Liberty to route 105 is still passable. It is a most evocative reminder that prior to European settlement the area of the central Maine coast was inhabited for millenniums. Once indigenous traders traveling west through Nova Scotia, Newfoundland or Labrador reached the Kennebec River in prehistory, there was only one ten mile portage obstructing passage down the St. Lawrence River valley through the Great Lakes to the Midwest and its deposits of copper, so greatly valued for decorative and ceremonial purposes by Native communities throughout the northeast and maritime peninsula. One map, one story, many maps, many stories.

1570 Map of Abraham Ortelius

Figure 1 Abraham Ortelius

Norumbega or New England

A section of the book jacket for Emerson Baker, Ed. (1994). *American Beginnings.* University of Nebraska Press, Lincoln, NE.

Abraham Ortelius, *Americae Sive Novi Orbis, Nova Descriptio,* 1570. Courtesy of Smith Cartographic Collection, University of Southern Maine.

Mercator's 1595 map

Figure 2 1595 Mercator Map

Norumbega as both Region and Community

Gerardus Mercator.

Some maps that were incomplete at his death were completed and published by his son Rumold Mercator in 1595.

Champlain's map of 1607

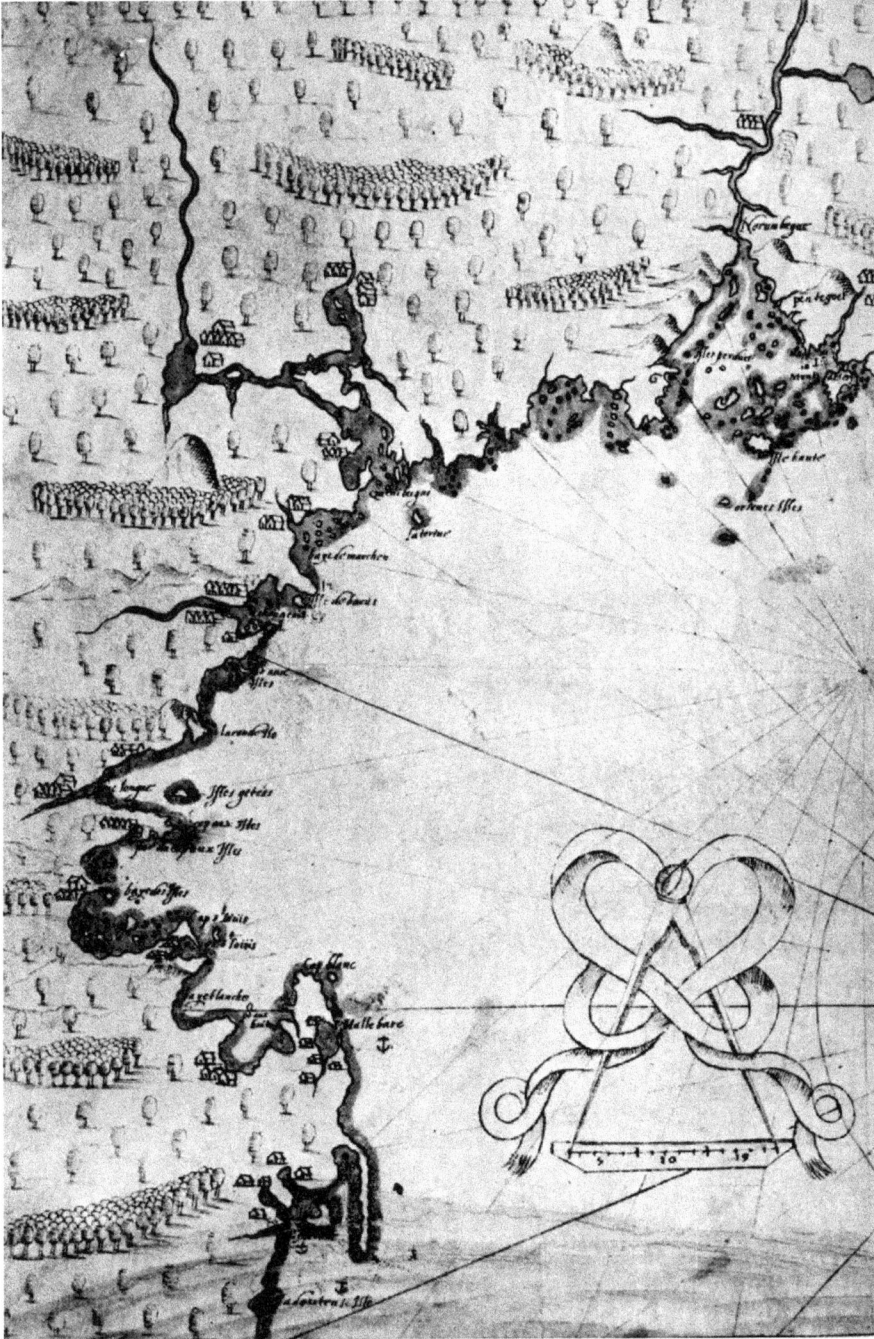

Figure 3 Champlain Map

The Unexplored Central Maine Coast

Samuel De Champlain's 1607 Illustrated Map from:

Viereck, Phillip, Ed. (1967). *The new land; discovery, exploration, and early settlement of Northeastern United States, from earliest voyages to 1621, told in the words of the explorers themselves*. John Day Co., New York, NY. Used with permission of Phillip Viereck.

The original copy is in the Library of Congress.

Figure 4 Enlargement of a section of the above 1607 Champlain map

A Tour of Norumbega near Bangor

Lescarbot map of 1609

Figure 5 Lescarbot map of 1609

The Etchemins of the Central Maine Coast

Close-up of map above

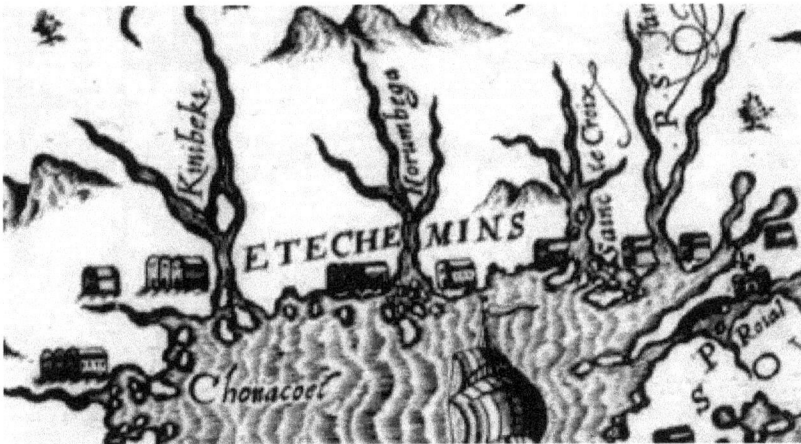

Figure 6 Close-up of Lescarbot map

Who Lived in those Houses in 1609?

Marcus Lescarbot, *Figure de la Terre Neuve Grande Riviere de Canada et Cotes de l'Ocean en la Nouvelle France*, 1609, Lescarbot Archives of Canada. (This is the map reprinted in Bourque, 2001, pg. 114).

Champlain's 1612 map

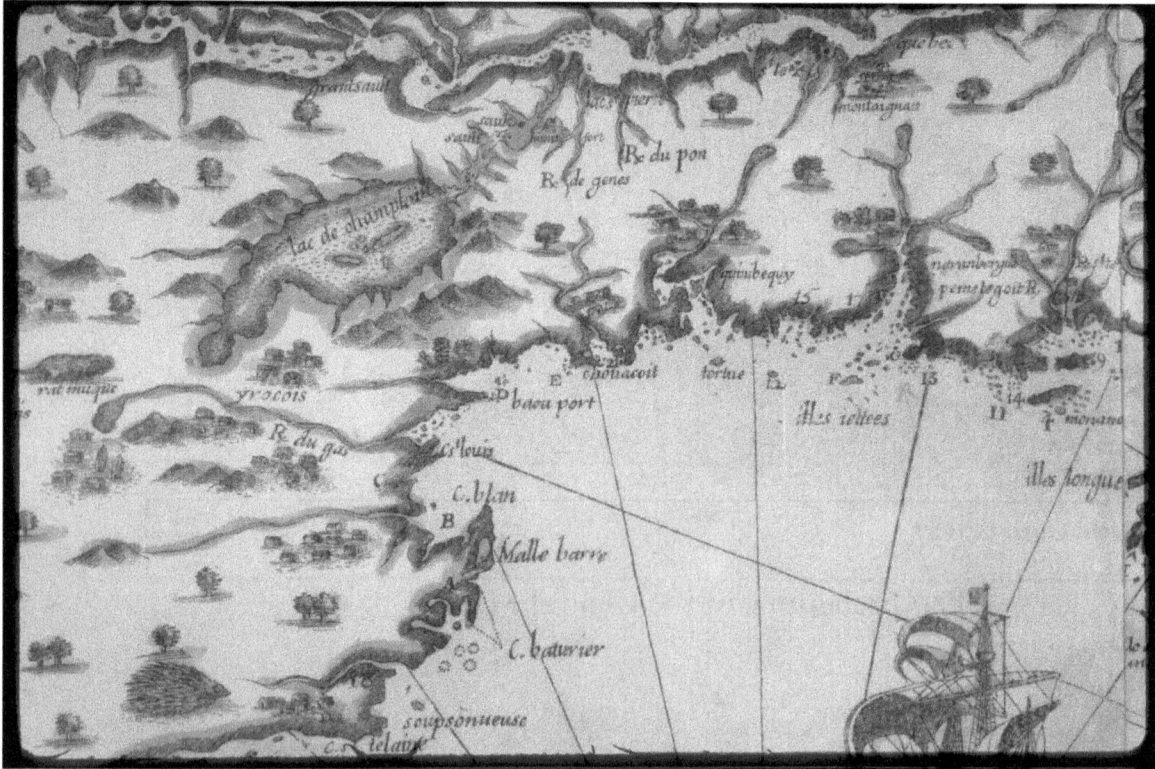

Figure 7 Champlain's 1612 map - Osher Library

The Unexplored Central Maine Coast II

CARTE GEOGRAPHIQUE DE LA NOVVELLE FRANSE . . .

faict len 1612
Facsimile of hand-colored engraving, 43.0 x 77.6 cm
Smith Collection

"Champlain merged his general information regarding the New England coast with his later explorations of the St. Lawrence valley (to 1612). The result is his large and ornate general map of New France" (Osher Map Library.)

Champlain 1613 Map from *Les Voyages*

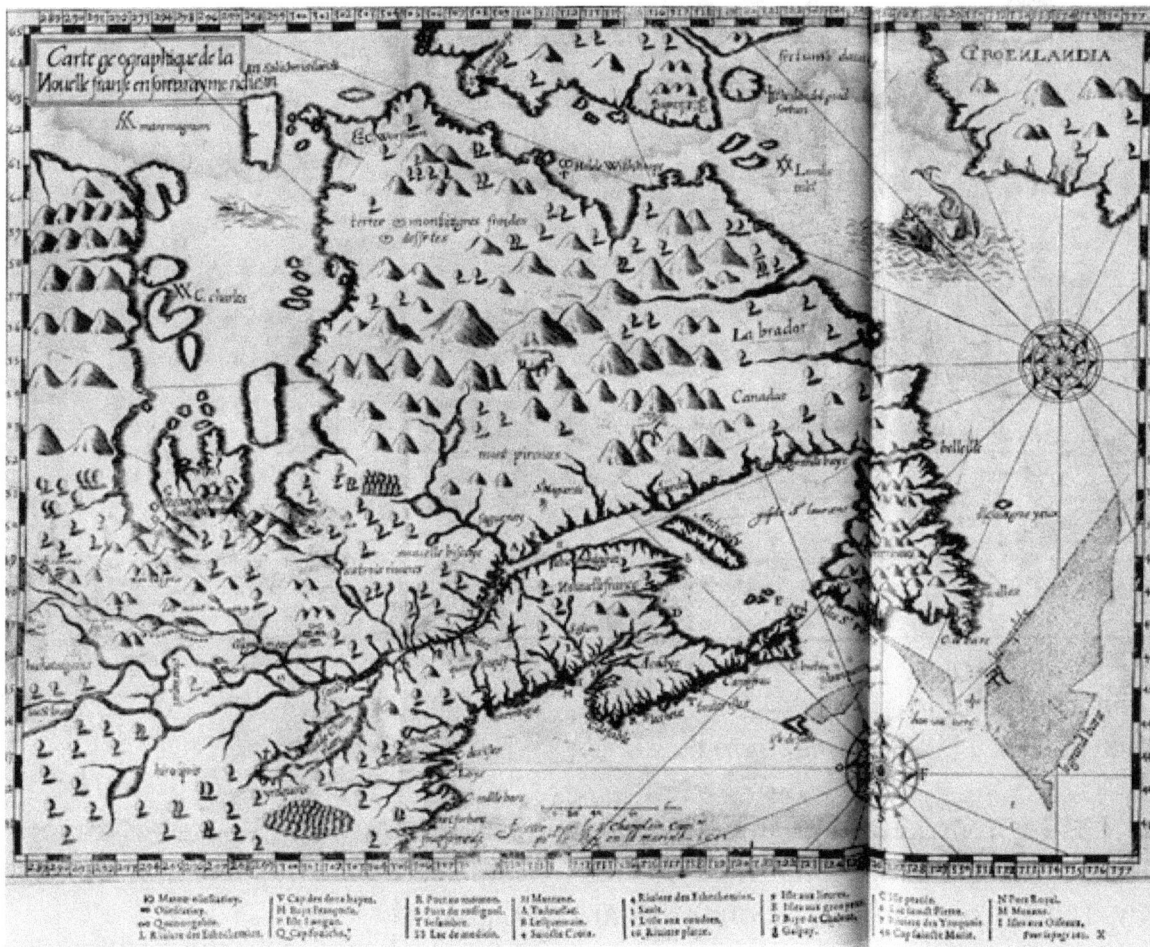

Figure 8 Champlain 1613 map

Norumbega as the Central Maine Coast

Baker, Emerson, Ed.. (1994). *American Beginnings*. Pg. 54-55.

This map of 1613 is reproduced in Baker, *American Beginnings* (pg. 54-55). Samuel de Champlain, *Carte geographique de la nouvelle franse en son vray meridian*, in his *Les Voyages,* 1613, Courtesy of National Library of Canada.

Champlain 1613 map close-up

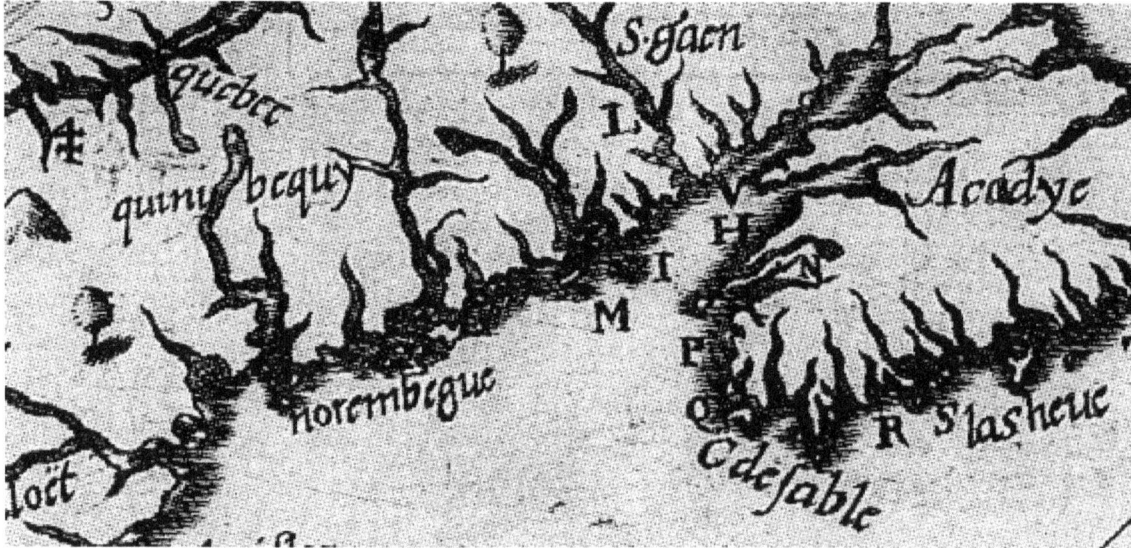

Figure 9 Close-up of Champlain 1613 map

A New River has Appeared

Baker, Emerson, Ed.. (1994). *American Beginnings*. Pg. 54-55.

This map of 1613 is reproduced in Baker, *American Beginnings* (pg. 54-55). Samuel de Champlain, *Carte geographique de la nouvelle franse en son vray meridian*, in his *Les Voyages,* 1613, Courtesy of National Library of Canada.

Champlain's 1632 map

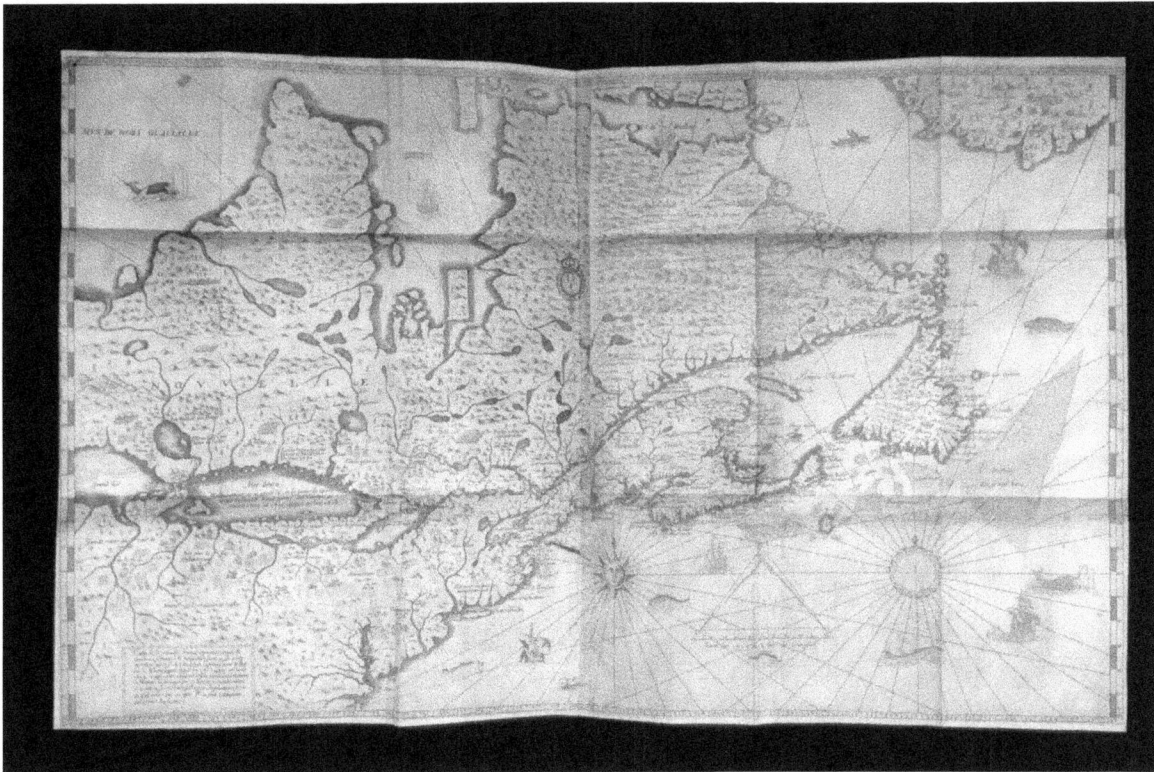

Figure 10 Osher Map Library copy of Champlain's 1632 map

Protohistory Becomes History

SAMUEL DE CHAMPLAIN (French, 1567-1635)
Carte de la nouuelle france …
In: *Les Voyages de la Novvelle France occidentale …* (Paris, **1632**)
Engraving, 52.2 x ca.96.5

"After constructing his map of 1612, Champlain returned to New France several times and acquired yet further information. The expansion of the French fur trade led to increasing interaction with, and the gathering of more geographical information from, the Hurons of the St. Lawrence valley. Champlain accordingly updated his map and expanded its geographical scope in this map made to accompany his general history of New France." (Osher Map Library).

Boisseau's 1634 copy of Champlain map of 1632

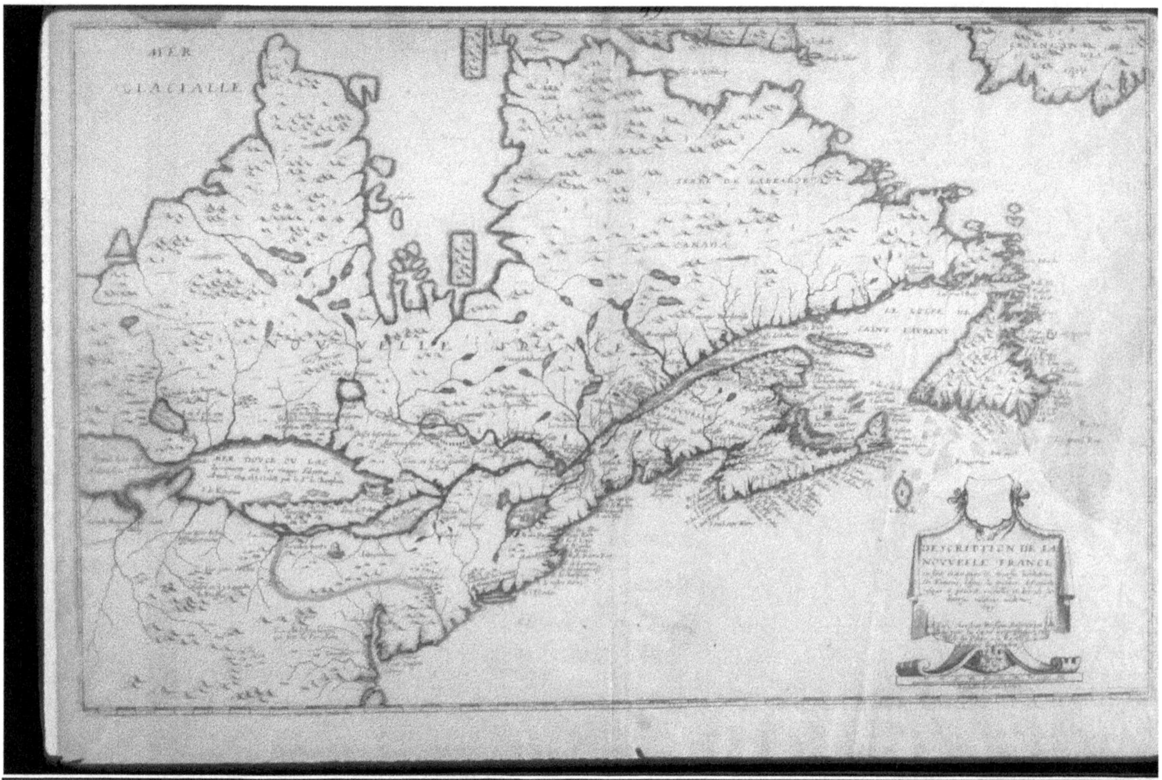

Figure 11 Complete image of Boisseau 1634 map.

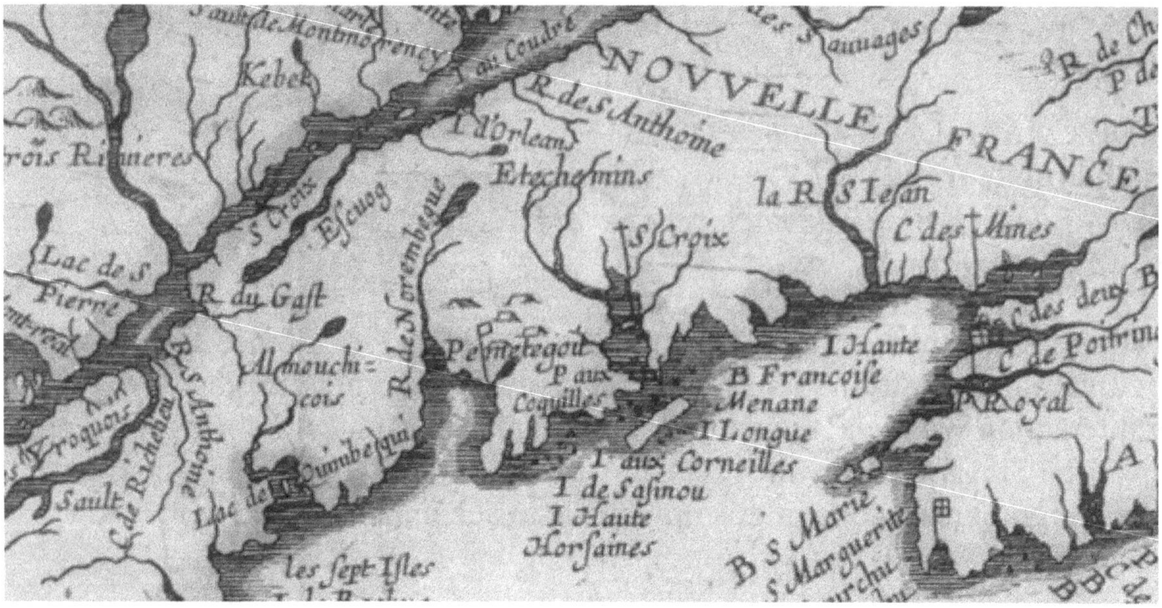

Figure 12 Close-up of Boisseau 1634 map

Almouchiquois west of the River of Norumbega

JEAN BOISSEAU (French, fl. 1637-1658)
DESCRIPTION DE LA NOVVELLE FRANCE
Paris: Jean Boisseau, 1643
Engraving, hand colored, 35.0 x 55.0 cm
Osher Collection

"Boisseau took Champlain's large map of 1632 and reduced it in size to make a more commercially viable product. He was, after all, a commercial cartographer and not a navigator. Although eleven years had passed since Champlain's original map had been published, Boiseau did not try to add any new details or place-names from any of the English or other French voyages. Instead, as has almost always been the case in commercial mapmaking, he simply copied his source directly." (Osher Map Library).

"Wôbanakik map"

Fig. 8. Wôbanakik and environs during the Years of the Moose and Log Ships. *Drawn by Frederick Wiseman.*

Figure 13 Wôbanakik map

Wobanakik Nation

Frederick Matthew Wiseman. *The Voice of the Dawn: An Autohistory of the Abenaki Nation*. Fig. 8, p. 32 © 2001 by Frederick Matthew Wiseman. Reprinted by permission of University Press of New England, Hanover, NH.

Caption: "Wôbanakik and environs during the Years of the Moose and Log Ships. *Drawn by Frederick Wiseman*."

Native American Ethnic Boundaries c. 1600

The Traditional Paradigm

Salisbury, Neal. (1982). *Manitou and Providence: Indians, Europeans, and the making of New England, 1500-1643.* Oxford University Press, NY, NY. Pg. 15. Used by permission of Oxford University Press.

Figure 14 Indian ethnic-linguistic boundaries c. 1600

Figure 15 Area of interest on Salisbury map

Snow's Tribal Region Map

FIGURE 2.1. Distribution of major cultural units in aboriginal New England around A.D. 1600. Each corresponds to a major language. Subdivisions and names that came into use in later times are not shown.

Figure 16 Snow's Map

Tradition Recapitulated

Reprinted from *The Archaeology of New England,* Dean R. Snow, pg. 26, Copyright (1980), with permission from Elsevier.

Relative Locations of Groups on the Maritime Peninsula

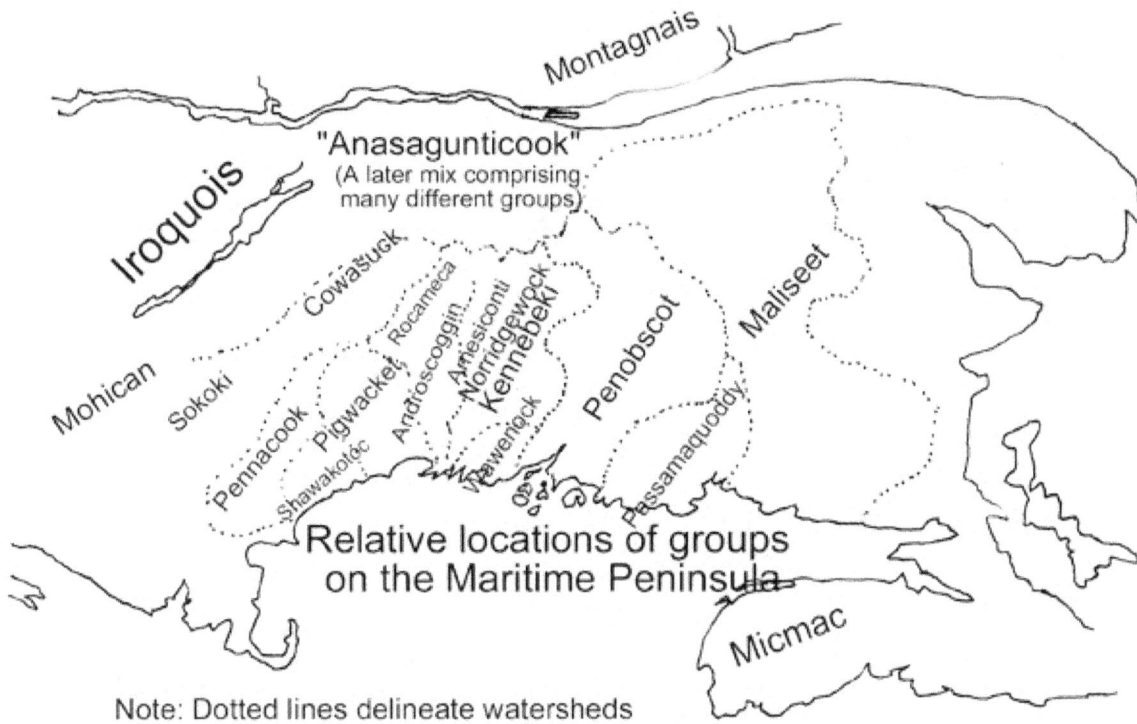

Montagnais

Iroquois

"Anasagunticook"
(A later mix comprising
many different groups)

Cowasuck

Mohican

Sokoki

Pennacook

Pigwacket

Shawakotóc

Rocameca

Androscoggin

Amesiconti
Norridgewock
Kennebeki

Wawenock

Penobscot

Maliseet

Passamaquoddy

Relative locations of groups
on the Maritime Peninsula

Micmac

Note: Dotted lines delineate watersheds

Figure 17 Relative locations of groups on the Maritime Peninsula c. 1600

Ethnicity in Retrospect

Courtesy of Kerry Hardy.

Maritime Peninsula

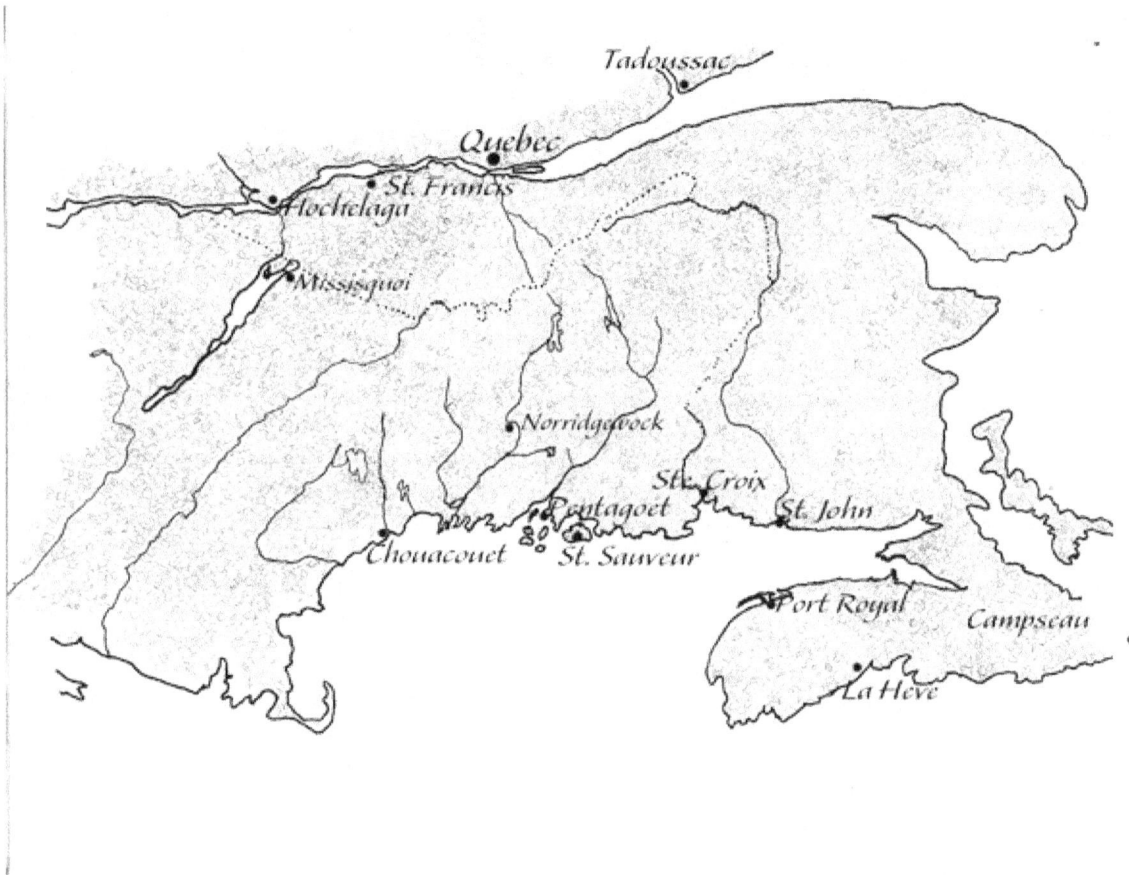

Figure 18 Maritime Peninsula

Ease of Access to the St. Lawrence River: A Proximity of Watershed

Courtesy of Kerry Hardy.

Map of Mawooshen

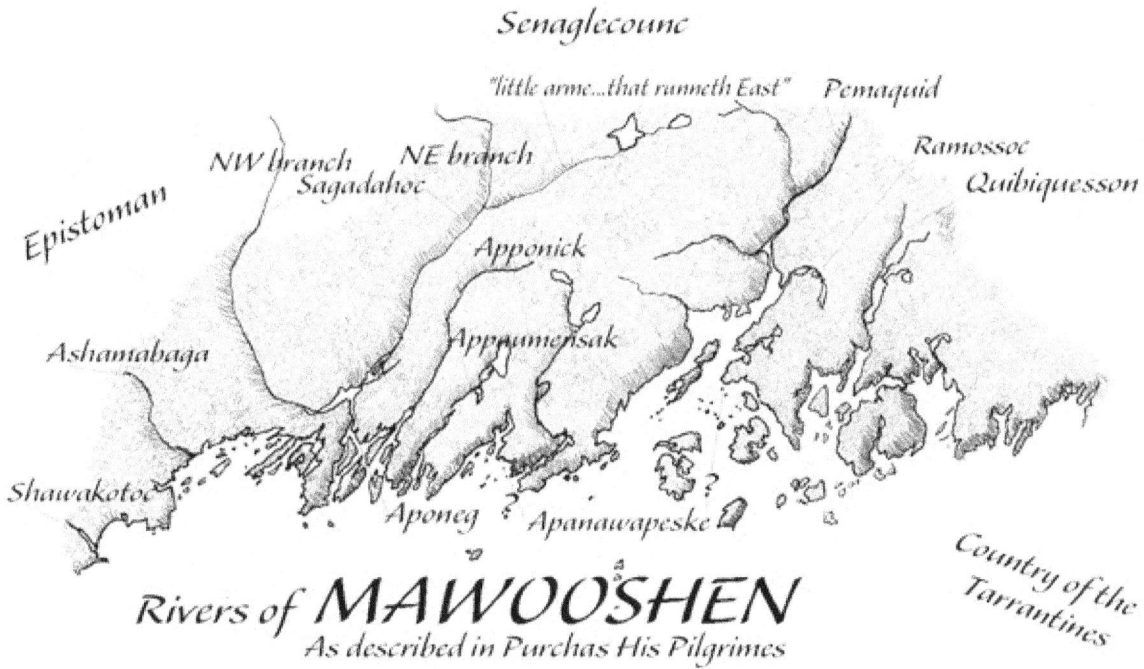

Figure 19 Map of Mawooshen

Ancient Domains New Paradigms: Pemaquid at Bangor

Courtesy of Kerry Hardy.

Wawenoc Homelands

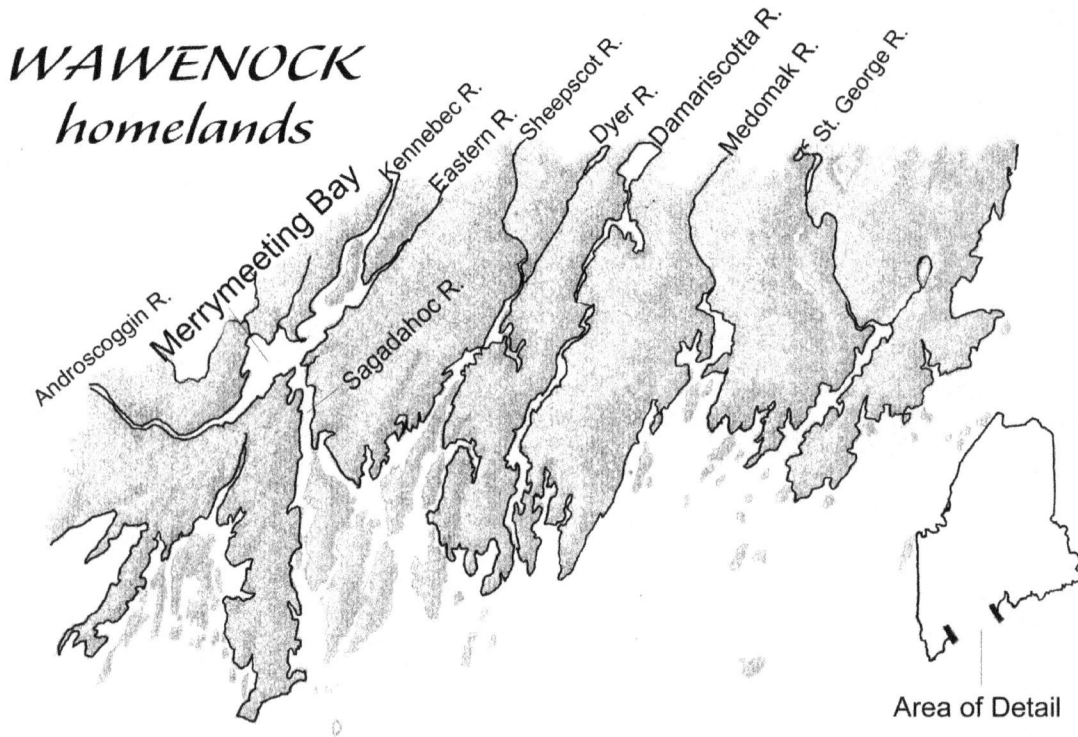

WAWENOCK
homelands

Androscoggin R.

Merrymeeting Bay

Kennebec R.

Eastern R.

Sheepscot R.

Sagadahoc R.

Dyer R.

Damariscotta R.

Medomak R.

St. George R.

Area of Detail

Drawn by Kerry Hardy, Merryspring Nature Center

Figure 20 Wawenock Homelands.

Canibas – Wawenoc – Penobscot. Who Shared which Watershed?

Courtesy of Kerry Hardy.

Wabanaki reprint of Snow's map

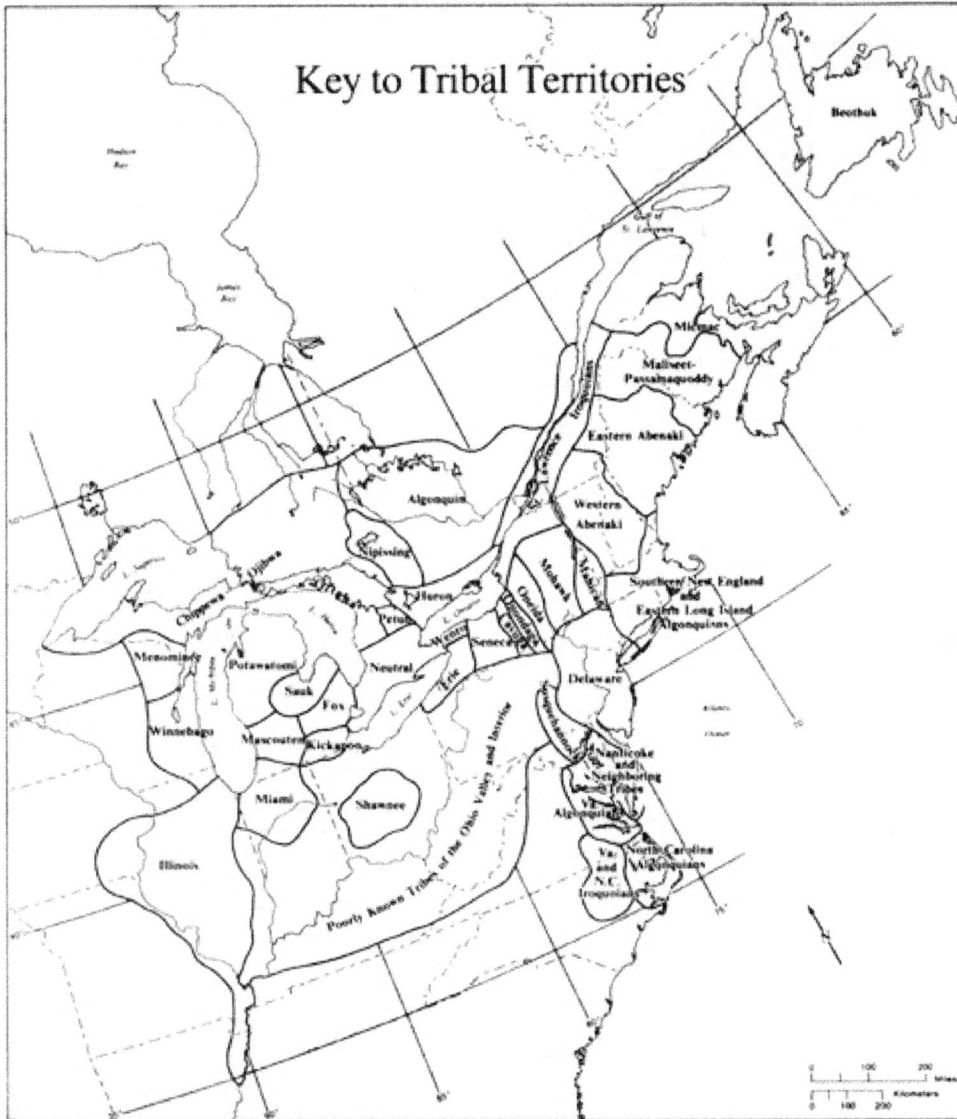

This map is a diagrammatic guide...rather than an authoritative depiction of tribal ranges. Sharp boundaries have been drawn and no territory is unassigned. Tribal units are sometimes arbitrarily defined, subdivisions are not mapped, no joint or disputed occupations are shown, and different kinds of land use are not distinguished. Since the map depicts the situation at the earliest periods for which evidence is available, the ranges mapped for different tribes often refer to quite different periods, and there may have been many intervening movements, extinctions, and changes in range. Boundaries in the western half of the area are especially tentative for these early dates.... Not shown are groups that came into separate political existence later than the map period for their areas. Map and caption reprinted, by permission, from Snow, Handbook of North American Indians. 1978a.

A-4

Figure 21 Wabanaki Tribal Territories

Conventional Overview

Maine Indian Program. (1989). The Wabanakis of Maine and the Maritimes: A resource book about Penobscot, Passamaquoddy, Maliseet, Micmac and Abenaki Indians. Wabanaki Program of the American Friends Service Committee, Bath, ME. Pg. A-4.

Hoffman's Native Territories in 1700

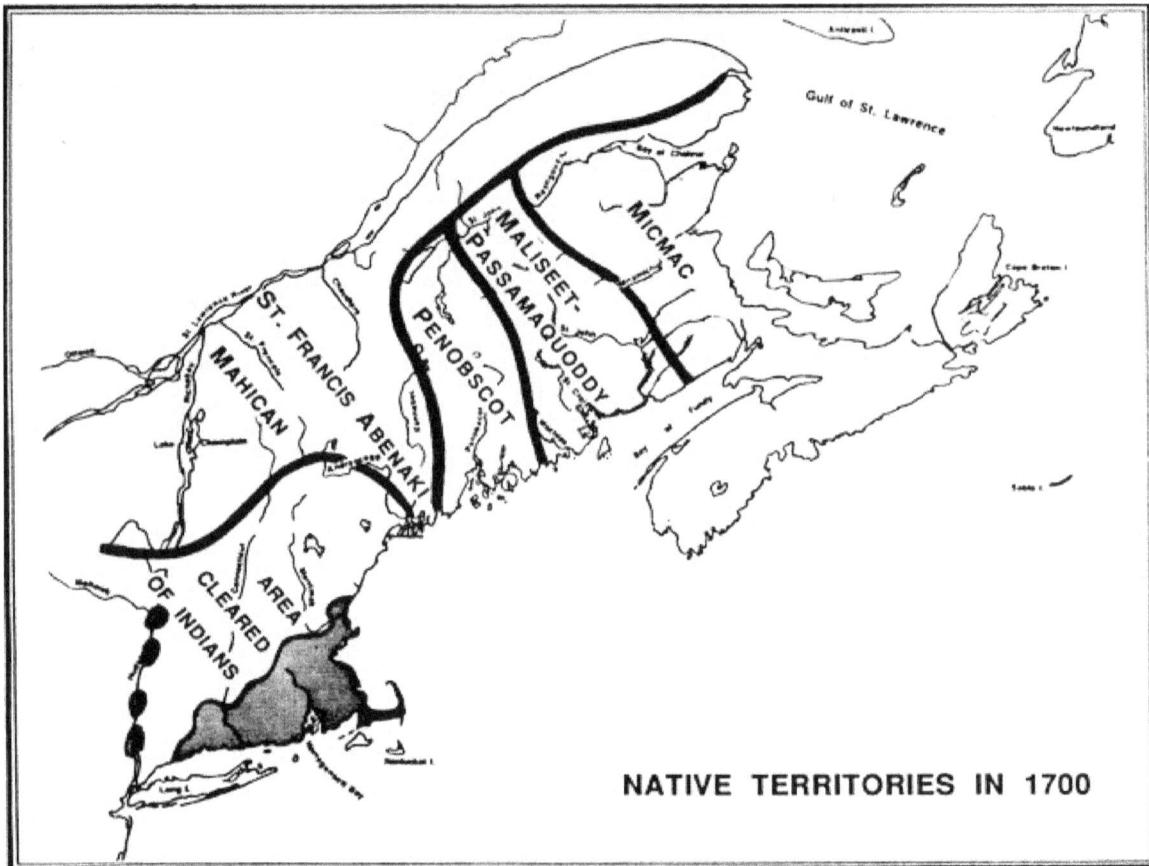

Map B. This map was redrawn from a map drawn up by Bernard Hoffman (Hoffman: 1955). Solid dark areas show areas of English and French settlement.

Figure 22 Native Territories in 1700

After the Apocalypse

Maine Indian Program. (1989). The Wabanakis of Maine and the Maritimes: A resource book about Penobscot, Passamaquoddy, Maliseet, Micmac and Abenaki Indians. Wabanaki Program of the American Friends Service Committee, Bath, ME. Pg. D-5.

French Map of 1719

Figure 23 French Map of 1719

New France in 1719: Carte de la Nouvelle France, ou le voit le cours des Grandes Rivieres de S. Laurens & de Mississipi Aujour d'hui S. Louis Aux Environs desquelles se trouvent les Etats, Pais, Nations, Peuples &c. de la Floride, de la Louisiane, de la Virginie, de la Marie-Lande, de la Pensilvanie, du Nouveau Jersay, de la Nouvelle Yorck, de la Nouv. Angleterre, de l'Acadie, du Canada, des Esquimaux, des Hurons, des Iroquois, des Ilinois &c. Et de la Grande Ile de Terre Neuve: Dreslee fur les memoires les plus nouveaux recueillis pour l'etablissement de la compagnie Francoise Occident.

This photograph, courtesy of John Sundberg, is of a section of his personal copy of a print of this map. The print is labeled: Reproduced from an engraving in the collection of Historic Urban Plans, Ithaca, NY.

Penobscot Tribe Map

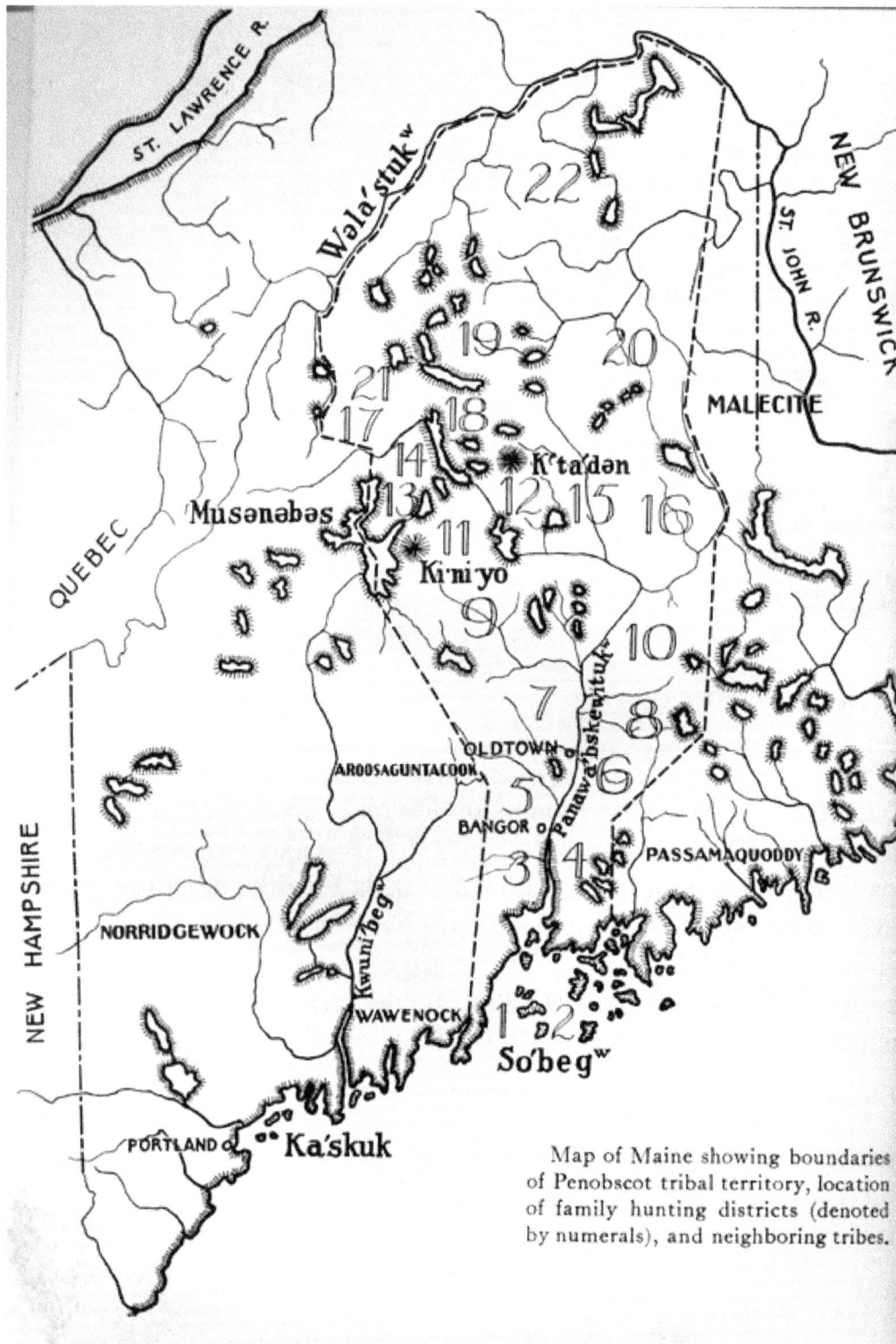

ST. LAWRENCE R.

NEW BRUNSWICK

Wəla'stuk^w

ST. JOHN R.

22

19

20

21

17

18

MALECITE

14

K'ta'dən

13

12   15   16

Mùsənəbəs

11

Ki'ni'yo

9

QUEBEC

10

7

OLDTOWN

AROOSAGUNTACOOK

Panawa'bskewituk

8

6

5

BANGOR

3   4

PASSAMAQUODDY

NEW HAMPSHIRE

NORRIDGEWOCK

Kwuni'beg^w

WAWENOCK

1   2

So'beg^w

PORTLAND   Ka'skuk

Map of Maine showing boundaries of Penobscot tribal territory, location of family hunting districts (denoted by numerals), and neighboring tribes.

Figure 24 Penobscot Tribe Map

What the Penobscot said to Frank Speck

A-26

Speck, Frank G. (1998). *Penobscot man: The life history of a forest tribe in Maine.* University of Maine Native Studies Series. The University of Maine Press, Orono, ME. Pg. 6. Reprinted by permission of the University of Pennsylvania Press.

Maine's Early Tribal Groups

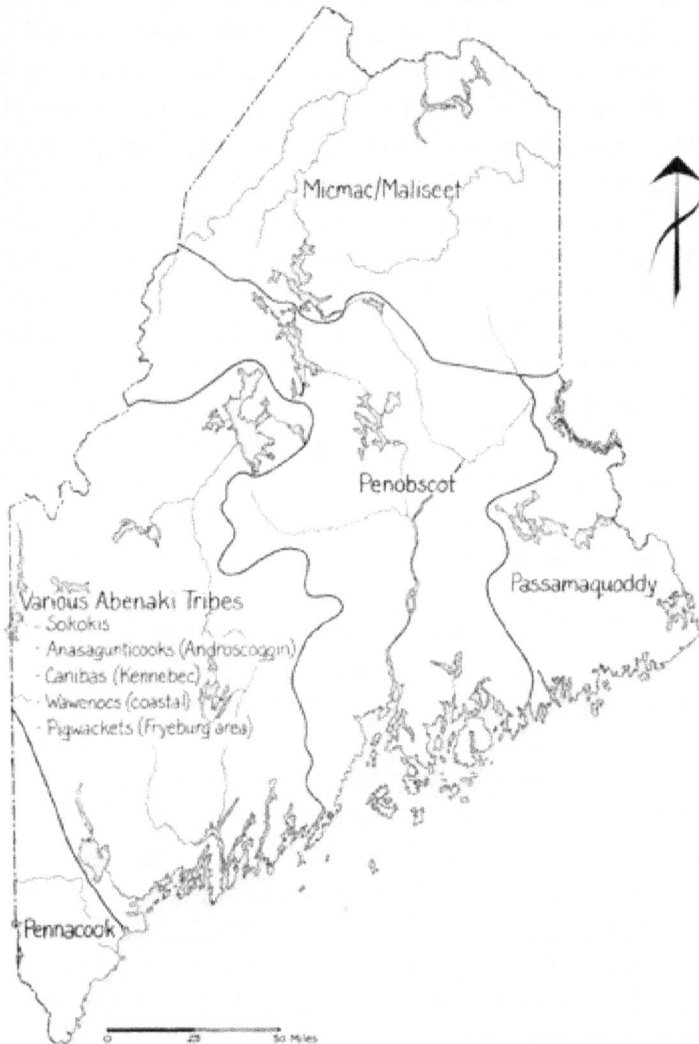

Micmac/Maliseet

Penobscot

Passamaquoddy

Various Abenaki Tribes
- Sokokis
- Anasagunticooks (Androscoggin)
- Canibas (Kennebec)
- Wawenocs (coastal)
- Pigwackets (Fryeburg area)

Pennacook

0   25   50 Miles

Figure 25 Early Maine Tribes

Contemporary Interpretation

Rolde, Neil. (2004). *Unsettled past unsettled future: The story of Maine Indians.*
Tilbury House Publishers, Gardiner, ME. Pg. 85. Used by permission of Orbis Maps
www.orbismaps.com.

Franquelin's Native Territories circa 1700

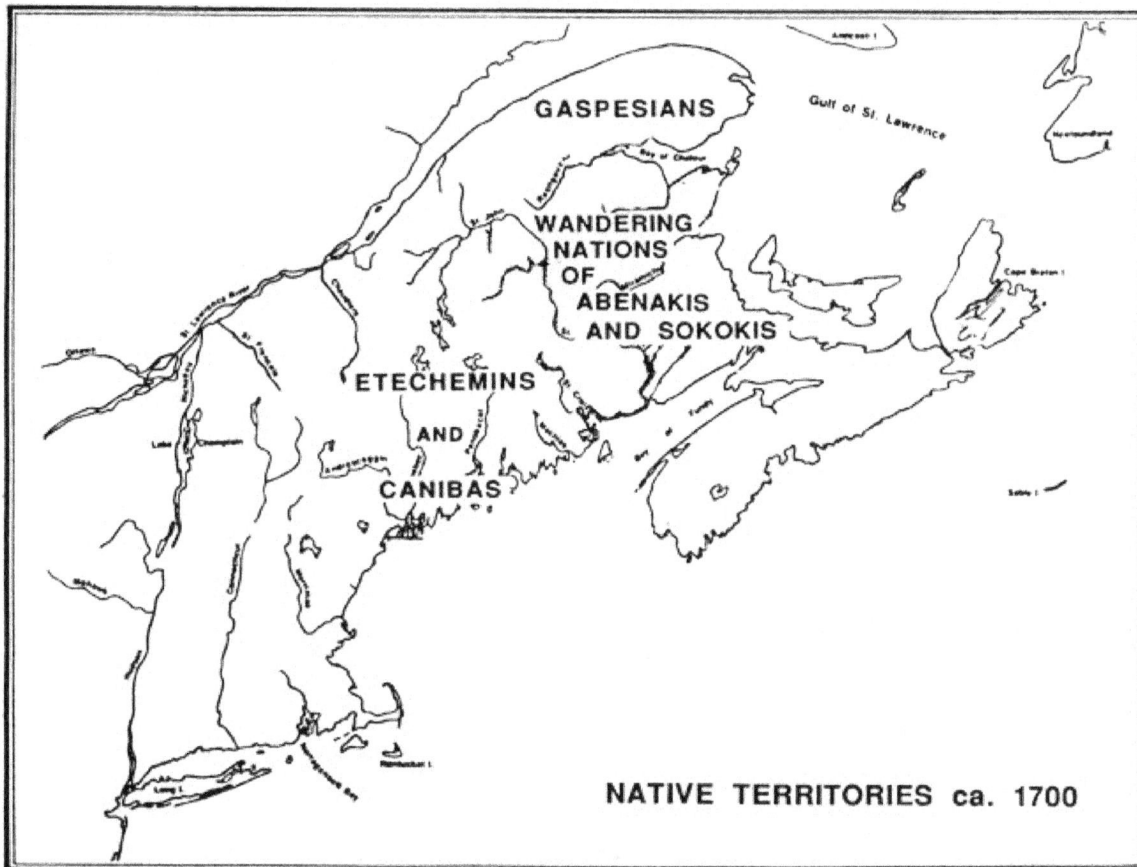

GASPESIANS

Gulf of St. Lawrence

WANDERING
NATIONS
OF
ABENAKIS
AND SOKOKIS

ETECHEMINS

AND

CANIBAS

NATIVE TERRITORIES ca. 1700

Map C. This map is redrawn from the Franquelin map, drawn up in 1702 from data collected on a voyage ca. 1678. The mapmaker did not travel to Nova Scotia. "Gaspesians" refers to Micmacs, and "Etechemins" are later called Passamaquoddies and Maliseets. (Jean-Baptiste-Louis Franquelin, National Map Collection, Public Archives, Ottawa, Canada.)

Figure 26 Wabanakis redrawing of Franquelin's Native Territories ca. 1700

Ethnic Mix

Maine Indian Program. (1989). The Wabanakis of Maine and the Maritimes: A resource book about Penobscot, Passamaquoddy, Maliseet, Micmac and Abenaki Indians. Wabanaki Program of the American Friends Service Committee, Bath, ME. Pg. D-6.

Tribal Territory in 1890

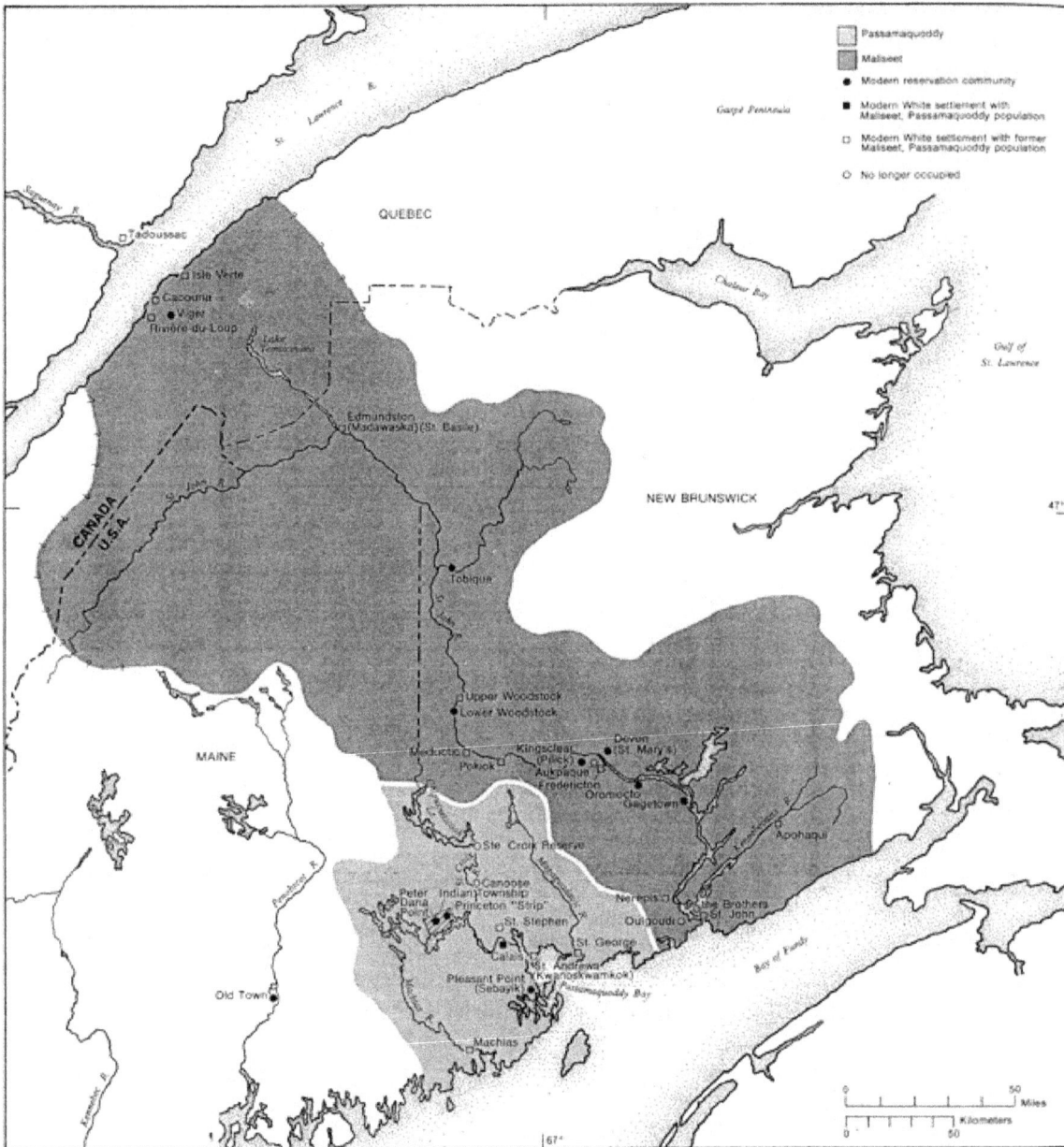

Fig. 1. Tribal territory about 1890.

Figure 27 Tribal Territory in 1890

A Traditional View of Etchemin Territory

Erickson, Vincent O. (1978). Maliseet-Passamaquoddy. In: *Handbook of North American Indians: Northeast*. Vol 15. Ed by Bruce G. Trigger. Smithsonian Institution, Washington, D.C. pg. 123-136. Used by permission of the Smithsonian Institution.

Abenaki Homeland

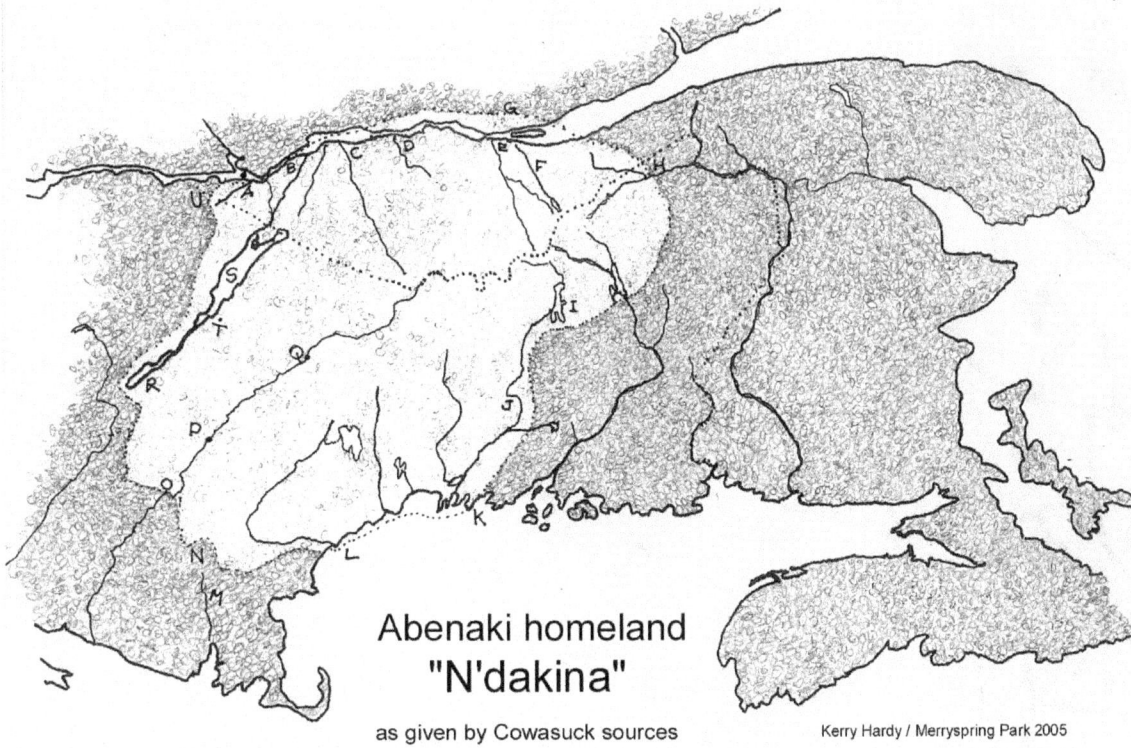

Abenaki homeland
"N'dakina"

as given by Cowasuck sources

Kerry Hardy / Merryspring Park 2005

Figure 28 Abenaki homeland N'dakina

Indigenous Voices

Courtesy of Kerry Hardy. Key to the map is in the Appendix: Abenaki Homeland Map Key.

Hoffman's Native Territories in 1590

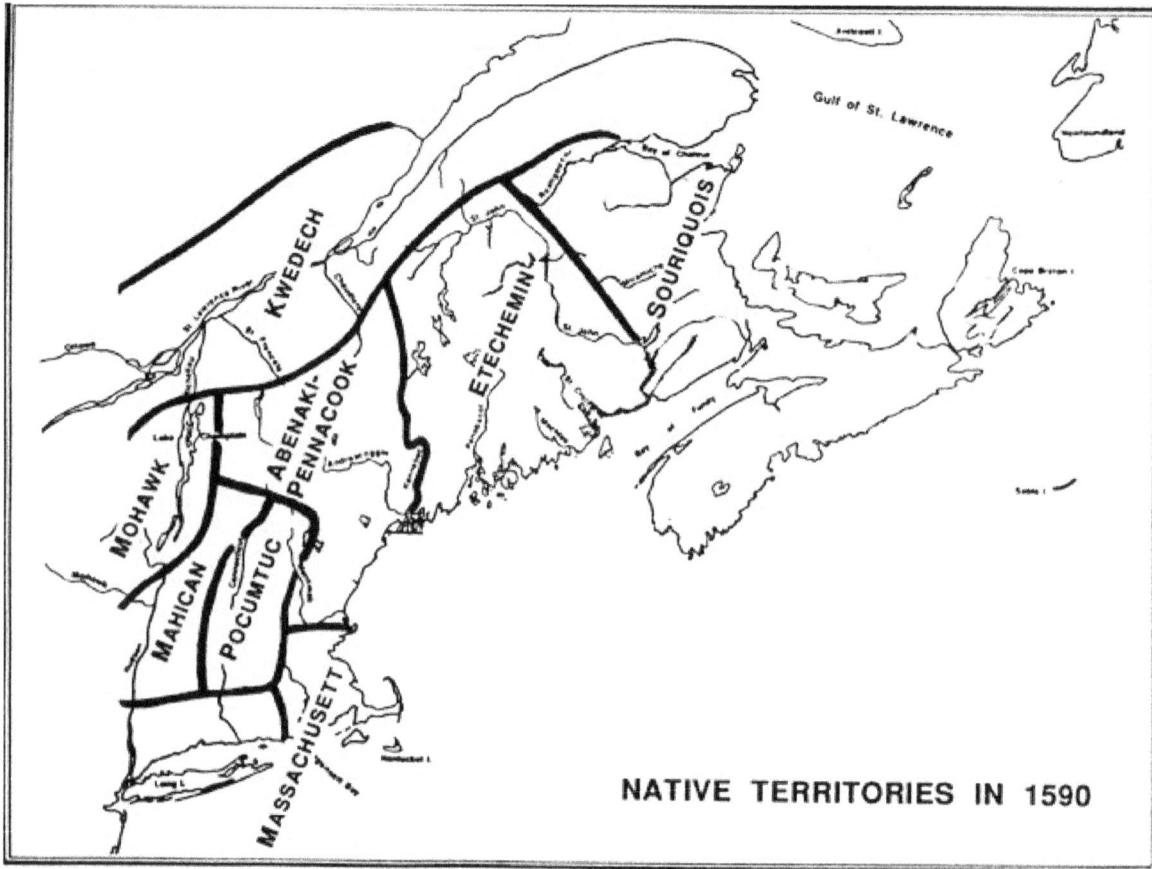

NATIVE TERRITORIES IN 1590

Map A. This map was redrawn from a map drawn up by Bernard Hoffman and included in his thesis (Hoffman: 1955). "Souriquois" was an early name for Micmacs, and "Etechemin" an early name for Maliseets and Passamaquoddies.

D-4

Figure 29 Hoffman's 1590 Native Territories Map Redrawn by Wabanakis

The First of the Revisionists

Maine Indian Program. (1989). *The Wabanakis of Maine and the Maritimes: A resource book about Penobscot, Passamaquoddy, Maliseet, Micmac and Abenaki Indians.* Wabanaki Program of the American Friends Service Committee, Bath, ME. Pg. D-4.

Algonkians in Maine

QUE.

MALISEET

M A L I S E E T

ME.   N.B.

N

QUE.

N.H. ME.

Norridgewock

Penobscot

Passamaquoddy

A B E N A K I

Arosaquntacook

Kennebec

Pejepscot

Wawenock

Pequaket

Ossipee   Saco   Casco

Newichewannock

ALGONKIAN TRIBES
OF MAINE

Figure 30 Algonkian Tribes of Maine

Abenaki Hegemony

Johnson, Steven F. (1995). *Ninnuock [The People]: The Algonkian people of New England.* Reprinted by permission of the Bliss Publishing Company, Inc., Marlborough, MA.

1826 map by a "Nathan Hale" of the roads in Maine

Figure 31 1826 map of Indian Trails

Vestiges of Ancient Trails

Courtesy of Kerry Hardy. "An 1826 map by a 'Nathan Hale' of the roads in Maine. I've used red dots to highlight those which converge on Augusta/Hallowell. Since most of our early roads were just widenings of Indian trails, I'm speculating that these roads reflect Indian travel patterns."

Modern-day maps

To help the reader, here are a few road maps:

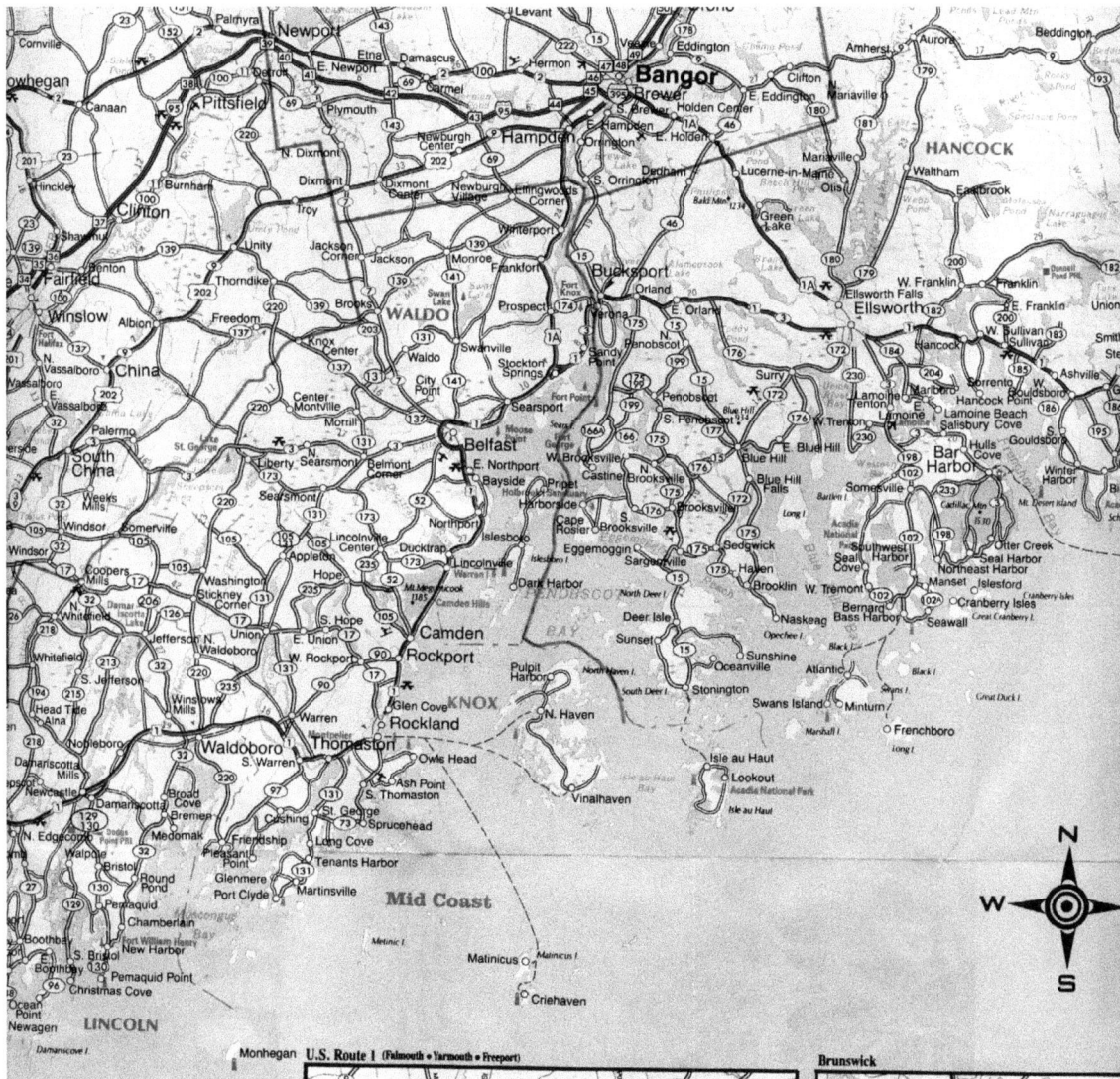

Figure 32 Midcoast Maine road map

East Mawooshen

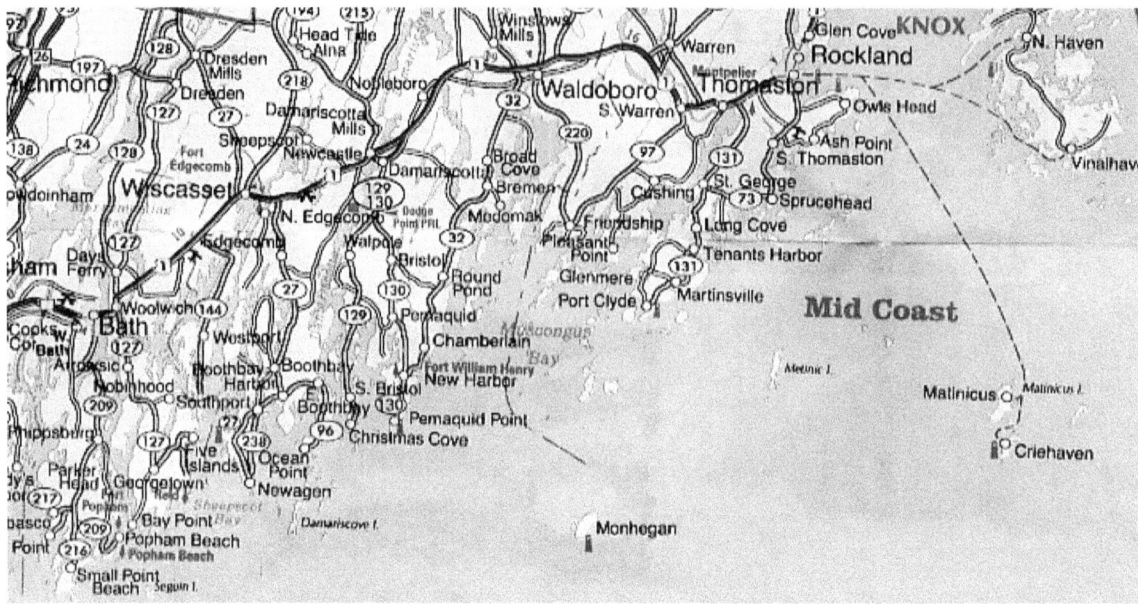

Figure 33 Road map of Midcoast Maine

Wawenoc Territory, Resettled

Midcoast area

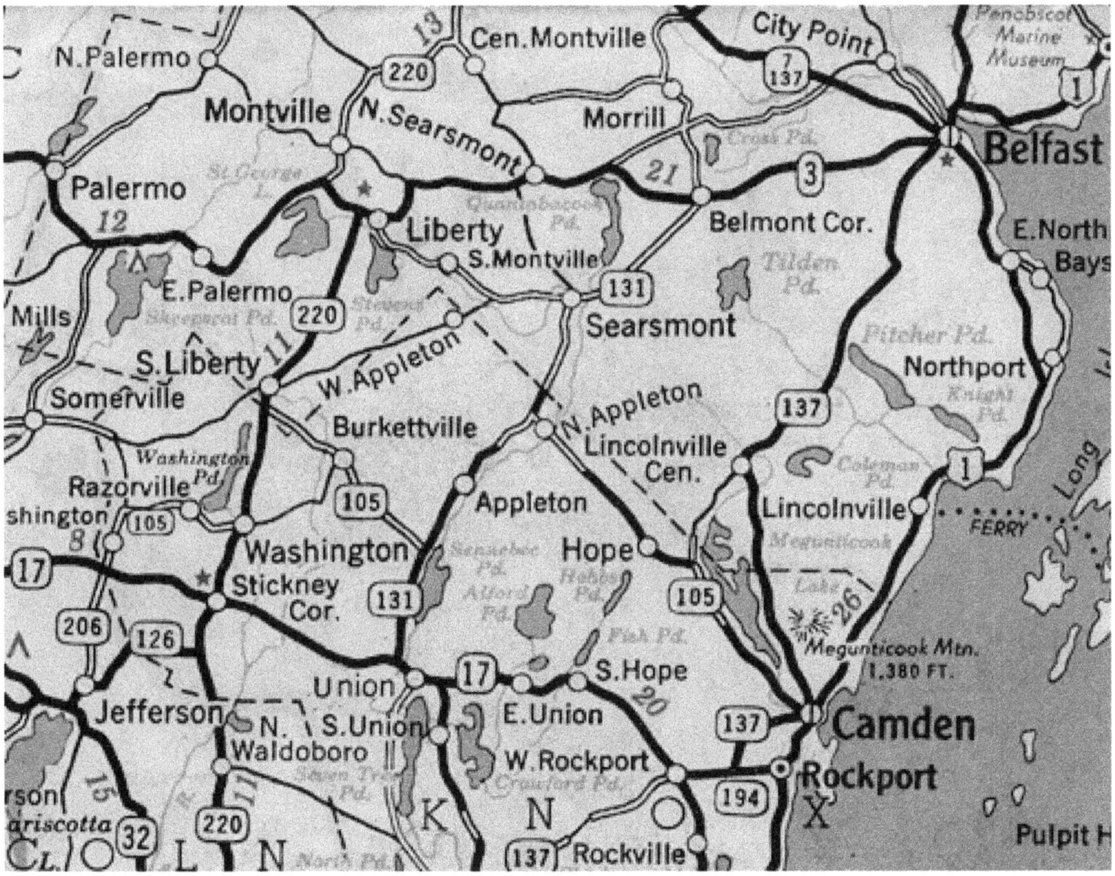

Figure 34 Old road map of midcoast Maine

The West Appleton – South Liberty Road: A Last Vestige of the Most Ancient
Dominion of Maine

New England Indian Tribes

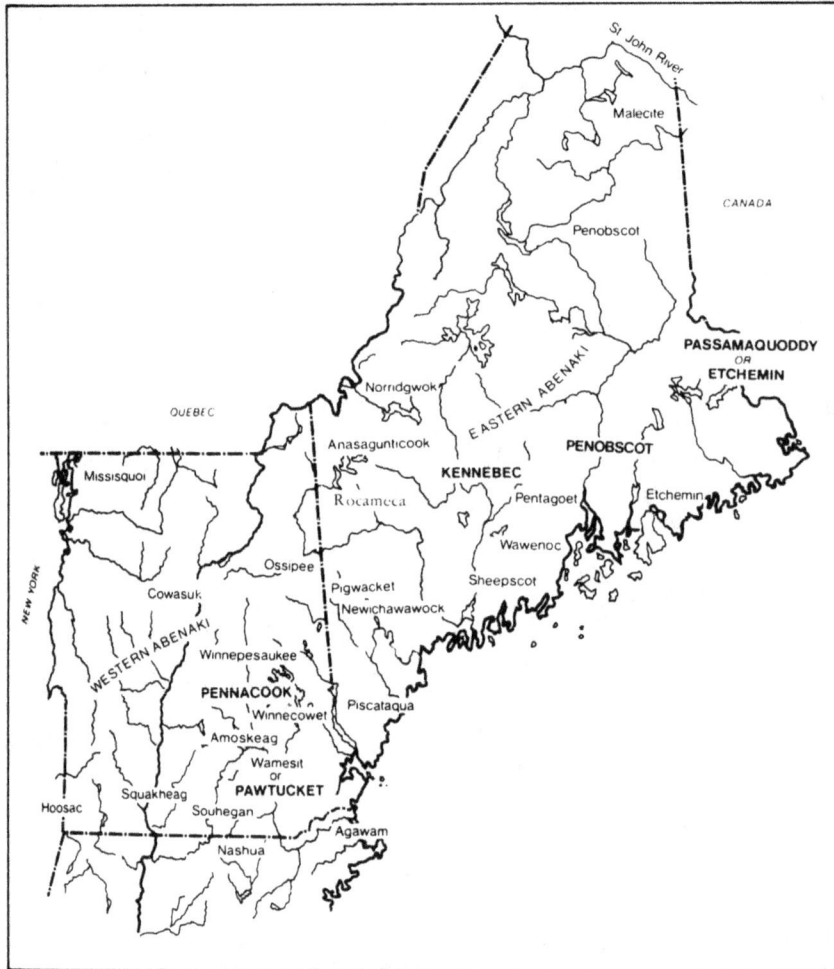

5. Approximate locations of certain Northern New England Indian tribes.

Figure 35 Russell's map of New England Indian tribes prior to European settlement.

Russell, Howard S. (1980). *Indian New England before the Mayflower*. University Press of New England, Hanover, NH. pg. 25. © University Press of New England, Lebanon, NH. Reprinted with permission figure 5 on page 25.

French Land Claims 1604-1763

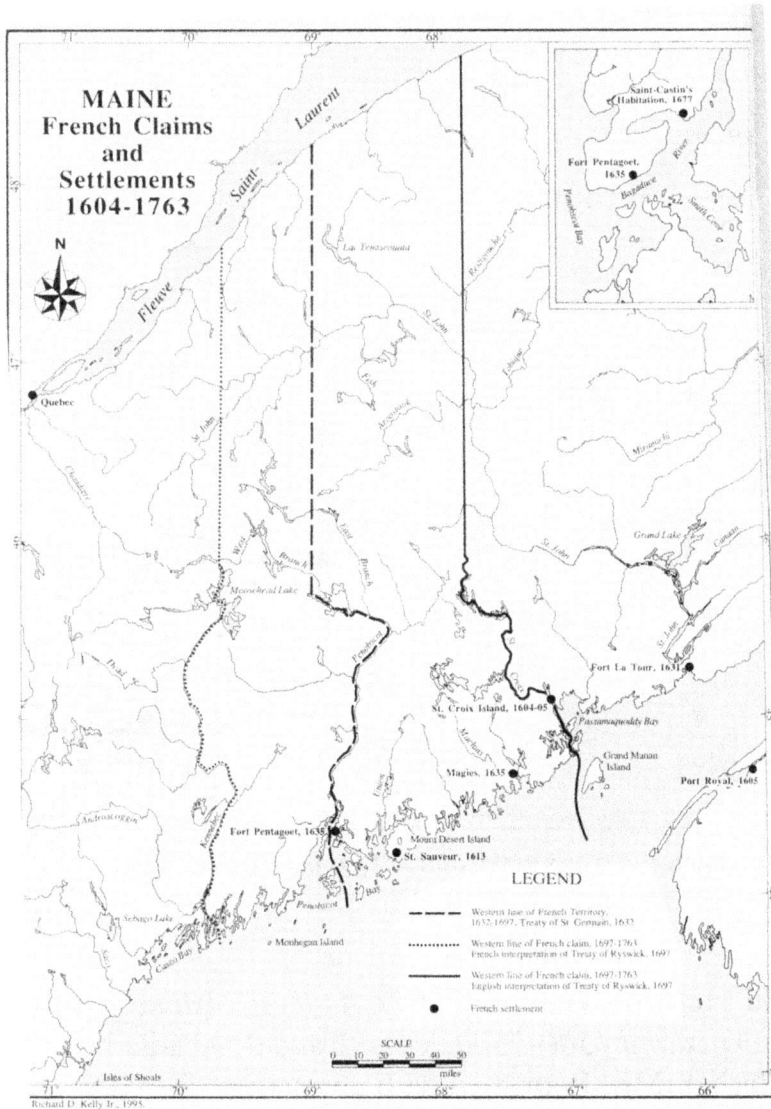

Figure 36 French land claims

Judd, Richard W., Churchill, Edwin A. and Eastman, Joel W., Eds. (1995). *Maine: State from prehistory to the present*. University of Maine Press, Orono, ME. pg. 78.

Ethnic Distribution at the Time of European Exploration

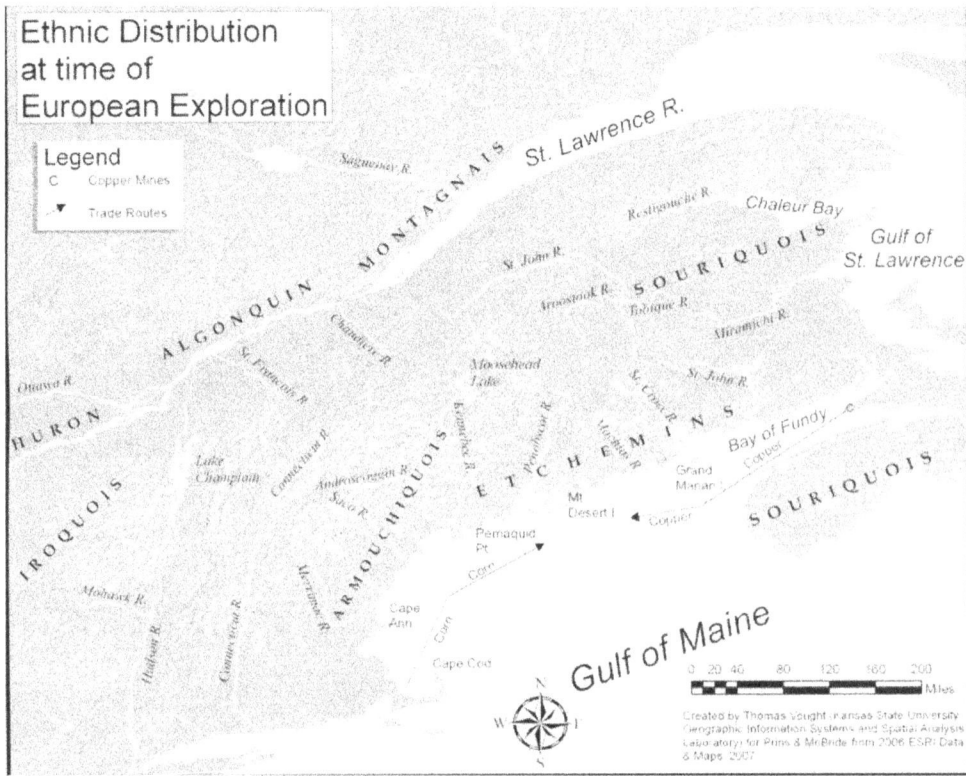

Figure 37 Distribution of tribes at the time of European Exploration.

Prins, Harald E. L. and McBride, Bunny. (2007). *Asticou's island domain: Wabanaki peoples at Mount Desert Island 1500-2000*. Vols. 1 and 2. Acadia National Park and The Abbe Museum, Bar Harbor, ME. Reprinted with permission from Dr. Harald Prins.

Prins and McBride's Map of the Mawooshen Confederacy

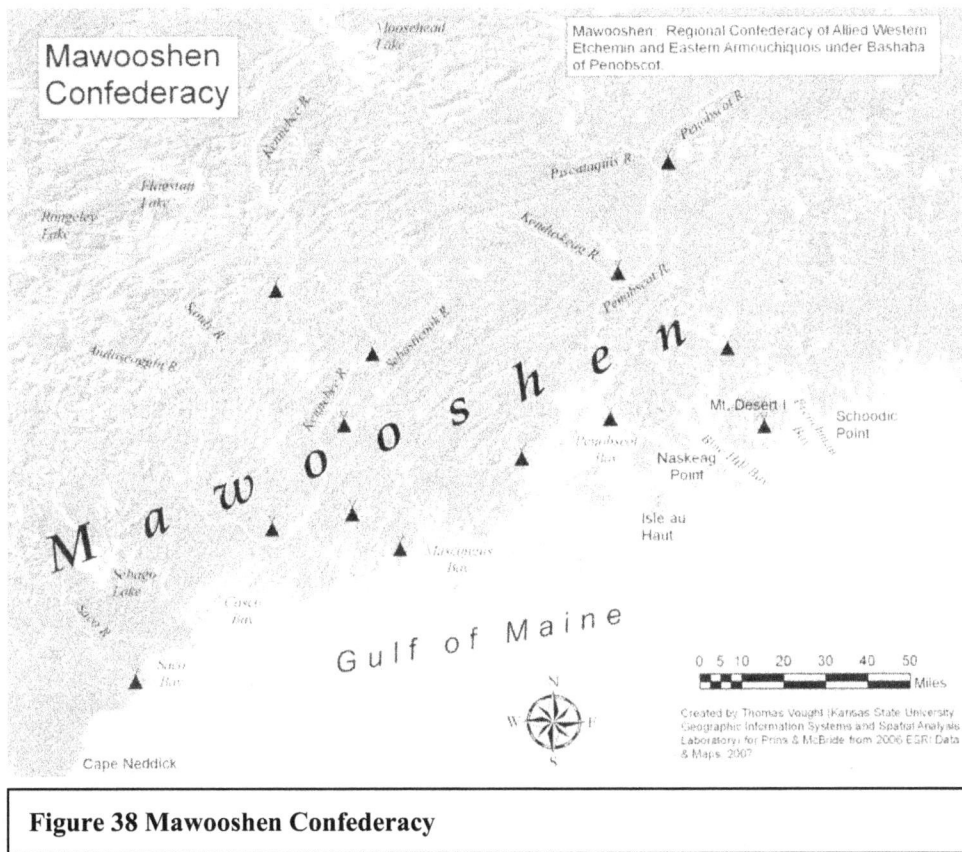

Figure 38 Mawooshen Confederacy

Prins, Harald E. L. and McBride, Bunny. (2007). *Asticou's island domain: Wabanaki peoples at Mount Desert Island 1500-2000*. Vols. 1 and 2. Acadia National Park and The Abbe Museum, Bar Harbor, ME. Reprinted with permission from Dr. Harald Prins.

Appendix B

Abenaki Homeland

A Native American Relation

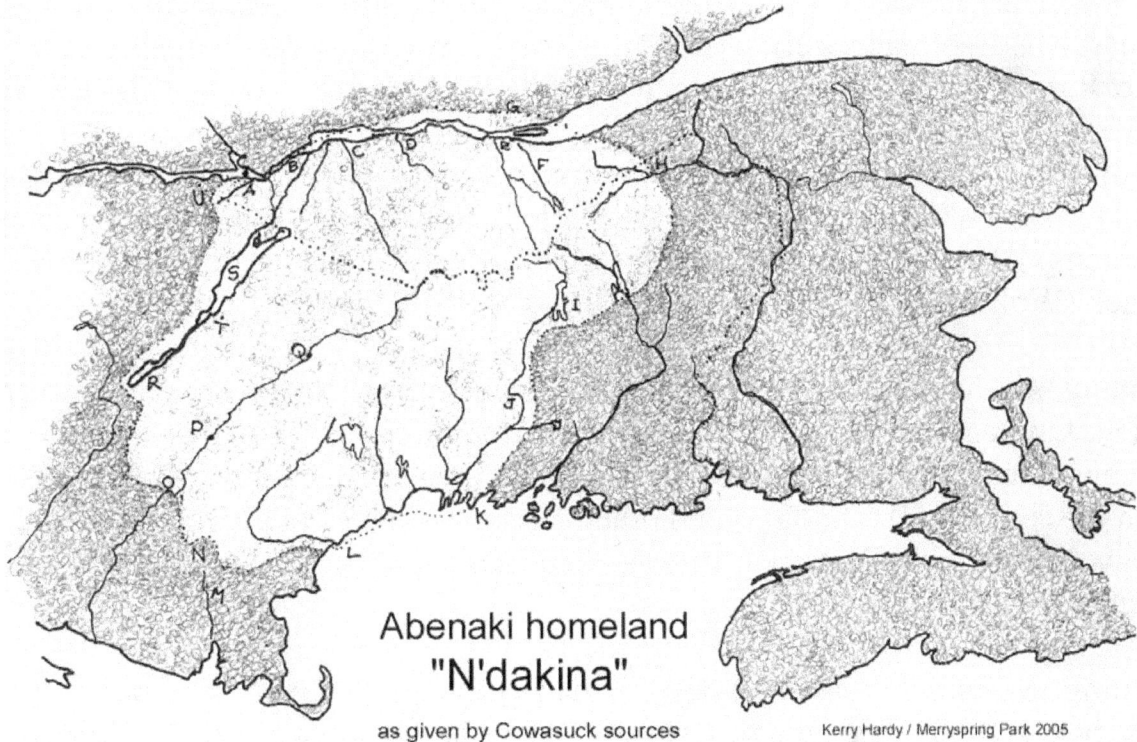

Abenaki homeland
"N'dakina"

as given by Cowasuck sources

Kerry Hardy / Merryspring Park 2005

Figure 1 Abenaki homeland N'dakina.

Map courtesy of Kerry Hardy.
The following **key to the map** is from the Cowasuck website:
http://www.cowasuck.org/history/ndakina.cfm

The following describes the boundaries of N'dakina by way of the rivers, lakes, landmarks, and the meeting points with the other First Nations People that border N'dakina. The primary descriptions of N'dakina are identified in the Aln8bad8wa (Abenaki) language.

At a starting point from - Nsawiwi pebonkik ta ali-nkihl8t (northwest from) where the Chateauguay River **[A]** and the Ktsitegok (great river) – Moliantegw (St. Lawrence River) meet near Molian (Montreal). The Os8ganek (Algonquin place) is the point where the lands of the Abenaki (N'dakina), Algonkin, and Mohawk nations (Magwak) meet.

Waji nahil8t (going easterly) along the Ktsiegok (great river) Moliantegw (St. Lawrence River), past the Bitawbagwizibok **[B]**(Richelieu River), past the Wigw8madenik (Yamaska River) and the village of both the Abenaki and Mohawk lived, past Masessolina (Sorel), past Pithiiganek (Nicolet) and the Pithiganitegw (Nicolet River), past Mad8balodnik and the village of Mad8balodniak (Three Rivers).

Continuing, Ali-nkihlot (easterly) past the Alsog8ntegok **[C]**(St. Francis River) and Welinaktegw or W8linaktegw (the river which has long turns - which causes delay by its windings) **[D]**(Becancour River) upon which Abenaki villages of Odanak and W8linack (Wolinak) are still occupied by the Abenaki People.

Continuing, Ali-nkihlot (easterly) along the Ktsiegok (great river) Moliantegw (great river) (St. Lawrence River) to the Kik8ntegok (river of fields) **[E]**(Chaudiere River) upon which the Abenaki villages of St. Joseph de Collraine and Kwanah8moik (long point in the river bend) (Durham) and other Abenaki villages along the Koattegok or Koattegw (pine river) (Coaticook River), Namaskonkik (fish field) (Megantic Lake) were settled.

Continuing, Ali-nkihlot (easterly) beyond the **[F]** Etchemin River (sand berries) and up to Kebek **[G]** (Quebec) and the Isle de Orleans at the point that the Abenaki and Ksitegwiiak (the land of the Hurons) meet near the village of Pamadenainak (Lorette), up to village of O'bamasisek (Yamachiche).

Going inland to the Big Black River to the point **[H]** that it joins the St. John River at the Notre Dame Mountains the point where the Abenaki meet the Moskwas (muskrat - Malecite - Maliseet - broken talker). Across the St. John River and along the the lands of the Malecite (Maliseet, Wulastegniak, Aroostook, St. John's - good river people) and further east to the land of the Passamaquody (Machias, Opanango, Pesmokant, Quoddy, Scotucks, Unchechauge, Unquechauge, St. Croix - plenty of pollock / pollock spearing place).

Sowanakik, (going southward) through the watersheds of the Allagash River, the Musquacook Lakes, the Chemquasabamticook Lake, the Churchhill Lake, the Chamberlain Lakes, the Caucomgomoc Lake, the Baker River, the Baker Lake, the Seboomook Lake, the Chesuncook Lake, the Moz8debinebesek **[I]** (Moosehead

Lake), and to the Kenebec (Kennebec River) and through Kwen8bagok (long lake - Kennebago Lake).

The Kenebec (deep river - Kennebec River) being the point where the Abenaki meet the Pan8bskaik (land of the Penobscot) Pana8bskaiiak (Penobscot Pentagoet, Panaomeska - plenty stones / rocky place / ledge place).

Going down the Kenebec (Kennebec River), past the ancient Abenaki village of Mol8joak (deep flow river) **[J]** (Norridgewock) and continuing to the Sobagwa (great ocean - Atlantic Ocean).

The Abenaki villages on the Laesikantgw (rock shelter river – Androscoggin River) are the villages of Amescana and Narakamik.

Sowanakik (going southerly) along the coast of the Sobagwa (Atlantic Ocean), past W8linak **[K]** (village on the bay - village of Wawenock), past Kaska, past Pejepskw (bad rock - Pejepscot), past the Laesikantegw (Androsooggin River), past the Presumpscot River, past Sokwakik (Saco) and the Zawakwtegok (Saco River), past Kinib8ka (rough ground) (Kennebunk), past the M'mosem (my moose river - Mousam River), past Ogwa8mkwik (at the accumulated sand -Ogunquit), past the village of Piscataqua on (great deer river) Pesgatakwa (dark river - Piscataqua River), to the outlet of the Mol8demak **[L]** (deep river - Merrimack River) at the Sobagwa (Atlantic Ocean).

The Mol8demak leads to the Pemijewasek (Pemigewasset River) and to the lake of Wiwinebesaki (lake around lake - Lake Winnepisaukee), the Abenaki villages of this area are Wiwinebesakik land around lake place - Winnepisaukee Village), Akwadocta, Asepihtegw (river alongside - Ossippee), and Apikwehkik). The Abenaki villages on the Mol8demak are the villages of (Wamesit (fishing place), Nanaskik (place of fish - Manchester), Penokok (down hill - Concord), and Senikok (at the rocks - Suncook), Wiwinijoanek (water flows around it - Dover).

The other area lakes and waters are: Massabeskik (large lake – Massabesikick Pond), N8wijoanek (long rapids - Salmon Fall River), Seninebik (rocky lake - Lake Sunapee), and W8bagok (clear lake - Lake Umbagog).

Ali-ali-nkihl8t (westward) along the Mol8demak (Merrimack River) past the village of Wamesit to the Pagontegok (Concord River), a one day's walk from the eastern shores of the Mol8demak (Merrimack) and Concord Rivers lands of the Pawtucket

(Agawam, Naumkeag, Saugus, Winnisinet) to the lands of the Msajosek (the great hill) (Massachuset Nation), Neponsit (Massachusett) and Shawmut (Massachusett), to the headwaters of the Concord, Sudbury, and Assabet, and Nashua Rivers lands of the Nsawiwi (between the rivers) (Nashua) (Nashaway, Washoc, and Nashoba) to the area known as the Narragansett corridor along the [M] Blackstone River and lands of the Nipmuc (Nipmuck) Nation.

Ali-ali-nkihl8t (westward) to Wachuset [N] (mountain of small / middle height - Mt. Wachuset) at the Warre River the meeting place of the Nipmuc and Abenaki.

Ali-ali-nkihl8t (westward) to Millers River, west to the Pokw8mtegok (very narrow river) (Pocumtuck River) and the land of the Pocumtuc.

Ali-nkihl8t (westward) crossing the Kwinitegok (long river – Connecticut River). The Abenaki villages along the Kwinitegok are the villages of Sokwakik [O] (southern place - Squakeag), Ktispontegok [P] (great falls - Bellows Falls, Vermont), Goasek [Q] (place of pines - Newbury, Vermont).

The rivers that feed the Kwinitegok are the 8manosek (fishing place -Ammonoosuc River), the Pasomkasik - Pemijoaswek (swift current - Pemigewasset River), and the Goategok (pine river - Coaticook River) (upper Connecticut valley).

The other lakes, rivers, and waters of N'dakina are the Menahanbagok, (island pond - Island Lake), Mamhiawbagok (wide water - Lake Mephramagog), Wasabastegok, Sobagwa (ocean - Sebago Lake), Nebiz8nnibizik (little medicine water - Alburg Springs), Mikazawitegok (black river - Black River), Bonsawinno (fire keeper - Lake Bomoseen), Pibesgantegok (roily river – Dead Creek), Nebiz8nnibik (medicine water - Highgate Springs), Massawippi (clear water - Holland Pond), Kwenosakek (pike place - mouth of Lamoille River), Kwenaskategok (long point river - La Platte River), Tamakwa (beaver – Maquam Bay), Masipskiwibi (flint water - Missisquoi Bay), Klahigantegok (wooden trap river - Nulhegan River), Pas8mkasik (clear sandy river – Passumpsic River), Kwenozasek (at the pike place - Pike River), and Wasabastegok (clear stream - White River).

Continuing, Ali-nkihl8t (westward) crossing the Kwinitegok to the Deerfield River and the lands of the Mahiganek (at the Mahigans) Mahican Nation.

Continuing, Pebonkik (northward) to Onegigwizibok (otter river – Otter Creek). The lands of the Green Mountains and Onegigwizibok (Otter Creek) and the lands beyond

[R] Lake George up to the western lands (Wawobzdenik, Senapskaizibok, and the lands of Ganienkeh) to the west of Bitawbagok [S] (lake between - Lake Champlain) are the Wawobadenik (white mountains - Adirondack lands and mountains) between the N'dakina (Abenaki) and Magwak (Mohawk) nations.

The Abenaki villages on Bitawbagok are the villages of Winoskik (onion place - Winooski), Mskitegwa (quiet water - Milton, Vermont), and Mazipskaik (flint place - Swanton, Vermont), and on the river Onegigwizibok is the village of Natami pontegok [T] (first falls - Vergennes, Vermont).

The rivers that feed the Bitawbagok are the Wazowategok (crooked river - Missisquoi River), the Wintegok (marrow river - Lamoille River), the Winoskitegok (onion river - Winooski River), the Seniganitegok (stone works river - Lewis Creek), and the Onegigwizibok (otter river - Otter Creek).

Continuing, Pebonkik (northward) up through the Bitawbagok (Lake Champlain) and all of its shores going north and west through the [U] water sheds of the Chateuaguay and Bitawbagwizibok (Richelieu) Rivers back to the Ktsitegwiiak (St. Lawrence River).

The major mountains of N'dakina are: Gawasiwajo (windfall mountain - Mt. Kearsage), G8dagwjo (hidden mountain - Mt. Washington), Menonadenak (stands alone mountain - Mt. Monadnock), Wawobadenik (White Mountains or Adirondack Mountains), Pemapskadena (rocky mountain - Mt. Ascutney), Mozeodebe wadso (moose head mountain - Mt. Mansfield), Mateguasaden (rabbit mountain - Mt. Philo), Pisgag (dark - Mt. Pisga) and Wachuset (mountain of small / middle height - Mt. Wachuset), Dowabodiwadjo (saddle mountain - Camel's Hump), Mozal8mo (calls like a moose - Mt. Moosalamoo), and Mozalhlakik (cow moose land - Mt. Mooselauke).

This describes the Abenaki homelands, N'dakina bordered by the Magwak (Mohawk) to the west, the Ksitegwiiak (the land of the Hurons) and Osoganek (Algonquin Place) to the north, the Moskwas (Malecite-Maliseet), Mikm8z (Micmac), (Passaamakwadi) Passamaquoddy, and Pan8bskaik (Penobscot) to the east, the Massacusett and Nipmuc to the south, and the Mahiganek (Mahican) to the west. This describes the N'dakina that the Abenaki People claim to be their sovereign homelands.

Search for the Wawenocks: Four Guides to the Past

Guest Essay by Kerry Hardy,
Park Director of Merryspring Park, Camden, Maine

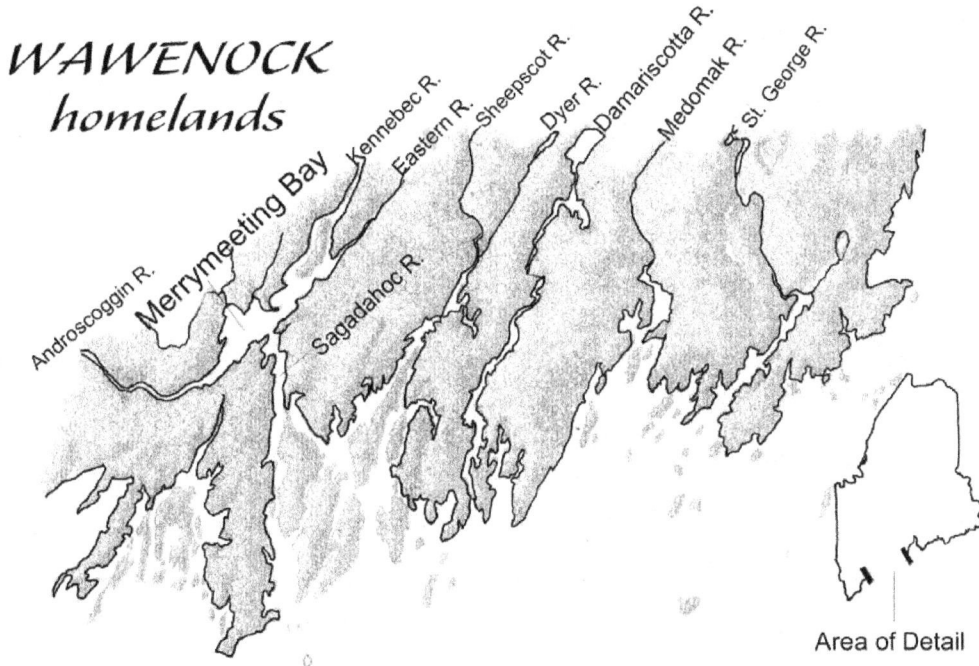

Drawn by Kerry Hardy, Merryspring Nature Center

Four Guides to the Past

I started out a few months ago innocently hoping to learn more about the history of a small slice of coastal Maine, in Camden and Lincolnville. In the time since then, I've learned a lot I never planned on and been drawn into much deeper water. Delving into history is a lot like attempting a small fix-up project on an old house—you'd better have lots of time or money on your hands if you want to do it right, because you'll just keep finding more that needs doing the deeper you dig.

Here's an example: I live on a street in Rockland, Maine called Limerock St.; it runs crookedly west from the harbor for about a mile. The quick story of this street is that it goes out to the old lime quarries; whence its name. Simple, until you wonder why it's crooked when all the other streets in town are straight.

A month or so of reading, ruminating, and observing the same pattern in other Maine towns will lead you to the discovery that it's a very old street; older than all the rest. In the process, you'll learn that Rockland used to be called Shore Village, and that Limerock Street—including portions of it now lost in the woods—was the road, or more likely, the path to the Upper Village of St. George, or present-day Warren. And you can stop there, unless in your digging into Rockland history you came across the name "Catawamteak" on an old map of the harbor, and wondered where *that* came from...

A bit more digging reveals that it means "great carrying place" in one of the Abenaki tongues. It turns out that there were three portages originating here—one led to the Wassaweskeag tidal marsh in South Thomaston, another to the head of tide on the Mill River in Thomaston, and one that went towards the head of tide on the St. George River—right past my house on present-day Limerock Street, as it turns out. And that would have been another good place for me to stop... except that a little part of me started wondering, what was up with this head-of-tide business? My background is in ecology, and I had some hunches.

I'll come back to that question, but I think by now you see what I'm getting at. Think back to my old house analogy—under the stained wallpaper you find crumbled plaster, because the laths have pulled out of the studs, which sagged when the sill under them rotted because of a leaky roof, and so it goes. You may be able to handle the wallpaper yourself, but chances are you'll need to bring a few other tradesmen in to do the whole job right.

My history project has now grown to the point where a few other tradesmen are needed, as well. I'll be the ecologist, but there needs to be a historian, an ethnologist, and an archaeologist too. Luckily for me, these guys all live on the Internet and work for free. By using a cross-disciplinary approach like this, different pictures emerge and occasionally reinforce each other in significant ways, suggesting new directions and sometimes even allowing leaps of insight. Like a rock climber who has just found and attained a new handhold, new routes, views, and possibilities suddenly appear to you. In this case, the routes go through exotic locales, with names like Majabigwaduce, Hochelaga, and maybe even Norumbega; and the views go back in time to before Columbus, before Christ, perhaps as far as ten thousand years. The possibilities are suggested by the collective thinking of all of the tradesmen, and if some of these can ultimately be confirmed by the archaeologist, then perhaps we can gain closure on one or two things we always wondered about.

One Boulder; Two Cultures

On the shore of Megunticook Lake in Lincolnville, at a spot where my family used to go swimming, there's a big granite boulder that sits right at the water's edge. One of our favorite kid-things to do was to splash water on it, in order to fill a little depression on the boulder with water. The heat stored in the rock would warm the water and make a tiny spa of sorts, which we would sit in quite happily. The sea breeze would kick in dependably every sunny afternoon, keeping the flies and heat at bay. It was a great place to spend the summer, and we probably weren't the first ones to think that.

Probably a family or small band of Native Americans had enjoyed the same place back in the sixteenth century. The same sea breeze soothed them and helped dry their fish, as the women poured corn into a small hollow on a large granite boulder, and beat it into meal with smaller hand-held rocks; smoothing the edges of our future spa as they worked. One part of my unfolding history-mystery is whether they grew their own corn, or traded to get it from tribes further south or west. My hunch is that they grew their own prior to 1500, but sometime thereafter found themselves gradually drawn out of agriculture and into a new trade-based economy.

The ecological underpinnings of my hunch are diverse clues like soils, alewives, and pine trees, which I'll elaborate on later. The historical clues are in places like the writings of Marc Lescarbot, a witty French visitor to these shores in the early 1600's, who learned from his native informants that they once grew corn but now spent their time trapping more beaver to trade with the Europeans. The ethnological evidence comes from men like Frank Speck, who lived among the Penobscot Indians at Old Town in the early 1900's, and recorded the name for May and June as ki'khadin, which translates to "planting time". The archaeological clues are finding stone mortars like the one I sat in as a child, or pestles like the one found on Appleton Ridge a couple of years ago. The combined weight of these and other bits of evidence raises a serious challenge to the conventional historical view that maize agriculture existed no farther north than the Kennebec River.

So maybe we have a new handhold. For most of my life, I saw this boulder through a child's eyes. It's nice to see it now through four different sets of eyes, and to think that it connects me to ancient people. History has a way of persisting on the face of the land, but it's also very good at hiding in plain sight. The more eyes you use in looking, the easier it is to find.

Meeting the Wawenocks

The Native Americans I spoke of a moment ago are a challenging group to put a name to. Most Maine historians refer to the mid-coast group as Wawenocks, and perhaps that will do for the present time. My first stabs at research on the Wawenocks indicated that they were either 1) non-existent, (2) a relatively unimportant coastal tribe located from the Sheepscot River to the St. George River, 3) the coastal allies of a once-powerful Abenaki nation whose leader, known as the Bashaba, ruled most of what we now call Maine in 1605, or 4) a "fusion" group with strong elements of western Abenaki culture overlaying a much earlier Delaware culture. Such is the spectrum of possibility!

The mystery gets even juicier when we consider that the very best minds in archaeology and ethnology cannot agree on the name or ethnic affiliations of these people, much less on the matter of their territorial limits. The Wawenock identity, it seems, is multi-faceted enough that one can see almost any side of them that one chooses to, and use that as "proof" that they were "like" this or that other group.

Once exposed to these divergent possibilities, I was intrigued enough to take up the trail left by the Wawenocks. There are precious few footprints left to follow, because most historians agree that a mid-coast chieftain called the Bashabas was in fact slain around 1615 (by either the English, the Micmacs, the Passamaquoddies, the Penobscots, or maybe someone else). Soon after his death, a plague in 1617 further decimated their numbers, and the few still surviving abandoned the mid-coast and headed inland, eventually finding shelter at Norridgewock or in Canada. Their troubles didn't end there, of course; ongoing warfare with the English and Mohawks continued to reduce their numbers, and all writers seem to agree that by the end of the 19th century Wawenock culture was virtually extinct.

To conclude this brief introduction to the Wawenocks, it's certainly appropriate to ask, "Where did that name come from?" The names most ethnic groups use for themselves usually translates to just "the people", so we tend not to use that. Instead, we select a name that Group B uses to describe Group A; such is the case here. Speck tells us that the Penobscots called them the Walinakiak, which he translates as "cove or little bay people". Others (like the archaeologists Arthur Spiess and Harbor Mitchell) assign the meaning "loop in the river" to the Penobscot word wawinok—this becomes quite relevant when you learn that there is in fact a loop in the St. George River, at the head of the tide in Warren, where artifacts dating all the way back to 9,000 years before present have been recovered. Another possibility might be the Abenaki word wowanal, which means eggs, perhaps in reference to the sea-bird eggs in their diets. The plot thickens when we check in on those survivors that straggled into Canada: They settled on a reservation on the modern-day Becancour River, Quebec; on a loop in that river, in a village now called Wolinak. A final intriguing possibility is the Abenaki word wawasi (holy, sacred), but here I start down the slippery slope of creative etymology that I decry in others.

Two more key questions about Indian words and names go hand in hand: Who's speaking the name, and who's writing it down? The Abenaki family of dialects has many sounds that seem intermediate to our English ears; one especially important example of this is the way that L sometimes equals R or W, or even N. Philologists refer to different Algonquin sub-groups as being "L-dialect" or "R-dialect", and it's one of the best ways of separating Abenakis (R-dialect) from their more easterly neighbors. The earliest recorded place names show "R"s west of Schoodic Point, and "L"s to the east in Nova Scotia (though the early French visitors, perhaps miffed at being called "Plangemon" instead of Frenchmen, freely substituted the R's back in). Similar blurring exists between K and G, P and B, T and D, and a few other judgement calls. To further complicate matters, Abenaki and English are equally haunted by the dreaded "schwa", which can turn any vowel into jelly. So, considering that both French and English listeners are hearing these words from one of ten or more Abenaki dialects, and then rendering them into spelled words, any of these candidates could be at the root of the name Wawenock. The historic record gives us Wawenoc, Wawenock, Weeweenock, Warrinok, and many other variations. One suspects that Elmer Fudd would have fit in nicely among these folks.

The last linguistic twist that I'll mention concerns the phenomenon of a name outliving the ones who bestowed it on a place. White people in the twenty-first century speak of "Damariscotta" and "Pemaquid", but those names obviously don't come from us; nor does using them make us Indian. In fact, those names may not have even come from the Wawenocks who lived there in 1600—the correct translation may be found among Micmacs, Narragansetts, Pennacooks, or a host of others who may have occupied the mid-coast before the Abenaki did.

Perhaps that's enough by way of introduction. The Wawenocks serve nicely to illustrate the fact that even the experts disagree about historical truth, and that the more points of view you consider, the closer you come to a workable version thereof. Thankfully, no one disputes that *somebody* was living along the coast between the Kennebec and Penobscot in 1600; it's the finer points that people disagree on. The balance of this essay will be an attempt to reconcile the various points of view as to just *who* and *what* they were.

A Closer Look at the Four Guides

Whether you're a trained archaeologist or just someone digging in a garden, finding artifacts is definitely fun. Harbor Mitchell III of Camden belongs to the former group, and spoke recently at the park where I work in that town. I had promoted his talk with a lurid press release asking the rhetorical question, "Was Maine's Macchu Picchu in Warren?" This probably got me in the doghouse with Harbor, but it also brought out a lot of curious folks from Warren; some who live right along the loop in the river. They all listened attentively as he told them of the incredible artifact density that this site contains, most of it not yet excavated.

After the talk, one of them came up and handed Harbor a thin rectangular stone about nine inches long by three wide. It was a stone adze, picked up along the river, which Harbor judged to be about 6,000 years old. That's the great thing about archaeology—the other disciplines generate theories, which can be right or wrong; but something as palpable as a stone tool that a human being made and used at that point in time and space can only be right.

For this reason, archaeologists usually get the last word. However, there's a whole lot of land out there if one were to just dig at random. Here's where the other three disciplines come in: They all identify reasoned scenarios, and collectively reduce the countless possible spots to the few most promising. If you remember the old Venn diagrams from grade school math, picture three circles that have a tiny area where they overlap each other—that's where you should dig.

The other disciplines have fun parts as well. By definition, ecology requires seeing the larger picture. An archaeologist may wonder why post-contact natives ate so few turtles compared to their ancestors; but an ecologist knows that you can't have turtles to eat if you've trapped all of the beaver out of the landscape—the two go hand in hand. Ecology recognizes that these ancient people were part of a larger system, and that the likeliest place for them to live would be where resources were concentrated. Not exactly rocket science there, but it takes maps to show this. Mapmaking is really fun; especially when you try to cram complex information into a simple, clear map.

Say, for instance, that both the historian and the ethnographer are convinced that these people depended on nuts as a part of their diet. The ecologist gets to figure out which species, where they grew historically, and present that analysis in map form. If he succeeds, anyone looking at his map will see at a glance the advantages of the mid-coast area. And that's only one of their dozens of food sources. By the time you've mapped clams, oysters, beavers, anadromous fish, waterfowl, wild rice, and so on, you have a body of evidence that draws a big fat bulls-eye around the region from Merrymeeting Bay to the Camden Hills. Simply put, this is a landscape where a man would have to work hard to starve. Significantly, that same region surrounds what most people consider to be the Wawenock homeland. It is also dead-center in the much larger region of Mawooshen, the confederacy of tribal land ruled by the aforementioned Bashabas, according to the accounts of five mid-coast Indians taken captive by George Waymouth in 1605.

History is fun too, if your idea of fun is spending a lot of time staring at a computer screen or visiting libraries. Fortunately, there is an Internet, and there are search engines, which enable me to sit at home and read documents that would have involved a lifetime of travel and research just fifty years ago. Care to know about Champlain's travels with Sieur des Monts in 1604? Try http://www.champlainsociety.ca, and read it from the man himself (as translated by H.P. Biggar). From the comfort of my desk chair, I can read a throwaway remark of Father Biard's -- "...the wicked *Ingres*, as they call the English."--that shows the Penobscot sagamores Bashabas and Asticou to be R-dialect Abenakis.

It's true that not everything has been digitized yet—like the Holy Grail of this project, Father

Rasles's Abenaki dictionary, or Frank Speck's *Wawenock Myth Texts from Maine*—but without the Internet, you'd be hard pressed to know that those two gems even existed. And when the historian taps the ecologist on the shoulder with stories about canoes in 700 AD, corn after 1000 AD, and European trade goods and germs entering the ecosystem via Newfoundland after 1520, we quickly realize that human ecology involves not just natural systems, but other shaping forces like travel, trade, disease, and warfare.

What about ethnology? If you read Frank Speck's *Penobscot Man*, the full richness of the people and their lifeways will become very real to you. Sometimes the tiniest scraps of knowledge prove useful in ways you'd never have guessed. Here's a quick example: All of the containers used for storing and cooking food by the Penobscots are either made of wood or birch bark. Their word for these pots is *seskidjou*, which translates to "earthen container". None of the old men can explain this discrepancy, but Speck recognizes that the word is a linguistic fossil that links them to ancestors from the Ceramic period. Here's another quick example: Historians debate about whether or not corn could have been grown in pre-contact Maine for reasons of growing season length; but an astute ethnobotanist will pounce on the last item in Father Rasles's list of corn varieties:

nenabiminar; *corn which comes quickly*

Frost, schmost!

Fine-grained information like this also comes from town histories, especially with regards to the nature of early landscapes, and the ancient place names that mapmakers have long since abandoned. Just as a single track in a vast forest is proof positive that a deer has been there, we can track history from single words, single events, obscure paths; or persistent anomalies in the landscape that shouldn't be there, but are. Modern maps show a small lake east of Newport as Pleasant Lake or Stetson Pond, but old town histories record its Indian name of Nexaongermek—"the lake between"—and this is a vital fact in reconstructing the busy waterways that linked the Penobscots and Kennebecs to one another.

These examples have been offered to give you an idea of the terrain, the clues, the sources, and the advantages to this collaborative approach to hunting for the past. The ecological richness of the mid-coast set the stage for human life, but human events like the development of the birchbark canoe, corn agriculture, warfare with neighboring groups, and trade with Europeans each led to major changes in where and how people lived here. When we look back in time four hundred years, we get tantalizing glimpses of the quarry; a dim shape moving around under many veils. There's something there, but what? Lifting those veils and convincing ourselves—and others—of what we see is the next step.

A Quick Review of Sources

Sifting through and selecting from the thousands of facts, legends, theories, and other bits of historical detritus available in books and cyberspace is daunting work, and I lay no claims to having done an exhaustive job of it. But I have done enough of it to at least feel conversant with the important primary sources—Verrazano, Cartier, Gosnold, Pring, Champlain, Rosier, the anonymous chronicler of the Popham Colony (1607), Lescarbot, Father Biard, John Smith, and the relations of the captive Indians presented in Purchas—to have some basis of an understanding of what they claim to have encountered. These are all extremely valuable, inasmuch as they give glimpses of the native culture before it was utterly upended by European contact. Next in line are later seventeenth-century sources like Christopher Levett, William Bradford, Father Druillettes, John Josselyn, and early colonial records from Maine and Massachusetts. Finally, Father Rasles's experiences at Norridgewock more than a century after European contact still offer considerable insight; particularly because language changes more slowly than lifestyle.

Especially valuable are the first attempts by these Europeans to spell the Indian words they were hearing. In this regard John Smith's accounts are particularly useful, for his travels took him all along the eastern seaboard and reveal some useful linguistic and cultural links. The real fun comes when you start seeing through the phonetic spellings, and recognize that the Indian village on Cheasapeake Bay which Smith renders as "Wigh Comoco" is the exact same word as Frank

Speck's "wigamagw", which means house in the Penobscot tongue. (Incidentally, Smith renders that bay as "Chisapeake", which John Huden points out was also the Abenaki name for Merrymeeting Bay). Today's Appomattox River, of Civil War fame, was "Apamatuck" to Smith's ear, and rings eerily like the rivers listed by Waymouth's captive Indians—Apponick, Apponeg, Apaumensek, and Apanawapeske. Incidentally, these Maine rivers, though 700 miles north of Chesapeake Bay, all had oysters. Halfway between, in Rhode Island, sits the island named Apponaug—"oyster place".

I've also dealt with a good many maps, thanks to places like the Library of Congress and its excellent American Memory collection. The Penobscot and the Kennebec River are clearly indicated in many of these early maps, but these were drawn by men of the sea; they don't tell us much about conditions on the mainland. The first Europeans saw our rock-strewn coast as a forbidding barrier—"A place to affright, rather than delight..", in the words of John Smith—and their maps often lead us to focus on the coastal strand too closely, and lose sight of the importance of the interior. The salmon that the Popham colonists saw jumping at the mouth of the Kennebec were destined to feed natives more than a hundred miles upstream from there. Indeed, a quick review of the information in Purchas's description of Mawooshen shows that, as of 1605, the inland villages had larger populations than those on the shore.

Early town histories are essential sources of point-specific data, since these writers are more interested in local minutiae than in solving larger regional questions. From them you get facts like where the first settlers found land already cleared, or how far inland different anadromous fish made their spawning runs, and in what numbers. For every artifact that makes it into a museum, there are probably five sitting on mantelpieces or in desk drawers around the state, and town histories are where you learn about these finds. I find them quite believable and useful – at least until they start offering their take on the meaning of native place names.

When that happens, it's time to turn to the Jesuit Fathers Rasles and Aubery, each of whom recorded an Abenaki dictionary prior to 1725; or Joseph Laurent's Dictionary, or more modern writers like Wilfred Ganong, Fannie Hardy Eckstorm, Frank Speck, or Gordon Day. The marvel of the two Jesuit works is that both are very early and are based on decades of living among the natives. Thus, we not only get significant linguistic data from the mouths of the last surviving Wawenocks and Kennebecs, but we also get it before many English or French words had crept in. By the time of Speck's work two centuries later, the Penobscots had plenty of French and English threads in their language and lifestyle; moreover, their mixing with more easterly cultures had converted them from having an R-dialect to an L-dialect. This leads to some comical juxtapositions, such as the Ramassoc River of 1605 becoming today's Narramissic River, which emanates from Alamoosook Lake—and it's all the same word.

Analyzing Indian place-names from modern maps without knowing the language is pretty challenging. Most of us wouldn't look at modern-day Damariscotta and Mattamiscontis, two places about a hundred miles apart from each other, and see them as the same name, but they actually are. Moreover, the ancient village of Amaseconti (today's Farmington Falls) is the same name again. The names tell us that at all three locations there were many alewives. Since alewives are both good food and good fertilizer for corn, name clues like this are definitely grist for our mill. For this work, John C. Huden's *Indian Place Names of New England* is an invaluable help, especially when buttressed by the works of Eckstorm and Day.

The archaeological record of Maine's coast is already bulging with sites and discoveries, and books like Dean Snow's *The Archaeology of New England*, or Bruce Bourque's *12,000 Years: Native Americans in Maine* offer good summaries of the important sites. Of course, the danger in knowing someone else's theory is that it might limit or bias one's own analysis. To know the Wawenocks, it's necessary to consider the Damariscotta oyster mounds at the center of their habitat. Moreover, the archaeological record has two significant time gaps —the disappearance of the so-called Red Paint people from the area, and the later abandonment of semi- permanent coastal sites at around 1,100 AD. How, or why, did this happen in the resource-rich mid-coast breadbasket? (*hint:* Corn.)

Another important site is Hart's Falls on the St. George River, which has most recently been examined by archaeologists Arthur Spiess and Harbor Mitchell, and has yielded artifacts that span nine millennia. Ongoing work there may shed further light on the question of continuous versus sporadic occupancy. So, with one more acknowledgement that my arguments rest on few, but reliable, sources; I'll plunge in and make my case. In a very few instances, when the vast majority of writers agree on a matter, I'll treat it as fact and not bore you with the details. Most of the time, it won't be that easy.

Part 1: The Setting
Most of what has happened to Maine's first people, as well as their landscape, since 1620 can be reconstructed from the written historical record. It's a story that needs telling another day, but the roots of my mystery are farther back, so the question is: what were the people and the land like prior to European contact?

Luckily, we have some documentation of this. Giovanni di Verrazano in 1524, and then Samuel de Champlain (accompanied by Marc Lescarbot) in 1604 and James Rosier in 1605, provided detailed observations about what they encountered. Better still, unlike most European explorers, these men actually went ashore and ranged over the land. Since Rosier apparently visited the Pemaquid to St. George River area, his account is especially useful. Moreover, the five natives captured by Rosier's captain (Waymouth) were taken back to England, and provided further information about their homeland and culture while they were living with Sir Ferdinando Gorges.

One of the things they described was a confederacy that the scribe rendered as Mawooshen (Moasham in other sources). They named nine rivers, supposedly in east-to-west order, that defined the boundaries of this confederacy; as well as the villages and sagamores, or chiefs, on each river. Consider closely the following claims, taken directly from Rosier's account:

"They shew the maner how they make bread of their Indian wheat, and how they make butter and cheese of the milk they have of the Rain-Deere and Fallo-Deere, which they have tame as we have Cowes."

Bear in mind that these Indians were taken most probably from somewhere near the mouth of the St. George River. The "Indian wheat" referred to, of course, is corn. Now, whether they grew it or traded for it doesn't much matter; either way, it seems to have been part of their diet. Faced with this, the logical mind sees two possibilities—either the claim is true, and they had corn, dairy, and tame venison in their diets; or the claim is false, whether through Rosier's devices or theirs, or merely through inefficient communication. Since the matter of corn is central to this search, let's take this primary source at face value for a moment and consider the land and its suitability for agriculture a bit further.

The St. George peninsula is the northernmost of about nine parallel ridges aligned from southwest to northeast, if you count the long islands around the mouth of the Kennebec River. Their geologic origin is the Acadian Orogeny, a continental collision that wrinkled the land in this linear fashion. Between the ridges, there are medium-sized rivers which drain the corrugated landscape and spill into long, narrow, island-filled, estuary-lined bays that eventually reach the open ocean.

Between the Kennebec to the west and the Penobscot to the east, there are four rivers that I wish to consider closely: the Sheepscot, Damariscotta, Medomak, and St. George. Smaller rivers, like the Eastern, Dyer, Pemaquid, Mill, Ducktrap, Passagassawaukeag, and Marsh Stream complete the mid-coast drainage; and though less suitable as canoe routes, they too had rich resources in historic times. The Megunticook River in Camden is uniquely different, since a steep waterfall at its entry to the sea bars most fish from running up it.

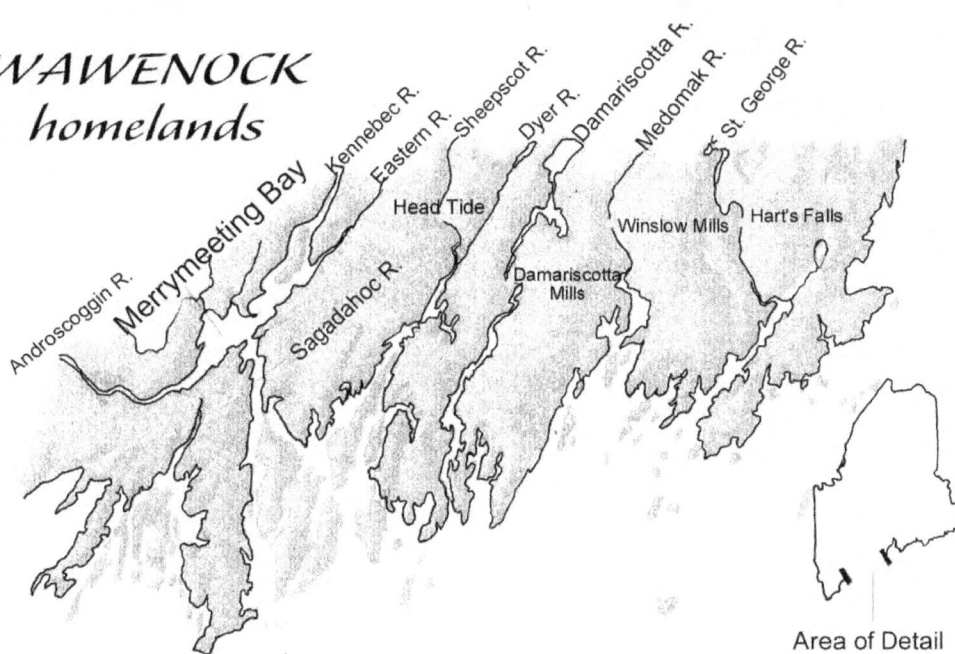

WAWENOCK
homelands

Androscoggin R.
Merrymeeting Bay
Kennebec R.
Eastern R.
Sheepscot R.
Dyer R.
Damariscotta R.
Medomak R.
St. George R.

Head Tide
Winslow Mills
Hart's Falls
Sagadahoc R.
Damariscotta Mills

Area of Detail

Drawn by Kerry Hardy, Merryspring Nature Center

These mid-coast peninsulas dovetail the land and sea in such a convoluted fashion that an incredible linear distance of edge habitat is created. A crow flying from Merrymeeting Bay will reach Owl's Head after forty miles, but a sandpiper walking the seashore between the same two points would cover more than five hundred miles. We'll see the full ecological significance of this later, but all this saltwater real-estate is not particularly well-suited to farming. Soils tend to be thin, excessively drained, and very acidic; better suited for growing spruce trees and blueberries than corn, beans, or squash.

Farther upstream, however, conditions are quite suitable for agriculture. The scouring effect of the glaciers served to move soil from the ridgetops into the valleys, assisted by the subsequent ten thousand years of erosion and gravity. Moreover, the heavy runs of anadromous fish provided natives with both sustenance at planting time and abundant fertilizer. A key convergence of these resources typically occurred at inland locations; specifically, the heads-of-tide where the first waterfalls impeded spawning fish and made for easy harvesting with spears and nets.

On the Sheepscot, such a location exists at Head-of-Tide in Alna. Damariscotta Mills is a parallel location on the next river, as is Winslow's Mills on the Medomak and Hart's Falls in Warren on the St. George. Visit any of these spots today, and you'll see that agriculture remains as a dominant land use.

Was it farmland in 1600, or for that matter, in 1500 A.D.? It's not clear from the historic record, because most explorers didn't venture far up Maine's rivers. Champlain ascended the Penobscot as far as modern-day Bangor, but not to the main village at Old Town. He was tantalizingly close—certainly within two miles—of the high ground on Fort Hill, which William Williamson says, "gave every appearance of having been the cornfields of the ancients". The following summer, Champlain observed and recorded fully the agricultural activities at the mouth of the Saco River, but that was a place where the corn was grown right at the seashore. While at the Kennebec, he heard of corn that was grown far upriver, for reasons of safety from sea-borne attacks. Champlain never made it to the heads-of-tide in any of the smaller mid-coast rivers, so we don't know if there were cornfields there or not.

Numerous other sources refer to agricultural centers far inland. Norridgewock and Waterville on the Kennebec (Narragooc and Ketangheannycke are the native names given in the Purchas relation of Mawooshen), as well as an alleged 700-acre cornfield in Canton on the Androscoggin, are identified as locations chosen for their safety against ocean-based raids. All of these villages are in areas of rich alluvial soil, and all are within the historic ranges of either alewives or shad. Perhaps most significantly, all were too far inland to have been visited or reported by the first Europeans. This raises the rhetorical question, "If a cornstalk falls in the forest but there's no Frenchman there to hear it, did it ever really grow?"

Further evidence of agriculture might the ubiquitous presence of tobacco in virtually every account provided by the first Europeans. The very name "tobacco"hints at the presence of other plants—*atebakw* is the Abenaki word for bean—and without doubt it was smoked, and presumably grown, everywhere from Virginia to the St. Lawrence River. If you're going to clear ground and nurture one crop, why wouldn't you grow others as well; especially since the "three sisters" were common horticultural practice all along the eastern seaboard? The broad-leaved tobacco of Appalachia was seen at Saco by Champlain, mentioned to Rosier while at Monhegan, and Lescarbot notes the natives growing it at Port Royal. All of this tobacco cultivation leaves little question that these natives knew which end of a hoe went into the ground.

In light of the foregoing, Lescarbot's assertion (History of New France, vol. lll, p. 250) deserves close attention: "The people of Canada and Hochelaga, in the time of Jacques Cartier, also tilled the soil after the same manner, and the land brought forth for them corn, beans, peas, melons, squashes, and cucumbers; but since their furs have been in request, and that in return for these they have had victuals without any further troubles, they have become lazy, as have also the Souriquois [as he called the natives of Nova Scotia] who at the same date practiced tillage". Inasmuch as his primary informant in these matters was the hundred-year-old sagamore Membertou, who claimed to remember Cartier's 1534 visit, I consider it vital evidence of corn agriculture throughout the Maritime Peninsula.

In short, the general physical characteristics of the mid-coast region appear to have been entirely suitable for agriculture, and the availability of large populations of fish, precisely at planting time, increase the likelihood. Add to this the numerous references that establish corn culture far inland on the large rivers, and it seems very likely that at least some agriculture was practiced upstream in the mid-coast river valleys. We know from the Jesuit Relations that Poitrincourt, accompanied by Father Biard, went from Nova Scotia to the heart of Wawenock territory (near today's Wiscasset) expecting to trade for corn in 1611. However, by the early seventeenth century, the fur trade with Europe was already well-established, and Maine's Indians' agricultural traditions were probably already in decline—at least among those coastal groups with easy access to European trade goods, which they could then trade for corn grown by their neighbors to the south, or by those upriver on the Androscoggin and Kennebec. By now, beavers had replaced corn as the staff of life.

Ecologically speaking, beavers were always more important than corn, Beavers are a keystone species in the ecosystem, since their ponds create gaps in the forest that benefit sun- loving plants, along with all the animal species that utilize them. Native Americans could eat the beavers, wear their skins, and hunt the margins of their ponds for edible aquatic plants, waterfowl, turtles, and the moose and deer that came there for succulent browse. The value of beavers was certainly apparent to the Indians, who took pains not to over-harvest any one area (this from Speck).

It's almost impossible to overstate the importance of beavers in the course of the European settlement of North America. Between 1550 and 1850, Europe's appetite for beavers and cod remained insatiable. European fishermen could harvest cod without much effect on native life, but the relentless extraction of beavers had profound implications for the land and its people.

We sometimes imagine European settlement as beginning on the east coast and diffusing gradually westward over a couple of centuries. More accurate is to imagine the newcomers as a hyper-aggressive "beaver cancer" that metastasized across the continent with lightning speed. Like a giant lymph system, the abundant waterways of the north facilitated this invasion, serving as both beaver habitat and as highways for commerce. From the Maritime Peninsula throughout the St. Lawrence watershed, to the far ends of Lake Superior, and northward to Hudson Bay, wherever beavers lived, a whole range of traders—Indians, voyageurs, and agents of the fledgling English and French governments—were all captive players in this trans-oceanic economy. English, French, and even Dutch interactions with Indians were almost always guided by economic motives relating to the fur trade.

Though the Canadian fur resource quickly eclipsed that of Maine, our mid-coast was nonetheless at ground zero of this culture clash. Verrazano in 1524 encountered Indians here with furs to trade, and an English vessel in 1527 encountered no less than fifty French, Basque, and Spanish boats along the Maritime Peninsula. Cartier in 1534 was greeted by a fleet of canoes, each filled with natives bearing their furs as trade goods. Though codfish were the main reason for these boats, the fishermen were quick to realize the profit potential of trading for native furs during the weeks they spent waiting for the fish to dry. Skins, or in later years the wampum they commanded, could be easily converted to kettles, cloth, knives, guns, food, and liquor, and the net effect of these commodities would alter the Indians' lifestyle irrevocably. Agriculture was abandoned, to a greater or lesser degree depending on the quantity of furs available in the region as trade goods.

Subsequently, the European commodities obtained in trade greatly amplified the status and power of those possessing them, and fur politics quickly became a destabilizing influence among tribes. Lescarbot details an encounter in 1605 between the Souriquois leader Messamouet and the Saco leaders Onemechin and Marchin, in which Messamouet feels slighted because his boatload of Euro goods doesn't command enough respect and compensation from the latter two chiefs. This is one of a series of events culminating in the 1607 war previously alluded to.

The final blow to the historic Indian lifestyle was the devastating epidemic in 1617-18 which killed perhaps as much as 90 per cent of the native population along Maine's coast. The work force needed to hunt, forage, grow and prepare foods—in short, to maintain their whole way of life-- simply wasn't there anymore; and trading beavers for sustenance and clothing was left as the only survival option. The conversion from self-reliance to wage slavery was hastened all the more by the promotion of a currency-based economy, with wampum serving in place of precious metals; and by the European traders' insidious use of alcohol to incapacitate the Indians at the trading table.

It seems likely that the network of trails leading to Cushnoc (modern-day Augusta) developed primarily in these times of beaver-and-wampum-based economy. Formally established in 1628 as a fur trading post, Cushnoc was a financial godsend to the nearly insolvent Plymouth Colony. Direct routes overland from modern-day Bangor, Hampden, Frankfort, Belfast, Lincolnville, Warren, and Wiscasset all converged there, as well as numerous trails from the north, west, and south. The ocean, as well as inland waterways, had always been used as highways between tribes, but the presence of Cushnoc—and with it, a growing Native dependence on the commodities to be traded for there—required overland trails as well, so that furs could be taken at any time of year. Indeed, the most valuable furs of all were taken in the winter, and that coincided with the Indians' season of greatest need for food and blankets. Most of these trails, whether in whole or in sections, are preserved even today in our system of roads.

It's also worth noting that trading at both Cushnoc and Pemaquid brought Indians from the Androscoggin, Kennebec, Penobscot, and all the intervening coast to the same locations, yet the historic record bears little evidence of any trade-related warring between these groups. Doesn't this indicate that they were on friendly terms, and at least imply a cultural affiliation?

Though the natives probably still tried to conserve a breeding population of beavers, white hunters and trappers were now joining the economy and had no such scruples. Competition for beavers led to mounting friction and occasional skirmishes between natives and whites, but the biggest losers were the beavers-- their numbers began a decline that neared extinction by the nineteenth century, and their absence in the ecosystem contributed to declines in many other species. Thankfully, a fashion whim in English high society, perhaps launched by Prince Albert's choice of a silk hat in 1850, would drastically reduce the demand for the North American beaver and start them on the road to recovery.

Ironically, the disappearance of beavers had one beneficial effect on the first white settlers. Abandoned beaver ponds dried up and became lush meadows, and were the only spots where livestock could be grazed immediately upon arrival in a wilderness. Thus the nucleus of many a Maine town, such as Lincolnville or Union, owes its siting to these abandoned beaver ponds.

Elsewhere in Maine, a sadly parallel phenomenon existed: the abandoned cornfields of the Indians, resulting from *their* near-extinction, offered similar footholds to arriving settlers. Thus the first white settlers in Leeds, on the Androscoggin, found vacant land consisting of fields with scattered large oak trees bearing mute testimony to its previous tenants. In other areas of Maine, including the mid-coast north and west of Fort St. George, these cornfields lay fallow for 150 years or more while wars raged between English settlers and the French-Indian alliance. Through the years, the wind-blown seeds of white pine reclaimed the fields, yielding names like Cowasesick— "place of small pines"—in Sheepscot. By the time of peace in the 1760's, these nearly pure stands of trees, some almost 200' tall, gave the impression that this was and had ever been a wilderness. In this regard, we would do well to recall the words of Gordon Day in his essay, *The Indian as an Ecological Factor in the Northeastern Forest*:
> "We must conclude that an area which was wooded when first seen by white men was not necessarily primeval; that an area for which there is no record of cutting is not necessarily virgin; and that a knowledge of local archaeology and history should be part of the ecologist's equipment."

All of this history must be known to understand what we're looking for today. Durable clues remain after four centuries that can still be perceived in each discipline. These include stone artifacts, words, place-names, historic records of anadromous fish runs, village locations, bones, seeds, shell middens, carbon layers, pollen grains and more. Clues can be direct—like a stone mortar—or indirect, like a grove of pines that replaced an abandoned cornfield, or a story handed down, or a word in a dialect that has a close parallel to another somewhere else. The task is to surmise what you're looking for, and where you might find it; to evaluate its authenticity when you find it, to be open to evidence that serendipitously finds you, and to resist cramming ambiguous facts into the places you'd like them to fit.

I've devoted about a year now to my little mystery, using the four different approaches outlined, and feel at last as though I can take a guess at answering a few basic questions about the Wawenocks.

Where did they come from, and when did they arrive?
If we were to look at the residents of a city like Boston and ask this same question, there wouldn't be any easy answer as to place of origin and time of arrival—people tend to come from different places, and at different times. This is worth keeping in mind, because even though they weren't as fluidly mobile as people are today, the American natives in pre-contact times certainly had ample means of expanding their horizons and gene pools. As with any other species, humans can exceed their habitat's carrying capacity, and when this happens there will be interactions, whether cooperative or hostile, with neighboring groups. Both kinds lead to cultural exchange, whether through intermarriage or hostage-taking.

To return to my Boston analogy briefly, consider another point: As a place becomes a center of commerce, cultural mixing increases. A growing body of evidence, collected at places like the Goddard site on Eggemoggin Reach, suggests that mid-coast Maine (and particularly Penobscot Bay) was an important pre-and post-contact trading location, from perhaps 1000 to 1650 AD, when places like Cushnoc, Pemaquid and Pentagoet were still more important than Boston. Corn and nutmeats from the west, lithics and furs from the north, and dried fish/shellfish from the east met conveniently in Norumbega. Wherever trade happens, cultural exchange happens too.

All of this regional trade can probably be traced to the development of the canoe, which made travel along the East Coast (and to it from Canada) possible. Rivers like the Androscoggin, Kennebec, Penobscot and St. John all pass within easy water access of the St. Lawrence, and allowed Canadian Algonquins to travel safely to the east of the Iroquois nation. When we consider the transportation and politics of 1500 AD, it seems almost inevitable that the region from Merrymeeting Bay to Penobscot Bay was a bulls-eye for trading in all of eastern North America. Consider, for instance, that the name Agguncia, which was applied to some unknown trade center in Penobscot Bay, is translated by John Huden as "island" -- in the *Huron* tongue!

As a European presence developed at Newfoundland after 1500, new locations like Tadoussac and Quebec became more important; such that by 1605, natives kidnapped by Waymouth could tell of going up the Penobscot to trade with Anadabiou at Tadoussac. This era also saw the Micmacs of Nova Scotia become important middlemen, bringing brass kettles and woolen cloth from Plaisence (Placentia) to the coast of Maine for trade. The superb cod fishing in the waters around Monhegan lured Europeans closer and closer, so that by 1680 colonists requesting support for the post at Pemaquid still considered it "the metropolis of these parts, as it has been long before Boston".

Traces of different cultures abound on the coast of Maine, and not just in the red-ochre lined graves so vigorously excavated by archaeologist Warren Moorehead in the early twentieth century. In ranging the coast between Saco and Mount Desert Island in the year 1605, Champlain encountered both hunter/foragers in birch-bark canoes and corn growers in dugout boats. Frank Speck notes the peculiar presence of *two* creation myths among the Penobscots, as well as power-sharing between two distinct groups of families: one with land-based totem animals, and another with marine-based totems. It is tempting to see this as a cooperative merging of two cultures; one which tapped the rich resources of the Gulf of Maine, and another which brought horticulture, or at least the memory of it. I suggested earlier that the Wawenocks might have Delaware-like origins overlaid with more recent Abenaki input, and I would extend the same theory to include the Penobscots.

Hints of an earlier group being pushed eastward by horticulturists from the northwest are found in the myth and language of the Penobscots, as well as the little we know of the Wawenock tongue. Maine historian Fannie Hardy Eckstorm, consulting with the best Canadian scholars of the day, reached the conclusion that some mid-coast place names predate the natives found living there at the time of contact. "The writer discovered that many place-names which Penobscot Indians could not translate were easily interpreted by Passamaquoddy and Micmac Indians. Some places had two names, one modern Abenaki and the other an older form readily explained by words still current among the tribes farther east." Thus names like Monhegan, Pemaquid, Chewonki, and Megunticook endure on the land; linguistic tracks left by those here before the Abenaki.

The first two names, Monhegan and Pemaquid, deserve fairly close examination. Huden gives Monhegan as being either Malecite or Micmac for "out to sea island", but also gives the Wampanoag name Monhiggin (Plymouth County, Mass.) as "place of islands". Eckstorm, supported by Ganong, makes it to be Micmac for "THE island". John Smith in 1614 gave it as Mona-higgen. None of these is entirely satisfactory; for the suffix –higan in Abenaki always refers to some kind of device, tool, manufacturing process, etc.; 'thingamajig', if you will. Where was the Abenaki translation for this important island in the heart of Abenaki territory? One possible translation lies buried in the Maine Historical Society, in a small handwriten notebook in which Rev. Michael O'Brien of St. Mary's Catholic Church in Bangor kept records of his conversations with Penobscot Indians. The entry "Mani-higan" is followed by this very specific statement: "Oil extracted from fish or meat, place where oil is so extracted." This intriguing entry suggests the island's long history as a place where whale and codfish oil, or train, was made; whether by Europeans or Native Americans.

As for Pemaquid, it too lends itself to translation in tongues other than Abenaki. Eckstorm saw it also as Micmac, as does Huden, for "extended land". Rosier heard it as "Bemmaquiducke" in 1605, which appears to have an Abenaki locative –uk ending on top of someone else's –quid, also a locative. It's as if the Abenakis of 1605 were calling it "long land place place"; just as we are redundant when we say "Sahara Desert". This increases the likelihood that someone before the Abenakis named it, and one obvious possibility has to be the Wampanoags. In their language, and in the very similar Narragansett, the root –aquid means "island", while a terminal –quid, -quit, -goet, -goit, -qut, and -cut all mean "place". The only occurrences of these various endings in Maine are all along the coast; moreover, many are ancient names that have been abandoned since the early 1600's. Peimtagoet, Pachipskut, Mecaddacut, Macquoit, Segocket, Saquid, Ogunquit, Pemaquid and other names from the coastal strand in Maine (and as far as Piziquid and Cobequid in Nova Scotia) may all indicate early coastal travelers that predate the Abenakis.

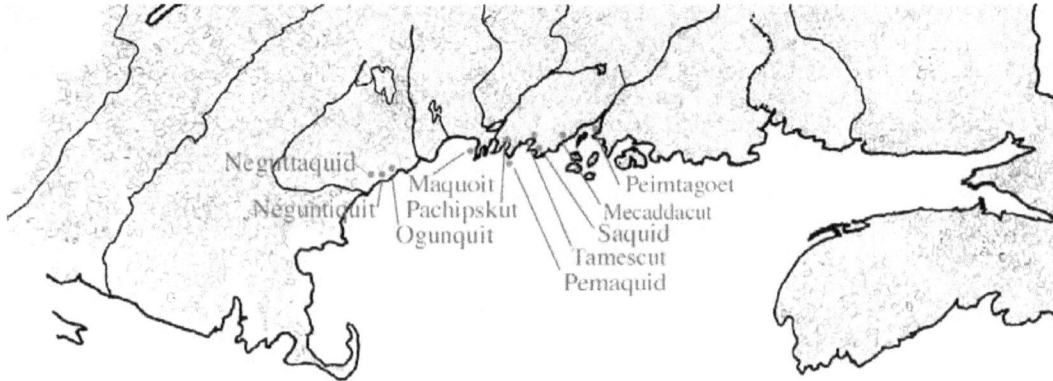

Negottaquid
Néguntiquit'
Maquoit
Pachipskut
Ogunquit
Peimtagoet
Mecaddacut
Saquid
Tamescut
Pemaquid

Early Maine place-names with
-quid, -quit, -goet, -goit, -cut, or similar endings

Clues like these suggest that a thorough investigation of multiple cultures—Micmac, Maliseet, Penobscot, Huron, Ottawa, and those from the seaboard to the south, like Narragansett, Mohegan, and Delaware will be needed to fully answer any questions about origins. I mention the Delaware because of their famous "Walum Olum", also known as the Red Record, which purportedly records more than two thousand years of that nation's history. In it, voyages to and from the north and east along the seacoast feature prominently.

The name Wawenock itself hints at the arrival of Abenakis, for it has some near-parallels: in Quebec (Wolinak, the village on the Becancouer River) and in the area of Westfield, Massachusetts; where a group known as the Woronoco (Waranokes, Waranoaks, etc.) are mentioned often in that state's early history. When conflicts with the English forced the Woronoco to retreat, they—just like our mid-coast Wawenocks—headed north and west, perhaps retreating to an ancestral homeland. From a haven on Missisquoi Bay at the north end of Lake Champlain, the Woronoco chieftain Greylock waged many successful strikes back at the English. In all instances, the root of these names has the same meaning of lands or waters twisting or turning about in dramatic fashion. Greylock's Indian name, in fact, was Wawanolet, and meant "the one who turns about", in reference to his reversing direction unpredictably, and to great advantage, during warfare.

Let's consider this "reversing of direction" theme as it relates to our area. In the mid-coast, any of the following features might inspire the name "Wawenock":

    -The S-curve in the Damariscotta River by the Great Salt Bay

    -The loop in the St. Georges River at Vaughan's Neck

    -Reversing tidal channels throughout the region especially noticeable at the reversing falls at Harpswell, Sasanoa, Sheepscot, Damariscotta, and Weskeag.

Of all these, I'm most interested in the reversing tidal falls. Champlain marveled at these, as tourists and kayakers still do today; why wouldn't they have also seemed amazing to Abenakis seeing (for the first time in their lives) something as mighty as a river apparently "turn on itself", i.e. reverse direction with the change in tide? The archipelago between Popham and Boothbay in particular has many passages where the waters reverse their flow; names like Hell's Gate and

Hockomock Point (from Hobbomocca, "Devil's Place") testify to both whites and natives thinking these waters bewitched. Inasmuch as Indian geography was usually based on the unique natural features of an area, it seems possible that these reversing waters might be the source of the name "Wawenock", meaning "turning-about place", and that it is of Abenaki (i.e. more recent) derivation.

An alternate theory of the name's origin appears when we search the historic record for the earliest uses of it. I can find no earlier usage than that traced by Frank Speck in his *Wawenock Myth Texts From Maine*, who notes Father Rasles mentioning "Warinakiens" sometime around 1700. Such a date is contemporary with the settlement at Wolinak on the Becancouer River, meaning that it could have originated at that point in time. Repeated trips from Canadian havens to the Maine coast, to visit ancestral sites and procure the ample marine food resources they had left behind, may have forged the link between these former coastal tenants and the name of their new home. The likelihood of this scenario increases when we consider that, in 1700, the letter "L" was probably not yet in use among the Wawenocks; thus their village at Becancouer would have been Warinok or Wawinok.

Moreover, there is a precedent for this, as Gordon Day pointed out in his analysis of the "Arosagunticook"—a name which properly belongs to the St. Francis River community in Canada, but which people mistakenly use to describe natives of the Androscoggin River. Because so many Indians fled that valley for the safety of the reservation on the St. Francis, the name of their new home stuck with them. When they launched raids from Canada against settlers in their former territory, the whites knew and feared them as "Arresagunticooks", and they knew that they had once lived along the Androscoggin; thus the two ideas were linked. Whatever the tribal boundaries may have been in 1600, it's safe to say that by the time of King Philip's War (1675) most of New England's Abenakis were settling into new homes and new relationships with each other.

If the Wawenocks are a similar case of Maine Indians being identified by a post-contact Canadian place name, perhaps we need to consider a more appropriate alternative. One thinks immediately of either Sagadahoc or Pachipskut as an accurate name from the center of their bioregion, and the latter has in fact been used (in its euphonized form of Sheepscot) since at least 1696 in colonial records. However, that may have to wait until we resolve one final question: How different were these mid-coast natives from the Kennebecs or the Penobscots?

In the case of the Wawenocks, at least in the seventeenth and early eighteenth centuries, relations seem to have been pretty friendly with their immediate neighbors. The language used by Kennebecs and Penobscots "differs little, no more than from one English county to the next", according to Canadian philologist J.H. Trumbull. As late as 1720, Father Rasles reported the Norridgewocks going to the seashore twice a year, to fish and visit the graves of their fathers, along routes that crisscrossed Kennebec and Androscoggin lands. Numerous colonial sources tell how the Penobscots would most commonly go to Canada by using the Sebasticook River to cross into the Kennebec watershed, and then follow the Kennebec to its end, where a short portage led to the Chaudiere River and ultimately Quebec. This report is confirmed in the name "Taconnick" (today's Waterville), which is a simplified version of "Keta kouan-auk", meaning "the great crossing place". Inasmuch as it already had a version of this name ("Ketangheannycke") in 1605, it seems safe to assume that Penobscots and Kennebecs had traveled freely among each other for a long time.

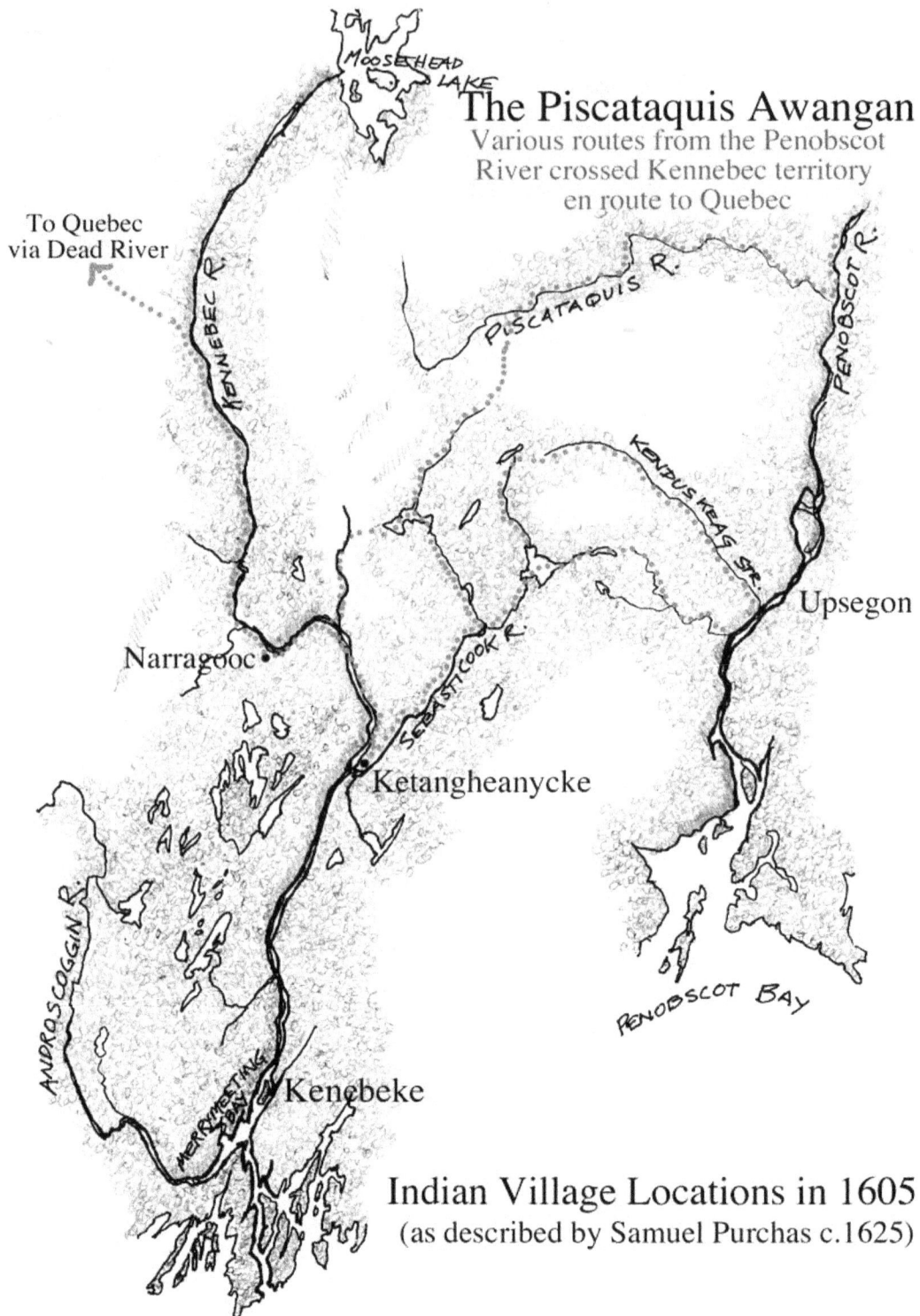

The Piscataquis Awangan
Various routes from the Penobscot River crossed Kennebec territory en route to Quebec

MOOSEHEAD LAKE

To Quebec via Dead River

KENNEBEC R.

PISCATAQUIS R.

PENOBSCOT R.

KONDUSKEAG STR.

Upsegon

Narragooc

SEBASTICOOK R.

Ketangheanycke

PENOBSCOT BAY

ANDROSCOGGIN R.

MERRYMEETING BAY

Kenebeke

Indian Village Locations in 1605
(as described by Samuel Purchas c.1625)

C-16

The historic record also indicates many instances of military alliance between these three groups, and offers almost no evidence of any enmity between Kennebecs and Wawenocks. The English, through long campaigns to divide and conquer, eventually managed to play the Penobscots against the Wawenocks (who by now had been assimilated into the mixed culture of post-1650 that included Norridgewocks, Pennacooks, Sacos, Pigwackets, Androscoggins, and Kennebecs), but it took extraordinary effort. Even as late as 1750, the Penobscots were showing outrage and demanding justice—to the point of threatening the English with war—over the killing and wounding of a few "Wiscasset Indians" by whites. We also know from Father Biard's 1611 meeting with "Meteourmite" in the Boothbay area that both Penobscots and "Armouchiqouis"(a Micmac term applied to those living anywhere from the Kennebec to the Merrimack) were allowed in the heart of the Wawenock homeland, though the great sagamore sends the westerners away for their bad manners before the visit's conclusion.

This sagamore, in fact, may be the keystone to understanding the Wawenocks' place in the Abenaki world. We encounter him in all of the primary accounts, though by many tortured spellings: Manthoumermer to Champlain, Meteourmite to Biard, Manawormet to Levett, Mentaurmet to Purchas, and finally "Natawormet", as he appears in a deed of 1648. It is worth considering the exact language very carefully, for in this deed his son Natahanda (one of Waymouth's original five captives, and now the apparent lord of the Kennebec) states his father's title: "old Natawormet, *sachem of Kennebec River*".

While it's true that by 1648 the Indians' plight was desperate enough that they might be compelled to say or sign anything for a blanket and a square meal, we can hardly overlook the importance of a primary source saying that he and his father, two of Maine's most famous "Wawenocks", are Kennebecs! However, in the Jesuit Relations for 1652, reference is made to the Norridgewock chief and "...a difference which he had with the captain of those who dwell at the mouth of our river," following which "...the old hatred which we had for the people stirred in our hearts, and we were on the point of cutting throats and making war." This "difference" might well have involved deeds of Kennebec lands to the English; it also makes it clear that the "saltwater Kennebecs" were a separate group from the Norridgewocks.

Micmacs, also known as Nova Scotia or Cape Sable Indians, are another matter entirely. Bad blood between Kennebec-area natives and Micmacs in the contact period culminated in the 1607 war at Saco. The Micmac version blames the Armouchiquois for killing Panounias, a Micmac trader; however, we know from Champlain that Panounias's wife was probably a stolen Kennebec, so there may well be more to the story. Whatever the causes, the various accounts that we have of this war (primarily Lescarbot, but also Davies) give us an idea of the alliances: Penobscots, Wawenocks, Androscoggins, and Sacos on one side; Micmacs, Malecites, Passamaquoddies and, most importantly, a few French muskets on the other. An important footnote occurs in the aftermath of this war: the Passamaquoddy sagamore Ouagimou and the Penobscot leader Asticou broker a peace the following year. Finally, lest we see the Micmacs as the villains of the piece, it's worth remembering the theory that they were probably among the displaced former tenants of the Kennebec-Penobscot archipelago, perhaps still harboring fond memories of the place.

In all that I've been able to find, there seems to a very practical model emerging: It made good sense for adjacent nations to find a way to get along, and they almost always managed to. Once beyond your immediate neighbor's land, relationships were much more shifting and treacherous, and wars of theft or vengeance were common. A notable exception to this latter occurred when faced with a powerful foe such as the Mohawks or the English (or both together, as eventually happened)—in such a case, the entire Abenaki nation could unite.

How did they make their living?
For years, historians have commented on what marvelous appetites the coastal Indians must have had, based on the phenomenal oyster-shell middens formed at Damariscotta more than a thousand years ago. However, when we think of these natives not just as foragers but as forager-traders, a different picture emerges. The shell- heaps speak of mass-production and specialization; of surpluses generated for the purpose of trade. From a survival point of view, everybody wins when

groups exchange diverse foods and durable goods; therefore, there is strong motivation to at least tolerate other cultures long enough to come together at a marketplace, just as different species tolerate each other at a waterhole in the desert. Corn, beans, dried fruits, nutmeats, smoked fish and oysters, and furs were all non- perishable assets that provided protection against winter, and to possess all of these was to be secure. Once kettles, knives, and muskets were added to the mix by Europeans after 1550 AD, the impetus to trade was even greater; and by 1650, when disease and Euro-economics had reduced the natives to beaver-trapping serfdom, trading was the only way to stay alive.

Prior to the arrival of Europeans and their diseases, ample resources existed in the Kennebec-Penobscot archipelago to ensure one's survival. Many writers have described the various ways that Indians used to derive food, shelter and medicine from the land. However, perhaps it is worth re-emphasizing one important condition of their existence: They were mobile enough to follow the resources around the landscape throughout the seasons. Their territories may have been fixed, but the people were by no means fixed within their territories. Unfettered by the mountains of belongings or notions of private personal property that limit our travels today, the Wawenocks and others like them ranged the landscape as their needs, and even their whims, dictated.

Our modern mindset is often vexed by this; we struggle to determine the Bashabas's residence, as though he might have been found at 150 Cedar Street on Indian Island. In fact, the earliest records are littered with references to empty villages; "non-sightings" if you will. The people could just as easily be at Farmington Falls (Amaseconti) as at Merrymeeting Bay; it all depended on what was in season. Thus it could happen that the same point of land (Castine) where Champlain saw nothing in September of 1604 could present, in November of 1611, "the finest assemblage of savages" that Father Biard ever saw: 300 natives, 80 canoes and a boat, and eighteen longhouses. The Indian's bioregion *was* his home, and it had many different rooms.

That said, we also know that there were some fixed village locations. Palisadoed forts are described throughout the Maritime Peninsula— at Saco, Little Swan Island in the Kennebec, Indian Island in the Penobscot, Chkoudon's village at the mouth of the Saint John, Membertou's at Port Royal, and others. These village locations were not always easily found from the water; the 1607 Popham expedition had to walk "neare a league" from the upper Kennebec's banks to reach the village that Sabenaw led them to. Were these Kennebecs just more timid than the Sacos, whose village Champlain easily saw from the shore, or was there a more compelling reason for their secrecy? Did it take almost a century of European influences to destabilize the Kennebecs' world, or did such defensive needs arise much earlier? Perhaps the need for security goes all the way back to the beginnings of trade. As in nature, any surplus of resources always needs to be defended, or trade will degenerate into outright taking by force. All indications are that conflicts of this nature were common long before contact, and were perhaps aggravated by the insistence on vengeance that all European observers noted in America's natives.

Located as they were at a favorable location for trade, the Kennebecs and Penobscots must have enjoyed all the benefits that could be drawn from the land and sea from Virginia to Newfoundland. Moreover, they commanded what was arguably the greatest concentration of natural resources north of Chesapeake Bay. Their shared interest in defending this area, together with the high degree of overlap in their culture and language, gave them ample reason to intermarry, trade, and live in peace with each other. Perhaps by 1500 AD they had collectively created the place known to Europeans as Arambeck or Norumbega, a flourishing trade center in the heart of a rich ecosystem.

I mention both names because each may relate to a different river—the Norumbega of early maps usually shows an area corresponding to the mouth of the Penobscot, but even earlier European references are to Ornbega, Aranbega, and Arambeck, which are all very close phonetic matches to a word—"Rimbegui"—used by Father Biard on three separate occasions, when referring to the Kennebec River. Whether there was such a name, or whether some translator simply misread his handwriting and made Kini to be Rim, remains to be ascertained.

Yet another intriguing possibility is that the –bega root, meaning an expanse of quiet water, refers to Merrymeeting Bay, and that "Norumbega" resolves to narra (above) bega, and "Aranbega" to aranm (below or under) bega—in other words, it's plausible that the Kennebec was the whole shooting match. Father Rasles's dictionary supports the above analysis; and for that matter, many of the earliest maps (such as *Norumbega et Virginia* by Cornelius Wytfliet in 1597) show a conspicuous forking of the "River of Norumbega"—might this not represent the parting of the Kennebec and Androscoggin, rather than the Penobscot?

And so...

I feel that my four guides to the past have led me on a fruitful journey, and that I have come to know the Wawenocks, or at least know them better, over the past year of searching. These people, whether you call them Wawenocks, Sheepscots, or Kennebecs, occupied the best habitat in New England; a land so rich that they could be justifiably scornful of the sedentary agricultural lifestyles that the European settlers espoused. The essence of their existence was the *place*; formed when two continents collided, dovetailing the land and sea so intricately that almost every kind of beast, bird or fish found a home here. Richness like this attracts people, and as fast as one culture settles in another one is knocking at the door, and a different kind of collision looms.

However, just as continental collisions melt, bend and reform the land, so do cultural collisions replace two old orders with a new one. The canoe allowed the Abenakis to travel east down the Kennebec and appropriate this rich coast for their own use, absorbing bits of the previous tenants' culture and driving the rest of it farther east or south; though in the oldest place names we still see hints of those here before them. They held their resource-rich territory in the same manner that all other cultures do, using diplomacy, economic savvy, and violence as necessary. The next cultural collision shook the whole continent, and drove most of the Abenaki culture back towards its origin. I say *most*; if that seems curious, just glance at any map of Maine—the Abenakis are still with us in hundreds of place names.

Perhaps future study of the area between Waterville and Rockland will confirm what I now believe, which is that these people (at the period of European contact) were the power elite of not just the Kennebec River, but of the whole Abenaki nation; and that they considered the Penobscots to be their brothers, and were largely at peace with them. The Bashabas of 1605 was the figurehead of the Abenaki nation, presiding from its all-important eastern front as the Europeans and Micmacs pressed against them; and that role transcended the question of being Kennebec, Penobscot, or something halfway between. Where did he live? Draw a triangle from Schoodic to Sheepscot to Old Town; that was his bioregion, that was where his nation's agenda was being played out, and that was where he lived. To require a more specific address is to undervalue the social organization of the Abenakis, and to underestimate the geopolitical scope of the issues he dealt with.

Today, the Wawenocks are almost gone. I say almost, because even though their bloodlines are long extinguished or mixed with others in Canada, their names live on here. The places they lived, and the great men who led them, are still known to us. I can jump in my rowboat at Owl's Head and in ten minutes time be holding a clamshell that was shucked by Wawenock hands five hundred years ago. I can climb Mount Megunticook, look off to the east towards Blue Hill, and imagine a fleet of canoes crossing Penobscot Bay by way of See-bur-essek, the "small waterway place", that we know today as the Fox Island Thorofare. Best of all, I can still hear their voices in the names of local places—Senebec, Arrowsic, Pachipscut, Matamiscowte, Winnegance, Netakamikus, and many more. Names like these, some of them still on today's maps, and others collecting dust in archives or floating in cyberspace, are the oral legacy that passed from the Wawenocks' culture to ours. They are worth preserving, and teaching to our children.

Appendix D

Lescarbot's Poem

Marc Lescarbot. (1609). *Les Muses de la Nouvelle France: à Monseigneur le Chancellier.* Chez Jean Millot, Paris.

This document contains the scanned text of Marc Lescarbot's poem. It is compiled here along with the title page for easy reading. This entire text is available on the internet at:

Early Canadiana Online (www.canadiana.org)
395 Wellington St Room 468
Ottawa ON K1A 0N4
Canada
613 235-2628
info@canadiana.org

This is a direct link to the title page. The poem is on pages 44 – 59 of the original document.

http://www.canadiana.org/ECO/PageView?id=5cfb3ed9fcedb8af&display=36653+0003

An English translation of this poem follows in the next appendix.

LES MVSES

DE LA NOVVELLE
FRANCE.

A MONSEIGNEVR
LE CHANCELLIER.

Avia Pieridum peragro loca nullius antè
Trita solo ----

A PARIS

Chez IEAN MILLOT, sur les degrez de
la grand' salle du Palais.

M. D. C. IX.

Avec privilege du Roy.

des anciennes Perſanes, leur remit le cœur au ventre, &
ſem blablement le pere dudit decedé, lequel impuiſſant
de ſes membres s'y eſtoit fait porter. En quoy ſe reco-
nioit combien ce peuple eſt âpre à la vengeance & d'un
cœur vrayment noble, de ne pouvoir ſouffrir vne injure impunie. *Membertou* deſiroit fort d'eſtre aſſiſté de
quelque nombre de François en cette guerre, mais il
n'y eut moyen d'y ſatisfaire, pource que nous eſtions
preſſez de reprendre la route de France. Neantmoins ſi
firent-ilz bonne diligence. Car ilz furent de retour le
neufiéme d'Aouſt deux jours auparavant le deparé
dudit Sieur de Poutrincourt, lequel dans vne chaloupe
vint lui neufiéme au long de la côte trouver la navire
qui nous attendoit au port de *Campſeau*, diſtant du Port
Royal (où nous avons hiverné) de 150. lieuës.

L'Au-
theur
veut dire
que cette
hiſtoire
n'eſt point
fabuleuſe.

E ne chante l'orgueil du geant *Eriarée*,
Ni du fier *Rodomont* la fureur enivrée
Du ſang dont il a teint préſque tout l'V-
niders.
Ni comme il a forcé les pivots des enfers:
Ie chante *Membertou*, & l'heureuſe victoire
Qui lui acquit naguere vne immortelle gloire
Quãd il joncha de morts les chãps Armouchiquois
Pour la cauſe venger du peuple Souriquois.
   Entre ces peuples-ci vne antique diſcorde
Fait que bien rarement l'un à l'autre s'accorde,
Et ſi par fois entre eux ſe traite quelque paix,
Cette paix ſe peut dire vn attrappe-niais.
,, Car oncques le renart ne changea ſa nature,
,, Et de garder la foy l'homme double n'eut cure.
Ceci n'a pas long temps ſe coneut par effect
Aux depens de celui qui me donne ſujet
De dire qui a meu *Membertou* & ſa ſuite
De faire pour ſa mort ſi ſanglante pourſuite.

Ce fut Panoniac (car tel eſtoit ſon nom) Sujet de la guerre.
Sauvage entre les ſiens jadis de grand renom.
Cetui cuidant avoir faite bonne alliance
Avecque ces mechans, alloit ſans deffiance
Parmi eux converſant: mémes il les aidoit
Bien ſouvent du plus beau des biens qu'il poſſedoit.
Mais pour cela la gent à mal faire addonnée
Sa mauvaiſe façon n'a point abandonnée.
Car ce Panoniac il n'y a pas dix mois
Les eſtant allé voir (pour la derniere fois)
Portant en ſes vaiſſeaux marchandiſes diverſes
Pour en accommoder ces nations perverſes,
Eux qui ſont de tout temps avides de butin, Armouchiquois ſont larrons.
Sans aucune merci aſſomment leur voiſin;
Pillent ce qu'il avoit & en font le partage.
Les compagnons du mort ſe ſauvans à la nage
Le cachent pour vn temps à l'ombre d'vn rocher,
N'oſans de ces mâtins à la chaude approcher.
Car, pour en dire vray, la meurtriere cohorte
Eſtoit contre ceux-ci & trop grande & trop forte.
Mais comme de Phœbus les chevaux haraſſez
Se furent retirez ſous les eaux tout laſſez,
Ces enragés en fin abandonnans la place
Laiſſerent là le corps tué à coups de maſſe,
Lequel à la faveur de la ſombreuſe nuit
Soudain par ſes amis fut enlevé ſans bruit,
Et mis, non, comme nous, en depoſt à la terre,
D'en vn coffre de bois, ni au creux d'vne pierre,
Ainſi il fut embaumé à la forme des Rois Les Sauvages conſervent les corps morts.
Que l'Ægypte pieuſe embaumoit autrefois.

    Le peuple Etechemin de cette mort cruelle
Receut tout le premier la mauvaiſe nouvelle,

D iij

D'où s'enfuivit vn dueil fi rempli de douleurs
Que le haut Firmament en ouït les clameurs.

Dueil des Sauuages

(Car lors que cette gent la mort des fiens lamente
Le voifinage enfemble à grans cris fe tourmente)
Mais ce ne fut ici le brayment principal,
Car quand ce pauure corps fut dans le Port Royal

Voy au ch. dern. de l'Hiftoire de la Nouv. France.

Aux fiens reprefenté, Dieu fçait cōbien de plaintes,
De cris, de hurlemens, de funebres complaintes.
Le ciel en gemiffoit, & les prochains côtaux
Sembloient par leurs echoz endurer tous ces maux:
Les épeffes foréts, & la riviere méme
Témoignoient en avoir vne douleur extreme.
Huit jours tant feulement fe pafferent ainfi
Pour refpect du François qui fe rit de ceci.

Les fervices rendus à l'ombre vagabonde
(Qui du lac Stygieux a desja paffé l'onde)
Et au corps là prefent, le Prince Souriquois

Exclama-tion ef-froyable de Mem-bertou.

Commence à s'écrier d'vne effroyable voix:
Quoy doncques, Membertou (dit-il en fon langage)
Laira-il impuni vn fi vilain outrage?
Quoy doncques Membertou aura-il point raifon
De l'excés fait aux fiens & méme à fa maifon?
Verrai-ie point jamais éteinte cette race
Qui de moy & des miens la ruine pourchaffe?
Non, non, il ne faut point cette injure fouffrir.
Enfans, c'eft à ce coup qu'il nous convient mourir,
Ou bien par nôtre bras envoyer dix mille ames
De cette gent maudite aux eternelles flammes.

Voy l'Hif-toire de la Nouv. France li. 2.c.43.

Nous avons prés de nous des François le fupport
A qui ces chiens ici ont fait vn méme tort.
Cela eft refolu, il faut que la campagne
Au fang de ces meurtriers dans peu de tēps fe baigne.

Actaudin *mon cher fils, & ton frere puifné*
Qui n'avez vôtre pere oncques abandonné,
Il faut ores s'armer de force & de courage,
Sus, allez vitement l'vn fuivant le rivage
D'ici au Cap-Breton, *l'autre à travers les bois*
Vers les Canadiens, *& les* Gafpeïquois
Et les Etechemins *annoncer cette injure,*
Et dire à nos amis que tous ie les conjure
D'en porter dedans l'ame vn vif reffentiment,
Et pour l'effet de ce qu'ilz s'arment promptement
Et me viennent trouver prés de cette riviere,
Où ilz fçavent que i'ay plantée ma banniere.

Membertou *n'eut pluftot à fes gens commandé,*
Que chacun prent fa route où il eftoit mandé,
Et fit en peu de temps fi bonne diligence,
Qu'il fembla devancer vn poftillon de France,
Si bien qu'au renouveau voici de toutes parts
Venir à Membertou *jeunes & vieux foudars*
Tous à ceci pouffez d'efperances non vaines
Souz l'affeuré guidon des braves Capitaines
Chkoudun, *&* Oagimont, Memembouré,
     Kichkou,
Meffamoet, Ouzagat, *&* Anadabijou,
Medagoet, Oagimech, *& avec eux encore*
Celui qui plus que tous l' Armouchiquois *abherre,*
C'eft Panoniagues, *qui a occafion*
De procurer mal-heur à cette nation
Pour de dur fouvenir de la mort de fon frere.
Quand tout fut arrivé, de cette mort amere
Il fallut de nouveau recommencer le dueil,
Et le corps decedé mettre dans le cercueil.

Chofe
merveil-
leufe de
faire fi
lōgs voya-
ges par
les bois.

                    C iij

Il n'y a que les Sagamos qui portent barbe entre les Sauuages

Le barbu Membertou lors prenant la parole:
Vous sçavez, ce dit-il, ô peuple benevole,
Le motif qui vous a conduit jusques ici,
C'est ce corps que voyés massacré sans merci,
De qui le sang versé vous demande vengeance.
Sans que par long discours ie vous en face instance.

Harãgue de Membertou. Membertou pouvoit avoir ouï cela de nous.

Et comme és siecles vieux quand au peuple Romain
Fut montré de Cæsar le massacre inhumain,
Tout à l'instant émeu d'vne ardente colere
Il voulut reparer ce cruel vitupere
Contre les assassins (ainsi que i'ay appris
Qu'il est mentionné és anciens écrits)
Ainsi vous devez tous à ce spectacle étrange
Estre émeus du desir de garder la loüange.
Que nos antecesseurs nous ont mis en depos,
Et par laquelle ilz sont maintenant en repos,
N'ayans point estimé estre dignes de vivre.
Sans de leurs ennemis les injures poursuivre.

Effect de la harangue.

    A ces mots vn chacun au combat animé
Sent un feu de vengeance en son cœur allumé,
Et eussent volontiers contre cette canaille,
(S'il y eut eu moyen) lors donné la bataille,
Mais il falloit premier le corps ensevelir,
Et du dernier devoir les œuvres accomplir.
Cette grand' troupe donc de douleur affollée

Funerailles.

A conduit le corps mort dedans son Mausolée,
En faisant sacrifice à Vulcan de ses biens

Matachiaz ce sont brasselets, carquans & joyaux

Masse, arcs, fleches, carquois, petun, couteaux & chiens,
Matachiaz aussi, & la pelleterie
Que d'epargne il avoit quand il perdit la vie.
Mais quant aux assistans, chacun à son pouvoir
Lui fit, devotieux, l'accoustumé devoir.

Qui donne des Castors, qui des couteaux, des roses,   *Presens*
Armes, Matachiaz, & maintes autres choses.   *faits aux*
Puis ferment le sepulchre, & laissent reposer   *morts.*
Celui duquel ilz vont la querelle épouser.
Le ciel qui bien-souvent les mal-heurs nous presage,   *Presages.*
Avoit auparavant par un triste presage,
Témoigné les effets de cette guerre ici,
Car ayant un long temps refrongné son sourci,
Il fit voir maintefois des torches allumées,
Des lances, des dragons, des flambantes armées.
Ainsi s'en va la flotte avec intention
De vaincre, ou de mourir à cette occasion,
Laissans de leurs enfans & femmes la tutele
A nous, qui en avons rendu conte fidele.

Quand des Armouchiquois les rives ils ont veu   *Armou-*
Ce peuple deffiant les a tot reconeu.   *chiquois*
Soudain les messagers volent par la campagne,   *aux alar-*
Et sonnent du cornet sur chacune montagne   *mes.*
Pour le monde avertir d'estre au guet, & veiller
Avant que l'ennemi les vienne reveiller.
Peuples de tous côtez à grand' troupes s'amassent
Tant qu'en nombre les flots de la mer ilz surpassent.
Mais pourtant Membertou ne s'epouvante point
Car il sçait le moyen de prendre bien à point.
L'ennemi, qui tout fier, voyant son petit nombre,
Se promet l'enlever si-tot que la nuit sombre
Aura dessus la terre étendu son rideau.
Membertou cependant approche son vaisseau   *Voy la fi-*
Du port de Choüacoet, ou la troupe adversaire   *gure de ce*
L'attendoit de pié-quoy, pour sçavoir quelle affaire   *Port en la*
Vers eux le conduisoit: mais il avoit laissé   *Charte*
Ses gens derriere un roc, & s'estoit avancé,   *geogra-*
   phique.

D iiij

Afin de reconoitre & le port & la terre
Qu'il vouloit ruiner par l'effort de la guerre.

Pourpar-
ler entre
deux en-
nemis.

He, he, ce fut le cri duquel il appella
Tout ce peuple attentif qui ferme attendoit là.
Yo, yo, fut répondu. Puis apres il demande
S'il pourroit seurement & sa petite bende
Traiter avecques eux, & amiablement
Vuider le different qui a si longuement
L'vn & l'autre troublé & reduit en ruine
Tandis que l'appetit de vengeance les mine
Et leur mange le cœur. Eux cuidans attrapper
Celui qui plus fin qu'eux les venoit entrapper,

Répense
des Ar-
mouchi-
quois.

Disent que librement de la riue il s'approche,
Et ses gens qu'il auoit laissé deuers la roche,
Qu'ilz n'ont plus grand desir que de voir vne paix
Solidement entre eux établie a jamais,
Afin qu'eux qui des Francs ont bonne conoissance
Leur facent part des biens dont ils ont abondance.
Et se puissent ainsi l'un l'autre secourir
Sans plus d'orenauant l'vn sur l'autre courir.

Accepta-
tion d'of-
fres.

Membertou reçoit l'offre, & quant & quãt otage,
Envoyant vn des siens par échange au rivage,
Puis recule en arriere, & va ses gens revoir
Qu'il trouve grandement desireux de sçavoir
En quelle volonté ces peuples ci estoient,
Et si à quelque paix encliner ilz sembloient.
Le Prince Souriquois ses suppots abordant
D'vn visage joyeux il les va regardant,
Disant, Ilz sont à nous: la farce s'en va faite:
C'est demain qu'il faut voir cette troupe defaite:
Et leur conte amplement ce qui s'estoit passé,
Et comment ilz s'estoient l'vn l'autre caresse.

Au surplus (ce dit-il) pensons de les surprendre,
Et en ce fait ici gardons de nous meprendre.
Quand nous sommes partis le conseil a esté
De leur faire present des biens qu'avons porté.
Et avec eux troquer de nôtre marchandise,
A fin que l'homme feint, soit pris en sa feintise.
Nous irons donc par mer la moitié seulement:
Le surplus en deux parts ira secrettement
Rengeant le long du bois en bonne sentinelle
Tant que, le temps venu, ma trompe les appelle:
Lors ils viendront charger, & nous seconderont,
Et tant que durera le jour ilz frapperont,
Sans merci, sans faveur, & sans misericorde,
Afin qu'ici de nous long-temps on se recorde.
Outre nôtre querele il y a du butin,
Ils ont du blé, des noix, de la vigne & du lin,
Tous ces biens sont à nous si nous avons courage,
Et si voulons avoir leurs femmes au pillage
Nous les aurons aussi.   Il estoit nuit encor
Et le clair ciel estoit tout brillant de clous d'or,
Quand Membertou (de qui l'esprit point ne repose)
A prendre son quartier tout son peuple dispose,
Et ceux-là qu'il conoit à la course legers
Il les fait essaier les terrestres dangers.
Ainsi Memembourré dispos à la poursuite
Est fait le general d'une troupe d'elite,
Medagoet d'autrepart hardi aux grans exploits
Choisit de tout le camp les plus forts & adroits.
Mais le grand Sagamos † pour tendre sa banniere
Attendit que l'Aurore eust épars sa lumiere
En tout son horizon: & lors que le Soleil
Eut esté reconduit au lieu de son reveil

Marginal notes:

Conseil pour surprendre l'ennemi.

Fruits de la terre Armouchiquoise.

Dispositiō pour attaquer l'ennemi.

† Capitaine, Duc, Roy.

Il met la voile au vent, tirant droit à la place
Où desja l'attendoit cette grand' populace,
Où estant arrivé, partie de ses gens
A descendre apres lui se montrent diligens.
Il saluë les chefs de cette compagnie,
Entre autres Olmechin, Marchin & leur mesgnie.

Mauuais appast.

Puis offre les presens dont i'ay fait mention,
Lesquels furent receus en iubilation,
C'estoient robbes, chappeaux, & chausses, & chemises,
Mais quand il fallut voir les autres marchandises,
Parmi les fers pointus, poignars, & coutelas,
Des trompes y avoit dont on ne sçavoit pas
L'usage, ni la fin du mal qu'elles couvoient.
Les autres cependant dans le bois attendoient
Soigneusement l'appel qui avoit esté dit,
Quand Membertou voulant étaller son credit,

Ruse de Membertou.

Il convoque ce peuple embouchant vne trompe,
Et trompant, les trompeurs trompeusement il trompe.
Car tout en vn instant lui qui n'avoit point d'armes
Oyant les siens venir feignit estre aux alarmes,
Et se trouvant garni de masses, & poignars,
D'arcs, fleches, coutelas, de picques, & de dars,
Il en saisit ses gens, & chacun d'eux commence
Sur l'heure à chamailler sans grande resistence.
Ils en font grand massacre, & cependant du bois
Arrive le surplus criant à haute voix

C'est, comme qui diroit Où est-ce.

He, he, oukchegouïa, & parmi la melée
Se voit incontinent cette troupe melée.
L'Armouchiquois voyant que de lui c'estoit fait,
S'il ne remedioit promptement à son fait,
A ce dernier besoin pense de se defendre
Plustot qu'à la merci de ceux ici se rendre.

Ils eſtoient la pluſpart ja de conteaux armez
Que de porter au col ilz ſont accouſtumez,
Mais ces armes bien peu leur ſervirent a l'heure.
Car Membertou muni d'vne armure plus ſeure,
D'vn bouclier de bois dur, & d'vn bon coutelas,
Ainſi que le trenchant d'vne faux met à bas
L'honneur des beaux épics: ſon epée de même
Moiſſonnoit l'ennemi d'vne rigueur extreme.
Les autres tranſportez de pareille fureur,
Suivans le train du chef, ne manquent point de cœur,
Mais rendans des grans cris & voix épouvantables,
Tuent comme fourmis ces pauvres miſerables,
Deſquels lors c'eſtoit fait s'ilz n'euſſent eu recours
Au bien qui vient par fois de tourner à rebours.
Ce peuple de tout temps addonné au pillage
Cuidoit ſur Membertou avoir tel avantage,
Que d'armes pour cette heure il ne leur fut beſoin,
Neantmoins en tout cas ils avoient eu le ſoin
D'en faire vn magazin au fond d'vne vallée,
Où la troupe fuiarde en fin s'en eſt allée.
Là chacun ſe fournir d'arcs fleches, & carquois,
De picques, de boucliers, & de maſſes de bois.
Là de tourner viſage, & d'vne face irée
Charger ſur Membertou & ſa gente enivrée
Du ſang Armouchiquois. A ce nouvel effort
Fut Panoniagués au danger de la mort
Bleſſé d'vn javelot environ la poitrine.
Chkoudun le courageux, y receut ſur l'echine
Vn coup qui l'atterra, & ſe vit en danger
(L'ennemi gaignant pié) de jamais n'en bouger.
Mais le fort Chkoudumech ſon frere, de ſa maſſe
Fendant la preſſe, fit bien-tot ſe faire place.

Sauvages
portent
vn cou-
teau pen-
du au col.
Comparaiſon.

Fuite des
Armouchiquois.

Ruſe d'iceux.

Nouveau
combat.

Pour le tirer de là : mais il y fut feru
D'un coup que lui chargea de toute sa vertu
Le cruel Olmechin. Mnesinou (dont la gloire
Par toute cette cotte est en tous lieux notoire)
Comme le plus hardi, s'efforce de son dard
Transpercer Membertou de l'une à l'autre part :
Mais le coup gauchissant par la subtile addresse
Du Prince Souriquois, a son fils il s'addresse,
Son fils Actaudinech, lequel il aime mieux
Que toutes les beautez de la terre & des cieux.
Ce coup doncques perçant le détroit de sa manche
Vite comme vn éclair lui porta dans la hanche :
Dequoy tout effrayé le Prince Membertou,

Ceci est
vne fein-
te Poeti-
que. Voy
l'Histoire
du Gou-
gou ci def-
fus liv 2.
ch. 28.

Il se remet aux jeux du monstrueux Gougou
Le duel ancien qu'en sa jeunesse tendre
Iadis son pere osa hazardeux entreprendre :
Et redoublant sa force il étendit son bras,
Et le fendit en deux de son fier coutelas.
Et comme vn chene haut abbattu de l'orage
Traine en bas quant & soy son plus beau voisinage,
Ainsi Mnesinou mort, maint des siens alentour
Alla voir de Pluton le tenebreux sejour.
L'Armouchiquois pourtant ne laisse de poursuivre,
Aimant mieux la mourir que honteusement viure
S'il arrivoit jamais que Membertou veinqueur
Leur laissat du combat l'eternel des-honneur.

Nouvel
effort des
Armou-
chiquois.

Ainsi se r'assemblans font des scares diverses
Qui à leur ennemi donnent maintes traverses.
Car jusques la encor n'avoient esté rangés,
Occasion que mal ilz s'estoient revengés.
Bessabez & Marchin ont les pointes premieres,
Qui venans attaquer avec leurs bendes fieres.

Le chef des Souriquois, vne grele de dars
En l'vn & en l'autre ôt tombé de toutes pars.
La clarté du soleil en demeure obscurcie,
Et le nombre des traits toujours se multiplie.
A cette charge ici quelques vns sont blessés
Parmi les Souriquois : mais plus de terrassés
Sont de l'autre côté : car de ceux-ci les fleches
A pointes d'os ne font de si mortelles breches
Comme de ceux qui sont plus voisins des François
Qui des pointes d'acier ont au bout de leurs bois,
Toutefois de nouveau voici nouvelle force   (force.
Qui des Membertouquois les bras, non les cœurs,
Go, go, go, c'est leur cri. Abejou, Olmechin,
Le fort Arbostembroet, & le fier Bertachin
En sont les conducteurs, qui de premiere entrée
Du vaillant Messamoet la troupe ont rencontrée
Messamoet (qui jadis humant l'air de la France
Avoit de guerroyer reconeu la science
Parmi les domestics du Seigneur de Grand-mont)
Apres mainte bricole avoit gaigné vn mont
D'où il pensoit avoir vit facile avantage
Pour mettre sans danger l'adversaire en dommage.
Mais cetui-ci rusé loin de la declina,
Et le gros escadron des Souriquois mena
Poursuivant vivement jusques dessus la greve
Où Neptune irrité à ses flots donne treve.
La Neguioadetch mere du decedé
Apres avoir long temps le combat regardé,
Voyant en desarroy de Membertou la troupe
Elle se met à terre, & sort de sa chaloupe,
Afin de donner cœur aux soldats etonnés
Qui leur premiere assiette avoient abandonnés.

Souriquois repoussez. La mere de Passniac estoit allée à la guerre.

Et comme des Perfans les meres & les femmes
Iadis voyans leurs filz & leurs marits infames
S'enfuir du Medois qui les alloit fuivant,
Courageufes foudain allerent au devant,
Sans honte leur montrer de leurs corps la partie
Par où l'homme reçoit l'entree de la vie,
Les vnes s'écrians: Quoy doncques voulez vous
Vous fauver ci dedans pour eviter les coups
De cil qui vous pourfuit? Les autres d'autre forte
Crians à leurs enfans: R'entrez dedans la porte
Du logis dans lequel vous avés eflé nés,
Ou contre l'ennemi promptement retournés.
Eux d'vn fpectacle tel fe trouvans pleins de honte,
Vn fang tout vergongneux à l'heure au front leur
Si bien que retournans leurs faces en arriere (monte,
A l'Empire Medois mirent la fin derniere.
Ainfi fit cette mere en voyant le danger
Où alloit Membertou & les fiens fe plonger.

Neguirouët fon mari ores paralytique,
Mais qui de bien combattre entendoit la pratique,
S'y eftoit fait porter: & bien reconoiffant
Le defaftre prochain qui les alloit preffant
S'il ne leur arrivoit quelque nouvelle force,
Se fait defcendre à terre, & lui-méme s'efforce
De marcher au combat afin de la mourir
S'il ne pouvoit au moins fes amis fecourir.
Etant au milieu d'eux il leur donne courage
Et les conjure tous de venger fon outrage.
Mes amis (ce dit-il) vous ne combattez point
Pour le fait feulement, helas! qui trop me point.
Il y va de l'honneur, il y va de la vie
Ces deux ici perdus, la perte en eft fuivie.

Des soupirs & regrets des femmes & enfans
De qui nos ennemis s'en iront triomphans
Tout ainsi que de nous. Ayez doncques courage,
Ie les voy ja branler: c'est ici bon presage.

Chance tournée contre les Armouchiquois.

A ces mots Membertou fait tirer les Mousquets
Qu'au partir les François lui avoient tenu prets.
Chkoudun en fait autant (car il a eu de méme
Deux Mousquets pour autāt que le François il aime)
Lesquels estoient parez pour la necessité
Comme vn dernier remede au corps debilité;
Aux coups de ces batons en voila dix par terre.
Et le reste effrayé au bruit de ce tonnerre.

Effect des coups de Mousquets.

Abejou, Chitagat, Olmechin, & Marchin
Quatre des plus mauuais de ce peuple mutin
A ce choc sont tombés. Chkoudun qui a memoire
Du coup qu'il a receu ne veut point que la gloire
En demeure au dōneur, mais d'vn trait donne-mort
Il attaque, hardi, Arbostembroet le fort,
Et presse le surplus d'vne roideur si grande
Qu'au seul bruit de son nom l'ennemi se debende.

Déroute des Armouchiquois.

Membertouchis aussi l'ainé de Membertou
A l'aile de son pere assisté de Kichkou,
Se faisant faire jour d'vn coup trois en renverse
Et ja deçà, delà, tout est à la renverse.
A cinq cens pas plus loin se trouvans Ouzagat
Et Anadabijou empechés au combat,
Ilz furent secourus par la troupe hardie
De Panoniagués, qui bien-tot fut survie
D'Oagimech & les siens; si bien qu'en peu de temps

Entiere déroute.

L'ennemi fut fauché comme l'herbe des champs.
Car sous ce qui restoit, quoy que puissant en nombre,
Ne porta gueres loin le malheureux encombre

Qui l'alloit talonnant: d'autant que Oagimont
Avec Memembouré estant au pied du mont
Que naguere i'ay dit, les fuyars attendirent,
Et valeureusement poursuivans les battirent.
Mais Oagimont s'estant eloigné de son parc,
Trop prompt, y fut blessé grievement d'vn trait d'arc.
Memébouré (trop chaud) préque en la méme sorte
L'ennemi poursuivant y eut la jambe torte,
Ce qui plusieurs en fit de leurs mains échapper,
Mais ne pewrent pourtant leur ennemi tromper.

Polyga-
mie. Car Etmeminaoet l'homme qui de six femmes
Peut, galant, appaiser les amoureuses flammes,
Et Metembroebit, Medagoet, Chichcobech,
Bituani, Penin, Actembroé, Semcoudech,
Tous vaillants champions, soldats, & Capitaines,
Acheverent du tout ces races inhumaines.

Victoire
sans perte Nais ce qui est ici digne d'étonnement,
C'est que des Souriquois n'est mort vn seulement.

    L'Armouchiquois éteint, cette armée de faite,
Membertou glorieux fit sonner la retraite,

Les bles-
sez. On trouve de blessés encores Pechkmeg,
Oupakour, Ababich, Pitagan, Chiskmeg,
Vmanuet, & Kobech, dont les playes on pense,
Tandis que du butin d'autre côté l'on pense,

Maniere
de guerir
les blessez La cure en est sommaire. Entre eux est vn devin,
(Ignorant toutefois) qu'on appelle Aoutmoin.
Cetui prognostiqueur de l'état du malade
Feint vers quelque demon pour lui faire ambassade,
Et selon sa reponse, en ceci comme en tout,
Il iuge s'il sera bien-tot mort ou debout.
Avec ce de la playe il va succant le sang,
Il la souffle, & soufflant il s'émeut tout le flanc:

                                         Ceci

Ceci fait, il applique au deſſus de la playe
Du roignon de Caſtor : & par ainſi eſſaye
(Le bendage parfait) ſon malade guerir.

 Le butin recuilli, avant que de partir
Des chefs Armouchiquois ils enlevent les têtes
Pour en faire au retour maintes joieuſes fêtes.
Ia ilz ſont à la voile, & approchent du port
Où ilz doivent donner à leurs femmes confort,
Leſquelles auſſi tot que de leur arrivée
Elles ont eu nouvelle, auſſi-tot la huée
Elles ont fait de loin, deſireuſes ſçavoir
Quel avoit eſté là de chacun le devoir.
Et en ordre marchans, qui en main vne maſſe,
Qui vn couteau trenchant (ayans toutes la face
De couleurs bigarrée) elles s'attendoient bien
Toutes ſur l'heure avoir vn Armouchiquois ſien,
Afin d'en faire tot cruelle boucherie,
Mais ſans cela convint faire leur tabagie,
Et apres le repas la danſe s'enſuivit,
Qui dura tout le jour, & qui dura la nuit,
Et toujours durera en s'écrians ſans ceſſe,
Chantans de Membertou la valeur & proüeſſe
Tant que leur eſtomach la voix leur fournira,
Ou que quelque malheur repoſer les fera.

Têtes des veincus enlevees.

Reception des victo-rieux.

Tabagie, c'eſt Fe-ſtin.

LA TABAGIE * MARINE.

COMPAGNONS, où eſt le temps
 Qu'avions nôtre paſſe-temps
 A deſcendre au plus habile
Sur le pié-ferme d'une ile,

Ceſt Bã-quet. Voy le ch. 47. ci-deſ ſus. pa. 633.

Voy le ch. Fourrageans de toutes pars
22.liv.3. Deça & delà épars
pa.882. Parmi l'epés des fueillages
Et des orgueilleux herbages
L'honneur des jeunes oiseaux
Qu'enlevions à grans troupeaux,
Le gros Tangueu, la Marmette,
Et la Mauve & la Roquette,
Ou l'Oye, ou le Cormorant,
Ou l'Outarde au corps plus grand
Ca (ce disoi-ie à la troupe)
Emplissons nôtre chaloupe
De ce oiseaux tendrelets,
Ilz valent bien des poulets.
Dieu! quelle plaisante chasse.
Amasse, garson, amasse,
Portes-en chargé ton dos,
Tu es alaigre & dispos,
Et revien tout à cette heure
Prendre pareille mesure,
Ne cessant jusques à ce
Que nous en aions assé

Voy les Car nous pourrions de cette ile
ch.2.& Fournir vne bonne ville.
7.du 2. Ie voudroy m'avoir couté
liv.pag. Vn karolus bien conté,
253.& Et estre en cet equipage
29 5. Avecque tout ce pillage
Au beau milieu de Paris,
O que i'y aurois d'amis,
Qui pour avoir pance grasse
Me suivroient de place en place.

Appendix E

Lescarbot's Poem - English Translation

Marc Lescarbot. (1609). *Les Muses de la Nouvelle France: à Monseigneur le Chancellier.* Chez Jean Millot, Paris.

This document contains the scanned text of a translation of Marc Lescarbot's poem *Les Muses de la Nouvelle France*.

The translation was done by Thomas Goetz, who was a faculty colleague of Alvin Morrison's at SUNY Fredonia (State University College). It was originally an appendix to Morrison's article [Membertou's Raid on the Chouacoet "Almouchiquois" - the Micmac Sack of Saco in 1607] for the Sixth Algonquian Conference (c. 1974).

Reprinted with permission from Alvin H. Morrison:
T H Goetz's translation accompanying A H Morrison's paper "Mem's Raid", pp 141-179 in W Cowan (ed) *PAPERS OF THE SIXTH ALGN CONF (1974)*, in CAN ETH SVC Paper No 23 (1975), Nat Mus of Man Mercury Series, Ottawa: National Museums of Canada.

THE DEFEAT OF THE ARMOUCHIQUOIS SAVAGES[1]

BY CHIEF MEMBERTOU AND HIS SAVAGE ALLIES, IN NEW FRANCE,

IN THE MONTH OF JULY, 1607

By Marc Lescarbot

In which one can recognize the ruses of war of said Savages,

    their funeral rites, and the names of several among them.

I do not sing the pride of the giant Briareus

Nor of the furious passion of the proud Rodomonte

Who has almost covered the universe with blood

Nor how he forced the gates of the underworld.

I sing of Membertou and the happy victory[2]

Which acquired for him a short time ago an immortal glory.

When he littered with dead the fields of the Armouchiquois

To avenge the Souriquois people.

Because of an ancient discord between these peoples

Rarely could they agree to get on well with one another,

And if occasionally they treat for peace,

This peace can be called a fool's trap.

"Because the Renard [fox] never changed his nature,

And the double-faced man took no heed to keep his word."

In fact, this lesson was taught these savages only recently

At the expense of the one who gives me subject

To say what moved Membertou and his followers

To undertake such a bloody pursuit for his death.

He was Panoniac (for such was his name)

Once a savage of great renown among his people.

E-2

Believing he had made a good alliance

With these wicked persons, he went unsuspectingly

To talk among them; he even aided them

Very frequently with the best of his possessions.

But for all that this people given to doing evil

Did not abandon their evil fashion of life.

Because this Panoniac ten months ago

Having gone to see them (for the last time)

Carrying in his boats some merchandise

To suit these perverse nations,

Who have always been greedy for spoils,

Without mercy they slaughter their neighbor,

Pillage what he had and divide it.

The companions of the dead man escape by swimming away and

Hide themselves for a time in the shadow of a rock

Not daring to approach on these warm mornings.

Because to tell the truth, the murderous band

Was much too large and too strong for them.

But as the over-ridden horses of Phoebus Apollo

Were drawn exhausted under the waters

These mad dogs finally abandoned the spot

Leaving there the cut up dead body

Which under cover of the dark night

Was suddenly carried away without noise by his friends,

And not put, as we are, in an earthly grave

Nor in a wooden coffin, nor in a stone hollow.

E-3

He was embalmed in the form of Kings

Whom the pious Egyptians embalmed in times past.

    The Etechemin people are the first

To receive the bad news of this cruel murder,

Whence followed a mourning so full of loud woes

That the high Heaven heard its clamor

(Because when these people lament the death

Of one of their own the people of these parts make

Strange clamors many days together.)

But this was not the principal mourning,

Because when this poor body was shown to his people

At Port-Royal, God knows how many cries,

Howlings, and funereal plaints there were.[3]

The air was filled with wails, and the nearby hills

Seemed by their echoes to endure all these ills:

The thick forests, and even the river

Gave evidence of being in extreme sadness.

Only eight days were spent in this fashion

Out of respect for the French who made light of this.

    Service paid to the wandering spirit

(Who has already passed the Styx)

And to the body present there, Prince Souriquois

Starts to cry out in a frightful voice:

What then, Membertou (he said in his language)

Will he leave unpunished such a vicious outrage?

What then, Membertou will not have satisfaction

For the excesses against his own and even his house?

E-4

Shall I never see extinguished this race

Who of mine and myself pursue the ruin?

No, no, one must not put up with this insult.[4]

Children, it is proper for us to die for such a blow,

Or else by our arm to send ten thousand souls

Of this accursed people to the fires of hell.

We have close to us the support of the French

To whom these dogs have done a similar wrong.

It is resolved, it is necessary that the countryside

Soon be bathed in the blood of these murderers.

Actaudin my dear son, and your youngest brother

Who have never once abandoned your father,

It is now necessary to arm yourselves with force and courage,

Now then, go quickly one following the shore,

From here to Cap Breton, the other through the woods

Towards the Canadians and the Gaspeiquois,

And the Etechemins to announce this insult,

And say to our friends that I beseech them all

To carry in their souls a spirited resentment,

With the result that they arm themselves promptly

And come to find me near this river,

Where they know I have planted my banner.

Membertou had no sooner commanded his people[5]

Than each took the route he was instructed to follow,

And made in a short time such good dispatch,

That they seemed to outdistance a French postilion

So well that in Spring from all directions

Young and old soldiers come to Membertou.

All drawn to him not by unreal hopes

Under the assured guidons of the brave Captains

Chkoudan, Oagimont, Mememboure, Kich'kou,

Messamoet, Ouzagat, and Anadabijou,

Medagoet, Oagimech and among them

The one who more than all others the Armouchiquois abhor.

He is Panoniaques, who has the chance

To bring misfortune to this nation

For the bitter memory of his brother's death.

When all had arrived, of this cruel death

It was necessary to start the mourning over again

And to put the body of the deceased in a coffin.

The bearded Membertou then started to speak:[6]

You know, he said, O benevolent people

The reason which has brought you here,

It is this body massacred without mercy which you have seen

Whose spilled blood asks for revenge,

Without my making long representations to you for it.

And as in centuries past when to the Roman people

Was shown the inhumanly massacred Caesar

(Membertou was able to have heard this from us.)[7]

All were moved immediately with an ardent anger.

They wished to redress this cruel vituperation

Against the assassins (as I have learned it is

mentioned in ancient writings).

Thus you must all by this strange sight

E-6

Be moved with the desire to keep the praise

That our ancestors have put in our trust,

And as a result of which they are now in peace,

Not having esteemed themselves worthy of living

Without having pursued their enemies for their insults.

At these words each felt moved to combat;

Each felt the fire of revenge ignited in his heart,

And would have willingly against the scoundrels

(If possible) thus joined battle,

But it was first necessary to bury his body,

And to accomplish the required last rites.

This great band thus maddened with sadness

Lead the dead body to its mausoleum,

And making sacrifice to Vulcan of his goods,

Bows, arrows, quivers, knives, and dogs

Matachias[8] also and his skins

All that he had saved when he lost his life.

But as for the mourners, each within his power

Paid him, devotedly, the accustomed duty.

Some cover him with beaver skins, some with knives, roses,

Weapons, trinkets, and many other things.

Then close the coffin, and allow to rest

The one whose quarrel they have just espoused.

The sky which very often warns us of misfortune,

Beforehand had by an ill omen,

Testified to the effects of this war here,

Because having frowned a long time,

It revealed many a time lighted torches,

Spears, dragons, flaming armies.

Thus went the fleet with the intention

Of vanquishing, or of dying on this occasion

Leaving the guardianship of their children and wives

To us, who took faithful care of them.

When they saw the shores of the Armouchiquois,

This wary people recognized them at once.

Suddenly messangers travel fast throughout the country,

And sound horns on each mountain

To warn everyone to be on the watch and to stand by

Before the enemy comes to awaken them.

Peoples from every direction gather in large bands

So numerous that they surpass the waves of the sea.

But still Membertou does not take fright,

Because he knows well how to take at the right moment

The enemy, who so proud, seeing his small band,

Promises themselves to do away with it as soon as the dark,

Shall have spread its curtain over the earth.

Membertou however draws his boat near

To the port of Chouacoet, where the adversary band

Was waiting for him with curiosity, to know what business

Brought him to them: but he had left

His people behind a rock, and had advanced

To reconnoiter the port and the terrain

That he wished to ruin by war.

He, he, this was the cry with which he called

E-8

All the alert people who were firmly waiting there,

Yo, yo was the answer. Then, after he asks

If he and his small band could safely

Treat with them and amicably

Settle the difference which for so long

Held each of them in endless war,

And ruined each others land.

They wildly believe to catch by surprise[9]

The one who shrewder than those he came to entrap,

Tell him he may freely approach the shore,

And his people that he had left near the rock,

That they have no greater desire than to see a peace

Solidly established between them forever,

So that they who know the French so well

May share the goods which they have in abundance,

And thus be able to succor one another

Without henceforth pursuing each other.

Membertou receives the offer and as a hostage

Sends one of his own in exchange to the shore.

Then he draws back and goes to see his people,

Whom he finds greatly desirous of knowing

What the will of these peoples was

And if they seemed inclined to some sort of peace.

Prince Souriquois approaching his followers

With a joyous face comes to them saying,

They are ours: the farce will take place,

Tomorrow we must see this band defeated:

And he gives them a full account of what happened,

And how they had greeted one another.

After all (he says) let us think of surprising them

And in this respect let us not make a mistake.

When we left the plan was

To make them a present of the goods we brought,

And to exchange our goods with them.

So that the deceitful man may be caught in his deceit,

Only half of us will go by sea:

The rest in two groups will go secretly

Spreading throughout the woods on sentry duty

Until the moment when my horn calls them:

Then they shall attack and come to our support,

And as long as the day shall last they will strike,

Without pity, without kindness, and without mercy,

So that here we shall be spoken of for a long time to come.

In addition to our quarrel there are some spoils,

They have wheat, nuts, vines, linseed,

All these goods will be ours if we are courageous,

And if we wish to sack their women

They will also be ours. It was still night

And the clear sky was brilliant with golden studs,

When Membertou (whose mind never rested)

Goes to his quarters and gives his people their assignments,

Those whom he knows to be quick runners

He tests with terrestrial dangers.

Thus Memembourre suited for pursuit

E-10

Is made the general of an elite band,

Medaqoet on the other hand brave in great feats of arms

Chose the strongest and the most skillful from the entire camp.

But the great Chief before raising his banner

Waited until Dawn had scattered its light

On all the horizon: and when the Sun

Had been escorted to the place of its waking

He sets sail, heading straight to the place

Where a great gathering of people was already waiting for him,

When having arrived, some of his people

Are anxious to follow him.

He greets the chiefs of this party,

Among them Olmechin, Marchin, and their households.

Then he offers the presents which I mentioned,

Which he offers as a mark of his esteem.[10]

There were dresses, hats, shoes, and shirts,

But when it was time to see the other goods,

Among the spears, daggers, and cutlasses,

There were some horns, of which they did not know

The use, nor the evil end they concealed.

The others, however, were in the woods

Carefully waiting for the planned signal,

When Membertou wishing to show his prestige

Calls his people by blowing a horn,

And in trumpeting, triumphantly deceives the deceivers.

Because in an instant he who had no arms

Hearing his people come he pretends to be alarmed

Finding himself provided with axes, knives,

Bows, arrows, swords, picks, and darts,

He attacks these people, and each of them begin

At once to defend themselves without great success.

They massacre many of them, meanwhile from the woods

The reinforcements arrive screaming:

He, he oukcheqouia,[11] and in the conflict

Soon find themselves mingled.

The Armouchiquois seeing that it was all over for them

If they did not promptly put their trouble right

Think of the need to defend themselves

Rather than of placing themselves at their mercy here.

They were for the most part armed with knives

Which they were accustomed to wear around their necks,

But these weapons were of little use at this time.

Because Membertou equipped with good armor

With a shield of hardwood and a good cutlass

Just as the swing of a scythe lays low

Honor in fine epics: his sword likewise

Reaped the enemy with extreme rapacity.

The others carried away with a like ardor

Following the chief's pace, do not lack courage

But with cries[12] and frightful voices

Kill these poor wretches like ants.

So that it was all over for them

If they did not find some way to reverse the situation.

These people who always loved pillage

Believed their advantage over Membertou so great

That there was no need of arms for this meeting,

Nevertheless had taken care just in case

To store an armory at the bottom of a valley,

Where the fleeing band finally went.

There each one armed himself with bows, arrows, and quivers,

With picks, shields, and wooden maces.

There they turn around and with angry faces

Charge Membertou and his people inebriated

With the blood of the Armouchiquois. In this counterattack

Panoniagues was in danger of dying

Wounded in the chest by a javelin.

Chkoudun the courageous, received on the spine

A blow which almost crushed him and saw himself in danger

Of never moving (the enemy was gaining ground).

But the strong Chkoudumech' his brother, with his body

Forcing his way through the crowd, soon made room

To take him out of there: but he was beaten

By a blow struck by the cruel Olmechin

Which taxed all his valor. Mnesinou (whose glory

Throughout these parts is well known)

As the boldest, strives with his spear

To pierce Membertou through:

But the blow dodged with subtle adroitness

By Prince Souriquois, to his son it directs itself,

His son Actaudinech' whom he loves more

Than all the beauty of the earth and sky.

E-13

This blow having pierced his sleeve

As quickly as a flash of lightning struck him in the hip:

Completely startled by this Prince Membertou

Recalled the eyes of the monstrous Gougou[13]

And the ancient duel that in his tender youth

His father once dared to undertake,

And redoubling his force he stretched out his arm,

And cleaved him in two with his proud cutlass.

And like a tall oak blown down by a storm

Drags down with it all the best in its neighborhood

So the dead Mnesinou fell, surrounded by many of his followers,

Went to see the sombre region of Pluto.

But the Armouchiquois do not allow themselves to be chased,

Preferring to die there than to live shamefully

If it ever happened that Membertou, victor,

Eternally dishonored them in this combat.

Thus reassembling themselves they make some attacks

And give their enemies many a set-back.

Because until then they had still not organized

For this reason they had badly revenged themselves.

Bessabes and Marchin, who have the first blows,

Come to attack with their proud bands

The Souriquois chief, a hail of arrows

Falls on both sides from every direction.

The sun's brightness remains obscured,

The number of arrows continually increasing.

In this attack some of the Souriquois

E-14

Are wounded: but there are more

Laid low on the other side: because their arrows

With heads of bone, do not make as mortal a wound

As those used by the neighbors of the French

Which have steel tips at the end of their wooden shafts.

Yet once more here is a new force

Which tries the arms, not the hearts, of the Membertouquois.

Go, go, go, is their cry, Abejou, Olmechin,

The strong Argostembroet, and the proud Bertachin

Are the leaders of it, who in their first encounter

Met the forces of the valiant Messamoet.

Messamoet (who once breathed the air of France

Had learned the knowledge of warfare

Among the domestics of the Lord de Grandmont)

After many a skirmish had gained the hill

From which he thought he had an easy advantage

To injure his adversary without danger to himself.

But this crafty foe stayed far from there,

And lead the main squadron of Souriquois

Who followed briskly to just above the shore

Where twice a day the tide rises.

There Nequioadetch' mother of the deceased,

After having watched the combat for a long time,

Seeing Membertou's followers in disarray

Comes to land and leaves her long-boat,

To give heart to the astonished warriors

Who had abandoned their first stable position.

And like those Persian mothers and wives

Of old seeing their infamous sons and husbands

Fleeing from the Medes who were following them,

Courageously went to the front suddenly,

Without shame to show them the part of the body

From which man receives his entry to life,

Some crying "What then, do you want

To save yourself in here to avoid the blows

Of those who chase you? Others in another way

Crying to their children: Return to the door

Of the dwelling place in which you were born,

Or return quickly against the enemy.

Finding themselves full of shame before such a spectacle,

The blood of shame now mounts to their faces

So well that in turning around

They put an end to the Empire of the Medes.

Thus did this mother in seeing the danger into which

Membertou and his followers were going to plunge themselves.

Neguiroet her husband now paralytic,

But who understood the practice of how to fight well

Had himself carried there: and well recognizing

The impending disaster which was going to beset them

If some new force did not arrive,

Had himself lowered to the ground, and himself tries

To march to combat, in order to die there

If he could not at least aid his friends.

Being in the middle of them, he gives them courage

E-16

And beseeches them all to avenge his outrage.

My friends (he said) you do not fight

Only for the fact, alas! which wounds me too much.

It is a question of honor; it is a question of life:

These two things lost, the loss is followed

By the regret and sorrow of the women and children

Of whom our enemies are going to be triumphant

As well as of us. Thus have courage,

I see them wavering there: it is a good sign.

At these words Membertou had the muskets fired

That at their departure the French had lent him.

Chkoudun does the same because he also had

Two muskets (for which he likes the French very much)

Which were prepared in case of necessity

As a last remedy for a debilitated body.

With their blows ten of them fell dead

And the noise of this thunder frightened the rest.

Abejou, Chitagat, Olmechin, and Marchin,

Four of the worst of this mutinous people,

Fell at this burst. Chkoudun who remembers

The blow he received does not wish the glory for it

To remain with the giver, but in a death dealing movement

Valourous he attacks the strong Argostembroet,

And sets on his followers with so great a severity

That at the sound of his name alone the enemy disbands.

Membertouchis as the oldest son of Membertou

Under the wing of his father assisted by Kichkou,

Gives three blows for everyone he receives.

And now here and there, everywhere the tide is turning.

Five hundred feet further away are Ouzagat,

And Anadabijou in the thick of combat.

They were aided by the brave band

Of Panoniagues, who was soon followed

By Oagimech' and his followers; so well that in a short time

The enemy was cut down like a field of grass:

Because all those who remained, although strong in numbers,

Hardly carried any further the ill-starred encounter

Which had followed on its heels: more especially as Oagimont

With Memembour staying at the foot of the hill

Where a short time ago I said, the panic-stricken waited,

And valorously pursuing fought them.

But Oagimont having assumed a distant position

Too promptly, was gravely wounded by an arrow.

Memembour (in hot pursuit) almost in the same way

Was wounded in the leg pursuing the enemy

As were several others attempting to escape from their hands

But who could not however fool their enemy.

Because Etmeminaoet the man who of six women

Can as a gallant lover appease the amorous flames,

And Metembroebit, Medagoet, Chich'cobech'

Bituani, Penin, Actembroe, Semcoudech',

All valiant champions, warriors, and captains

Completed the ruin of this inhuman race.

But what is here worthy of astonishment,

Is that not a single Souriquois died.

The Armouchiquois extinguished, their army defeated,
Membertou glorious has sounded retreat,
They find still more wounded: Pech'kmeg,
Oupakour, Ababich, Pitagan, Chich'kmeg,
Vmanuet, and Kobech', whose wounds they dress,
While they think of the spoils of the other side.[14]
The cure is improvised. Among them is a soothsayer
(Ignorant nevertheless) whose name is Aoutmoin.
A prognosticator of the state of sickness
He feigns towards some demon to be his ambassador
And according to his answer, in this as in everything else,
He judges that he will soon be dead or cured.
Thereupon from the wound he sucks blood,
He spits it out, and while spitting it out shakes his sides:
This done, he applies over the wound
The kidney of a beaver (the perfect bandage)
And thus tries to cure his patient.

The spoils gathered, before leaving
They sever the heads of the Armouchiquois chiefs
So as to make of their return a time of joyous feasting.
Now they are sailing and approach the port
Where they must give comfort to their wives,
Who as soon as they have news
Of their arrival, shout from

E-19

And marching in order, some with spiked staffs

Others with sharp knives (all having

Their faces mottled) they were all waiting

Their turn to have their own Armouchiquois,

To butcher him cruelly.

But without that agreed to feast

And after the banquet followed the dance,

Which lasted all the day and the night,

And which goes on with unending cries

Singing the valor and prowess of Membertou

As long as their stomachs support their voices,

Or until some illness makes them rest.

Translated from the French
by Thomas H. Goetz
State University College
Fredonia, New York

E-20

Hakluytus Posthumus or Purchas His Pilgrimes
Contayning a History of the World in Sea Voyages and Lande Travells by Englishmen and others
by Samuel Purchas
Volume XIX
Glasgow
James MacLehose and Sons
Publishers to the University
MCMVI

Description of Mawooshen
A.D. 1623

The following is a transcription from this text, pg. 400 - 406. The text contains notes in the margins; these are also included in italics, as they are in the original.

The description of the Countrey of Mawooshen, discovered by the English in the yeere 1602. 3. 5. 6. 7. 8. and 9.

This description of Mawooshen I had amongst M. Hakluyts papers. Climate and quantitie. Tarantines are said to be the same with the Souriquois.

1. Quibequesson River.

[IV. x. 1874.]

Asticon Sagamo.
A great Lake.

MAwooshen is a Countrey lying to the North and by East of Virginia, betweene the degrees of 43. and 45. It is fortie leagues broad, and fiftie in length, lying in breadth East and West, and in length North and South. It is bordered on the East side with a Countrey, the people, whereof they call Tarrantines: on the West with Epistoman, on the North with a great Wood called Senaglecounc, and on the South with the mayne Ocean Sea, and many Ilands.

In Mawooshen it seemeth there are nine Rivers, whereof the first to the East is called Quibiquesson; on which there is one Towne, wherein dwell two Sagamos or Lords, the one called Asticon, the other Abermot. In this Towne are fiftie houses, and 150. men. The name of which Towne is Precante; this River runneth farre up into the Mayne, at the head thereof there is a Lake of great length and breadth; it is at the fall into the Sea tenne fathoms deepe, and halfe a mile over.

2.
Pemaquid river.

The next is Pemaquid, a goodly River and very commodious all things considered; it is ten fathoms water at the entrance, and fortie miles up there are two fathoms and a halfe at low water; it is halfe a mile broad, and runneth into the Land North many daies journey: where

A great Lake.

is a great Lake of 18. leagues long and foure broad. In this Lake are seven great Ilands: toward the farthest end there falleth in a River, which they call Acaconstomed, where they passe with their Boates thirtie daies journey up, and from thence they goe over Land twentie daies journey more, and then come to another River, where

Anadabis.

they have a trade with Anadabis or Anadabiion, with whom the Frenchmen have had commerce for a long time. Neere to the North of this River of Pemaquid are three

Three townes. Bashabes.

Townes: the first is Upsegon, where Bashabes their chiefe Lord doth dwell. And in this Towne are sixtie houses, and 250. men, it is three daies journey within

Caiocame.

the Land. The second is Caiocame; the third Shasheekeing. These two last Townes are opposite one to the other, the River dividing them both, and they are two daies journey from the Towne of Bashabes. In Caiocame dwelleth Maiesquis, and in Shasheokeing Bowant, two Sagamos, subjects to Bashabes. Upon both sides of this River up to the very Lake, for a good distance the ground is plaine, without Trees or Bushes, but full of long Grasse, like unto a pleasant meadow, which the Inhabitants doe burne once a yeere to have fresh feed for their Deere. Beyond this Meadow are great Woods, whereof more shall be spoken hereafter. The River of Pemaquid is foure dayes journey from the mouth of Quibiquesson.

3.
Ramassoc.

The third River is called Ramassoc, and is distant from the mouth of Pemaquid foure daies journey; it is twentie fathoms at the entrance, and hath a mile over; it runneth into the Land three daies journey, and within lesse then a daies journey of the dwelling of Bashabes: upon this

Panobscot a Towne.

River there is a towne named Panobscot, the Lord whereof is called Sibatahood; who hath in his Town fiftie houses, and eightie men.

4.
Apanawapeske.

The fourth River Apanawapeske, lying West and by South of Ramassoc, at the entrance whereof there is twentie fathoms water, and it is a mile broad: it runneth up into the Countrey five daies journey; and within three daies of the mouth are two Townes, the one called Meecombe, where dwelleth Aramasoga, who hath in his Towne fiftie houses, and eightie men. The other is Chebegnadose, whose Lord is Skanke, and hath thirtie houses and ninetie men. The mouth of Apanawapeske is distant from Ramassoc three daies journey.

5.
Apanmensek.

To the South-west foure daies journey, there is another excellent River; in the entrance whereof is twentie fathoms water, and it is a quarter of a mile broad, it runneth into the Land two daies journey, and then there is a great fall, at the head whereof there is a Lake of a daies journey long and as much in breadth. On the

A Lake.
Another Lake.

side of this Lake there is a Strait, and at the end of that Strait there is another Lake of foure daies journey long, and two daies journey broad; wherin there are two Ilands, one at the one end, and another at the other end. I

All the Lakes
full of Fish,
Beeves, and
sweet Rats.

should have told you that both these Lakes, as also the rest formerly spoken of, doe infinitely abound with fresh water fish of all sorts, as also with divers sorts of Creatures, as Otters, Beeves, sweete Rats, and such like.

6.
Apponick.

The sixt River is called Apponick, on which there are three Townes; the first is called Appisham, where dwelleth Abochigishic. The second is Mesaqueegamic, where dwelleth Aminquin, in which there is seventie houses and eightie men; the third is Matammiscowte, in which are eightie houses and ninetie men, and there dwelleth Narracommique.

7.
Aponeg.

To the Westward of this there is another River called Aponeg: it hath at the entrance ten fathoms water, and is a mile broad: it runneth up into a great Sound of fresh water. Upon the East side of this River there are two Townes, the one called Nebamocago, the other called Asshawe. In the first dwelleth Mentaurmet, and hath in his Towne 160. housholds, and some 300. men. In the second dwelleth Hamerhaw, and hath in his Towne eightie housholds and seventie men. On the West side there is another Towne called Neredoshan, where are 120. housholds, and 100. men. There is a Sagamo or Lord called Sabenaw.

8.
Sagadahoc.

Three daies journey from Aponeg to the Westward, there is a goodly River called Sagadohoc: the entrance

Two Lakes.

[IV. x.
1875]
A great Iland.

Kenebeke.

whereof is a mile and an halfe over, holding that breadth a daies journey, and then it maketh a great Sound of three daies journey broad: in which Sound are six Ilands, foure great and full of Woods, and two lesse without Woods: The greater are called Sowaghcoc, Neguiwo, Niewoc. And in the verie entrance of this River there is another small Iland: from the West of which Iland to the Maine, there is a Sand that maketh as it were a bar, so that that way is not passable for shipping: but to the Eastward there is two fathoms water. This Sound divideth it selfe into two branches or armes, the one running North-east twentie foure daies journey, the other North-west thirtie daies journey into the Maine: At the heads whereof there are two Lakes, the Westermost being eight daies journey long, and foure daies journey broad; and the Eastermost foure daies journey long, and two daies broad. The River of Aponeg runneth up into this Sound, and so maketh as it were a great Iland between Sagadahoc and it. From the Iland upward the water is fresh, abounding in Salmons, and other fresh-water fish. Some thirteene or fourteen daies journey from the entrance in the North-east branch, there is a little arme of a River that runneth East some daies journey, which hath at the entrance foure fathoms water. Upon this arme there is one over fall, which standeth halfe a daies journey above this branch: upon this arme there are foure Towns: The first is called Kenebeke, which hath eightie houses, and one hundred men. The Lord whereof is Apom- hamen. The second is Ketangheanycke, and the Sagamos name is Octoworthe, who hath in his Towne ninetie housholds, and three hundred and thirtie men. This Towne is foure dayes journey from Kenebeke, and eight dayes journey from   To the Northward is the third Towne, which they call Naragooc; where there are fiftie housholds, and one hundred and fiftie men. The chiefe Sagamo of that place is Cocockohamas. And on the small branch that runneth East standeth the fourth Towne, named by Massakiga; where there are but eight housholds, and fortie men. Upon the Northwest branch of this Sound stand two Townes more: The first is called Amereangan, and is distant from Kenebeke six dayes journey. In this place are ninetie housholdes, and two hundred and sixtie men, with two Sagamoes; the one called Sasuoa, the other Scawas. Seven daies journey hence there is another Sagamo, whose name is Octoworokin, and his Townes name Namercante, wherein are fortie housholds, and one hundred and twentie men. A dayes journey above Namercante there is a downefall, where they cannot passe with their Cannoes, but are inforced to carrie them by Land for the space of a quarter of a mile, and then they put them into the River againe: And twelve dayes journey above this Downfall there is another, where they carrie their Boates as at the first; and sixe dayes journey more to the North is the head of this River, where is the Lake that is of eight dayes journey long, and foure dayes broad before mentioned. In this Lake there is one Iland; and three dayes journey from this Lake there is a Towne which is called Buccawganecants, wherein are threescore housholds, and foure hundred men: And the Sagamo thereof is called Baccatusshe. This man and his people are subjects to the Bashabez of Mawooshen, and in his Countrey is the farthest limit of his Dominion, where he hath any that doe him homage.

9. *Ashamahaga.* To the Westward of Sagadahoc, foure dayes journey there is another River called Ashamahaga, which hath at the entrance sixe fathoms water, and is halfe a quarter of a mile broad: it runneth into the Land two dayes journey: and on the East side there is one Towne called Agnagebcoc, wherein are seventie houses, and two hundred and fortie men, with two Sagamos, the one called Maurmet, the other Casherokenit.

10. *Shawakotoc.* Seven dayes journey to the South-west of Ashamahaga there is another River, that is sixe fathoms to the entrance: This River is named Shawakotoc, and is halfe a myle broad; it runneth into the Land fiftie dayes journey: but foure dayes from the entrance it is so narrow, that the Trees growing on each side doe so crosse with their boughes and bodies on the other, as it permitteth not any meanes to passe with Boates that way: for which cause the Inhabitants that on any occasion are to travell to the head, are forced to goe by Land, taking their way upon the West side. At the end of this River there is *A Lake foure dayes journey long & 2. broad* a Lake of foure dayes journey long, and two dayes broad, wherein are two Ilands. To the North-West foure daies journey from this Lake, at the head of this River Shawakatoc there is a small Province, which they call Crokemago, wherein is one Towne. This is the

Westermost River of the Dominions of Basshabez, and Quibiquisson the Westermost.

Appendix G

Dean Snow's Eastern Abenaki Tribal Names

The following excerpt about Eastern Abenaki tribal names is from
A chapter by Dean R. Snow, *Eastern Abenaki*, pg. 146.
In: *Volume 15, Northeast*. Bruce G. Trigger, Volume Editor
In the series: *Handbook of North American Indians*. William C. Sturtevant, Series
Editor
1978, Smithsonian Institution, Washington, DC.

Snow's comments on Eastern Abenaki tribal names is reprinted as an appendix for the information he provides about the ethnicity of the indigenous communities of the Maritime Peninsula at the time of European contact, and especially because of his comments in paragraph five on the Wawenoc community at Bécancour. After having one or more personal communications with Frank Siebert, Dean Snow came to the opinion that Wawenoc, as noted, was a village name, not a tribal or dialectical division. Frank Siebert was a collector and an expert on Abenaki material culture, but never published any widely distributed texts or essays on the Native Americans in Maine with whom he had such close contact during his professional career. Prior to Snow's comments on Siebert's opinion that no community of Wawenocs existed occupying the central Maine coast in pre or protohistory, this editor is not aware of any other writer or commentator who shared Siebert's view. Snow's opinion on the insignificance of the Wawenocs, whom he "lumps" with the Canibas in the *Archaeology of New England* may now be considered the dominant view among Maine archaeologists and ethnohistorians. Snow suggests that the Penobscot word wáwinak (Wawenoc) refers to a nearby island in the St. Lawrence River, and not to any community along the central Maine coast. According to Carol Smith Fisher (personal communication, 2005) Siebert was skeptical not only of the long standing assertion that the Wawenocs were one of the four important Abenaki communities in Maine (Williamson, 1832), but also often expressed the opinion that the confederacy of Mawooshen was romantic bunk invented by early English narrators and writers who mistook a village site on the Mousam River (just west of Kennebunk Beach) for the confederacy of Native American communities described to Ferdinando Gorges and printed by Purchas in 1625. In this context, and considering the whole spectrum of often contentious opinion about the ethnicity of the indigenous communities of coastal Maine in protohistory, Siebert represents one extreme of this spectrum. His skepticism lends itself to a reductionism that minimizes the historical significance, size, social organization and complex trading networks of the indigenous communities of central Maine. Future ethnohistorians may prove Siebert correct: there was no Wawenoc community living on the central Maine coast in pre and protohistory. The name instead derives from a community of refugees who settled at Bécancour during and after the French and Indian wars. Siebert, though virtually unpublished, by virtue of his influence on the much more well known Dean Snow, has had a vast impact upon how we now view the ethnicity of the central Maine coast at the time of European contact. Though Bruce Bourque strongly disagrees with Dean Snow's riverine theory of the lifestyles and locations of Maine's indigenous communities, he clearly agrees with Snow's assertion of the unimportance and the lack of separate cultural identity of Native Americans living between the Penobscot and Kennebec rivers at the time George Waymouth encountered 286 warriors (from which indigenous community?) near Cushing and then kidnapped 5 Native Americans who were brought to England and recounted the narration of Mawooshen. This reductionist view of Maine's ethnohistory now predominates in classrooms, museum displays and textbooks. It also raises more questions than it answers, not only about the Native Americans encountered and kidnapped by the Waymouth expedition, but about the large indigenous population that lived between the Penobscot and Kennebec rivers and now has no name and no cultural identity. If the Wawenoc nation never existed, who was it that George Waymouth, John Smith and others encountered in such great numbers? And even more puzzling, what indigenous community was responsible for creating the huge archaeological site at the loop in the St. Georges River in Warren, Maine, in the heart of Mawooshen?

The following text reprints Snow's comments on tribal names in the *Eastern Abenaki* chapter in Bruce Trigger's *Northeast*.

Table 2 lists the major synonyms for the Eastern Abenaki and their four major divisions. The table is necessarily simplified. There are many more spelling variants; it is not unusual for an early document to contain four or five spellings of the same term. In addition, many more meanings have been attached to the synonyms than the five clear-cut definitions used here. Researchers are cautioned to proceed carefully through primary sources and to distrust all secondary sources.

The earliest use of the term Abenaki in its various spellings appears to be French. Champlain, the *Jesuit Relations*, and other sources use the term after about 1630, abandoning the earlier extension of Etchemin (Maliseet-Passamaquoddy) to include them. Many later writers lumped them with the Western Abenaki under the heading Openango (spelled variously). English writers of the seventeenth century usually called the Eastern Abenaki simply Eastern Indians. In the nineteenth century the term Tarrantine, a seventeenth-century English name for the Micmac, was revived (as Tarratine) and erroneously applied to the Penobscot (Siebert 1973). Various other obscure and confusing identifications also exist, usually as single instances.

Pigwacket is preferred to Pequawket, the other major form, because it more closely approximates the original pronunciation. As used here, the term includes the Ossipee and the Presumpscot River Indians, but probably excludes the people of the lower Saco River and the Sokoki. The Pigwacket may be the inhabitants of the "Shawakotoc" on the list published by Purchas. The Pigwacket are not clearly isolated in English documents until the treaty of 1690. French sources make specific references to them shortly thereafter (JR 67:31). Pigwacket derives from the Eastern Abenaki word *apík^{w}ahki* 'land of hollows' (F. T. Siebert, personal communication 1974), not from a term meaning 'punched-up-through hill' (Eckstorm 1936:378-379).

Arosaguntacook and Arossagunticook represent Eastern Abenaki *alessíkantek^w* 'river of the cliff dwellings or rock shelters'; the form Androscoggin (River) probably is a corruption or analogical contamination with the name of Massachusetts governor Edmund Andros. The modern Penobscot name for the Saint Francis Abenaki is *alessikántek^{w}eyak*, the Arossaguntacook being one ancestral element in the Saint Francis population. The meanings 'river abounding in shellfish' (Speck 1940:18) and 'fish-curing place' (Eckstorm 1941:147) are erroneous (F. T. Siebert, personal communication 1974).

Kennebec appears in the Purchas publication as Kenebeke, a village name, as well as in the earliest French sources (Champlain 1907; Lescarbot 1928). It represents Eastern Abenaki *kínipek^w* 'large body of still water, large bay', probably primarily referring to Merrymeeting Bay (F. T. Siebert, personal communication 1974). It has since been broadened as a name for the entire river and its inhabitants. The Kennebec of the eighteenth century were usually called Noridgewock after their last surviving village. The Amaseconti were a subdivision from the Sandy River, most of whom migrated to Becancour, Quebec, in 1704. The Wawenock were the people of Bécancour, called *wáwinak* in Penobscot, evidently meaning 'round or oval island' (perhaps from a nearby island in the Saint Lawrence River); it is a village name, not a tribal or dialectal division (F. T. Siebert, personal communication 1974).

Penobscot appears first to identify, apparently correctly, a village near modern Orland (Purchas 1625, 4:1873-1875). The French form Pentagoet (Champlain 1907:46) was applied to the river generally and to the site of modern Castine specifically, beginning in 1604. Later usage by both the French and English applied the term to the river and virtually any location on it. Many contemporary students believe (incorrectly) that Penobscot has always identified the village at Old Town. The Penobscot River was called Pemaquid by some early English explorers. That term was soon shifted to Pemaquid Point, to the confusion of later historians. Penobscot derives from *panáwahpskek* 'where the rocks widen, open out, spread apart' (F. T. Siebert, personal communication 1974).

Most of the forms discussed above appear frequently as plurals. The number of published variants of these, their subdivisions, and village names runs to at least 1,000.

APPENDIX H

Donald Soctomah's Chapter in *One Land Two Worlds*

The following chapter "A Wabanaki Perspective" is from the Island Institute's 2005 text *A symposium to celebrate one land - two worlds: Maine Mawooshen 1605 - 2005: The 400th anniversary of George Waymouth's voyage to New England* published by Island Institute, Rockland, ME, pages 29-31.

SPONSORED BY:
ATLANTIC CHALLENGE, FARNSWORTH ART MUSEUM, ISLAND INSTITUTE, PENOBSCOT MARINE MUSEUM, STRAND THEATRE, & THOMASTON HISTORICAL SOCIETY

A Wabanaki Perceptive On the Voyage of George Waymouth

By Donald Soctomah

Living along the coast of Maine for the last 50 years has made me aware of the strength of nature and the effects of mankind. Gradual change took place after the glacier retreated from the area. But for Native people the landscape has dramatically changed in the last 400 years and at an accelerated rate in the last 20 years.

Was Maine this remote unused wilderness, as George Waymouth saw from his ship? For the First People of Maine, the Wabanaki, this was home for over 12,000 years. Legend has it that as the land was first made, so were the First People of this land. This creation legend makes it clear that the environment and its surroundings shaped the Native people. A bond closely connected the people to their surroundings, for the same creator made them all. Creation stories do vary from one tribe to another, but the understanding of what was a being, and beings having a soul or spirit, is the same for all Tribal people. All spirits were given respect in many of the sacred ceremonies; a true connection was formed in this relationship. Land is also viewed as a gift from the Creator, which furnished everything for the people. Native people see the earth as "Mother" and regard it as being sacred. The burning of medicinal plants serves as a means of thanking the Creator for this gift.

The voyage of George Waymouth set the stage for many other voyages, but the result of his first encounter with Native people had a ripple effect along the coast and then across North America. Waymouth's kidnapping of Native people set a negative impression of the English that would stay in the minds of Native

ABOVE N.C. WYETH (DETAIL)

29

people forever.

The English viewed and treated the Native people not as humans but more as sub-beings, because the Native societies did not conform to the English concept of a society. This concept evolved in Europe from the belief that European society was superior, and that all other cultures were less highly evolved. The belief justified their reasoning for taking land from the Wabanaki people and also the killing of Native people. The less a Native culture resembled English culture politically, socially and economically, the easier it was for English society to deny the rights of the Wabanaki societies. From the first encounters between English explorers and the Wabanaki people, the cultural conflict between the two groups has been resolved in favor of the colonizers, despite the fact that English settlements relied greatly on Native people.

For many years the governments of England and France were at war, and no matter how hard the tribes tried to remain neutral, they were drawn into these conflicts. Native people had never regarded the French as possessing title to the lands they explored, but welcomed them as allies. The French, in turn, relied on Native peoples as allies and as trading partners and were careful not to advertise their claims to Native lands. The French were delicate in their dealings with the Wabanaki people, hoping to increase anti-English feeling among them. The Waymouth voyage was an issue that was commonly brought up during these times.

The lack of understanding of the Native culture by the English played an important role in how the Wabanaki people were treated for the next 400 years. It is amazing that the Wabanaki people still exist, surrounded by an alien culture and outnumbered 100,000 to one. Having endured the world's largest genocide, the Wabanaki people still exist. This is a topic that is not discussed in today's world because people would have to do some hard thinking on the displacement of Native people.

With the coming of the English began the lumber trade and the destruction of the Native hunting grounds. The woodsman's axe resembled the Tribal legendary forest giant known as Chee-bal-ok, whose sound in the forest brought death to the hearer. Every tree cut in the forest reduced the area of the hunting grounds that the hunters inherited from their fathers. Every day Natives saw the opening of fields and meadows, narrowing the circle of hope. Native people became strangers, aliens in their own land --- outcasts robbed of birthrights by another race. War and diseases decimated the Wabanaki population, and efforts to stop the advance of the white race were ineffective.

Most Native people remained on the land that was their aboriginal territory. Maine Indian treaties frequently contain rights that Native people reserved for themselves, while allowing the buyers to also enjoy the fruits of the land. The land deeds with the rights reserved show that the Tribes intended to live right where they had previously lived. It seems clear that the Maine treaties and land deeds meant one thing to the Maine Natives and quite a different thing to the English or Massachusetts land buyers. A misunderstanding of different values and uses was a major conflict.

The Native people's natural instinct for survival allowed them to endure colonialism. Their language has survived and so has the culture. It is clear that the time has come for Western societies to accept this Native relationship, which has always existed, and to acknowledge that it is unlike what exists in Western societies. Today the tribes continue to deal with a society that does not understand the Native people of this land. We look at the Maine Land Claims Settlement Act as one of those misunderstandings, reflecting interpretations from two different worlds. Today's society does live on "one land but in two different worldviews," when it comes to Native people.

Deep in the subconscious of many Native people is the unfinished story that begins with the exploration of the European powers and the way things could have been before that. Would things have changed if the Waymouth voyage brought friendship and acceptance of the Native societies? We only can wonder about what would have happened. But when dealing with reality, today's Native people will continue to adapt to the existing conditions, as our ancestors adapted to the changes in their environment, for the future survival of the Wabanaki people.

Donald Soctomah directs the Passamaquoddy Tribal Historic Preservation Office.

H-3

Appendix I

Maine Native American Links

Abbe Museum: Bar Harbor, 04609, (207) 288- 3519, fax (207) 288-8979. http://www.abbemuseum.org

Friends of the Abenaki (NE-DO-BA): http://www.avcnet.org/ne-do-ba/menu_his.shtml

- Abenaki culture and history, focused on western Maine.

Hudson Museum: University of Maine, Orono, (207) 581-1901. http://www.umaine.edu/hudsonmuseum

- Maine Indians: A Web Resource List for Teachers
- Tribal websites:

    The Houlton Band of Maliseet Indians (www.maliseets.com)
    The Aroostook Band of Micmac (www.micmac.org)
    The Penobscot Nation (www.penobscotnation.org)
    Passamaquoddy Tribe at Pleasant Point (www.wabanaki.com)
    Passamaquoddy Sovereign Nation (www.peopleofthedawn.com)

Native Trails, Inc.: PO Box 240, Waldoboro, ME 04572, (207) 832-5255. http://www.nativetrails.org

Penobscot Nation Museum: 5 Downstreet St., Indian Island, Maine 04468, (207) 827-4153. http://www.penobscotnation.org/museum/indox.htm

SEBAGO-PRESUMPSCOT ANTHROPOLOGY PROJECT: Lakes Region of Maine: Mawooshen Research. http://www.lakesregionofmaine.gen.me.us/sebago_anthro/index.html

Waponahki Museum and Resource Center: Pleasant Point, PO Box 295, Perry, ME 04667, (207) 853-4001.

Other Interesting Native American Sites

Abenaki History: Lee Sultzman. http://tolatsga.org/aben.html

The Abenaki Language: http://www.hmt.com/abenaki/language.htm

American Language Reprint Series: Evolution Publishing, c/o Arx Publishing, LLC, 10 Canal Street, Suite, 231, Bristol PA 19007-3900, (215) 781-8600. http://www.evolpub.com/ALR/ALRhome.html

- Dedicated to the preservation of early Native American linguistic records

Cowasuck Band of the Pennacook-Abenaki People: COWASS North America Inc., PO Box 554, Franklin, MA 02038. http://www.cowasuck.org/

- This website includes a detailed listing of the labyrinth of Abenaki communities and their geographic boundaries throughout New England. http://www.cowasuck.org/history/ndakina.cfm.

First Nations Seeker: Directory of North American Indian portal websites

Interactive ALR (American Language Reprints): http://www.evolpub.com/interactiveALR/home.html

- "The Interactive ALR is a powerful online resource for the comparative study of Native American languages."
- "After December 31, 2003, the full functionality of the database will be available via subscription. Special reduced rates are available to recognized tribal institutions and members of SSILA."

Journal of Prophecy of Native People Worldwide: http://www.wovoca.com/

- Well worth a visit for information on Native Americans, plus links to other sites.

Library and Archives of Canada: http://www.collectionscanada.ca

Mashantucket Pequot Museum & Research Center: 110 Pequot Trail, PO Box 3180, Mashantucket, CT 06339-3180, (800) 411-9671. http://www.mashantucket.com

Native American Genealogy: http://www.accessgenealogy.com/native/

- Indian Tribes of Maine: http://www.accessgenealogy.com/native/maine/

Native Languages of the Americas: PO Box 130562, St. Paul MN 55113-0005. http://www.native-languages.org/

- Wabanaki Confederacy (Wabenaki, Wobanaki): http://www.native-languages.org/wabanaki.htm

National NAGPRA: National Park Service, 1849 C Street, NW (2253), Washington, D.C. 20240, 202-354-2201. http://www.cr.nps.gov/nagpra/INDEX.HTM

- "The Native American Graves Protection and Repatriation Act (NAGPRA) is a Federal law passed in 1990."

NativeTech: http://www.nativetech.org/

- "Dedicated to disconnecting the term 'primitive' from perceptions of Native American technology and art."

North American Indian Center of Boston: 105 South Huntington Avenue, Jamaica Plain, MA 02130, (617) 232-0343. http://www.bostonindiancenter.org/

The Northern Plains Archive Project: 519 Otis Ave. N., Saint Paul, Minnesota 55104. http://www.hiddenhistory.com/home1.htm

Mikmaq.com: http://www.mikmaq.com/

Native American Navigator: Columbia University. http://www.ilt.columbia.edu/k12/naha/nanav.html

- "An interface for geographical, historical, topical and keyword-based student inquiry on topics related to Native American history and culture in the United States."

Mocotagan: A nice website describing crooked knives. http://members.aol.com/mocotagan/index.html

Northeast Wigwam: A Short History of the Waponahkiyik Nations. http://www.newigwam.com/wwwboard/history/messages/24.html

Oyate: "A Native organization working to see that our lives and histories are portrayed honestly, and so that all people will know our stories belong to us." http://www.oyate.org

- This site includes a list of books to avoid, ones that contain incorrect stereotypes.

Peabody Museum of Archaeology and Ethnology: http://www.peabody.harvard.edu/default.html

- Located at Harvard University, this site includes lists of several archival collections, both photographic and paper.

The Wabanaki Confederacy: People of the Dawn:
http://www.wabanakiconfederacy.com/

- "Information regarding events for the Wabanaki Confederacy, specifically for actual members of our Wabanaki Nations."

WWW Virtual Library - American Indians: Index of Native American Resources on the Internet: http://www.hanksville.org/NAresources/

- A site full of great links to Native American stuff.

Appendix J

Annotated Bibliographies

Note each bibliography section is alphabetical and separate from the others. Due to the lengthy annotations following many of the citations the traditional all inclusive bibliographic format has been modified and the bibliography subdivided into several sections.

Table of Contents

Native Americans in Maine
Principal References

For information on Native Americans outside of Maine, also check our Archaeology bibliography page.

Axtell, James. (1985). *The invasion within: The contest of cultures in colonial North America.* Oxford University Press, NY, NY. IS.

Banks, Ronald R., Ed. (1969). A history of Maine: A collection of readings on the history of Maine, 1600-1970. Third edition. Kendall/Hunt Publishing Co., Dubuque, Iowa. IS.

- See annotations in the Maine history: contemporary bibliography.

Baker, Emerson W., Churchill, Edwin A., D'Abate, Richard S., Jones, Kristine L., Konrad, Victor A. and Prins, Harald E.L., Eds. (1994). *American beginnings: Exploration, culture, and cartography in the land of Norumbega.* University of Nebraska Press, Lincoln, NB. IS and also W.

- A great read and the most important of all recent texts on the cartography of the Maine coast.
- The many contributors express a wide range of opinions about Maine's ethnohistory in the years of exploration and early settlement.

- See annotations in the Maine history: principal sources bibliography as well as our comments in the text of *Norumbega Reconsidered*.

Baxter, James Phinney, Ed. (1884). *Sir Ferdinando Gorges and his Province of Maine*. 3 vols. Hoyt, Fogg, and Donham, Portland, ME. Reprinted in 1890 as *The life and letters of Sir Ferdinando Gorges*. Prince Society Publications, 18 - 20, Boston, MA. Reprinted in 1967, NY.

- See annotations in the Maine history: Antiquarian bibliography.

Baxter, James P. (1891). The campaign against the Pequakets. *Maine Historical Society Collections 2*. Series 2. pg. 353-371. X.

- "One hundred and fifty Penobscot Indians, converts of Thury, the Jesuit priest, set out on this expedition, and were joined by a body of Indians from the Kennebec. Traveling on snow-shoes, the expedition reached York, which, in the early dawn, they attacked and destroyed; Dummer, the venerable minister of York, was shot dead at his door, and his wife subjected to the hardships of a captivity which she did not survive. One of the savages it is said arrayed himself in the clerical garb of the dead minister, and delivered a mock sermon to his howling associates." (pg. 354).
- "The country of the Pequakets was to be Lovewell's objective point. The principal seat of this tribe was upon the shores of the Saco, near the present village of Fryeburg. The Pequakets had in former wars been active against the English, and were considered especially dangerous to the settlements exposed to their attacks. Their premeditated treachery at the time the Casco treaty was made, and their subsequent cruelties had not been forgotten..." (pg. 363).
- "So great was the terror inspired by Lovewell's attack upon them, that the savages abandoned their seat at Pequaket and took up their abode in Canada." ... "To Lovewell, then, we may accord the honor of having ended a war, which might have been prolonged for years and caused much bloodshed and suffering, by his brave fight at Pequaket." (pg. 371).

Baxter, James Phinney. (1906). *A memoir of Jacques Cartier: Sieur de Limoilou: His voyages to the St. Lawrence*. A Bibliography and a facsimile of the manuscript of 1534 with annotations, etc. Dodd, Mead & Company, New York, NY.

- "Like many other Indian tribes of North America, the Hochelagans used no salt whatever in their food, which comprised game and fish, maize, beans, peas, pumpkins, cucumbers, and wild fruits." (pg. 33).
- "And we having arrived at the said Hochelaga, more than a thousand persons presented themselves before us, men, women, and children alike, the which gave us as good reception as ever father did to child, showing marvelous joy; for the men in one band danced, the women on their side and the children on the other, the which brought us store of fish and of their bread made of coarse millet, which they cast into our said boats in a way that it seemed as if it tumbled from the air." (pg. 161).

- "There are within this town [Hochelanga] about fifty long houses of about fifty paces or more each, and twelve or fifteen paces wide, and all made of timbers covered and garnished with great pieces of bark and strips of the said timber, as broad as tables, well tied artificially according to their manner." (pg. 164).
- "Likewise they have granaries at the top of their houses where they put their corn of which they make their bread, which they call *carraconny*, and they make it in the manner following: they have mortars of wood as for braying flax, and beat the said corn into powder with pestles of wood; then they mix it into paste and make round cakes of it, which they put on a broad stone that is hot; then they cover it with hot stones, and so bake their bread instead of in an oven. They make likewise many stews of the said corn, and beans and peas, of which they have enough, and also of big cucumbers [crooked-neck squash] and other fruits. They have also in their houses great vessels like tuns, where they put their fish, namely eels and others, the which they dry in the smoke during the summer and live upon it in the winter. And of this they make a great store, as we have seen by experience. All their living is without any taste of salt." (pg. 164-165).
- This book is now in Google Book and the entire text is searchable.
- See more annotations for this citation in the Ancient Pemaquid bibliography.

Berkhofer, Robert. (1978). *White Man's Indian: Images of the American Indian from Columbus to the present*. Alfred A. Knopf, NY, NY. IS.

Biggar, Henry P., Ed. (1911). *The Precursors of Jacques Cartier, 1497-1534: A collection of documents relating to the early history of the dominion of Canada*. Publications of the Public Archives of Canada, #5, Ottawa, Canada.

Biggar, Henry P., Ed. (1922-1936). *The works of Samuel de Champlain*. 6 vols. Reprinted in 1971 by Toronto University Press, Toronto, Canada. X (partial Xeroxed copy only).

- See annotations in the New England and US History: Antiquarian bibliography.

Biggar, Henry P. (1937). *The early trading companies of New France: A contribution to the history of commerce and discovery in North America*. University of Toronto Library, Toronto, Canada.

Bourque, Bruce J. (1989). Ethnicity on the Maritime Peninsula, 1600-1759. *Ethnohistory*. 36(3). pg. 257-284. IS.

- "Challenges Speck's classification of Maine's Native Peoples. Discusses French understanding of tribal identities vs. Speck classifications." (Ray, *The Indians of Maine*, pg. 31).
- This is among the most important of all essays pertaining to the interpretation of the ethnohistory of Maine and the maritime provinces. The "Bourquian era" of Maine's ethnohistory can be dated from the publication of this thesis.

- Bourque's version of Maine's ethnohistory remains virtually unchallenged since the publication of this article; almost all commentary and museum exhibitions have utilized his term "Etchemins" to describe the ethnicity of the indigenous population of the central Maine coast east of the Saco River at the time of contact with Europeans.
- Extensive excerpts from this landmark essay are commented on in the main text of this publication (Norumbega Reconsidered).

Bourque, Bruce J. (1995). *Diversity and complexity in prehistoric maritime societies: A Gulf of Maine perspective*. Plenum Press, NY. IS.

- Beginning with a site-specific analysis of the Turner Farm site on North Haven Island, Bourque explores the ethnohistory and life-style adaptations of Maine's Native American maritime communities over a period of five millennia. This is the first of two comprehensive publications by Bourque on Native Americans in Maine and contains an excellent bibliography and photographs of lithic, bone, shell and ceramic specimens from this site.
- "The Turner Farm site is located on North Haven Island, one of the Fox Island group in Penobscot Bay off the central Maine coast. Large-scale excavations there during the 1970s, followed by over a decade of analysis, have produced a body of data that, in its age, size, and comprehensiveness, is probably unparalleled among coastal sites in North America. It spans five millennia, from 5000 B.P. to the early historic period, and includes 6,500 catalogued artifacts of stone, bone, and fired clay, as well as 1,800 bone samples from which over 20 thousand vertebrate specimens have been identified. ...the Turner Farm data set is doubly useful, for it provides a record of human coastal adaptation during the entire recent Holocene epoch at a single location." (pg. vii.).
- "The discovery of the Susquehanna tradition cemetery was a landmark event for eastern North American archaeology. There, for the first time, were preserved the uncremated human remains and bone technology of a people whose now boneless cemeteries have often been encountered in the Northeast, and whose technology so closely resembles that found among Archaic peoples throughout much of eastern North America (Appendix 3). ... A comparison of the isotope values from this sample with others from central coastal Maine ranging in age from 4300 to 400 B.P. revealed one of the biggest surprises of the whole project: the site's Susquehanna tradition occupants, surrounded by the riches of the sea, apparently made little use of them, consuming less marine protein than any other coastal population known to us." (pg. 2).
- "Ground slate point technology in the Northeast still has not been reliably traced back before about 5500 B.P., although a few variable and generalized specimens have been recovered from various contexts dating to about 7000 B.P. After about 5500 B.P. the technology ramified throughout much of the Northeast with specimens occurring as far west as Michigan, eastward down the St. Lawrence Valley, along its tributaries, and up and down the Atlantic coast from northern Labrador to the Kennebec River. It was during this post-5500 B.P. florescence that distinct styles developed. Although no ground slate points have been found at the Turner Farm site (and very few have been found in the handful of other early shell middens either), the presence there of bayonets made of swordfish rostra provides a new perspective on the possible origins of the ground slate point." (pg. 7).

- "Radiocarbon dates then available suggested that the Moorehead phase dated between about 4500 and 3800 B.P. A few habitation sites, including shell middens, were identified as having Moorehead phase components, and evidence for swordfish hunting was noted from some of these sites. I saw the Moorehead phase as characterized by discrete cemeteries of red ocher-filled graves -- often richly furnished -- a sophisticated heavy woodworking technology, ground slate bayonets, plummets, and nonutilitarian symbolic artifacts." (pg. 223).
- "The analyses presented in Chapters 4 and 5, as well as data from other sites discussed below, reflect my increasing confidence that the historic roots of the Moorehead phase extend back to Middle Archaic populations in the Gulf of Maine region to the south of both the Gulf of St. Lawrence and the domain of the Laurentian tradition. What follows is a summary of the Moorehead phase origin debate." (pg. 225).

Bourque, Bruce J. (2001). *Twelve thousand years: American Indians in Maine.* University of Nebraska Press, Lincoln, Nebraska. IS.

- The most comprehensive and up-to-date summary of the ethnohistory of Native American communities in Maine in the pre-historic as well as in the historic period. Bruce Bourque is Maine's preeminent archaeologist; this text supplements and expands his previous publication *Diversity and Complexity in Prehistoric Maritime Societies,* which remains a basic reference for exploring Maine's Native American pre-history.
- Bourque begins his historic survey by noting the traditional emphasis on predictable sequence and cultural continuity in previous accounts of Native Americans in Maine. Bourque instead postulates the existence of complex and dynamic Native American communities, which experience "...rapid population expansion, culture change and innovation that strain against explanations based upon passive cultural adaptation. (pg. xvi).
- "In my view, the primary explanation for the cultural dynamism of the Maine region is the long standing importance of the sea and the rich resources it provided." (pg. xvi).
- "A second factor that contributed to Maine's cultural dynamism is its geographical situation. Maine is positioned astride a larger geographic formation known as the Maritime Peninsula..." (pg. xvi).
- Bourque's description and photographs of ceramic fragments (chapter III, The Ceramic Period) located during his archaeological explorations provide the best summary available of pottery production in the late prehistoric era.
- Chapters VI, VII and VIII are the strongest parts of Bourque's comprehensive survey of Native American's in Maine, and provide an excellent summary of each of the Indian Wars and the era of missionary activity that followed. These chapters will be particularly useful for secondary school teachers preparing courses on Maine history or Native American history as a component of the Native Education Bill.
- Of a more controversial nature is Bourque's description of the Native American communities in the Maritime Peninsula just before and at the time of contact with Europeans (Chapter IV, An Introduction to the Historic Past). "The early French sources name four ethnic groups on the Maritime Peninsula. As is the case for colonized peoples throughout the world, however, the names used by the French were not generally those these groups used for themselves.

Eastward from the Gaspé and St. John River lived the Souriquois, who were apparently named for a river called the Souricoa..." (pg. 106).

- "West of the Souriquois, between the St. John and Kennebec Rivers, lived the Etchemins... By 1605 members of this group were also engaged in the fur trade and in providing guides to the French. In the late seventeenth century, the Etchemins came to be referred to by the French as the Maliseets (or Malicites) between the St. John and Penobscot Rivers and as the Canibas between the Penobscot and the Kennebec Rivers." (pg. 106).

- "West of the Kennebec and as far to the southwest as Massachusetts lived a third people, whom the Souriquois referred to as Almouchiquois -- literally 'dog people' -- with whom they had been at war. This group's territory began at the Androscoggin River, which John Smith later named the Almouchicoggin. They were linguistically and culturally distinct from their neighbors to the east, wearing different clothing and hairstyles, using some dugouts in addition to birchbark canoes, and practicing horticulture. The French soon abandoned this epithet, and the calamitous epidemics and warfare that broke out during and soon after their initial visit so disrupted the region that it is unclear who, if anyone, remained in former Almouchiquois territory." (pg. 106-107).

- "Champlain later described a fourth group, the Abenakis, who lived eight days travel south of the newly founded settlement of Quebec at Norridgewock, on the Kennebec River. They lived in 'large villages and also houses in the country with many stretches of cleared land, in which they sow much Indian corn.'" (pg. 107).

- "In later years, as all the region's coastal populations became increasingly oriented to Quebec, the term Abenaki was extended to all, even the Micmacs at times. The Abenakis proper, however, remained distinct enough to be distinguished from their neighbors until around 1700." (pg. 107).

- Bourque's brief chapter IV adds a particularly interesting element to his comprehensive survey of Native Americans in Maine by either contradicting or ignoring traditional English sources. Local Maine historians such as William Williamson, Francis Greene, Rufus King Sewall and many others provide a description of Native American communities in central coastal Maine at the time of contact that differs radically from Bourques. Maine's town and state histories as well as its literature are filled with descriptions of the Wawenoc Indians as living in a series of robust semi-sedentary villages in the heart of Mawooshen between the Penobscot and Kennebec rivers prior to and during the early years of European contact. Bourque alleges that Etchemins lived in this region and that the Canibas living to the north on the Kennebec River were also Etchemins. While Bourque consistently presents arguments for ethnohistoric complexity as well as dynamic change, the reduction of all communities living east of the Saco River to the convenient label of Etchemin is a radical simplification of a much more complex ethnohistorical reality, and one that contradicts the huge body of written and oral history of thousands of English settlers and their descendants. In one brief paragraph Bourque has eliminated one of Maine's most important Native American communities of the late prehistoric past. Is this because the Wawenoc Indians had no significant role to play after 1620, having been decimated both by Micmac (Tarrentine) massacres and the epidemics that followed? (See Bourque's comments on the Bessabez and the Tarrentines quoted below.)

- Bourque's description of the ethnohistory of Native American communities in Maine in the 15th and 16th centuries in the central coastal region is contradicted by his description of the

Bessabez in the excerpt on page 119. English sources frequently note the alignment of the Etchemins with the Tarrentines in their conflict with Native Americans living west of the Penobscot - conflicts that arose as a result of the intense European demand for furs. Bourque quotes from Sir Ferdinando Gorges (below) but also fails to mention the confederacy of Mawooshen that Gorges along with so many other English sources describe, and which Gorges is essentially describing in this excerpt. The only Native American description of Mawooshen, printed by Samuel Purchas in 1626, is reprinted in its entirety in the Appendix.

- Bourque's description of Etchemin's living to the east of the Almouchiquois and the Androscoggin River cuts Mawooshen into two diametrically opposed halves, not only eliminating the Wawenoc Indians from our history texts but contradicting without adequate explanation a huge body of historical narrative by English speaking writers. The controversy thus delineated in this brief chapter makes Bourque's book all the more interesting; how boring it would be if there was nothing to disagree with in this fast moving narrative of *Twelve thousand years: American Indians in Maine.* Bourque and other writers continue to refer to surviving Native American communities in the maritime provinces by the designations these communities use to describe themselves: Penobscot, Passamaquoddy, Maliseet, Micmac. The elimination of Wawenocs from our history texts and the description of Canibas as Etchemins constitute a new ethnohistorical interpretation of Maine's protohistoric past that needs further documentation.

- "Early English explorers in the Gulf of Maine described a rivalry that reflects the emergence of European influence there during the late sixteenth and early seventeenth centuries. On one side was Bessabez, the supreme Etchemin sagamore whom English sources describe as the preeminent leader of a domain that extended from Frenchman's Bay at least to Saco and possibly as far west as Lac Mégantic in Quebec. On the other side was a group that lived to the east of Bessabez. Known to the English as Tarrentines and to the French as Souriquois, they were mainly the ancestors of those who would later be called Micmacs. In 1658 Sir Ferdinando Gorges, a prime backer of the 1607 effort to colonize present-day Popham, described the rivalry and its causes as follows: [Bessabes] had under him many great Subjects ... some fifteen hundred Bow-Men, some others lesse, these they call *Sagamores*....[He] had many enemies, especially those to the East and North-East, whom they call *Tarrentines*.... [H]is owne chief abode was not far from *Pemaquid*, but the Warre growing more and more violent between the *Bashaba* and the *Tarrentines*, who (as it seemed) presumed upon the hopes they had to be favored of the *French* who were seated in *Canada*[.] [T]heir next neighbors, the *Tarrentines* surprised the *Bashaba* and slew him and all his People near about him." (pg. 119).

- One particularly interesting aspect of the controversy Bourque inadvertently highlights in chapter IV pertains to a most important contemporary study of Native Americans in New England which Bourque omits in his bibliography, Kathleen Bragdon's *Native People of Southern New England.* Bragdon postulates three patterns of settlement in southern New England:
  - An inland culturally conservative hunting and gathering society with little or no focus on semi-sedentary villages -- very similar to the mobile hunting and gathering Etchemins Bourque postulates as living in central coastal Maine and on the Kennebec River.

- River valley based sedentary villages with horticultural activities, a description one would think would aptly apply to the Canibas Indians living on the Kennebec River as well as the Native American communities living on the Saco River at the time of European contact, and one which coincides with Champlain's observations when he first visited this area in 1604/5.
- Of most importance, Bragdon postulates a third settlement type that she calls "conditional sedentism" -- semi-sedentary communities relying upon the extensive marine resources of the southern New England coastal area.

- One of the ironies of Bragdon's important text is her rejection of the use of tribal designations, which she strongly advocates at the beginning of her book. Bourque must to some extent agree with her since he drops reference to all of the Native American tribes who did not survive contact with Europeans in significant numbers (Wawenoc, Cannabis, Pigwacket, etc.) Both Bourque and Bragdon then also follow the politically correct and probably safest course of action and carefully refer to all the tribes surviving in significant numbers in the historic period by the tribal designation they themselves use: e.g. Pequot, Pennacook, Penobscot, and Passamaquoddy.

- Bragdon's more complex model of settlement patterns in New England contrasts with the more pervasive oversimplified view of Native communities in Maine as being either wandering hunters and gatherers living east of the Saco River or horticultural communities from the Saco River west. One can't help ask the question in view of the huge antiquarian literature on the Wawenoc Indians: Isn't there at least a reasonable possibility that the robust semi-sedentary marine resource dependent communities of coastal southern New England extended further than Saco and included the central coastal communities of Maine so prominently documented in Samuel Purchas' description of Mawooshen? In fact, aren't many of the communities described in this important early narrative located in tidewater locations that exactly match Bragdon's description of **non-horticultural** coastal communities dependent on marine resources? In an era of global warming, before the little ice age, circa 1350, why wouldn't these semi-sedentary communities also characterize the central coast of Maine? Aren't the presence of these communities verified by the extensive shell heaps and other archaeological sites that Bourque has so carefully documented in his lifetime of research on the Maine coast? Would Bourque contend, in fact, that the huge shell heaps of the Damariscotta River and those scattered about the coastal reaches of Maine including Frenchmans Bay, result from the activities of mobile hunting and gathering Etchemins lacking semipermanent village sites?

- While skipping over the interesting descriptions of the Native American communities of coastal Maine contained in both Purchas' narrative of Mawooshen (1623) and Dean Snow's (1980) *Archaeology of New England*, Bourque inadvertently comments on their demise by including a Jesuit map of 1715 illustrating the last of the semi-sedentary Native American communities in New England at Pigwacket (Saco River), Narakamogou (Androscoggin River), Amaseconti (Farmington Falls, Sandy River), Norridgewock (Kennebec River), Panawamské (Penobscot River) and Meductic (upper St. John's River). (pg. 182). These villages, rather than being located at the head of tide, reflect the fact the Native Americans had withdrawn from coastal locations and were making a last stand at riverine locations well inland from their original tidewater village sites.

- What would William Williamson (1832) say about this revisionist view of ethnohistory which substitutes Etchemins for the Wawenocs and identifies the Kennebec Indians as Etchemins? Was the Confederacy of Mawooshen really cut in half in the manner described by Bourque? Would Dean Snow also agree with this new paradigm, which cuts the communities he describes after Purchas in *The Archaeology of New England* into two diametrically opposed components? Doesn't the cultural and linguistic differences noted by Bourque for the Almouchiquois also describe the Wawenoc Indians? Didn't Champlain encounter some horticultural activity when he visited the Wawenocs at Wiscasset in 1604? Didn't he note their radical cultural differences from the more eastern tribes during this visit? Didn't George Waymouth also note this difference when he encountered the coastal Indians near Pemaquid? Didn't Samoset, who greeted the Pilgrims, share the cultural characteristics of the Almouchiquois rather than the Etchemins? Is the history of the Native American communities living between the Kennebec and the Penobscot in the 15th and 16th centuries (and earlier) so simple that it can be described as Bourque does in just one sentence?
- Bourque was recently the source of a justifiably adulatory review article in the Bangor Daily News (Alicia Anstead, Nov. 17/18, 2001, pg. E1-E2). Bourque is quoted thusly "Bourque might say that 'change' is part of his underlying thesis in 'Twelve Thousand Years.' Based on his own research, analysis and interpretation fusing archaeology and history, he posits that Maine was the site of dynamic and divergent cultural traditions, and that native people were at the vanguard of those shifts." and "'There is a perception that the people were isolated here and not in touch with the rest of the world,' said Bourque. 'Prehistorically, they were in touch with people all over North America. And natives here were in on the earliest visitors from Europe. There was a connectedness. All people who have ever lived here were connected to much larger regions. Maine's perception of itself has never been more isolated than it is today. Maine was important and Indians were players up here for a long, long time.'" These comments contradict Bourque's easy identification of most indigenous residents of central coastal Maine in the late prehistoric period as being simply Etchemins whose primary location has always been the Passamaquoddy and Medutic areas.

Bourque, Bruce J. and Cox, Steven L. (Fall 1981). Maine State Museum investigation of the Goddard site, 1979. *Man in the Northeast*. 22. pg. 3-27. IS.

- "By far the most intense Archaic component preserved at the site is one which can be referred to the Moorehead phase (Bourque 1971:78-81).
- It is characterized by small, narrow stemmed points, small stemmed and usually barbed ground stone points, plummets, adzes, gouges and pecking stones (Plate I:f-n)." (pg. 7).
- "The culture/historical sequence of the ceramic period in Maine is known only in broad terms." (pg. 12).
- "The archeological evidence at hand from the Goddard site indicates that it was a major summer village during the period of Norse visits to North America and that its population participated in extensive trade networks ultimately reaching as far north as Ramah Bay, Labrador. The archeological sample from the site is unusually large. These factors suggest several possible scenarios which could have led to the [Goddard] coin's deposition." (pg. 23).
- Bourque is referring to the notorious Norse coin found at this location.

Bourque, Bruce J. and Whitehead, Ruth Holmes. (1985). Tarrentines and the introduction of European trade goods in the Gulf of Maine. *Ethnohistory*. 32(4). pg. 327-341.

- A key document for students of the contact period in Maine history. Bourque and Whitehead contend that the numerous trade goods found in the possession of 15th century Native American inhabitants of coastal Maine derived not from direct contact with English, Basque, French or other traders or fishermen, but only from Micmac traders (Tarantines) who were intermediaries between the coastal natives and the European visitors. This revisionist interpretation insists such contacts did not take place until after 1600.
- See our comments on this contemporary view of Maine history in the Ancient Pemaquid: Voyages of Humphrey Gilbert, etc. section.

Bragdon, Kathleen J. (1996). *Native people of southern New England, 1500 - 1650*. University of Oklahoma Press, Norman, OK. IS.

- "The anthropological and historical literature on southern New England has also been obscured by the use of various sociopolitical labels, most notably the term *tribe*, to characterize the nature of governance and sociopolitical organization in that region. ...The reality of this vaguely conceived entity in 'prehistoric' North America has been vigorously questioned by numerous scholars, and its applicability in southern New England is likewise questionable." (pg. xvi).
- "In summary, archaeological evidence for the Late Woodland period suggests three distinct settlement types, associated with specific eco-regions: estuarine 'conditional sedentism' based on reliance upon a wide variety of marine and estuarine resources; riverine village-based sedentism, with a heavier dependence on corn-beans and squash horticulture; and a culturally conservative uplands lacustrine adaptation. Whether some or all uplands peoples were connected in some way to coastal or riverine groups is unclear;..." (pg. 77).
- "Many scholars have suggested, for example, based on the descriptions of early explorers and settlers, that the Natives of southern New England occupied settled village sites, dependent on maize horticulture. In opposition to this 'ethnohistorical' model, Ceci and others have more recently argued that maize horticulture and settled village life in coastal regions were in fact a response by Native people with a band-like sociopolitical organization to the development of trading relations with Europeans, but that prehistorically such Natives were part of mobile groups with egalitarian social structures." (pg. xviii).
- "Native people soon observed that certain European explorers were absolutely without conscience regarding Native property or persons. Dozens of people were captured and transported to Europe and especially England during the late sixteenth and early seventeenth centuries, and only a handful ever returned. Sailors looted Native graves, and stole their seed corn, tools, and household goods. Exploring parties deployed vicious dogs, discharged guns, and built forts, displaying their hostility with every gesture (Brasser 1978:80-83)." (pg. 6).
- "Three related issues continue to occupy archaeologists and ethnohistorians studying the fifteenth through the seventeenth centuries A.D. in southern New England: the extent and onset of reliance on maize horticulture, the nature of settlement, and the level of sociopolitical integration there." (pg. 31).

- "Both the expansion of the Hopewellian-Ohioan state to the west and the arrival of Europeans in the Northeast have been invoked as causes in the development of complex societies in coastal southern New England (e.g., Thomas 1979:400; Ceci 1990). ...it is clear that the forces leading to complexity in southern New England were in operation centuries before the European presence was established there." (pg. 48).

- "Both Eleanor Leacock and Karen Sacks suggest that gender asymmetry is due to women's loss of control over the means of production and over their own labor--losses resulting from the expansion of production for exchange and the emergence of hierarchical societies." (pg. 51).

- "If, particularly in the contact period, accumulation of capital in the form of wampum and other scarce goods facilitated a patrilineal organization, women's status (with the exception of that of sachem women) among the Ninnimissinuok may well have been on the decline, particularly in coastal regions." (pg. 53).

- "It is difficult not to conclude, for example, when examining descriptions of women's habitual work among the Ninnimissinuok, that their status was not commensurate with their important contributions to the indigenous economy." (pg. xvi).

- "Fragile and bounteous, estuarine ecosystems comprise some of the most unique and significant environments of southern New England. Generally semi-enclosed coastal bodies of water with connections to the open sea, estuaries are characterized by varying mixtures of fresh, brackish, and salt waters. ...True estuaries consist of multiple zones, beginning with the water column itself, then extending inland over mudflats exposed only at low tide, which merge with an intertidal zone where marsh grasses flourish, succeeded in turn by a zone of mixed salt and freshwater plant species." (pg. 55-56).

- "Once called 'ecotones,' or 'regions of transition between two or more diverse communities' (Odum 1971:157), estuaries are now celebrated for their remarkable biotic diversity. Dincauze (1973, 1974), Barber (1979), and Kerber (1984) argue that estuaries represent uniquely rich habitats for human populations because of the way in which they link diverse ecosystems. Zones ranging from terrestrial to freshwater riverine, freshwater marsh, and salt marsh, are all easily accessible within a relatively narrow strip running from the sea inland. The estuarine ecotone also benefits from what E. P. Odum calls the 'edge effect,' or 'the tendency for increased variety and density at community junctions' (1971:157). Estuaries and other intertidal regions are associated with a number of diverse habitats of great importance to Native subsistence and diet, including the water column itself, the strandflats, tidal rivers, and salt marsh." (pg. 57).

- "The focus on settlement near estuaries, which manifests itself with the stabilization of sea-level rise, was accompanied through time by an increasing diversification of resource use, as well as increased cultural modification of the landscape. ...Ceramics, frequently associated with sedentism in the archaeological and ethnographic literature, are manifestly unsuited to a mobile way of life, being both fragile and cumbersome, and although traditionally associated with maize horticulture, appear long before maize-use can be documented in southern New England." (pg. 64).

- "The arrival of maize in coastal southern New England has been called a 'non-event' in the sense that it had little immediate effect on settlement patterns or on previously established subsistence practices." (pg. 83).

- "It appears that the richness and diversity of coastal estuaries both permitted and encouraged large, conditionally sedentary populations, but that the carrying capacity of these estuarine regions was ultimately surpassed, putting stress on natural resources and necessitating the adoption of alternative food-producing strategies." (pg. 86). Horticulture then becomes a necessary adjunct to estuarine adoption.
- "The archaeological data suggest that the tripartite model of settlement was overlain, or interconnected by, intraregional networks of trade, and that territorial boundaries were established in order to control that trade and protect vital resources within constricted environmental settings. Both trade and the desire to protect restricted resources may have served to encourage the coalescence of territorially based 'ethnic' groupings and the rise of chiefly families and hereditary leadership..." (pg. 101).

Brasser, T.J. (1978). Early Indian European contacts. In: *Handbook of North American Indians*, vol. 15. Trigger, Bruce G., Ed., Smithsonian Institution, Washington, D.C.

Braun, Esther K. and Braun, David P. (1994). *The first peoples of the Northeast.* Moccasin Hill Press, Lincoln, MA. IS.

Brereton,John. (1602). *A brief and true relation of the discovery of the North Viriginia, etc. made this present year 1602, by Captain B. Gosnold, Capt. B. Gilbert, etc by the Permission of the Hon. Knight, Sir W. Raleigh.* In MaHSC, 3rd series, vol 8, pgs. 83-123.

Brockman, Mark E. and Georgiady, Jeffrey. (2005). Prehistoric lithic resources of the coastal volcanic belt, Washington County, Maine. *Maine Archaeological Society Bulletin.* 45 (1). pg. 5-23. IS.

Burrage, Henry S., Ed. (1887). *Rosier's relation of Weymouth's voyage to the coast of Maine, 1605.* Gorges Society, Portland, ME.

- See our information file for a reproduction of James Rosier, *A True Relation of Captain George Weymouth his Voyage. Made this Present Yeere 1605.*

Burrage, Henry S., Ed. (1906). *Original narratives of early English and French voyages 1534-1608.* Charles Scribner's Sons, NY, NY. Also reprinted in 1930 as *Early English and French voyages, chiefly from Hakluyt, 1534-1608.* Reprinted in 1969.

- See annotations in the New England and US History: Antiquarian bibliography.

Burrage, Henry S. (1914). *The beginnings of colonial Maine 1602-1658.* Marks Printing House for the State of Maine, Portland, ME.

- See annotations in the Maine History: Antiquarian bibliography.

Burrage, Henry S. (1923). *Gorges and the grant of the Province of Maine, 1622*. Printed for the state, Augusta, ME.

Byers, Douglas S. (1959). The Eastern Archaic: Some problems and hypotheses. *American Antiquity*. 24. pg. 233-256. IS.

- "The Micmac, once makers of pottery and tillers of corn, had abandoned both arts when the French arrived, and, with their neighbors to the north, were living examples of the Archaic stage of culture." (pg. 234).
- "The fact remains that until 1936 the dwelling places of the people who buried their dead with red ochre were never excavated. ...In recent years these formerly mysterious people have begun to fit into their proper place in the Northeast. Sites at Ellsworth Falls have been instrumental in accomplishing this feat." (pg. 243).
- An extensive description of the Ellsworth Falls site begins on page 243.
- "On a larger scale the same principle applies to the entire Boreal Archaic. This would include Frontenac, Brewerton, Vosburg, Vergennes, Tadoussac, the Moorehead complex, Newfoundland Aberrant, and the Old Stone culture of Labrador. All show points in common. They are as familiar as a contemporary class picture from another school -- the clothes and poses are familiar, but the faces are different." (pg. 254).

Cadillac, Antoine de la Mothe, Sieur de. (1930). *"Memoir on Acadia" [1692]*. In W.F. Ganong, ed. "The Cadillac Memoir on Acadia of 1692.", Collections of the New Brunswick Historical Society, no. 13, New Brunswick , Canada. pp 77-97.

Calloway, Colin G., Ed. (1991). *Dawnland Encounters: Indians and Europeans in northern New England*. University Press of New England, Hanover, NH. IS.

Campeau, Lucien. (1967). *La premiere mission d'Acadie (1602 - 1616)*. Presses de l'Universite Laval, Quebec, Canada.

Champlain, Samuel de. (1922). *The works of Samuel de Champlain*. Edited by H. H. Langdon and W. F. Ganong. 6 Vols. Champlain Society, Toronto, Canada.

- There are numerous editions of the works of Samuel de Champlain. The Langton and Ganong edition is the definitive edition and is the one reprinted by the University of Toronto Press in 1971 under the auspices of the Champlain Society and edited by H. P. Biggar. This edition is electronically accessible at: The Champlain Society (http://www.champlainsociety.ca/). This edition is the sole source cited by Bourque in his definitive *Twelve Thousand Years*.
- Champlain began compiling his first volume in 1599, volume II in 1603, volume III in 1613, volume IV, V and VI in 1632.
- Another frequently cited edition of Champlain's work is that compiled by Grant in 1914.

Charlevoix, Pierre F.X. de. (1900). *History and genreal description of New France*. 6 vols. F. P. Harper, New York.

Cronon, William. (1983). *Changes in the land: Indians, colonists, and the ecology of New England*. Hill and Wang, NY, NY. IS.

- Among the most important of all information sources about the lifestyles and environmental impact of New England's indigenous inhabitants prior to contact with European explorers, traders and settlers.

Davies, James. (1880). *Relation of a voyage to Sagadahoc, 1607 - 1608*. American Journeys Collection. Document No. AJ-042. Reprinted in 2003 by Wisconsin Historical Society Digital Library and Archives. www.wisconsinhistory.org. X.

- This is the same document as the one cited below by DeCosta. James Davies was the navigator of Gilbert's vessel the Mary and John, and is almost certainly the author of the first part of this relation. The Rev. B. F. DeCosta was the person who discovered the manuscript in London in 1875; the document has now been reprinted a number of times.
- A copy of this is available in the Davistown Museum library.
- Davies Relations has also been reprinted by the Hakluyt Society (1849), the Massachusetts Historical Society (1880), in *New American World: A documentary history of North America* (1979) and in David and Alison Quinn's *The English New England Voyages 1602 - 1608*.

Day, Gordon M. (1962). English-Indian contacts in New England. *Ethnohistory*. 9(1). pg. 24-40. X.

- "...the central problem of New England ethnohistory, namely, that of identifying the ethnic units within the region, establishing their affinities, locating them at the time of discovery, and following their movements, their partitions, regroupings, and mergers through the violent dislocations which followed European contact." (pg. 26).
- "The English also exhibited a tendency to create a distinct band for each river, village, or fishing camp as their acquaintance with the country grew. Perhaps we should, pending the unraveling of the nomenclature by a concordance of historical and linguistic data, place more trust in the entities recognized by the French among their northern New England allies and in those recognized by the English among the southern New England coastal tribes." (pg. 26).
- "Of course, King Philip's War, that cataclysm in New England history, changed everything. When the smoke had cleared away, southern New England contained only what might be called reservation Indians, who had made some kind of peace with the English, and northern New England would contain southern New England refugees for the next one hundred and twenty-five years." (pg. 28).
- "...we can not profitably study the effect of European contact on New England Indian cultures unless we know what the pre-contact cultures were and unless we can identify the several entities with which they were associated. When we can surely identify our ethnic

units, we shall have a framework on which to hang the data of ethnographic studies." (pg. 32).

Day, Gordon M. (1981). The identity of the Saint Francis Indians. *Canadian Ethnology Service Paper no. 71*. National Museum of Man Mercury Series, Ottawa, Canada. pg. 237-247.

- "The Pennacooks, among many other New England tribes, came as refugees to the St. Francis, Odanak community." (Ray, *The Indians of Maine*, pg. 34).
- See the annotations for Day's *In Search of New England's Native Past* below.

Day, Gordon M. (1995). *Western Abenaki dictionary*. Canadian Museum of Civilization, Hull, Quebec, Canada.

Day, Gordon M. (1998). *In search of New England's Native past: Selected essays by Gordon M. Day*. Foster, Michael K. and Cowan, William, Eds. University of Massachusetts Press, Amherst, MA. IS.

- Essential background information for understanding the destination of any Wawenocs who survived the 1616 pandemic, this book of essays contains important information about Maine's Arosagunticook and Androscoggin tribes, among other subjects.
- "Saint Francis, ... was founded as a Catholic mission in the 1660s. From the beginning, the majority of its inhabitants were Western Abenaki refugees, who arrived there from various locations in the New England interior during the colonial wars of the eighteenth century and well into the nineteenth century." (pg. 1).
- "...he established, ... the fundamental role of groups in the middle and upper Connecticut River valley (the Sokokis, Penacooks, and Cowasucks), *with some increments from the Eastern Abenaki area,* [italics added] in building the Saint Francis community in its early stages." (pg. 23).
- The focus of most of the text is on the Western Abenaki; there is only one reference to the Wawenocs, which, unlike the Penobscots, are not shown on the map on page 29.
- "The plagues of 1616-1619 and 1633-1634 killed thousands of people in southern New England and countless more in the interior. But it was really the disastrous King Philip's War (1675-1676), named for the Wampanoag leader who rallied New England's Indians to take up arms against the English, that began the final dispersal of interior groups such as the Sokokis, Penacooks, Pocumtucks, Pigwackets, and others to the west and north, swelling the ranks of refugees at the village of Schaghticoke, a haven created for them on the Hudson River by New York governor Edmund Andros, and at the French missions, including Saint Francis, in Quebec. Well into the eighteenth century, Saint Francis received refugees from Maine; the upper Connecticut River valley; Schaghticoke; and especially Missisquoi, near present-day Swanton, Vermont." (pg. 9).
- "To complicate the historian's task further, there were reverse movements of people at different times from Saint Francis back to Schaghticoke and Missisquoi." (pg. 9).

- "Because most of interior New England underwent severe dislocations and depopulation before the groups involved were documented, locations that persisted throughout the period, such as Missisquoi, Schaghticoke, and Saint Francis, have assumed special importance for the historian and dialectologist." (pg. 9).
- "The impression that Saint Francis was settled by people from central and western Maine derived some of its impetus from the fact that in 1705-1706 the community had received refugees from the similarly named Saint-François-de-Sales mission on the Chaudière River, which empties into the Saint Lawrence about 75 miles below the mouth of the Saint Francis River. Many of the Chaudière people were originally attracted to that mission from the Kennebec and other rivers in Maine, some from as far east as the Penobscot area, and most of them spoke Eastern Abenaki dialects." (pg. 17).
- "Specifying who the Sokokis were and where they were located in early colonial times is important for Western Abenaki history, because they were the principal founding group at Saint Francis and have remained a significant presence there. Past historians often assumed that the Sokokis migrated to Quebec from the Saco River in western Maine, in part because of the vague similarity between the names. However, examination of seventeenth-century French and English documents reveals variants of the name such as *Sokokiois, Suckquakege,* and *Suckquakege,* and *Squakey* that appear to equate with *Squakheag,* the name of a village and a tribe in Northfield, Massachusetts. If the equation is valid, this places the Sokokis in the middle Connecticut River valley rather than western Maine." This paper, which demonstrates the value of place-name analysis for piecing together the history of a poorly documented region, was originally published in *Ethnohistory* 12(3):237-249 (1965). (Chapter 8: The Identity of the Sokokis, pg. 89).
- "The English also learned of the Saco River in 1605 from the Indians whom George Waymouth took captive to England, but they recorded no name for the tribe (Purchas 1905-1907 4:1873-1875). Captain John Smith visited the mouth of the Saco with one of Waymouth's Indians in 1614, but neither he nor Ferdinando Gorges's men who wintered there in 1616 left us any tribal name (J. Smith 1836 2:2, 42; Gorges 1837 5:57). The Indians at the head of the river were known as Pigwackets from the time they were visited by Gorges and Richard Vines in 1642 (Winthrop 1853 2:89). Throughout the seventeenth century, the English referred to the Indians on the lower river simply as Saco Indians, and they were still called 'the Saco tribe' in the 1726 census when there were only four men left (Wendall 1866)." (pg. 89-91).
- "For another thing, the Saint Francis Indians were a tribe of mixed origins, ...Saint Francis had received practically the whole Caniba (Norridgewock), Arosagunticook, Pigwacket, Cowasuck, Pocumtuck, Schaghticoke, and Missisquoi tribes, as well as individuals and fragments of bands broken by the wars in southern New England." (Chapter 2: Dartmouth and Saint Francis, pg. 50).
- "In approaching the history of English-Indian contacts in New England, we are faced with the fact that contact commenced long before significant records were made. For the casual reader, the history of New England began in 1620 with the landing of the Pilgrims on Plymouth Rock, yet he is confronted with the anomaly of Samoset's greeting, 'Welcome, Englishmen.' We may search hopefully in the relations of the voyage of 1602 (Archer 1843; Brereton 1843), but our quest for the precontact Indian is hardly satisfied by the Indians who met Captain Gosnold then at Cape Neddick, clad in European clothes and rowing 'in a

Baskeshallop,' or by the Cuttyhunk natives who tossed off in English such phrases as 'How now are you so saucie with my Tabacco?'" (Chapter 5: English-Indian Contacts in New England, pg. 65).

- "The mere thought of historical ethnographies, however, brings up a problem which is perhaps the central problem of New England ethnohistory, namely, that of identifying the ethnic units within the region; establishing their affinities; locating them at the time of discovery; and following their movements, their partitions, regrouping, and mergers through the violent dislocations which followed European contact." (Chapter 5: English-Indian Contacts in New England, pg. 66).

- "In the latter half of the seventeenth century, an Indian village sprang up on the east bank of the Saint Francis River a few miles above its junction with the Saint Lawrence. The subsequent history of this village, although known only imperfectly, shows complex population changes, characterized by immigration of many increments from tribes in Maine, New Hampshire, Vermont, and Massachusetts; attribution by war and disease; and emigration and reimmigration. The inhabitants of this village are known in history as the Saint Francis Indians." (Chapter 6: The tree nomenclature of the Saint Francis Indians, pg. 72).

- "It appears from the data obtained on trees and other plants that those men who in their youth lived the old hunting and fishing life and maintained lifelong contact with the woods as guides have preserved a very full corpus of plant lore in spite of the acculturated condition of the band. Whatever additional knowledge of medicinal and other plants which may be the possession of the elder women of the band has not been investigated." (Chapter 6: The tree nomenclature of the Saint Francis Indians, pg. 83).

- "Bécancour now contains only three families and practically no linguistic recollections. The descendants of those Bécancour families that migrated to Lake Saint John are now Montagnais in culture. Speck (1928) caught the last gasp of native language at Bécancour in 1912, but his naming it 'Wawenock' should be queried pending a thorough study of the history of the band." (Chapter 10: Historical notes on New England languages, pg. 104-105).

- "Linguistic and ethnographic data which cannot be assigned to a definite, named group at a definite time and place are at best useless and at worst a fruitful source of confusion and false theory." (pg. 223).

- "'There is a great many Indians in *Canada* that have not been out this Summer, both of *Kennibeck* and *Damarascoggin*, therefore a great many of these Indians at *Kennibeck* do intend to go to Canada in the Spring to them.' Thus we have Kennebec and Androscoggin Indians somewhere in Canada in the summer of 1675 and more planning to join them in the spring of 1676, since the Indians on the Kennebec at that time included Androscoggin and Saco River Indians under Squando (Hubbard 1865 2:204)." (Chapter 22: Arosagunticook and Androscoggin, pg. 225).

- "Therefore, until and unless I see new evidence to the contrary, I favor the position that (1) the Androscoggin River Indians were the Amarascoggins, not the Arosaguntacooks; (2) Arsikôntegok was the name of the Saint Francis River and village, derived from its characteristics, not from the founding tribe, and probably given by the Eastern Abenakis from the Chaudière in 1700; and (3) the Arosaguntacooks who appear in the Maine treaties were merely delegations from Saint Francis, whose ethnic composition at that time was probably predominantly Western Abenaki." (pg. 227-228).

- The best summary of the history of the St Francis Abenaki, some of whom migrated to Canada from Maine.
- The bibliography in this text is extensive and contains many citations not included in The Davistown Museum bibliographies.

DeCosta, Benjamin F., Ed. (1880). The Sagadahoc Colony. *Proceedings of the Massachusetts Historical Society,* 18. pg. 82-117.

- A relation of a voyage to Sagadahoc, printed from the original manuscript in the Lambeth Palace Library. James Davies is the author.

DeCosta, Benjamin F. (1884). Norumbega and its English explorers. In: Winsor, Justin, Ed. *Narrative and critical history of America.* Vol 3. Houghton, Mifflin and Co., Boston, MA. IS.

- This whole chapter has been scanned and is available in our Norumbega information file for you to read.

Denys, Nicolas. (1908). *The description and natural history of the coasts of North America (Acadia) [1672].* Edited and translated by W.F. Ganong. The Champlain Society, Toronto, Canada.

Druillettes, Gabriel. (1857). *Narritive of a voyage, made for the Abenaquiois mission, and information acquired of New England and dispositions of the Magistrates of that republic for assistance against the Iroquois. The whole by me, Gabriel Druillettes, of the Society of Jesus, translated and edited by John Gilmary Shea.* Collections of the New York Historical Society, 2nd series, vol. 3, part 2, New York, NY. pg. 309-320.

Eckstorm, Fannie Hardy. (1945). *Old John Neptune and other Maine Indian shamans.* The Southworth-Anthoensen Press, Portland, ME. A Marsh Island reprint in 1980, University of Maine at Orono, Orono, ME. IS(2).

- "The statements of many historians and near historians are so full of errors and so contradictory that it is useless to cite them as evidence, needless to demolish them as errors. Nearly all say that the Penobscots are Tarratines. They are not. Some say that the Passamaquoddies are Tarratines. They are not. Others say that the Wawenocks were exterminated. They were not." (pg. 73).
- "The Wawenocks were not exterminated. After the Norridgewock disaster they removed to Canada and most of them stayed there. Within a few years Dr. Frank Speck has found a remnant of the tribe and has studied the dialect." (pg. 74).
- "According to Dr. Speck, the name is not *Wan-noak,* 'very brave': it comes from *Walinakiak,* the 'People of the Bays,' their old homes having been along the deeply indented coast

between the Kennebec and St. George's Rivers, whence their other name of 'Sheepscot Indians.'" (pg. 74).

Erickson, Vincent O. (1978). Maliseet-Passamaquoddy. In: *Handbook of North American Indians: Northeast.* Vol 15. Trigger, Bruce G. Ed., Smithsonian Institution, Washington, D.C. pg. 123-136. X.

- "The Maliseet and Passamaquoddy speak mutually intelligible dialects of the same language." (pg. 123).
- "These virtually identical people differed primarily in their economic adaptation. The Maliseet were inland hunters, living along the Saint John River drainage in New Brunswick and Maine; the Passamaquoddy were sea mammal hunters, living along the coasts of New Brunswick and Maine. (pg. 123).
- "The Passamaquoddy had long occupied and used the territory on the south and east shores of Passamaquoddy Bay for maple sugaring (Eckstorm 1941:226), marine hunting, and fishing (Sabine 1852:100) and used Lewis (Lewey's) Island near Princeton for inland hunting and fishing (Ganong 1899:223)." (pg. 125).
- "In June the Maliseets went to one of the islands in the Saint John to camp, first to spear bass and later sturgeon. Several trips were made back and forth from garden plots to fishing sites in the summer. After corn was hilled the Maliseets went out to spear fish including salmon by torchlight at night. Fish, wild grapes, and roots provided the summer diet. In fall corn was harvested, and the portion that was dried was either stored in subterranean pits lined with bark or taken along on the migratory winter hunt. This hunt for moose or bear was done by groups of 8 to 10 people, two of whom were adult men. Until spring, the group continually traveled over a large area of Maine, New Brunswick, and the Gaspé Peninsula in search of game." (pg. 127).
- "Passamaquoddy subsistence activities and annual cycle resembled the Maliseet in most details for the three periods outlined. Spring found the same fishing and planting sequences, but June precipitated a movement to the seashore. Men, two to a canoe, paddled into the open seas of the Bay of Fundy to shoot porpoise and seal (Verrill 1954:96). While it is not universally agreed that porpoise and seal hunting was aboriginal among the Passamaquoddy, Eckstorm (1932:15) suggests that seal and porpoise oil were used by Maine Indians during the ceramic period. Whales were enticed by men in canoes to swim into shallow areas where they became stranded and were more easily killed. Excursions were made to neighboring islands to fish, to gather clams and lobsters, or to collect the eggs of sea birds. Winter hunting and trapping follow most details of the Maliseet." (pg. 127).
- "Porcupine-quill embroidery was lost about the time the splint basket replaced the birchbark container." (pg. 129).
- "Other types of political organization reflect changes associated with the formation of the Wabanaki Confederacy. Essentially an alliance established in the mid-eighteenth century among the Micmac, Maliseet, Passamaquoddy, Penobscot, and Abenaki, it embraced other tribes allied to the French and had its 'great fire' or principal meeting place at Caughnawaga, Quebec. ...The Wabanaki Confederacy ceased to meet sometime in the second half of the nineteenth century." (pg. 132).

Fitzhugh, William W., Ed. (1985). *Cultures in contact: The impact of European contacts on Native American cultural institutions A.D. 1000 - 1800*. Smithsonian Institution Press, Washington, DC. IS.

- "The lack of archeological information on contact-period Indian cultures is only one side of the coin, for archeological attention to the more mundane aspects of rural colonial life has been equally deficient. ...Is the paucity of archeological data really attributable to site destruction from colonial land-use practice, village and urban sprawl, and dam and highway construction, or is this frequently heard claim just a rationalization for neglect?" (pg. 4).
- "Little attention, however, has been given to archeological studies of early contact from the native point of view. ...we decided therefore to attempt an archeological perspective on the earliest period of contact -- primarily the sixteenth and seventeenth centuries -- and to concentrate not on changing material culture and technology per se, but rather on the effects of European contact on the institutions that organized native societies. By doing so, we hoped to identify structural change in the organization of these groups and to relate changes in economic and social organization, religious beliefs, settlement patterns, subsistence, land use, and other systems to various contact and acculturation phenomena." (pg. 5).
- "More recently, a growing awareness of native life and history has led to the view that the virtual annihilation of many of these cultures and their people is attributable to the merciless and unconscionable economic, military, political, and spiritual exploitation of native American groups by European explorers and colonists competing for nationalistic and mercantile dominance in the New World. This view holds that Indian groups were unwitting witnesses to their own destruction or, at best, ineffectual defenders of their rights in the face of broken treaties and unfavorably balanced transactions. History supports the validity of many elements of this perspective." (pg. 8-9).
- "Societies ranged from small, nomadic hunting groups to complex chiefdoms and regional confederacies controlled by tribal councils and powerful sachems, sagamores, and shamans. At the time of contact native groups interacted in various ways in coastal areas and inter-tribal economic exchange systems dispersed utilitarian as well as socially valuable commodities throughout the region, many destined for prestigious individuals." (pg. 100).
- "By the time Gosnold visited the coast of Maine in 1602, natives were wearing large copper breastplates and European costumes including waistcoats, breeches, hose, and shoes in seafashion style." (pg. 101).

Ganong, William Francis. (1917). The origin of the place-names Acadia and Norumbega. *Proceedings and Transactions*. Royal Society of Canada, 3rd series, XXXI, ii. pg. 105-119. X.

- "Thus the late A. S. Gatschet, a trained philologist and expert in the Indian language, has also written in connection with Norumbega: 'The name does not stand for any Indian settlement, but is a term of the Abnáki languages, which in Penobscot sounds nalambígi, in Passamaquoddy nalabégik -- both referring to the 'still, quiet' (nala--) stretch of a river between two riffles, rapids, or cascades; --bégik, for nipégik, means 'at the water'. On the larger rivers and watercourses of Maine ten to twenty of these 'still water stretches' may occur on each' (*National Geographic Magazine*, VIII, 1897, 23). A root -BEGA, in the locative case -BEGAK or BEGAT, is very common in place-names of Maine and Eastern Canada associated with standing water, as manifest by the fact that the sixth paper of a series appearing in these transactions, gives a list of approximately one hundred of them; and a root NOL- or NOLUM- occurs in words meaning STILL or QUIET, referring to water (Hubbard, *Woods and Lakes of Maine*, 205)." (pg. 108).

- "Thus De Costa, repeating the explanation above given by Ballard, adds that of Sewall who makes it mean PLACE OF A FINE CITY. Sewall, in his *Ancient Dominions of Maine*, made the word apply to an Indian village westward of the Penobscot, as did an Indian mentioned by Godfrey." (pg. 108).

- "Champlain in his *Voyages* of 1613 uses the form NOREMBEGUE, and identifies the river with the Penobscot; but his personal experience showed the falsity of the old stories, and his common sense comments, aided by the wit of Lescarbot, swept Norumbega from the maps. It is easy to find the source of Champlain's *Norembegue*, for this form of the name, and the stories he controverts, occur in a popular book which ran through seven editions prior to 1605 -- about the time when Champlain was writing (Harrisse, 155), viz., *Les Voyages avantureux du Capitaine Jan Alfonce*. This work was founded on Alfonse's well-known Ms. *Cosmographie* of 1544, in which he describes a cape, river, and city of NOROMBEGUE in the region of the present Maine." (pg. 109).

- "Thus we are led back to the narrative of 1539 which says that NORUMBEGA was the name of the country used by the inhabitants. The statement has an air of finality, but grave difficulties attend its acceptance. First, we know that the American Indians did not themselves use names for extensive territories, as the civilized white man does, but only for specific localities having some connection with their lives or interests. Our surviving Indian names for territories were adopted and extended by the whites from more limited geographical features." (pg. 110).

Ganong, William F. (1933). *"Crucial Maps in the early cartography and place nomenclature of the Atlantic coast of Canada. V: The Compiled , or Composite Maps of 1526-1600"*. Transactions of the Royal Society of Canada, Series 3, vol. 27, sect 2, pp. 149-195. Ottawa, Canada.

Gorges, Ferdinando. (1658). *A briefe narration of the originall undertakings of the advancement of plantations into the parts of America. Especially showing the beginning, progress and continuence of that of New England.* E. Brudenell for Nath. Brook., London, England. Reprinted in 1890 by Publications of the Prince Society, Boston, MA. W.

- "This Bashaba had many enemies, especially those to the East and North-East, whom they called <u>Tarentines</u>, those to the West and South-West, were called <u>Sockhigones</u>, but the Tarentines were counted a more war-like and hardy People, and had indeed the least opportunity to make their attempts upon them, by reason of the conveniency and opportunity of the Rivers and Sea, which affoarded a speedy passage into the <u>Bashabaes</u> Country, which was called <u>Moasham</u>, and that part of the Country which lay between the <u>Sockhigones</u> Country and Moasham was called <u>Apistama</u>: The Massachisans and Bashabaes were sometimes Friends and sometimes Enemies as it fell out, but the Bashaba and his People seemed to be of some eminence above the rest, in all that part of the Continent; his owne chief abode was not far from Pemaquid, but the Warre growing more and more violent between the Bashaba and the Tarentines ... the Tarentines suprised the Bashaba, and slew him and all his People near about him, carrying away his Women, and such other matters as they thought of value..." (This quote from Gorges was reprinted in Siebert, 1973, pg. 71.)

- Gorges or one of his associates interviewed several of the Wawenoc Indians captured by George Waymouth. The narrative was given to Hakluyt who died before publishing it. Samuel Purchas published it in 1625 (Morey, 2005).

Grant, W.L., Ed. (1907). *Voyages of Samuel de Champlain: 1604 - 1616*. Charles Scribner's Sons, NY, NY.

- Champlain's narrative of his voyages to Maine are the primary source for the Bourque/Snow thesis that the Bashaba, titular head of the mysterious confederacy of Mawooshen, was an Etchemin and lived on the Penobscot in the vicinity of Bangor. (Also see Baird's letters.) This point of view is in fact directly contradicted by the very text that is used to verify its truth, e.g. below Champlain makes very clear that while visiting the Bangor area he found no evidence of any significant community of Native Americans, Etchemins being such a nomadic tribe that they had no permanent place of residence. Champlain never explored the rivers of Norumbega with any thoroughness, not having visited the Medomak, Damariscotta and much of the Sheepscot basin with the exception of a single trip to Wiscasset, where he noted Armouchiquois of a different lifestyle and dress than the Souriquois of eastern Canada. Based upon this lack of accurate exploration of the heartland of the Wawenocs, the conclusion that the Native Americans living west of the Penobscot River were Etchemins is based only upon a single encounter on the Penobscot near Bucksport and is contradicted by a large body of oral and written history from primarily English rather than French sources. Champlain's narrative further supports the English point of view by the obvious error of calling the Kennebec Indians Etechemins ("This nation of savages of Quinibequy are called Etechemins, as well as those of Norumbegue", pg. 50.) If Champlain thought the Kennebec Indians were Etchemins, he certainly could have easily been mistaken about the Bashaba as well as his brethren, the Wawenocs of "Norumbegue." The Kennebec Indians (Cannabis) are considered to be Armouchiquois by both Antiquarian and contemporary historians.
- This controversy is given further fuel by W.L. Grant in his footnote pertaining to the domain of the Bashaba as being in the region around Rockland, an area Champlain called Bedabedec, see below. This footnote supports the English and colonial observations that the stronghold of the Wawenocs and their Bashaba was in the Pemaquid/Rockland region. The Bourque/Snow thesis would seem to hold that the Wawenocs, in fact, never existed, were it not for Snow's one and only comment on the Wawenocs in his *Archaeology of New England*: "Wawenoc Indians, who appear in many later documents, were simply residents of the coastal drainages between the Kennebec and Penobscot that I have chosen to lump with the Kennebec." (pg. 61). The Wawenocs may appear in "many later documents" but seem to disappear in contemporary texts, most graphically in that most comprehensive of all studies of the Native Americans of North America, Trigger's *Handbook of North American Indians*. In Volume 15, Snow's chapter on the Eastern Abenaki identifies the Bashaba as an

Etchemin/Penobscot chief, with no mention of his historic association with the Wawenocs of Mawooshen. The following observations by Champlain provide a very meager basis for this contention.

- While visiting Mount Desert Island (Sept. 6, 1604): "On the morning of the next day they came alongside of our barque and talked with our savages. I ordered some biscuit, tobacco, and other trifles to be given them. These savages had come beaver-hunting and to catch fish, some of which they gave us. Having made an alliance with them, they guided us to their river of Pentegoüet, [Penobscot] so called by them, where they told us was their captain, named Bessabez, chief of this river. I think this river is that which several pilots and historians call Norumbegue, and which most have described as large and extensive, with very many islands." (pg. 46).

- "The Isle des Monts Déserts forms one of the extremities of the mouth, [of the Penobscot] on the east; the other is low land, called by the savages Bedabedec, to the west of the former, the two being distant from each other nine or ten leagues." (pg. 46-47).

- "Some two or three leagues from the point of Bedabedec, as you coast northward along the main land which extends up this river, there are very high elevations of land, which in fair weather are seen twelve of fifteen leagues out at sea." (pg. 47).

- The editor, W.L. Grant, adds this footnote: "An indefinite region about Rockland and Camden, on the western bank of the Penobscot near its mouth, appears to have been the domain of the Indian chief, Bessabez, and was denominated Bedabedec. The Camden Hills were called the mountains of Bedabedec and Owl's Head was called Bedabedec Point." (pg. 46).

- "And I will state that from the entrance to where we went [Bangor], about twenty-five leagues, we saw no town, nor village, nor the appearance of there having been one, but one or two cabins of the savages without inhabitants. These were made in the same way as those of the Souriquois, being covered with the bark of trees. So far as we could judge, the savages on this river are few in number, and are called Etechemins. Moreover, they only come to the islands, and that only during some months in summer for fish and game, of which there is a great quantity. They are a people who have no fixed abode, so far as I could observe and learn from them." (pg. 48).

- Grant follows with this footnote: "The Souriquois are the Mic-Macs of Nova Scotia. Closely akin to them were the Etechemins, who extended from St. John, N.B., to the neighborhood of Mount Desert. South of these were the Almouchiquois or Armouchiquois." (pg. 48).

- September 16, 1604: "The 16th of the month there came to us some thirty savages on assurances given them by those who had served us as guides. There came also to us the same day the above-named Bessabez with six canoes. ...Bessabez, seeing us on land, bade us sit down and began to smoke with his companions, as they usually do before an address. They presented us with venison and game. I directed our interpreter to say to our savages that they should cause Bessabez, Cahahis, and their companions to understand that Sieur de Monts had sent me to them to see them, and also their country, and that he desired to preserve friendship with them and to reconcile them with their enemies, the Souriquois and Canadians." (pg. 49-50).

- "The 17th of the month I took the altitude, and found the latitude 45° 25'. This done, we set out for another river called Quinibequy, distant from this place thirty-five leagues, and nearly twenty from Bedabedec. This nation of savages of Quinibequy are called Etechemins, as well as those of Norumbegue." (pg. 50).

- "The 20th of the month we sailed along the western coast, and passed the mountains of Bedabedec, when we anchored. The same day we explored the entrance to the river, where large vessels can approach; but there are inside some reefs, to avoid which one must advance with sounding lead in hand. Our savages left us, as they did not wish to go to Quinibequy, for the savages of that place are great enemies to them. We sailed some eight leagues along the western coast to an island ten leagues distant from Quinibequy, where we were obliged to put in on account of bad weather and contrary wind [Monhegan Island]." (pg. 51).
- "And in consideration of the small quantity of provisions which we had, we resolved to return to our settlement [at St. Croix] and wait until the following year, when we hoped to return and explore more extensively. We accordingly set out on our return on the 23d of September, and arrived at our settlement on the 2d of October following. The above is not an exact statement of all that I have observed respecting not only the coasts and people, but also the river of Norumbegue; and there are none of the marvels there which some persons have described. I am of opinion that this region is as disagreeable in winter as that of our settlement, in which we were greatly deceived." (pg. 51-52).

Greene, Francis B. (1906). *History of Boothbay, Southport and Boothbay Harbor, Maine 1623 - 1905 with family genealogies.* Loring, Short and Harmon, Portland, ME. IS.

- Greene is one of the last of the traditional historians utilizing Williamson as a primary source of information and retaining the tribal specific name Wawenoc for the Native American inhabitants living between the Kennebec and Penobscot rivers.
- "The Indian inhabitants of Maine were divided into two great confederacies; the Abenaques and the Etechemins; and the Penobscot River was the line of demarcation. The Abenaques dwelt westerly and the Etechemins along the banks and east of this river. The former were divided into four large tribes; the latter into three. The Sokokis, the smallest tribe among the Abenaques, were settled upon the Saco River; and their principal abode was Indian Island, just above the Lower Falls, also a settlement in the present town of Fryeburg and another on the Great Ossipee. The Anasagunticooks dwelt along he Androscoggin River, on the west side, from its sources to Merrymeeting Bay; their principal resort being at Pejepscot, now Brunswick. The Canibas lived on the Kennebec River, from Norridgewock to the sea, and Kennebis, the paramount lord of the tribe, lived on Swan Island; but there were several other points along the river where settlements of some size were indicated, notably at Norridgewock and Teconnet, now Winslow. The Wawenocks occupied the remaining space between the two great rivers, Kennebec and Penobscot, their principal settlements being on the Sheepscot and Damariscotta..." (pg. 35).
- "The principal dwelling places of the Wawenocks must have been those spots here and there alongshore which have shown the greatest amount of offal deposit." (pg. 38).
- "The two great centers of Wawenock settlement were where the Damariscotta oyster shell deposit exists and about the lower Sheepscot waters, though there were many minor ones. Indications point to this Damariscotta locality as the Norumbegua or Arambec of the ancients, and also as being the residence of the Bashaba, more strongly than any other place. ... There are several reasons why this place is indicated as the chief point in old Mavooshen.

It shows to have been the center and abode of a mighty horde of eaters, much greater in extent than any other in America, and one of the largest in the world; it was as nearly central in their territory as any place that could be selected; the quality of the food was better than any other section has shown, being oysters instead of clams, and the ruling element usually takes the best in either civilized or barbarian life; lastly, when the Popham and Gilbert colony was visited by a delegation from the Bashaba, consisting of his brother Skidwares and Nahanada, extending an invitation to visit him, a locality northerly from Pemaquid was indicated by them, and not the lower Sheepscot, where the next greatest aggregation of offal deposit exists." (pg. 39 - 40).

- "At the head of the cove which penetrates Sawyer's Island from the north, more than half the distance across it, were in early times quite well-defined cooking pots, cut in the rocks, which in later years have crumbled and sloughed off. It is supposed that they were used for cooking maize and vegetables by immersing hot stones in the pot holes when filled with water and the articles to be cooked." (pg. 40).
- Commenting on Verrazzano's 1524 visit to the shores of Maine: "He skirted the coast along, touching near the site of Portsmouth, and then made his cruise along the shores of the Gulf of Maine. He stated that while at the South he found the natives agreeable and gentle, here, on the Maine coast, they were in an irritable state, rude and ill-mannered. No navigator of his time knew better than Verrazzano just what localities had been visited up to that date by voyagers and fishermen, and he interpreted it at once as an indication that the Indian race, in these parts, was disaffected from treatment they had received from European visitors. He noted another peculiarity of the Indians on this coast, which strengthened his suspicions; while at the South the natives were pleased with any trinket or ornament, here they wanted nothing but fishhooks, knives, or some iron or steel instrument that would cut, and appeared as though they had learned the use of such articles. He concluded that European barter with the natives had commenced before his visit." (pg. 45).

Hakluyt, Richard. (1582). *Divers voyages touching the discoverie of America*. London. Facsimile reprint in 1967 by Theatrum Orbis Terraram, Amsterdam.

Hakluyt, Richard. (1589-1601). *The principall navigations, voiages and discoveries of the English nation*. George Bishop and Ralph Newberrie, London, England.

- The Davistown Museum library has a copy of a modern reprint in its library: Hakluyt, Richard. (1985). *Voyages and discoveries: The principal navigations voyages, traffiques and discoveries of the English nation*. Edited, abridged and introduced by Jack Beeching, Penguin Classics, Penguin Books Ltd., London. IS.
- See annotations in the General History Sources: Antiquarian bibliography.

Hakluyt, Richard. (1877). *A discourse concerning western planting: Written in the year 1584 by Richard Hakluyt; now first printed from a contemporary manuscript, with a preface and an introduction by Leonard Woods, Ed., with notes in the appendix, by Charles Deane*. Press of J. Wilson, Cambridge, MA.

Hardy, Kerry. (2006). Personal communications. Director of Merryspring Park, Camden, ME.

- Kerry Hardy is also the author of the essay: "Four Guides to the Past."
- Thank you to Kerry for many helpful suggestions in the preparation of this publication by email, telephone conversations, snail mail, carrier pigeon and messages in a bottle.

Hardy, Kerry. (2009). *Notes on a lost flute: A field guide to the Wabanaki.* Down East Books, Camden, ME. IS.

- *Notes on a Lost Flute* is a lyrical in-depth survey of the ecology and multiplicity of natural food resources in the homeland of a major Eastern Woodlands people, specifically the Wabanaki communities of coastal Maine.
- Kerry Hardy has more knowledge of the ecology of coastal Maine in both the pre-contact and post-contact periods than any other contemporary writer or ethnohistorian, and reinforces the literary excellence of his text with his familiarity with the linguistic origins of surviving Algonquin terms and names.
- His index on this subject, "part glossary and part sounding board for some proposed translations that I think deserve further scrutiny" (pg. 137) is, along with his ecological and ethnohistoric studies and insights, a major contribution to the ongoing efforts of public schools to further the study of the indigenous communities of Maine.
- This publication is an absolutely essential component of any public, private, or home school presentation dealing with the history of Native Americans in Maine.
- "The world needs all kinds of boats and all kinds of books. This book is a canoe, and from it I hope to show you a lively mix of ancient New England and the people who lived here. We'll see caribou and swans, oysters and sturgeon, wood lilies and groundnuts. Penobscots and Maliseets; and in true canoe fashion we'll travel fast and light, without much baggage… the first section of the book offers compressed background history and terminology that will help you make sense of the chapters that follow. The last section discusses the sources of information that I've relied on in my research." (pg. 10).
- "After three years of intensive study of [the Wabanaki community of Maine's] history, language, culture, and ecology… I hope that these resurrected glimpses of an original American landscape and its people do justice to both." (pg. 11).
- "Do not assume that these accounts offer pictures of precontact Maine. They don't. The Maine that Rosier and Davies saw was a war zone, and had been for a period of years. Tremendous upheavals had taken place in the prior century, and bigger ones were still to come, as different native factions struggled to control trade and gain influence with the Europeans." (pg. 45).
- "The five natives that Waymouth kidnapped and took back to England described a confederacy called Mawooshen that represented the peak of Abenaki influence over their eastern neighbors. It seems to have spread eastward quickly, and it would retreat just as quickly in the following two decades as the Micmac and Maliseet, or 'Tarrantines' as their enemies knew them, pushed back. The years from 1607 to 1615 marked the height of the struggle, and the culminating battle saw the death of a legendary figure known alternately as Bessabes, Beshabe, Bashabas, or The Bashaba." (pg. 46).

- "The Sebasticook traditionally had the most spectacular alewife runs in the state, and it flows through miles of rich alluvial soils that were, and are, perfectly suited for cornfields. Such a location would jibe with the Penobscot oral tradition that their ancestors traveled west along the Sebasticook each spring and fall to plant and harvest corn in cooperation with Kennebec River natives." (pg. 65-6).
- "I'm no archaeologist, but I do have a pretty strong belief that corn was just about everywhere on the Maritime Peninsula by 1550." (pg. 69).
- A final interesting word is Etchemin, which is how Champlain and Lescarbot's Micmacs referred to those living west of them. The first two syllables of this word, preserved today in the Passamaquoddy word skidjim, mean simply Indian; but the final syllable of –min usually indicates a seed of some kind. Consider the following names for Indian corn collected from various groups around New England (collector in parentheses): weatchiminneash (Trumbull), eachimmineach (Cotton), ∞iatchimanes (Mathevet), ew-chim-neash (Williams). Calling groups to their west 'corn-growers' would make sense for the Micmacs in 1605 – they had abandoned the practice by then, as they told Lescarbot, but the Abenaki (and probably the Meductic Maliseets) had not." (pg. 75).
- A compelling reanimation and reexamination of one of America's richest ecological bioregion 400 years before the dawn of the age of biocatastrophe. A most important addition to the ethnohistorical literature reviewed in this publication.

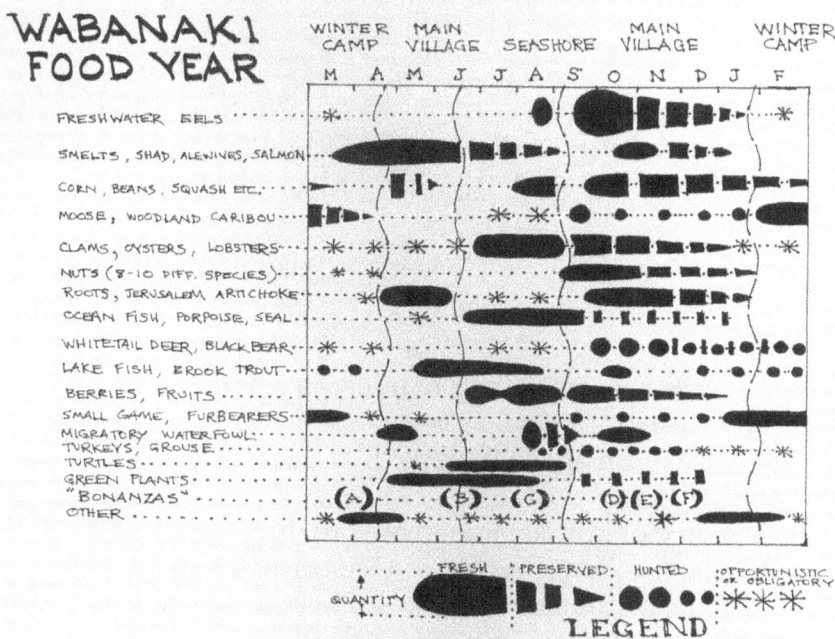

(pg. 58).

Hoffman, Bernard G. (November 1955). Souriquois, Etechemin, and Kwedech -- a lost chapter in American ethnography. *Ethnohistory*. pg. 65-87.

- "...historical evidence that at the time of the Cartier voyages the St. Lawrence Iroquois of the Montreal-Quebec-Tadoussac region were engaged in an ancient war against southern Indians named by them Toudaman..." (pg. 78).

- "... legendary but consistent materials from the Micmac of Nova Scotia and New Brunswick to the effect that they were one engaged in a bitter war with Iroquois Indians named by them Kwedech..." (pg. 79).
- "After the great plague of 1617 a large section of the Etchemin country was completely depopulated and was reoccupied by Abnaki-speaking peoples moving in from the west, and by Micmac-speaking peoples moving in from the northeast. The Abnaki speakers eventually coalesced into the Abnaki of the Kennebec and Penobscot drainages." (pg. 79-80). This is not presently considered an accurate summary of intertribal movements in the seventeenth century.
- Hoffman is the first of the revisionists asserting Etchemin occupation of the Wawenoc territory between the Kennebec and Penobscot rivers. The map he published with his Ph.D. thesis is reproduced in the Maps Appendix of Norumbega Reconsidered and is a precursor of the Bourquian revolution that began in 1989. This interpretation of the ethnicity of the central Maine coast would imply that there was no Wawenoc community prior to the great pandemic and that Abenaki occupation east of the Saco River is a post-pandemic event.

Hubbard, William. (1677). *The present state of New-England: Being a narrative of the troubles with the Indians in New-England from Pascataqua to Pemmaquid*. London. Facsimile reproduction with introduction by Cecelia Tichi in 1972, York Mail-Print, Bainbridge, NY.

Hubbard, William. (1865). *The history of the Indian Wars in New England, from the first settlement to the termination of the war with King Phillip 1677*. (Originally published in 1680?) 2 vols. Dranke, S.G., Ed., W. Eliot Woodward, Roxbury, MA.

Innis, Harold A. (1962). *The fur trade in Canada*. Yale University Press, New Haven, CT.

- "The fur trade in the first half of the sixteenth century was of minor importance and incidental to fishing. By the end of the century a revolution had occurred and the agricultural Indians of the Huron-Iroquois family had been driven from the St. Lawrence valley apparently by hunting Indians." (pg. 12).
- "Once they had secured access to a source of iron supplies, more primitive implements disappeared and the methods of making them were forgotten. Guns displaced bows and arrows. They required periodic mending and ammunition was in constant demand. As old cultural traits fell gradually into disuse and old ways of getting a livelihood were forgotten, the Indian became increasingly dependent on the products of the specialized equipment of Europe and increasingly dependent upon his supply of furs." (pg. 17-18).
- "Indian middlemen were able to exercise greater bargaining power over more remote tribes with the use of European weapons. Consequently, they were extremely jealous of any attempt of the French or the Dutch to trade guns with these remote tribes. On the other hand, a supply of guns for more remote tribes enabled the European trader to break the monopoly of the middlemen. The net result was continuous and destructive warfare. The disastrous

results of these cultural changes were shown further in the spread of European diseases, especially smallpox, and the decimation of the Indians." (pg. 21).

Island Institute. (November 2004). One Land - Two Worlds: Maine. Mawooshen 1605-2005: The 400th Anniversary of George Waymouth's Voayage to New England. Rockland, Maine. IS.

Jennings, Francis. (1975). *The invasion of America: Indians, colonialism and the cant of conquest.* University of North Carolina Press, Chapel Hill, NC. IS.

- "The invaders of strange continents assumed an innate and absolute superiority over all other peoples because of divine endowment; their descendants would eventually secularize the endowment to claim it from nature instead of God, but would leave its absolute and innate qualities unchanged." (pg. 5).
- "Decent men with pigmentless skins no longer overtly espouse delusions of peculiar grandeur, but the myths created by the cant of conquest endure in many forms to mask the terrible tragedy that was Europe's glory." (pg. 6).
- "The historian cannot wholly free himself from the outlook of his own cultural tradition. In perceiving and reflecting upon the interaction of two cultures, he necessarily adopts a viewpoint somewhere in his own. The idea of a neutral ethnohistory is itself a product of the scientific tradition of European culture. Because of this inescapable bias of outlook, reinforced by the historian's dependence for source materials on the literate Europeans' corpus of documents, it seems desirable to make a special effort of imagination to see things as Indians might." (pg. 14).
- "*European explorers and invaders discovered an* inhabited land. Had it been pristine wilderness then, it would possibly be so still today, for neither the technology nor the social organization of Europe in the sixteenth and seventeenth centuries had the capacity to maintain, of its own resources, outpost colonies thousands of miles from home. Incapable of conquering true wilderness, the Europeans were highly competent in the skill of conquering other people, and that is what they did. They did not settle a virgin land. They invaded and displaced a resident population." (pg. 15).
- "The basic conquest myth postulates that America was virgin land, or wilderness, inhabited by nonpeople called savages; that these savages were creatures sometimes defined as demons, sometimes as beasts 'in the shape of men'; that their mode of existence and cast of mind were such as to make them incapable of civilization and therefore of full humanity; that civilization was required by divine sanction or the imperative of progress to conquer the wilderness and make it a garden; that the savage creatures of the wilderness, being unable to adapt to any environment other than the wild, stubbornly and viciously resisted God or fate, and thereby incurred their suicidal extermination; that civilization and its bearers were refined and ennobled in their contest with the dark powers of the wilderness; and that it all was inevitable." (pg. 15).
- "Unfortunately, however, the price of repressing scruples has been the suppression of facts." (pg. 15).
- "The so-called settlement of America was a *re*settlement, a reoccupation of a land made waste by the diseases and demoralization introduced by the newcomers." (pg. 30).

- "A basic rule was that any given Englishman at any given time formed his views in accordance with his purposes. ...In short, like the most modern of architects, the Englishman devised the savage's form to fit his function." (pg. 59).
- "Before European invasion most eastern Indians subsisted largely on the products of their farms and fishing. A nutritionist has concluded that the Indians of southern New England ate only about half as much meat per capita as Americans do today. A Dutch colonist reported that the Indians 'do not eat a satisfactory meal' without cornmeal mush. (pg. 63).
- "...as has been noticed, Indians created pasture land that attracted grazing animals. After contact with Europeans some Indians came to speak of the deer as their 'sheep.' ... Indian pasture was made by communal effort, English by private. Actually the colonists of the early contact period avoided the heavy labor of clearing woods whenever possible, bending their chief efforts instead to acquiring the lands already cleared by Indians." (pg. 65).
- "Whether hunters or farmers, all Indian bands or other organized community groups lived in territories marked by specific natural boundaries such as mountains or streams. Their lives were governed by cycles of movement within their territories. When fish shoaled, plants fruited, and animals seasonally migrated, Indians revisited familiar spots. Both hunters and farmers gathered at certain seasons in tribal centers or villages for the performance of unifying rituals and public business as well as for simple sociability." (pg. 67).
- "Whether searching for food or commodity, the Indian hunter always returned after the chase to his native village." (pg. 71-72).
- "About the journey to distant hunting territories, two facts may be noted: the hunters moved over networks of trails that were soundly enough laid out to serve as the basis for the wagon roads and automobile highways of times to come; and the journey was made in all sorts of weather." (pg. 91).
- "The collapse of intertribal trade in Indian commodities surely contributed to a general increase in hostilities by establishing competition as a greater source of advantage than cooperation. There can be no doubt at all of the increase in hostilities stimulated by the arrangements of the new trade with Europeans. Although the resulting carnage has been called the 'beaver wars,' it might be as justifiably called the 'firearm wars,' 'kettle wars,' or 'blanket wars.'" (pg. 95).

Johnston, John. (1873). *A history of Bristol and Bremen.* Joel Munsell, Albany, NY.

- " Capt. Levett too, who visited Capmanwagan (now Southport), in the winter of 1623, and saw there numbers of the Pemaquid Indians, with Samosett their chief, frequently speaks of beaver and otter skins as common articles of trade." (pg. 13).
- "Those who first became acquainted with the natives of this region speak of a *bashaba*, or great ruler, whose authority extended over many tribes, and the sachems of those several tribes acknowledging him as their common sovereign. The country over which he ruled was called *Mavooshen*, and probably extended from the Piscataqua river to the Penobscot or even farther east. The chief residence of the *bashaba* is said, by some, to have been at Pemaquid, but by others it is thought to have been somewhere on the Penobscot. If his residence was on the Penobscot, it is certain that he belonged to the Abenakis; and it is probable that he was slain, and his kingdom broken up, during the wars between the western and the eastern Indians, about 1612-1617." (pg. 14).

- "It is certain that he was living and in full possession of his acknowledged authority, in the autumn of 1607, when the Popham expedition made their landing at the mouth of the Kennebec. They had been there only a few days when a large company of the natives, in nine canoes, made them a visit: and among them were Nahanada and Skidwares, both of whom had spent some time in England, having been kidnapped by Waymouth two years before. The Indians were desirous that the white men should make a visit to the *bashaba*, for whom they appeared to entertain great respect; and it was arranged that Capt. Gilbert, commander of one of the ships of the expedition, with some attendants, should be sent as representatives of the colony. ... On account of several unfavorable circumstances, it was six days before Capt. Gilbert and company reached Pemaquid, when they found, to their great mortification, Nahanada, and the other Indians, whom he expected to accompany him, had already departed for the Penobscot, where the *bashaba* resided. They immediately followed, in the hope of joining their Indian friends in the immediate precinct of the *bashaba's* court; but having spent two days in a vain search for the mouth of the river, and their supply of provisions failing, they turned again to the new settlement." (pg. 14-15).
- "But the tribe more especially interesting to us, in connection with this work, was the *Wawenocks*, whose territory extended along the coast, from the mouth of the Kennebec, on the west, to the river St. George, on the east, and perhaps quite to the Penobscot. The great bashaba is believed to have been of this tribe. Their principal residence, when the European adventurers first became acquainted with them, was probably near Pemaquid, but, at a later period, it was at Sheepscott, and they became known as the *Sheepscott* Indians. According to Capt. Francis, a Penobscot chief, the name Wanneocks, or Wawenocks signifies *fearing nothing, very brave*, which seems to accord well with their general character. Smith, who visited the place in 1614, says; 'they were active, strong, healthful, and very witty. The men had a perfect constitution of body, were of comely proportion, and quite athletic. They would row their canoes faster with five paddles than our own men would our boats with eight oars.'" (pg. 16).
- "The people of this tribe were, like the Kennebec Indians, more mild and gentle in their dispositions, and less inclined to war than some of the neighboring tribes; and for many years no serious difficulty occurred between them and the English. So far as is known, the Wawenocks and Kennebecs, were always on good terms with each other, and in the Indian wars, they were always allies." (pg. 16).
- "In the great and devastating Indian war, which, as we have seen, occurred about 1615 or 1616, the Wawenocks were greatly reduced; and the dreadful epidemic of 1617, affected them still more seriously. Nothing is heard of the great bashaba, after this period, and it is supposed that he was slain in the war. From this time, they gradually dwindled away; and according to Douglass, in 1747, there were only two or three families remaining. These, a year or two afterwards, emigrated to Canada, and joined themselves with the St. Francis Indians." (pg. 16).

Josephy, Alvin M. Jr. (1991). *The Indian heritage of America*. The American Heritage Library. Houghton Mifflin Company, Boston, MA. IS.

Judd, Richard W., Churchill, Edwin A. and Eastman, Joel, W. Eds. (1995). Maine: The pine tree state from prehistory to the present. University of Maine Press, Orono, ME. IS.

- This history is frequently cited in Norumbega Reconsidered. See in particular the preface, which provides an overview of recent Maine history texts and their relationship to the questions of ethnicity discussed in this text.
- Comments and observations by Harold Prins are quoted within Norembega Reconsidered; see in particular, for example, our comments on this text in the chapter entitled "The Current Paradigm".

Leach, Douglas Edward. (1958). *Flintlock and tomahawk: New England in King Philip's War.* The Norton Library, W.W. Norton & Company, Inc., New York, NY. IS.

Lepore, Jill. (1998). *The name of war: King Philip's War and the origins of American identity.* Alfred A. Knopf, Inc., NY, NY. IS.

Lescarbot, Marc. (1609). *Les Muses de la Nouvelle France: à Monseigneur le Chancellier.* Chez Jean Millot, Paris.

- This contains Lescarbot's poem recounting a Native American battle that is discussed in the Davistown Museum publication *Norumbega Reconsidered.*
- This text is available online at Early Canadiana Online.

Lescarbot, Marc. (1609). *Nova Francia: A description of Acadia, 1606.* P. Erondelle, tr. London. Reprinted in 1928 by Routledge, London.

Lescarbot, Marc. (1911-1914). *The history of New France (1609-1612).* 3 vols. The Champlain Society, Toronto, Canada.

Lescarbot, Marc. (1974). *The defeat of the Armouchiquois savages by Chief Membertou and his savage allies.* Translated by Thomas Goetz. In: *Papers of the sixth Algonquian conference,* Cowan, William, Ed. Carleton University, Ottawa, Canada. pg. 141-179.

Levett, Christopher. (1847). Voyage into New England, begun in 1623, and ended in 1624. (1628). *Collections of Maine Historical Society* (CMeHS), 1st series, vol. 2, Portland, Maine. pg. 73-110.

Locke, John L. (1859). *Sketches of the history of the town of Camden, Maine; including incidental references to the neighboring places and adjacent waters.* Masters, Smith and Co., Hallowell, ME. IS.

Maine Indian Program. (1989). *The Wabanakis of Maine and the Maritimes: A resource book about Penobscot, Passamaquoddy, Maliseet, Micmac and Abenaki Indians.* Maine Indian Program of the New England Regional Office of the American Friends Service Committee, Bath, ME. IS.

- "An excellent resource for classroom use. Includes lesson plans for grades 4-8. Developed as a cooperative venture with the tribal education committees in Maine." (Ray, *The Indians of Maine*, pg. 33).
- Pages D-8 and D-9 summarize the names used by Europeans to refer to different Wabanaki groups. This program makes the following classifications which are generally followed today in most contemporary texts: Micmacs, Maliseets, Passamaquoddies, Penobscots, the four groups that survive today in Maine. Major groups in Maine that no longer survive are listed as Kennebecs, Androscoggins and Sacos. Emigrants to Canada include the Becancour Abenakis (Quebec), the St. Francis Abenakis (Quebec) and the Swanton Abenakis in Vermont. Wawenocs are listed twice, first under Kennebecs but in parentheses (as extinct?) then as Becancour Abenakis, where the few Wawenoc survivors went in the 18th century.
- In the above listing Androscoggins are noted as including Arosaguntacooks and Anasaguntacooks, both in parentheses. Survivors of both of these tribes emigrated to Quebec and are also listed as St. Francis Indians. The Saco Indians are listed as including Presumpscots, Pigwackets and Pequawkets.
- Here, as elsewhere, Wabanaki is defined as "People of the Dawn".
- "Historians are unable to agree on just where different groups of Wabanaki people were living in the sixteenth, seventeenth, and early eighteenth centuries. Written records are confusing, for Europeans were not always able to distinguish among Wabanaki groups, nor were they familiar with areas that were far from their settlements or the coast. In addition, many areas were used by more than one Wabanaki group, something that Europeans did not always recognize." (pg. D-4).
- The editors of this book illustrate the above observation by giving an ethnohistoric description of the inhabitants of Maine in 1590 as containing two groups: Abenaki-Pennacook, living east of the Kennebec River as far as the Merrimac River, with all the remaining lands of Maine, including its coastal regions, as Etchemin. No reference is made to Wawenocs on this map. (pg. D-4). This misinformation is followed by a more accurate map of native territories in 1700 that lists Micmac, Maliseet-Passamaquoddy and Penobscot as survivors along with St. Francis Abenaki with a tiny foothold at the mouth of the Kennebec. The remaining sections of central and southern New England are listed as "cleared of Indians" by 1700.
- "Later movements of Native people were in response to epidemics, English settlement, and warfare. ... The purpose of including these contradictory maps is not to confuse, but to introduce the idea that Wabanaki and other Native cultures were not static, as well as to point out the fact that many issues in Wabanaki history are just beginning to be addressed today." (pg. D-5).
- Another among many texts which perpetuate the erasure of the tribal identity of the Wawenoc Indians.

McBride, Bunny. (1999). *Women of the dawn*. University of Nebraska Press, Lincoln, NB. IS.

- This book is the subject of the exhibition "Four Mollys: Women of the Dawn" at the Abbe Museum, Bar Harbor, Maine, opening January 31, 2002.

- "Native American women have played critical roles in assuring the economic, social, religious, and political well-being and survival of their tribes, despite their repeated absence in the written record." (pg. 135).
- *Women of the Dawn* tells the stories of four remarkable Wabanaki Indian women who lived in northeast America during the four centuries that devastated their traditional world. Their courageous responses to tragedies brought on by European contact make up the heart of the book." (jacket).
- "The narrative begins with Molly Mathilde, a mother, a peacemaker, and the daughter of a famous chief. ...she provided a vital link for her people through her marriage to the French baron of St. Castin.
- The saga continues with the shrewd and legendary healer Molly Ockett and the reputed witchwoman Molly Molasses. The final chapter belongs to Molly Dellis Nelson (known as Spotted Elk), a celebrated performer on European stages who lived to see the dawn of Wabanaki cultural renewal in the modern era." (jacket).
- On Molly Mathilde (Pidianiske) McBride notes, "Her mother was an Abenaki from a chieftain family of the Kennebec River valley to the southwest. Her father [Madockawando] was a Maliseet whose band roamed between the Penobscot and the St. John Rivers to the northeast." The identity and tribal affiliation of Molly's mother is never made clear.
- "In fact, it was the ship of Giovanni da Verrazano, an Italian navigator hired by the king of France in 1524 to find a passage to China. In the course of the century, a handful of other European explorers steered ships into Penobscot Bay and nosed around the river's mouth. Their brief encounters with Penobscot River folk were fraught with tension as well as mutual wonder, and they almost always included a bit of ceremonial barter. These early visits enlivened stories told around wigwam hearths, but otherwise life here continued as it had for more than a hundred thousand moons."
- This passage, in conjunction with the synopsis on the jacket: "...in the mid-1600s, when Wabanakis first experienced the full effects of colonial warfare, disease, and displacement." reflect the current disinclination of some contemporary ethnohistorians to confront and document the tumultuous and disastrous encounter of Native Americans in Maine with Europeans that occurred before 1620. It remains a disconcerting conceit of white Europeans that the "full effects" of contact occurred after 1650. The more convivial encounter implied in this excellent text omits mention of the death of 90% of the Wabanakis living east of the Penobscot during the 1617 epidemic.
- "One thing seems clear. If we limit ourselves to documented records alone, the life histories of Native American women -- especially those who lived prior to this century -- will remain largely unwritten. Neither diplomats nor warriors, they were not on the cutting edge of tribal relations with those members of colonial society who kept written record of individuals and events. Rarely and barely noted, they remain hidden beyond the historical horizon. Yet it seems obvious that these women, as much as native men, participated in the struggle for survival from generation to generation. They too made vital choices concerning adaptation and resistance in the face of colonial aggression. If we make no effort to research the stories of Native American women and incorporate them into the wider historical picture, our images of the past will remain incomplete and therefore inaccurate." (pg. 138-189).

McBride, Bunny and Prins, Harald E. L. (2009). *Indians in Eden: Wabanakis and rusticators on Maine's Mount Desert Island, 1840s-1920s*. Down East Books, Camden, ME. IS.

- "As 'People of the Dawn,' Wabanakis were organized in bands of extended families, each forming part of larger ethnic groups called tribes or nations. Today, Wabanakis are divided into five distinct tribes: Penobscot, Passamaquoddy, Maliseet, Mi'kmaq, and Abenaki." (pg. 1).
- "One of their favorite sites was strategically located at Manchester Point (Northeast Harbor) by the entrance to Somes Sound. In the early 1600s, Wabanaki families under the leadership of Chief Asticou camped here in the summer. Other long-used coastal sites in Asticou's domain can be found at Bar Harbor and Hull's Cove, as well as on neighboring islands such as Great Cranberry, Swan's, Gotts, and Long, and also on the shores of Blue Hill Bay (such as Naskeag Point or nearby Flye Point). Included among the dozens of additional encampment sites in this domain is one by the Union River near Ellsworth Falls and another at Waukeag Neck on upper Frenchman Bay." (pg. 3).

Miller, Virginia. (Spring 1976). Aboriginal Micmac population: A review of the evidence. *Ethnohistory*. 23(2). pg. 117-127. IS.

- This is a particularly important journal article because it discusses and documents extensive dislocations in the Micmac populations of eastern Canada in the mid to late 16th century due to the trauma of contact and trade with the French. Of particular interest is the impact of European diseases well before the great pandemic of 1616 - 1619 that devastated the coastal populations of Native Americans in New England including the Wawenocs.
- Also discussed is the immediate deleterious impact of trade goods and their effective undermining of the traditional subsistence patterns of the Micmacs. Rampant alcoholism among the Micmacs is well documented prior to any European contact with the Indians of Maine.
- Miller's most significant observation pertains to the availability and use of firearms by the Micmacs, which were provided by the French in trade for furs. The combination of the intense demand for beaver pelts and other furs and the availability of firearms to the Micmacs appears to have played a major role in the later attacks (1607 f.) of the Micmacs (Souriquois) on the Indians of Massachusetts, the Saco River and the Wawenoc Indians.

Mitchell, Harbour, III and Spiess, Arthur E. (Spring 2002). Early archaic bifurcate base point occupation in the St. George River valley. *Maine Archaeological Society Bulletin*. 42(1). pg. 15-24. IS.

- "Site 28.53 is a multi-component site located along a section of the St. George River known as Hart's Falls in Warren, Maine. Site 28.53 represents only a small percentage of a much larger archaeological presence along the Harts Falls section of the river. This presence, herein referred to as the Hart's Fall Archaeological Complex, is believed to involve at least

25,000m2 of surface area, and can extend to at least 80cm below surface in stratified alluvium." (pg. 15).

- The Hart's Falls archaeological complex may be among the most important Native American village sites in central coastal Maine. Warren K. Moorehead excavated a number of cemetery sites in this location in the 1920's (1922 - *A Report on the Archaeology of Maine*). The whole complex was subject to extensive vandalism and pot hunting throughout the 19th century, as well as to extensive further collecting after Moorehead's excavations. Mitchell and Spiess note the Overlock and Archie McLaughlin collection - dozens of other individuals have collected artifacts during the 20th century from this, one of the largest and longest inhabited archaeological sites in the midcoast area.
- Part of this extensive site includes the "Wowinak", a Penobscot term for "loop in the river", this is the probable location of what may have been the largest of all Wawenoc semipermanent village sites. Mitchell and Spiess note a radiocarbon age of 9030 years B.P. in charcoal infused paleosol; evidence of nearly continuous settlement is noted through the late ceramic period.
- Numerous references are made to a residence of the bashaba, chief of the confederacy of Mawooshen, by early writers beginning with Rosier, Gorges etc., as being located to the north of Pemaquid, but inland and to the west of Penobscot Bay. The root of the word "Wawenoc", according to Snow (1980), is the Penobscot word "Wowinak" - "loop in the river" - the exact location of the Hart's Falls archaeological complex on the St. George River. Could this be the location of the ancient "Arambec", a term possibly synonymous with "Norumbega". Europeans called the whole section of the Maine mid coast "Norumbega": Native Americans allegedly never used generalized regional names, but only metaphors as specific place names. Hart's Falls: a most intriguing component of Norumbega Reconsidered.

Moorehead, Warren K. (1922). *A report on the archeology of Maine: Being a narrative of explorations in that state, 1912-1920, together with work at Lake Champlain, 1917.* Department of Anthropology, Phillips Academy, Andover, MA.

- One of the important early sources of information on the archaeology of Maine, Moorehead is also considered in some circles to epitomize the era of "vandalism archaeology". His famous cursory hit and run excavations of important Red Paint cemetaries destroyed much more archaeological evidence than they uncovered. He is nonetheless immortalized by the use of his name as in "Moorehead phase" to describe the Red Paint culture of Maine. This archaic culture, which utilized red ochre in its burials, is much more appropriately called Maine Maritime Archaic, and differs slightly from its nearby cousin, the Canadian Maritime Archaic. For more comments on the confusing and sometimes inappropriate titles of the prehistoric cultures of Maine, see the chronologies listed in the Historical Overview Section.
- Moorehead made significant finds at the Halls Falls Archaeological complex on the St. Georges River: see the essay "Wawinak" in *Norumbega Reconsidered*.

Morey, David C. (May 2005). *The Voyage of Archangell: James Rosier's Account of the Waymouth Voyage of 1605 - A True Relation.* Tilbury House, Publishers, Gardiner, Maine. IS.

- Published in May 2005, this text is a comprehensive essay on the background of George Waymouth's 1605 voyage to the Maine coast and is particularly helpful in explaining the historical context of the journey as one of a series of trips to "North" Virginia for the purpose of both exploration and settlement sponsored by private but well connected English entrepreneurs like Sir John Popham and Sir Fernando Gorges.
- Morey presents persuasive arguments for Penobscot River and not the St. Georges as the river explored by Waymouth and observed by Rosier. In one fell swoop, Morey has altered wide-spread perception based on the writings of Prince and Cushing in the 19th century that Waymouth explored the St. George River.
- Excellent annotations of the Rosier's "A True Relation", Rosier's account of the Waymouth voyage of 1605: an exact description of the specific islands, harbors, and campsites of Waymouth's visit.
- Morey makes interesting comments on Samoset, as one of the native Americans kidnapped by Waymouth, and also as son of Mentaurmet, "Sagamore of Mebamocago" (Indian town island, Boothbay) pg. 101, as well a brother of Tehanedo, one of the other Wawenocs captured by Waymouth. Morley avoids mentioning the word "Etchemin", but following English sources, as well as Rosier's narration, clearly describes the Native Americans visiting Waymouth as occupying a village at the tip of Cushing's Pleasant Point (Segocket, map pg. 39), as well as to the *west* at Pemaquid and on the Sheepscot River. Samoset's father is noted as the same Sagamore visited by Champlain the previous year (1604) at Wiscasset.
- Excerpts from this publication are reprinted in the Penobscot maritime Museum's Summer Symposium on Waymouth's voyage, "One Land - Two Worlds: Maine - Mawooshen 1605-2005". The excellent museum exhibition provides a nice introduction to the land of Mawooshen, while at the same time, utilizes Lescarborts 1606 map of the coast of Maine, showing both Norumbega as a village site near Bangor, and the Etchemins as living in the area between the Penobscot and Kennebec Rivers occupied by the Wawenoc (Abenaki) indians kidnapped by Waymouth.
- A number of excerpts from this publication are quoted within the main text of *Norumbega Reconsidered.*

Morison, Samuel Eliot, Ed. (1963). *Of Plymouth Plantation: 1620 - 1647 by William Bradford: A new edition.* Alfred A. Knopf, New York, NY. IS.

- Samuel Eliot Morison's annotations, introductions and comments make this the most useful republication of Bradford's history of Plymouth Plantation. A number of quotations from both Morison and Bradford are excerpted in the text of the Norumbega Reconsidered essay.
- One among many of Morison's interesting footnotes illustrates the extent of the pandemic of 1617 that swept the New England coast, wiping out the entire population of the Patuxet tribe living at Plymouth with the exception of Squanto, who apparently had been to England, learned the English language and may have acquired immunity to the pathogens that caused the pandemic. "Squanto or Tisquantum appears to have been the sole survivor of the Patuxet tribe. Kidnapped there by Capt. Thomas Hunt in 1614, he had the curious career that Bradford says; he jumped Capt. Dermer's ship in 1618 and made his way to the site of Plymouth, where he found himself to be the sole survivor of his tribe, wiped out in the pestilence of 1617." (footnote, pg. 81).

Morison, Samuel Eliot. (1971). *The European discovery of America: The northern voyages A.D. 500-1600.* Oxford University Press, NY. IS.

- Morison is one of the first and most vocal advocates of the myth of Norumbega -- that is, the concept of Norumbega is a conceit that is entirely the invention of European explorers hoping to duplicate the treasure troves that the Spanish explorers found in south America. Morison's point of view reappears again and again in contemporary Maine history texts, most especially in Baker, et. al. *American Beginnings.*
- Most interesting considering his disparagement of the myth of Norumbega is his repeated descriptions of what Norumbega meant to Native Americans. "Norumbega, apart from the name, which means 'quiet place between two rapids' in Algonkin, was wholly created by European imagination." (pg. 464).
- Later in the notes to the same chapter Morison says "*Nolumbeka* in the Abnaki tongue means either a stretch of quiet water between two rapids, or a succession of rapids interspersed by still waters. This exactly fits the Penobscot River above Bangor." (pg. 488).
- In view of the stubborn insistence of contemporary Maine historians, including Morison, a long time resident of Northeast Harbor and author of the wonderfully brief *History of Mount Desert Island,* that Norumbega is a myth of European origin, one can't help but ask the following question: what's so controversial about Norumbega meaning exactly what the Algonquin Native American community in Maine described it as: quiet waters between or near waterfalls? The Algonquin description not only matches the Penobscot River, it even more exactly describes the vast network of bays and river basins lying between the Kennebec and Penobscot River. It especially describes the Damariscotta Lakes region and the areas of the Damariscotta shell middens, which by long oral tradition have always been considered the heart of Norumbega. The region between the Kennebec and the Penobscot is a virtual archaeological treasure trove of accidental durable remnants left by the thousands of residents in the numerous tide water villages of Mawooshen. The Penobscot is the focus of the European myth, but there is much less archaeological evidence for an extensive community of Native Abenaki in the late pre-historic period in this area.
- See our excerpts from Morison in the General History: Contemporary Sources bibliography and Ancient Pemaquid essays. Also see our information file on Morison's excellent description of the wet and dry fisheries of Labrador and Newfoundland, as well as Morison's colorful description of David Ingram's trek through Maine from the gulf coast and the role he played in the evolution of the myth of Norumbega.

Morris, Gerald E., Ed. (1976). *Maine bicentennial atlas: An historical survey.* The Maine Historical Society, Portland, ME. IS.

- "The Wawennocks, although seen several times by explorers in the Pemaquid region, are not included on Plate Six because it seems probable that they were members of the larger Kennebec or Penobscot sub-tribes, most likely the former. If so, they would have summered in the Pemaquid region and then moved inland during the winter season." (pg. 3).
- See the other annotations for this text in the Maine History: Primary Sources bibliography, comments about its information on early settlers' trading posts in the Introduction to the

Ancient Pemaquid section and some of the plates in the Maps section: geography of ancient Pemaquid.

Morrison, Kenneth M. (1984). *The embattled northeast: The elusive ideal of alliance in Abenaki-Euramerican relations.* University of California Press, Berkeley, CA.

- "Abenaki refers to the various tribes that inhabited the river basins of New Hampshire, Maine, and New Brunswick. From west to east these peoples were the Pennacook, Saco, Androscoggin, Kennebec, Wawenock, Penobscot, Passamaquoddy, and Maliseet." (pg. 5).
- "According to English documents, the westernmost Abenaki--Pennacook, Saco, and Androscoggin--bore the brunt of the first war with New England and their self-defense ignited the second. After that, little is known about them. During the third war most migrated to Canadian mission villages or went to live with eastern neighbors." (pg. 5).
- "With the destruction of Norridgewock during the fourth war the Penobscots emerged as leaders of a new intertribal alliance." (pg. 5).
- "Pressed by hostile frontiersmen and by English expectations that they submit, the Abenaki found themselves fighting a defensive war." (pg. 89).
- "This extension of King Philip's War spelled an ecological disaster for the Abenaki. In the first place, it undercut the tribes' postcontact hunting economy, which by 1675 required European arms and ammunition. ...Faced with English refusal to sell them ammunition, the Abenaki experienced a severe shortage of major food sources. To make matters worse, the war also threatened Abenaki horticulture. In the fall of 1675 the English settlers so frightened the Kennebec that they fled to the Penobscot River, leaving their fields unharvested. Finally, the war barred the Abenaki from access to the animal and marine resources of their coastal lands. The Wawenock, who could not withdraw because of the short rivers of their territory, found themselves hard pressed by English hostiles who controlled the shore near Pemaquid peninsula." (pg. 89).

Nicolar, Joseph. (1893). *The life and traditions of the red man.* C.H. Glass, Printers, Bangor, ME. W.

Parkman, Francis. (1865). *France and England in North America: Volume 1: Pioneers of France in the New World; The Jesuits in North America in the Seventeenth Century; La Salle and the Discovery of the Great West; The Old Regime in Canada.* The Library of America, New York, NY. Reprint in 1983 of the first four volumes of what was originally an 8 volume set. IS.

- Parkman has important observations pertaining to the Abenaki communities in Maine, whose existence has been questioned by Bourque and others. Commenting on the Jesuits in North America, Parkman recounts the several journeys of the Jesuit Druilletes on his missions to Maine. The Abenakis, after visiting the Christian Indians of Sillery near Quebec, requested that a missionary be sent. Druilletes first trip was in August of 1646 where he "reached the waters of the Kennebec and descended to the Abenaqui villages" (pg. 624). After visiting the trading post at Augusta, he continued to the Penobscot, where he found "several Capuchin friars, under their superior Father Ignace" (pg. 624) who were apparently acting as missionaries to the Penobscot Indians.

- Three years later, in the summer of 1650, he again visited the Kennebec and went as an envoy charged with the negotiation of a treaty pertaining to the second round of intertribal fur trade wars now so widespread in New York and southeastern Canada. While his attempt to get the colony of Massachusetts to join in opposition to the marauding Mohawks failed, Parkman has this interesting comment: "Druilletes set forth from Quebec with a Christian chief of Sillery, crossed forests, mountains, and torrents, and reached Norridgewock, the highest Abenaqui settlement on the Kennebec. Thence he descended to the English trading-house at Augusta, where his fast friend, the puritan Winslow, gave him a warm welcome." (pg. 626).

- Parkman in his description of the Native tribes of New England in this volume notes that after the travel pushes northward and passes the Piscataqua River and the land of the Penacooks, upon crossing the river Saco "...a change of dialect would indicate a different tribe or group of tribes. These were the Abenaquis, found chiefly along the course of the Kennebec and other rivers, on whose banks they raised their rude harvests..." (pg. 347).

- Parkman is almost entirely dependent on the same French sources that Bourque uses in his 8 volume survey France and England in North America yet his observations about the Abenakis in Maine are consistent with the English sources, who describe Abenaki communities as far east as the Penobscot River. Parkman clearly notes Druilletes' observation that Norridgewock was the northernmost of the Abenaki settlements even as late as 1650.

Penhallow, Samuel. (1726). *The history of the wars of New-England with the Eastern Indians, or a narrative of their continued perfidy and cruelty, from the 10th of August 1703, to the peace renewed 13th of July, 1713. And from the 25th of July, 1722, to their submission 15th December, 1725, which was ratified August 5th, 1726.* Boston Edition. Reprinted in 1859 with a memoir, notes and appendix for Wm. Dodge by J. Harpel, corner Third & Vine Sts., Cincinnati, OH.

- No mention of the Wawenoc Indians.

Petersen, James B., Blustain, Malinda and Bradley, James W. (2004). "Mawooshen" revisited: Two Native American contact period sites on the central Maine coast. *Archaeology of Eastern North America.* 32. pg. 1-71. IS.

- "Analysis of Contact period artifacts from several archaeological sites on the central Maine coast was undertaken as part of the process of repatriation related to NAGPRA at the Robert S. Peabody Museum of Archaeology. Native American and European mortuary goods, including rare plant-fiber perishables, other perishable artifacts and nonperishable specimens, were recovered together with human burials by Warren K. Moorehead and the Sandy Point and Walker's Pond sites in 1912 and 1914. These samples document the diversity of indigenous garments, ornaments and utilitarian artifacts used as mortuary goods during the time of early contact before European colonization, combining Native and European elements in an indigenous fashion. Along the Maine coast, substantial contact between Natives and Europeans began during the late sixteenth and early seventeenth centuries, and somewhere around A. D. 1580-1600 at these sites based on the stylistic and technological evidence. This portion of the Maine coast was situated within the territory of a historically recorded native confederacy at the time, the 'Countrey of Mawooshen.' Representing some of the earliest Contact period mortuary remains known in the far Northeast, they are presented in detail and situated regionally for the first time here." (pg. 1).

- "Broadly speaking, this was the 'Countrey of Mawooshen' during the early seventeenth century, the large Native confederacy under the leadership of Bashabes, who lived on the Penobscot River toward the eastern edge of Mawooshen and its boundary with the Eastern Etchemin. The meaning of the Native term Mawooshen is unclear, but it has been tentatively explained as a 'band of people walking or acting together'. Regardless of the precise meaning of this name, Bashabes apparently controlled the entire region of Mawooshen on some level, primarily including the region from Cape Neddick (modern-day Saco, Maine) to Schoodic Point near the Union River (just to the east of Mt. Desert Island). Mawooshen also perhaps extended as far west as Lake Megantic in modern day Quebec and southwestward to Massachusetts. In part because Bashabes has been described as the 'first among equals,' some analysts consider Mawooshen a short-lived, historically contingent Native confederacy on the Maine coast, representing the extraordinary circumstances of the early Contact period when trade and competition enhanced the power of certain leaders. Yet, Mawooshen may have been built on previous forms of political leadership and it is not difficult to conceive of its indigenous origin during late prehistory." (pg. 6).

- "In fact, prehistoric and early historic leadership in Mawooshen was likely based, in part, on control of regional trade on some level. The Etchemin were certainly involved in regional trade during the earliest 1600s. At least one extraordinary prehistoric site, Goddard, would support local participation of the ancestral Etchemin (Maliseet-Passamaquoddy) in a far-reaching regional trade network long before the Contact period. Situated on Naskeag Point at the eastern end of Eggemoggin Reach, Goddard is closer to Blue Hill Bay and Mt. Desert Island than it is to Penobscot Bay proper. Nonetheless, Goddard is rather close to both Sandy Point and Walker's Pond, quite likely representing a direct socio-cultural link with both of them. Goddard was also the scene of a few Contact period burials, along with others in the local area." (pg. 6).

- "Goddard is primarily attributable to the early-middle portion of the Late Woodland (Ceramic) period, dated about 300-600 years before Sandy Point and Walker's Pond, that is, primarily A. D. 1000-1300 for Goddard, with some earlier and scant later occupations. Goddard can be interpreted as the setting of an intensive prehistoric 'trade fair' and it is not obviously matched anywhere within the broad Gulf of Maine region. If this local trade fair nexus can be verified, then the Mawooshen confederacy had prehistoric roots long before Bashabes came upon the scene and this would be something rather different than most scholars recognize for Mawooshen. At the other extreme, some analysts suggest that Mawooshen was primarily an invention of the English and not a true confederacy, since French chroniclers such as Champlain mention Bashabes by name, but not Mawooshen at all. This example well reflects the types of problems faced by ethnohistorians and it again demonstrates the difficulty of linking archaeology and history." (pg. 6).

- "In spite of all this, we believe that during the earliest 1600s Mawooshen represented a confederacy of some sort, or a 'superconfederacy,' as it has been called, minimally stretching over much of central and western coastal Maine. This area minimally represents about 2/3 of the Maine coast in linear distance, or about 210-220 km 'as the crow flies' parallel to the convoluted coastline, which actually constitutes a much larger area. Bashabes reportedly could marshall 1500 warriors, as recorded ca. 1605-1609, and perhaps as many as 10,000 Native people lived in Mawooshen all told. At the time, Mawooshen was described as an area 'fortie leagues [120 miles] in bredth, and fiftie [150 miles] in length [comprising] nine rivers'" (pg. 6).
- "The Souriquois/Micmac (Mi'kmaq) killed Bashabes in 1615, perhaps because of his growing position in regional trade and the loss of their own middlemen status, thereby helping to destroy the Mawooshen confederacy. Regardless of one's interpretation of the precise details, this example clearly demonstrates the complexity of cross-cultural events caused by European-Native contact, as well as the instability of different indigenous structures at the time." (pg. 7).
- "The wealth and power of some Native traders must have been quite tangible, if short lived in relative terms. It seems quite likely that the political position of Bashabes, the 'superchief' of Mawooshen, was enhanced by his participation in and control over an indigenous trading network that stretched from the central Gulf of Maine across some portion of the far Northeast and even beyond." (pg. 59).
- "From the time when regular European contact first began on the central Maine coast, as many as 25-50 years (+) many have passed before the French and English actually colonized the area during the early 1600s. Initial devastation caused by introduced diseases would have gone largely undocumented, except perhaps in indigenous oral history, if direct of indirect regular contact began this early. The earliest epidemics surely appeared well before the first well recorded epidemic/pandemic of ca. 1616-1619, for example, during which time the decimation of coastal communities from Cape Cod northward to the central Maine coast was very widespread. The fact that more than 70% of the individuals interred at Sandy Point and Walker's Pond were children, many suffering from poor health, suggests a population with very different mortality statistics than known among most pre-contact Natives in local and broad regional contexts. Burials at these two sites, ca. A. D. 1580-1600, seemingly predate these documented events and almost certainly provide evidence of European-induced trauma in this part of the Gulf of Maine before local European colonization." (pg. 59).
- This article contains a very comprehensive bibliography on this topic.

Platt, D. Ed. (2005). *One land - two worlds: A symposium to celebrate the 400th anniversary of George Waymouth's voyage to New England.* Island Institue, Rockland, ME.

Prins, Harald. (Fall 1992). Cornfields at Meductic: Ethnic and territorial reconfigurations in colonial Acadia. *Man in the Northeast.* 44. pg. 55-72. IS.

- "...native crop cultivation was introduced to the area, probably in the 1670s - 1680s. It appears that the introducers were Abenaki refugees from the central New England region, rather than French missionaries or colonists." pg. 55.

- Cornfields "...appearance at Meductic in the 1680s was the direct consequence of inter-ethnic mobility due to unstable geopolitical conditions in the area." pg. 55.
- "Until the second half of the seventeenth century, Abenaki horticulturalists remained within their habitual range west of the Penobscot River, whereas Maliseet hunting bands generally roamed the region between the Penobscot and St. John rivers. However, especially from the late 1640s onwards, intertribal 'beaver wars' turned the region into mayhem." pg. 57.
- "When King William's War broke out in 1688, events in Acadia took a dramatic turn. Waves of native refugees from New England's frontiers moved into the valleys of the Penobscot, St. Croix, and St. John, and beyond -- until then primarily inhabited by those still referred to by the French as 'Etchemins'." pg. 63.
- "...in contrast to the migratory Maliseet food collectors, the semisedentary Abenaki cultivated crops in their aboriginal territories southwest of the Penobscot. ...large communal lodges in palisaded villages were typical for early seventeenth-century horticulturists in southern Maine and beyond, ...Abenaki refugees introduced the horticulture complex to the St. John River valley after the catastrophe of New England's Puritan 'war of extermination'." pg. 67.

Prins, Harald. (1996). Chief Rawandagon, alias Robin Hood: Native "Lord of misrule" in the Maine wilderness. IN: Grumet, Robert S., Ed. (1996). *Northeastern Indian lives, 1632 - 1816*. University of Massachusetts Press, Amherst, MA. W.

- "Traditionally, native subsistence activities in this region were based on hunting, fowling, and fishing. In contrast to *migratory bands living east of the Kennebec,* [italics added] tribal villagers from this river westward also planted gardens of corn, beans, squash, and tobacco. When Rawandagon was born, Abenaki traditional life was about to be upset and radically transformed." (pg. 97).
- "Some Mi'kmaq entrepreneurs turned into fur-trade middlemen. Engaging in long-distance trading voyages, they learned to sail small, open boats called shallops (sloops), taking valuable European trade goods to remote villages in order to get high-quality furs. ... Soon, coastal Maine turned into hotly contested territory. In addition to the Mi'kmaqs, who not only traded but also raided the corn-and-fur-producing Abenakis and their neighbors, some English, French, and Basque explorers, traders, and fishers began venturing into the region." (pg. 97-98).
- "Soon, Rawandagon's people were getting European manufactures such as copper kettles, steel knives, swords, cloth, and woollen blankets directly from the Europeans. Cut from the profitable trade loop, the Mi'kmaq middlemen quickly turned to violence. Newly equipped with French muskets, Mi'kmaq marines swept over the coastal Abenaki region, killing several local chieftains of Saco River in battle before retreating." (pg. 98).
- "Meanwhile, on the heels of yet another punishing raid by Mi'kmaqs that swept through the Penobscot valley in 1615, an apocalyptic event struck Rawandagon's world: a two-year pandemic of bubonic plague, coupled with what has been suggested was hepatitis, scourged the area from Penobscot to Cape Cod. Although precise figures are lacking, this pandemic may have killed over ninety percent of the coastal population. In 1619, small and beleaguered remnant bands of kinsfolk and associated families regrouped, joining surviving sagamores such as Rawandagon's father, Chief Manawormet, at Sheepscot." (pg. 98-99).

- Prins assiduously avoids making any reference to the ethnic identity of Rawandagon's community. Rawandagon's sound strategy and widespread influence in the mid-17th century echoes the presence and influence of the Bashabas c. 1600. Since he was the son of Manawormet, he was most likely of Wawenoc descent (see pg. 96).
- In a later chapter in the collection, Prins has no difficulty identifying Molly Ockett as a Pigwacket.

Prins, Harald. (1996). The Mi'kmaq: Resistance, accommodation, and cultural survival. Harcourt Brace College Publishers, Fort Worth, TX. IS.

- "He includes a valuable description of Mi'kmaq social organization as a family band comprised of extended kin who collectively practiced seasonal mobility across their homeland using a variety of subsistence sources. This sets the stage for a discussion of contact with Europeans." (Micah Pawling. Winter 2000-01. Book review. Maine History. 39(4). pg. 273. IS).
- On the Mi'kmaq - Abenaki war Prins has this comment: "On his second exploration voyage along the coast from Passamaquoddy Bay to the Kennebec River in the summer of 1605, Champlain employed Panoniac, who was of Chief Membertou's band. With the help of Panoniac, who was married to an Abenaki woman from southern Maine (Champlain 1:280), the French began searching for a better settlement site. Panoniac took them across the Bay of Fundy to a place near one of his band's favorite seasonal camping grounds. Here the French established Port Royal. The following summer Messamoet accompanied Champlain again, this time sailing his own shallop in tandem with the Frenchman. They sailed from Passamquoddy Bay south to Saco Bay, where Messamoet hoped 'to make an alliance with those of that country by offering them sundry presents' (Champlain 1:394). At Saco, Messamoet negotiated with the local Abenaki chieftain, Olmechin. In return for trade goods 'gained by barter with the French, which they came thither to sell--to wit, kettles, large, medium, and small, hatchets, knives, dresses, capes, red jackets, peas, beans, biscuits, and other such things.' Messamoet received 'a canoe laden with what [Olmechin's people] had, to wit, corn, tobacco, beans, and pumpkins [squash]...' (Lescarbot 2:324). To his great displeasure, he received no furs from his Abenaki hosts. That summer, already strained Mi'kmaq-Abenaki relations turned openly hostile when a party of Mi'kmaq warriors under Chief Iouaniscou killed some Abenakis on the Maine coast (Champlain 1:442). Unaware of the brutality committed by fellow tribesmen, Panoniac sailed with a cargo of French trade goods from Passamaquoddy Bay south to Penobscot. There, in revenge for their slain kinsmen, Abenakis killed the innocent Panoniac." (pg. 108-109).
- "Because Panoniac's killing could not be left unavenged, the old chief assembled a fighting force of about 40 Mi'kmaq and allied Maliseet warriors. Armed with spears, tomahawks, bows, and iron-tipped arrows and newly equipped with French muskets, the warriors boarded their shallops and sailed to Saco Bay, where they defeated the local Abenakis. They returned home knowing that sooner or later they would suffer an Abenaki counterattack." (pg. 109).
- On the Mi'kmaq - Maliseet war Prins has this comment: "Fur-trade competition also fueled hosilities between Mi'kmaqs and Maliseets (including Passamaquoddies) of the central Maine coast. Their powerful leader, Bashaba, lived in the Penobscot Valley and was even recognized as a paramount chief by neighboring Abenakis. Maliseet relations with the

Mi'kmaqs were already strained in 1604, when Champlain first sailed up the Penobscot River. Bashaba's followers told the French explorer that 'they wished to live in peace with thier enemies, in order that in future they might hunt the beaver more than they had done, and barter these beavers with us in exchange for things necessary for their usage' (Champlain 1:295-96). Unwilling to give up their privileged positions as fur-trade middlemen, Mi'kmaqs tried to intimidate thier neighbors, determined to get by raiding what they could not get by trading. From thier Gulf of Maine stronghold at Mount Desert Island, sailing in shallops and armed with muskets, they staged lighting raids against coastal Maliseets unwilling to engage in barter." (pg. 109).

- "In 1615 Mi'kmaq warriors 'surprised the Bashaba, and slew him and all his people near about him, carrying away his women and other such matters as they thought of value' (Gorges, 90). With Bashaba and so many of his great warriors dead, the confederacy collapsed." (pg. 109).

Prins, Harald E. L. and McBride, Bunny. (2007). *Asticou's island domain: Wabanaki peoples at Mount Desert Island 1500-2000*. Vols. 1 and 2. Acadia National Park and The Abbe Museum, Bar Harbor, ME. http://www.nps.gov/acad/historyculture/ethnography.htm. X.

- Currently available only as an unedited book on the National Park Service's website, this text is a comprehensive survey of the history of Native Americans visiting and living on Mount Desert Island (MDI). This 600 page text is the source of Bunny McBride and Harald Prins (2009) *Indians in Eden*, which has been extracted from chapters 10 - 13.
- The first nine chapters constitute the most comprehensive survey of Native Americans and their rapidly changing social and political milieu from 1600 - 1840 in the region from the eastern shores of Penobscot Bay to the Narraguagus River. While the first five chapters are full of redundancies, this comprehensive survey of Native Americans in eastern Maine is worthy of republishing in a shorter format. While focusing on Asticou as the last of the grand chiefs of the Native American communities of the Maine coast, Prins and McBride provide an excellent summary of the political and tribal alignments and eventual fate of the confederacy of Mawooshen in the early 17th century. The authors have minimal commentary on the confederacy of Mawooshen prior to 1600; their time line commentary for this date is: "Inter-tribal trading and conflicts have led to the formation of Mawooshen, a political confederacy of Abenaki corn-growing villages between Kennebunk and Kennebec, and Etchemin migratory bands from the Kennebec to the Narraguagus River. MDI forms the 'eastern door' of Mawooshen, whose chiefs all recognize Bashaba of Kadesquit (Bangor) as grandchief." (pg. xv).
- The remaining chapters (14 - 21) in this voluminous text provide an excellent survey of material culture, food and medicinal uses of plants and animals on MDI as well as animal and plant populations, archaeological sites, encampments, and local and regional canoe routes. This National Park study is, in fact, the most detailed analysis and site specific survey of Native American activities and seasonal movements in any eastern United States location.
- "As sakom of a Wabanaki community inhabiting the Mount Desert Island area, Asticou headed a district that formed part of a political confederacy known as Mawooshen. Headed by a grandchief, Bashaba of Penobscot, this was an inter-tribal alliance of neighboring

Wabanaki groups in Maine, each with their own districts and headed by their own chiefs. Mawooshen's political boundaries were Narraguagus River in the northeast and Moussam River (at Kennebunk) in the southwest." (pg. ii).

- "The newcomers [Europeans] brought with them not only trade goods, but also killer diseases, including smallpox, cholera and influenza. These scourges, added to the lethal combination of firewater and firearms, almost wiped Maine's indigenous coastal peoples from the face of the earth. Within a few decades, up to 90 percent of the Wabanaki perished in this American Indian holocaust." (pg. ii).

- "To confront the complex challenges of survival in the contested colonial borderlands, Madockawando and other indigenous leaders forged new political alliances, in particular the Wabanaki Confederacy. A successor to Mawooshen, this intertribal alliance, comprised of Algonquian-speaking ethnic groups from Maine to Newfoundland, was formed in the late 17th century to defend ancestral homelands against English aggression. A political force in this coastal region for almost 200 years, the Confederacy gave its support to the American Revolution. After that war, a newly designated border between Canada and the United States sliced right through Wabanaki homelands. Under government pressure, the Confederacy was dissolved around 1870." (pg. iii).

- "At the time of first contact with European seafarers over 400 years ago, the Atlantic Northeast was inhabited by perhaps as many as 50,000 Wabanaki Indians. Based on linguistic and cultural differences, two major groupings are distinguished: Eastern Wabanakis, who fully depended on hunting, fishing and gathering, and **formed migratory bands ranging the vast woodlands and coastal domains from Newfoundland to the Kennebec River valley**; and Western Wabanakis, semi-sedentary villagers who survived not only on hunting, fishing and gathering, but also on growing corn, squash and beans in large gardens near their villages located between the Kennebec and Merrimac River valleys. There were about equal numbers of Western and Eastern Wabanakis, but territories inhabited by the latter group were much larger and, consequently, had a much lower population density." (pg. 1-2).

- "Wabanaki tribal communities formed part of three major groupings identified in early French documents as the Etchemin, Souriquois and Armouchiquois. Each of these groupings could be distinguished from their neighbors by distinctive cultural features, including different speech. Etchemin foragers ranged primarily through the **vast woodlands between the Kennebec** and St. John River valleys. Thus, Mount Desert Island is clearly situated in the center of the Etchemin coast. To their northeast were Souriquois bands—better known as Mi'kmaq from the late 1600s onwards—ranging the area to southern Newfoundland. Southwest of the Etchemin were communities collectively known as Armouchiquois, corn-growing peoples whose **villages could be found in the Kennebec valley** and far beyond. These Armouchiquois consisted of several different ethnic groups, **including Abenakis traditionally inhabiting territories** from the Kennebec to the Merrimac Rivers. As **semi-sedentary corn-growing villagers**, these Abenakis are here distinguished as Western Wabanakis, whereas the Etchemin and Mi'kmaq, as migratory foragers, are grouped together as Eastern Wabanakis." (pg. 2).

- "Asticou, the sakom of the Western Etchemin community inhabiting Mount Desert Island and its surrounding foraging domain, was closely allied to Bashaba, a neighboring Etchemin chieftain. Bashaba's strategically located seasonal encampments were situated at Kadesquit

(Bangor) and Pentagoet (Castine), just west of Asticou's. Regional sakoms, representing tribal communities speaking closely related Algonquian languages and dialects, collectively elected Bashaba as their leader, recognizing him as grandchief of Mawooshen, an Algonquian term for 'alliance' or 'confederacy.' **This regional Wabanaki alliance included almost two dozen independent tribal communities with their territorial districts situated between the Narraguagus River and the Mousam River (Kennebunk)."** (pg. 36).

- "This political alliance between a coastal group of **Western Etchemin and Abenaki** sakoms encompassed nine rivers, covering a stretch of coastal territory about 120 miles wide." (pg. 37).

- "Connected by ties of kinship and friendship, they belonged to an ethnic group historically known as the Etchemin. Organized in several self-governing migratory bands, Etchemins ranged primarily between the Kennebec and St. John Rivers. Although these bands shared the same culture and speech, regional differences existed. Here we distinguish between **Western Etchemins (ranging from the Kennebec to the Narraguagus River) and Eastern Etchemins (from the Narraguagus to the St. John valley).** The regional dialects spoken by Eastern Etchemins are still heard in Maliseet, Passamaquoddy and even Penobscot communities today." (pg. 39).

- "Asticou succeeded Bashaba as grandchief of Mawooshen after this fellow Western Etchemin chieftain was attacked and killed by Mawooshen's Tarrentine enemies (Mi'kmaq and allied Eastern Etchemins). **Western Etchemin and Abenaki chieftains heading communities from Mount Desert Island to Cape Porpoise** acknowledged Asticou as leader of the confederacy during its final years." (pg. 62).

- "Since the **Eastern Etchemin headquartered at Passamaquoddy Bay and the St. John River** did not form part of Mawooshen, but were instead loosely allied with their Mi'kmaq neighbors across the Bay of Fundy, they were lumped together as Tarrentines by the people of Mawooshen and their neighbors south of Cape Porpoise. **Like the Mi'kmaq, they also were in conflict with the Abenaki corn-growers inhabiting the Kennebec and Saco valleys.**" (pg. 64).

Purchas, S. (1625). The description of the countrey of Mawooshen, discovered by the English in the Yeere 1602.3.5.6.7.8. and 9. In: *Hakluytus posthumus or Purchas his pilgrims*. Vol 4. Henry Fetherston, London.

- The most important of all antiquarian narratives on the Native American communities of the Maine coast.
- See annotations and a listing of some other versions of this publication in the General History: Antiquarian Authors bibliography. A transcription of this text, pg. 400 - 406, is in our information files.

Quinn, David Beers. (1977). North America from earliest discovery to first settlements: The Norse voyages to 1612. Harper and Row, NY, NY.

- See annotations in the US History: contemporary bibliography.

Quinn, David Beers. (1990). Explorers and colonies: America, 1500-1625. Hambledon Press, London.

- See annotations in the US History: contemporary bibliography.

Quinn, David Beers. (1995). The early cartography of Maine in the setting of early European exploration of New England and the Maritimes. In: *American beginnings: Exploration, culture, and cartography in the land of Norumbega*. Baker Emerson W. et al. Eds. University of Nebraska Press, Lincoln, NB.

Quinn, David Beers and Skelton, R.A. (1965). *Richard Hakluyt, the principall navigations (1589)*. 2 vols. Hakluyt Society, Extra Series 39.

Quinn, David Beers, Quinn, Alison M. and Hillier, Susan, Eds. (1974). England and the discovery of America, 1481 - 1620. In: *New American world: A documentary history of North America to 1612*. 5 vols. Arno Press, NY, NY.

Quinn, David Beers and Quinn, Alison M., Eds. (1983). *The English New England voyages, 1602-1608*. 2nd series, no. 161. Hakluyt Society, London.

Rasle, Father Sebastien. (1833). A dictionary of the Abenaki language in North America, [1690-1722] with an introductory memoir and notes. In: Pickering, John, Ed. *Memoirs of the American Academy of Arts and Sciences*. pg. 375-565.

- "The Lenápe is the most widely extended of the languages spoken eastward of the Mississippi. It is found, in various dialects, throughout Canada from the coast of Labrador to the mouth of Albany River, which falls into Hudson's Bay, and from thence to the Lake of the Woods. All the Indians, indeed, who now inhabit this portion of the continent (with the exception of the Iroquois, who are by far the least numerous, and are mostly within the limits of Canada,) speak dialects of the Lenápe. When the Europeans arrived in America, these Indians were in possession of the *eastern* coast of this continent, from Virginia to Nova Scotia; and hence, as we are informed, they were called *Wapanachki*, or Abenakis, that is, *Men of the East*, or Eastlanders. By La Hontan and some other writers they were called *Algonkins,* or as more usually written by the French travellers and historians, *Algonquins*." (pg. 372).

Ray, Roger B. and Faulkner, Gretchen F. Ed. (1994). *The Indians of Maine: A bibliographic guide: fourth edition*. The Maine Historical Society, Augusta, ME.

- See the annotations in the bibliography of Other Author's Bibliographies.

Rolde, Neil. (2004). *Unsettled past unsettled future: The story of Maine Indians*. Tilbury House Publishers, Gardiner, ME. IS.

- "With the exception of the May-Quays, it is impossible in reading Joseph Nicolar to recognize our latter-day names for the Indian tribes of Maine history. The same holds true for his labelling of the landscape, which stretches from *Mik-mark-keag* to *Odur-wur-keag*. The names we know -- Penobscot, Passamaquoddy, Micmac, Maliseet, Kennebec, Saco, Androscoggin, and even less familiar ones like Wawenoc and Pigquacket -- are of our own making. They are what we think we heard the Indians call themselves and their surroundings, honed by our continued usage through several centuries." (pg. 81).
- "To compound the confusion, a third language is also encountered -- namely, the interpretation the French gave to the Indian sounds they heard. At least one of their labels has stuck -- *Iroquois* -- for a large grouping that refers to itself as the *Haudenosaunee*. Others -- the ones in Maine -- *Souriquois, Etchemin, Armouchiquois*, remain vivid only to historians. Translating this French-Indian into English-Indian, we have respectively: Micmac, Maliseet-Passamaquoddy, and Eastern Abenaki (particularly Saco, maybe Penobscot, too)." (pg. 81).
- "The *Pennacooks* were the southernmost tribe in Maine, spreading across the Piscataqua River from New Hampshire. In the small town of York, where I live, they were wiped out by 1614 due to smallpox or maybe measles that reached them from the English mariners and fishermen who had made a summer headquarters out on the Isles of Shoals. Cleared, deserted fields met the hardy Anglo settlers who ventured into the area around 1630. South of the Saco River it was warm enough for the tribes to practice extensive agriculture. But the Pennacooks had vanished, leaving only the memory of their great chief Passaconaway and his name to grace a famed Victorian tourist hotel at York Beach." (pg. 83).
- "To the west, in the shadow of the White Mountains, lived a branch of the Pennacooks called the *Pigquackets*. Or maybe they weren't Pennacooks and thus not *Eastern Abenaki*, say some experts, but in actuality *Western Abenaki*. (pg. 83).
- "Moving north, after the Saco, the next great flowage is that of the Androscoggin. The main tribe there, although usually called *Androscoggins*, can trip you up because some historians will refer to them as *Anasagunticooks* and others *Arosaguntacooks*. One reason may be the enormous reach of these people when they were still a viable entity -- occupying land all the way west to Lake Umbagog, well into New Hampshire, and east toward the Atlantic, debouching into Merrymeeting Bay where it joins the Kennebec at Topsham -- a length of 210 miles and a drainage of 3,430 square miles, with 7 tributaries and 83 lakes and ponds. The Androscoggins have been depicted as a 'powerful, warlike, relentless tribe, characterized as the first to make war and the last to conclude peace.' Various subsets of this same group existed under names such as *Rockomekas, Pejepscots, Sabbatis,* and *Amascontees* at particular geographic points along the Androscoggin River. The principal village early on was at Canton Point..." (pg. 84).
- "On a modern-day website created by the Davistown Museum of Liberty, Maine, an unnamed book reviewer vents considerable spleen at those authors who would deny the Wawenocs their space in history. He angrily charges that a particular writer 'in one brief paragraph...has eliminated one of the most important Native American communities of Maine's late prehistoric past,' thus, as is claimed, contradicting 'the huge body of written and oral history of thousands of English settlers and their descendants.' Seeking an answer to this atrocity, the reviewer asks rhetorically: 'Is this because the Wawenoc Indians had no

significant role to play after 1620, having been decimated both by Micmac (Tarrentine) massacres and the epidemics that followed?'" (pg. 88).

- "Some of the scholarly dithering on this subject is due to the role in history of a shadowy Indian figure known as the *Bashabas*, or alternatively, as *Bessabes*. This fellow was either a great chief who bore the title, like *emperor*, of the Bashabas or was an individual named Bessabes, whose force of personality made him an imperially great chief, with a realm stretching from Hancock County to York County. Was he a Penobscot, as Dean R. Snow has stated, locating him in a village at Kenduskeag Stream near Bangor? Our Wawenoc patriot, in his review of Snow's book, pounces immediately upon this (to him or her) a bad idea." (pg. 88).

Rosier, James. (1605). *A true relation of the voyage of Captaine George Waymouth.* Reprinted in Burrage, Henry, S. Ed. (1930). *Early English and French voyages chiefly from Hakluyt 1534-1608.* Charles Scribner's Sons, NY, NY.

- The most important of all early documents about the explorations of the Maine coast.
- See Morey, 2005, for a recent re-evaluation of Waymouth's voyage.
- See our information file reproduction of this text by James Rosier, *A True Relation of Captain George Weymouth his Voyage. Made this Present Yeere 1605.*

Rosier, James. (1843). A true relation of the most prosperous voyage made this present year, 1605, by Captain George Waymouth on the discovery of the land of Virginia. *Massachusetts Historical Society Collections.* 3rd series. 8. Boston. pg. 125-127.

- The most significant original source of information about the first contacts of Europeans with the Indians of Maine.
- Another republication of the text listed above.

Russell, Howard S. (1980). *Indian New England before the Mayflower.* University Press of New England, Hanover, NH. IS.

- The single most important and comprehensive source of information on the Native Americans of New England prior to and during the contact period (1500-1620).
- Published in 1980, it's one of the last important contemporary publications on New England's Native American history to mention the existence of the Wawenocs as residents of the region between the Kennebec and the Penobscot rivers. Most earlier references include the Sheepscot Indians as synonymous with the Wawenocs; Russell's map on page 25 implies they are two different tribes, which is not the case. This discrepancy helps illustrate the fact that there exist wide variations among major historians in their definitions of the names and locations of the Indian tribes of Maine. This may help explain why Baker, et.al., Churchill, et. al and other writers lump all the tribes together as Wabanaki; this is easier than explaining which tribes have been dislocated and why.
- Russell denotes three major groupings of eastern Abenaki: Passamaquoddy, Penobscot and Kennebec in Maine; the latter of which Russell places around Norwidgewock and Waterville.

Salisbury, Neal. (1982). *Manitou and Providence: Indians, Europeans, and the making of New England, 1500-1643*. Oxford University Press, NY, NY. IS.

- The most important summary of Indian - European relationships in the 16th and early 17th centuries; a particularly comprehensive description of the epidemic that swept through the Native American villages of the New England coast in 1617.
- Of particular interest is Salisbury's tribal-specific description of Indian - European relations in southern New England. For Native American's living in northern New England, including Maine, Salisbury follows the current convention and labels everyone as Eastern Abenaki. Salisbury's index does not list the Wawenoc, Kennebec or Androscoggin Indians of Maine. Detailed descriptions of inter-tribal relationships in southern New England are provided throughout this text.
- "The fruit of the Indian experience was an ethos in which relationships in the social, natural, and supernatural worlds were defined in terms of reciprocity rather than domination and submission. Developed centuries earlier when hunting and gathering were the primary modes of subsistence, this ethos had survived and continued to prevail as agriculture brought larger populations and more sedentary settlement patterns to the southern portion of New England." (pg. 10-11).
- "They overlooked important evidence for both north and south, particularly an anonymous description of upper New England written in 1605 and included by Samuel Purchas in his *Hakluytus Posthumus* (1625) and pre-epidemic estimates for southern New England obtained by Daniel Gookin in the 1670s and first published in 1792. 'The description of the Countrey of Mawooshen,' as the document published by Purchas was entitled, locates villages, identifies their leaders, and estimates the number of adult males and houses in each. Dean R. Snow has carefully correlated this information with that provided in other pre-epidemic accounts and concluded that about 11,900 Eastern Abenaki inhabited the river drainages from the Union River to the Saco in what is now the state of Maine." (pg. 23-24).
- "Agriculture, then, was the key to southern New England's departure from the Archaic patterns that still prevailed to the north. By the seventeenth century Indian women from the Saco River southward had developed a variety of crops, including several types of maize, beans, and squash, as well as pumpkins, cucumbers, Jerusalem artichokes, and tobacco." (pg. 30).
- "Underlying the nascent southern trade was a striking degree of unity among the Indians, based in part on economics. Smith reported that southern farmers were supplying corn to Abenaki hunters. At least part of the return for this corn was presumably European goods which the Abenaki, far less populous but vastly richer in furs, were beginning to acquire. Though built on pre-contact patterns of exchange, such a trade had revolutionary implications once Europeans were involved. By obtaining corn from their southern neighbors, the Abenaki could intensify the specialized hunt for furs while averting the perennial food shortages suffered by the Micmac." (pg. 76-77).
- "For all their planning and effort, the English made no headway among the Indians during the first decade and a half of the century. Initial native resistance to colonization and settlement was broken here, as in much of the Western Hemisphere, not by superior numbers, enterprise, technology, or military skill but by that most lethal of Europe's weapons, it diseases." (pg. 86).

- "The elimination of the French colonial presence, however, did not mean the end of their trading presence and its effectiveness among the indians. This fact was grasped by the man who was Virginia's second and greater, if unintended, contribution to New England colonization--John Smith. Coasting from above the Penobscot to Cape Cod in 1614, he found that French traders had largely exhausted the supply of furs at every harbor except Pemaquid, where Francis Popham had succeeded in trading (literally) on his late brother's good reputation." (pg. 97).
- "The reciprocity that Indians sought to maintain in economic, political, and spiritual relationships was seriously undermined in southern New England by the sequence of English actions and the plague epidemic. The propensities of English visitors (with the limited exception of the Pophams) toward violence and kidnapping, and their refusal to enter into and maintain reciprocal relationships, finally succeeded in arousing the hostility of most coastal Indians from the Penobscot to Cape Cod. Then the epidemic so reduced the coastal peoples in numbers and strength that their ability to maintain autonomy and, thus, real reciprocity with outsiders was largely lost. The once powerful Pawtucket, Massachusett, and Pokanoket were reduced to terror and humiliation before the numerically tiny Micmac as well as the formidable Narragansett, who now enjoyed important advantages in the competition for trade with Europeans. Even more critically, the epidemic enabled the hitherto inept English to establish a foothold for settlement." (pg. 109).

Sanger, David, Ed. (1979). *Discovering Maine's archaeological heritage.* Maine Historic Preservation Commission, Augusta, ME. IS.

- In the introduction, Sanger provides the following PaleoIndian chronologies: "11000 - 10000 B.P.; early archaic 10000 - 7000 B.P.; middle archaic 7000 - 5000 B.P.; late archaic 5000-2000 B.P.; ceramic period 2000 B.P. to European contact." (pg. 9). Sanger notes a scarcity of archaeological sites in Maine before 3000 B.C. (5000 B.P.) (see chapter 3).
- "During this century of contact there apparently occurred a change in aboriginal settlement and subsistence, so that the summer-interior/winter-coastal pattern of seasonal movement became reversed, probably in response to the summer voyages of Europeans and the developing trade in furs (Bourque 1973; Sanger 1971; Sanger and Sanger 1974). This reversal tended to emphasize the hunt and de-emphasize the importance of fishing. It seems apparent, however, that when one plots the distribution of sites in Maine there emerges a high correlation between large sites and good fishing spots. Sites such as Hirundo are prime examples of this very common pattern (Sanger and other n.d.)" (pg. 30-31).
- "No Maine cemetery, with the exception of the ambiguous radiocarbon dates for the Hathaway site, can be securely dated. ...Recent discoveries in Canada have helped the situation. In 1968 and 1969 James A. Tuck excavated the Port au Choix site in western Newfoundland (Tuck 1970, 1971). The red ochre-covered skeletons and characteristic Moorehead complex tools linked the Port au Choix cemetery with the Maine sites. Especially close relationships are seen between the Port au Choix and the Nevin sites, the latter near Blue Hill, Maine." (pg. 69).
- Long the standard reference for the nonprofessional interested in Maine archaeology, this publication has been supplanted by Bourque's *Diversity and Complexity in prehistoric*

maritime societies: A Gulf of Maine perspective. Still particularly relevant for anyone concerned with Paleo-Indian history and the important Paleo-Indian sites outside of Maine.

Sanger, David. (Fall 2000). "Red Paint People" and other myths of Maine archaeology. *Maine History.* 39(3). pg. 145-167. IS.

- "As I define the Moorehead burial tradition, it includes the development of cemeteries usually separated from habitation sites, a preference for sandy land forms, usually overlooking water, the inclusion of substantial amounts of red ocher and, perhaps most importantly, the tendency to include as grave offerings a highly selective suite of artifacts. ... Participants in the Moorehead burial tradition interred in the graves a number of well-crafted, ground and highly-polished tools, few of which ever appear in habitation sites. ... From 6000 B.C. until 1800 B.C. the emphasis was clearly on ground stone tools, many never used for daily tasks." pg. 152-153.

- "To recapitulate, what has been known as the 'Red Paint People' since the early decades of the 20th century is not a distinct race at all. ... They simply practiced a burial tradition connected with a set of spiritual beliefs unknown to us. Evidently those beliefs underwent a dramatic change about 1800 B.C. when red ocher all but disappeared from Maine graves, many of the distinctive artifacts dropped out of the archaeological record, and cremation replaced inhumation." pg. 154.

- "Archaeological research in the last two decades has led to a re-examination of the traditional seasonal migration idea. During the late 1960s, research in Penobscot Bay by Bourque and Ritchie, and simultaneously by me in Passamaquoddy Bay detected unmistakable signs of winter occupation on the coast. Indeed, I even went so far as to suggest that year-round coastal occupation might be represented. The evidence for winter habitation sites consisted of the presence of birds, such as ducks like oldsquaw, that today only winter on our coast. Large numbers of tom cod bones, a species that spawns in fresh water in the dead of winter, was also a good indicator. ... Another useful indicator is the fact that male deer drop their antlers in the winter. The finding of skull bones in which the antlers have been shed indicates a winter kill. On the other hand, antlers hacked from a deer taken in the summer will leave tell-tale cut marks on the skull bones. These indicators led to recognition of near year-round occupation at the Turner Farm site, ca. 2500 B.C., on North Haven Island, Penobscot Bay." pg. 155-156.

- "We now have records from well over 1,000 soft shell clams recovered from shell middens ranging from Passamaquoddy Bay to Casco Bay. In those areas where we have conducted detailed survey and testing, we can demonstrate both summer and winter occupation on the coast based on shells and other indicators." pg. 158.

- "...Native people lived year-round in the coastal zone, moving from site to site in response to resource availability and the need for shelter in the cold seasons. This reconstruction is very different from the traditional model derived from documents produced by the first European visitors to the coast of Maine, and echoed in *Penobscot Man*. If this reconstruction is accurate, it would leave very little time for the Native peoples to create sites in the interior. Therefore, we then have to face the question of who left all the archaeological sites in the interior of Maine." pg. 158-159.

- "Unfortunately, seasonal indicators for the interior are much diminished in the archaeological record, such that the currently available evidence cannot either support or deny what I call 'the two population model.'" pg. 159.
- "...a review of artifacts we consider to have potential to reflect the maker's traditions, such as pottery and flaked projectile points (arrow and spear heads), supports a long-standing separation of interior and coastal peoples. ... For example, archaeologists have recognized that starting around 6000 B.C. the Kennebec River has formed a cultural boundary. East of the Kennebec, and including the Maritime Provinces, we see many similarities in the cultural province of the Maritime Peninsula. The reasons for this remain speculative; however, it is clear that west of the divide the archaeological cultures remind us more of southern New England. 'Two Maines' has a long history!" pg. 161.
- "Although artifact style undoubtedly says something about the maker and his or her traditions, it is a leap of faith from there to ethnic assignment at the level of a named tribe with respect to the archaeological record. ... The point is when asked, 'What tribe lived here in pre-European times?' we ought to admit we cannot say. In my opinion, the bits and pieces left behind in archaeological sites cannot support a conclusion as complicated as ethnic identity." pg. 161-162.
- "Yet there is one overriding problem with *Penobscot Man* that is a product of its time: namely, an attempt to derive what is sometimes referred to as the 'ethnographic baseline,' a period in which Native cultures were not yet impacted by Europeans." pg. 162.

Schultz, Eric B. and Tougias, Michael J. (1999). *King Philip's War: The history and legacy of America's forgotten conflict.* The Countryman Press, Woodstock, VT. IS.

Sewall, Rufus King. (1859). *Ancient dominions of Maine.* Bath, ME.

- This text contains an extensive description of the abandoned Wawenoc sites in the Wiscasset area and, along with Williamson, is the most important antiquarian information source on Wawenoc history.
- Rufus King Sewall has been relegated to the rubbish bin of history not only for his romanticism pertaining to the Wawenoc Indians as a "lost race" but especially for his stubborn insistence that Waymouth sailed up the Kennebec River rather than the St. George River to plant his cross commemorating his visit to Maine. After George Prince (1860, just after the publication of the *Ancient Dominions*) printed his commentary on Rosier's *Narrative of Waymouth's Voyage to the Coast of Maine*, Sewall was the last stubborn holdout who, throughout his lifetime, did not acknowledge Prince's now universally accepted observation that Waymouth's exploration took place in the St. George River and his famous hike in full armor on a very hot summer day was in the direction of the Camden Hills, not Mt. Washington. Sewall nonetheless remains an important source of information about the Wawenoc Indians and their confederacy of Mawooshen, which has been recently written out of Maine's history.
- "These island-lawns are covered with the remains of a vast primitive population, whose bones, blackened, broken and decayed, are everywhere diffused in the offal of their subsistence; and the soil of their planting grounds, where clustered their lodges, is full of the fatness of the ashes of the unnumbered and forgotten dead!" (pg. 20).

- A "'Norubegua,' contemporaneous with the aboriginal Mavooshen, is one of the earliest of ancient names on our shores." (pg. 30-31).
- The early historian, Ogilby, described Norubegua to be "the ruins of an ancient town, which the natives called Arambec, and had deserted." (pg. 32).
- Quoting Purchas, vol. 4, pp. 1620-1625, Sewall notes: "This book, of two and a half centuries ago, describes Norombegua 'as a city toward the north, which is known well enough by reason of a fair town and a great river.' at the mouth of the river 'is an island very fit for fishing******and the region that goeth along the sea, doth abound in fish.'" (pg. 32).
- "Damariscove, or Monhegan Island, lying east and west of each other, and off the mouth of the Damariscotta River-islands remarkable for their advantages in fishing, ...lay off the mouth of the river, on the margins of whose waters the fair town of Norumbegua stood, ...or the ruins of the deserted Arâmbec lay ...have an intimate connection with the enormous oyster offal deposites we have described in the remains of these edible bivalves, at the head-waters and along the margins of the lower basins of Damariscotta River. (pg. 34).
- That "Norembegua of our aboriginal history was a fair town and not a Province, here located is more fully confirmed from the facts recorded ...of the earliest nature of this region." (pg. 35).
- As Waymouth's "ship lay under Fisherman's Island, west of Pemaquid, in Boothbay harbor, they signified that the 'Bashaba' (i.e. their king,) sent them with an invitation, that Capt. Weymouth should bring his '*Quiden*' (as they called it,) or ship, up to the Bashaba's house, being as they pointed, up on the main, toward the east, from whence they came." (pg. 38). This is to say, up the river at the present location of Damariscotta and Newcastle.
- Sir Ferdinando Gorges "...also tells us 'the native government was Monarchical, the king bearing the title of Bashaba, whose own chief abode and was not far from Pemaquid.'" (pg. 41).
- "The bone-made darts and javelins, and offensive weapons of this manufacture, the knowledge and use of copper ornaments and utensils, together with the use of tobacco in such extravagant forms; the costume and array of their persons; the mode of dressing the hair of their heads; ornamental hair work as a part of the Royal vesture, or court costume of the great officers of state; the evidences of permanency of abode and of a people 'who would eat nothing raw;' eminently a people of culinary tastes and habits, discoverable in the sites of ancient and eloquent ruin at the head-waters of the Damariscotta and on the Sheepscot at the entrance of the harbor of Boothbay...clearly and palpably establish an identity between the barbaric aboriginal inhabitants of the lower waters of the Sheepscot, and the upper water settlements of the Damariscotta, together with the women and children of the people visiting Weymouth's ship, and the residents of the island dwellers on the Sheepscot, if not also with the savages of Gosnold's shallop vision!" (pg. 42-43).
- "...the Capital of the native Sovereign of Lincoln was within the precinct, not far from, but not at Pemaquid. ...the royal abode of the Bashaba and Norumbegua were identical; ...the ruins at the head-waters ...mark the seat of ancient empire--of which the island city of lodges on the Sheepscot, at the 'Ne-krangan' of native travel through the harbor below, was a sea-board town." (pg. 44).
- "Menikuk and Arambec were sister cities; and of the residents in both places, were the ancient people visited and outraged by George Weymouth in the spring and summer of 1605." (pg. 46).

- "Were they of that race ... known in history as the 'Wa-wen-nocks,' whose very name endows them with the highest   excellence of humanity--'as a people very brave, fearing nothing'? the immediate subjects of the Bashaba, the grand sovereign of the east--the sway of whose scepter from its center near Pemaquid, to the boundaries of Massachusetts, was all potent? to whose court all the subordinate tribes paid savage homage, from the banks of Penobscot to the shores of the Merrimac? whose prowess the fierce Tarratine alone dared to brave.?" (pg. 47).
- Sewall follows Williamson using an incorrect spelling of Tarrantine.
- "It is a point of heroism with the savage brave, to rescue and bury the body of his fallen comrade; and the remarkable non-observance of the custom here, clearly points to surprise, consternation and death at the hands of unexpected enemies..." (pg. 50).
- "Both of these agencies may have operated. To the east and north-east of the dominions of the Bashaba, dwelt the people of the Tarratines, enemies of the Bashaba, who had many. The Wawenocks, his subjects, dwelt on the Sheepscot and Pemaquid; but the fierce Tarratines occupied and held the waters of the Penobscot." (pg. 50-51).
- "Pestilence trod hard on the heels of war, till the utter desolation of the Bashaba dominions was completed. Arambec and Menikuk may have been the chief towns of the Wawennock race..." (pg. 51).
- "Samoset was a native of Pemaquid--the Lord of Monhegan-an eastern prince--the great chief and original proprietor of the town of Bristol, whose conveyance of the same to John Brown is the first landed title by deed acknowledged, ever given to a white man." (pg. 101).

Siebert, Frank T. Jr. (1973). The identity of the Tarrentines, with an etymology. *Studies in Linguistics*. 23. pg. 69-76. IS.

- Siebert observes how William D. Williamson misspelled Tarrentines and then mistakenly identified them as Penobscots and then notes that Alden T. Vaughn more recently misidentified them as Abenakis in general.
- "The Abnaki-Micmac or Armouchiquois-Souriquois war lasted from 1607 to the end of 1616, and resulted in the death of Bashabes and the destruction of several Abnaki villages on the coast of Maine. Later the Micmacs extended their forays further to the south and made raids against the Massachusett Indians until c.1633." (pg. 71).
- Siebert's article also contains several important footnotes: "Smith's Mecadacut is Penobscot /amehkáyihtekok/ 'at a stream below a height (or mountain)', which is better retained by the modern spelling found in the present Megunticook River. Near-by is Mt. Megunticook which rises to a height of 1380 feet, and is the southern-most mountain or headland of the Appalachians to stand directly on the Atlantic coast. The Penobscot village which Smith visited here was probably destroyed by the Micmacs in 1616 and never re-occupied." (pg. 74).
- "It is interesting to note that the Penobscot village located at present Castine, Maine, given by Purchas as Chebegnadose was spared by the Micmacs, evidently because of the beginning settlement there by Claude de Saint-Etienne de La Tour. ...The Penobscots did not abandon their village adjoining the small fort and settlement at Castine until about 1743 at the beginning of King George's War." (pg. 74).

- "There is adequate documentation demonstrating the presence of large numbers of Basque fishermen in North Atlantic waters from Newfoundland and the Gulf of St. Lawrence southward to Cape Cod during the sixteenth and seventeenth centuries. The Basques ...together with the Bretons held an early monopoly on the whale and cod fisheries in that area. (Reade 1889:21-39)." (pg. 72-73).

Smith, John. (1616). *A Description of New England: Or the observations, and discoueries of Captain John Smith (Admirall of the Country) in the north of America, in the year of our Lord 1614: With the success of sixe ships, that went the next yeare 1615; and the accidents befell him among the French men of warre: With the proofe of the present benefit this Countrey affoords: Whither this present yeare, 1616, eight voluntary ships are gone to make further tryall.* Printed by Humfrey Lownes, for Robert Clerke, London. X.

- The Davistown Museum has a xerox copy of Smith's text in its special collections library (24 pages long).

Smith, John. (1837). A description of New-England. *Collections of the Massachusetts Historical Society*, 3rd series, 6. pg. 103-140.

- Along with Rosier, Purchas and Davies, this is one of the key documents providing early English observations of the Maine coast and its inhabitants in the years before English settlement.
- A number of excerpts from his description are reproduced in the Davistown Museum's *Norumbega Reconsidered* publication.

Snow, Dean R. (1968). Wabanaki "family hunting territories". *American Anthropologist.* New series. 70. pg. 1143-1151. IS.

- "Such political developments as the Wabanaki confederacy in Maine and at the Maritimes developed out of this base as a response to later pressures by European settlers. Prior to these relatively late developments, there had been no formal political organization above the hunting band level." (pg. 1143).
- "Archeological evidence from Maine alone indicates that the beaver and other sedentary fauna were of considerable importance aboriginally. ...in the case of the Wabanaki, the fur trade lead to the crystalization of family territories along the lines of preexisting pattern of economic exploitation." (pg. 1145).
- "...the Wabanaki defined individual territories in terms of drainage areas such that lakes and streams were at the nucleus rather than the periphery of each of them." (pg. 1146-1147).
- Snow also has this to say about the term Wabanaki or Dawn-Land-People. "This convenient term is usually used to refer to the Micmac, Malecite, Passamaquoddy, Penobscot, Abnaki, and Pennacook, although there is some question regarding the inclusion of the last (Dodge 1957:68-69)". (pg. 1147).

- "The distribution of Wabanaki Indians appears to have followed a dendritic pattern that coincided with major streams and tributaries." (pg. 1147).
- "The Abnaki probably had a system similar to that of the Penobscot. Morgan obtained a list of fourteen band names from an unknown informant among the St. Francis, Quebec, Abnaki in about 1878 (Morgan 1907:174). These names parallel those known for Penobscot bands, and therefore indicate that these two closely related tribes had similar forms of 'territoriality.'" (pg. 1147).
- Snow also quotes Joseph Chadwick (1889) on the propensity of the "Wabanaki" Indians to conserve their resources. "...that it was their rule to hunt every third year and kill two-thirds of the beaver, leaving the other third part to breed, and that their Beavers were as much their stock for a living as Englishman's cattle was his living; that since the late war English hunters kill all the Beaver they find on said streams, which had not only impoverished many Indian families, but destroyed the breed of Beavers, etc." (pg. 1149).
- This article illustrates that the propensity to not mention the Wawenoc Indians was well established by 1968.

Snow, Dean R. (1976). The Abenaki fur trade in the sixteenth century. *The Western Canadian Journal of Anthropology.* 6(1). pg. 3-11. IS.

- "Conclusions focus on increasing dependence upon European goods, rescheduling of subsistence activities, involvement in food-redistribution networks, and settlement nucleation." (pg. 3).
- "As it happens, I agree with Innis (1962:12) that 'the fur trade in the first half of the sixteenth century was of minor importance and incidental to fishing.'" (pg. 3).
- "A Portuguese presence along the Maine coast in the first quarter of the sixteenth century raises the possibility that they began the fur trade with the Eastern Abenaki. Indeed, Bourque (1973) has argued that data from late prehistoric coastal sites and the earliest European sources suggest shifts in seasonal scheduling and settlement patterns during this period, and that these shifts are best explained by the emergence of a pattern of summer coastal trade with European vessels." (pg. 4).
- "...felt hats ...became the fashion rage in the court of Elizabeth I around 1560. ... By that time, the European beaver survived in only a few places in southern Europe. It was scarce everywhere on the continent by the end of the century. Thus, demand for pelts rapidly outstripped the supply after 1560." (pg. 5).
- "The English and other northern Europeans did not have easy access to cheap salt, and consequently they established land stations [in Newfoundland] for the purpose of drying their catches before returning home." (pg. 5).
- "...during the period Smith was on the Maine coast, he reports that 25,000 pelts were sent back to France (Smith 1905:214-234). It must have been clear to Smith that the only way the English could beat the French at this game was to set up their own trading posts and offer better prices. However, a horrible and unexpected epidemic altered the system dramatically." (pg. 8).

Snow, Dean R. (1976). *The archaeology of North America: American Indians and their origins.* Thames and Hudson, London. IS.

Snow, Dean R. (1976). The ethnohistoric baseline of the eastern Abenaki. *Ethnohistory* 23(3). pg. 291-306.

- "Sources on the Eastern Abenaki dating to about 1600 are crucial in establishing the ethnohistorical baseline, the initial cultural state from which all subsequent historical changes occurred. ...original inhabitants of the Penobscot, Kennebec and adjacent river drainages were occupied by the Abenaki rather than by the Malecite-Passamaquoddy as some have stated." [Hoffman, 1955 and Morrison, 1978] (pg. 291).

- "In the 17th century, the Eastern Abenaki controlled an area that is almost entirely contained within the modern State of Maine. Their major divisions coincided with four major river drainages within the larger area. From west to east, those divisions were Pigwacket, Arosaguntacook, Kennebec, and Penobscot corresponding to the Presumpscot, Androscoggin, Kennebec and Penobscot drainages. Colonial period sources provide a staggering number of synonyms and misnomers for the Eastern Abenaki and their various subdivisions, but these four seem to be the common denominators. Only the Penobscot survive in place today. Descendants of the others can be found in the old Abenaki refugee colonies of St. Francis and Becancour, Quebec." (pg. 291).

- "Verrazzano sailed eastward along the Maine coast, and for us the real significance of his voyage is that a map that resulted identifies the Penobscot River as 'ornbega.' This term, which is clearly a native word identifying the lower portion of the Penobscot River, is the only native name on the map." (pg. 292).

- "As Morrison (1974:21) points out, 'Almouchiquois' is an almost meaningless general term that lumps together what must have been several Algonquian communities in southern New England. I see no reason why Champlain's 'Etechemin' should be considered to have a more precise and historically meaningful definition since Champlain used both at the same level of descriptive abstraction." (pg. 296).

- "In 1625, Samuel Purchas published a description of what he called the country of 'Mawooshen.' Gorges (1890:76) calls the same place 'Moasham.' Both references are to the area later clearly identified as belonging to the Eastern Abenaki. The Purchas list in particular is quite explicit. He defines the area in terms of a series of river drainages extending from Mount Desert Island on the east to the upper portion of the Saco River on the west." (pg. 298).

- Snow argues that the Bashabes so frequently mentioned in early writings as the chief of all of Mawooshen (the area from the Saco River to Schoodic Point) was actually from an Indian village located at the Kenduskeag Stream where it joins the Penobscot at the present site of Bangor. Earlier writers had insisted that the Bashabes lived in the area of Pemaquid; in which case the Bashabes would have been a Wawenoc. There is no direct evidence that the Bashabes lived at Kenduskeag and there is no archaeological evidence extant for a significant Indian village at that location. The current paradigm derives from an interpretation of Champlain's voyage up the Penobscot, and it is essential that the Bashabes is not a Wawenoc, but rather, a Penobscot, if one is to believe that the Wawenocs were an insignificant community of little or no importance. In fact, it would follow from the current paradigm that most of the contact with natives along the shores between the Penobscot and the Kennebec reported by early writers would then have to have been with Penobscot Indians. Kenduskeag Stream is quite remote and distant from the highly populated areas of the Sheepscot,

Medomak and St. George's Rivers, including the Pemaquid area where numerous early writers place the Bashabes. Why would the Bashabes live in an area so remote from the highly populated coastal regions where he was so admired and so often referred to by the natives as reported by the early writers?

- "The death of Bashabes is as controversial a subject as anything else about him. Lescarbot (1928:101) states flatly and without elaboration that he was killed by the English. Gorges (1890:76) discusses the matter at greater length, but says without any equivocation that Bashabes was killed by the Micmac." (pg. 302).
- "Bashabes was replaced by a man named Asticou. ...but he disappears from history during the epidemics that preceded 1618. ...In summary, the political organization of the Eastern Abenaki at the beginning of the 17th century appears to have been based upon a loose confederation of ethnically related groups stretching from Mount Desert Island to the Saco River in Maine. Local groups were defined on the basis of the river drainages they occupied, and each was led by a chief sagamore." (pg. 303).
- "We know, for example, that by 1620 Samoset (Somersett) was an important sagamore living on the Damariscotta, but we do not know whom he succeeded or in which (if any) of the three villages listed by Purchas he lived." (pg. 304).

Snow, Dean R. (1978). Eastern Abenaki. In: Trigger, Bruce G., Volume Ed. *Volume 15, Northeast*. In: *Handbook of North American Indians*. Sturtevant, William C., Ed., Smithsonian Institution, Washington, DC.

- "An anonymous description published by Samuel Purchas in 1625 indicated that in the early part of that century, the Eastern Abenaki were confederated under the leadership of a man called Bashabes. The name appears elsewhere in various early sources and in several forms including Bessabez and Betsabes. He was one of 23 'sagamores' named for 21 villages on 11 rivers. He appears to have been first among equals, the acknowledged leader of all the Eastern Abenaki." (pg. 137).
- "The 'countrey of Mawooshen,' as it is described by Purchas, was composed of villages on Mount Desert Island, and the Penobscot, Orland, Bagaduce, Muscongus, Damariscotta, Sheepscot, Kennebec, Androscoggin, Presumpscot, and upper Saco rivers." (pg. 137).
- "There are enough sources to allow the reconstruction of Eastern Abenaki culture for the period just before the epidemics of the early seventeenth century. Samuel de Champlain and John Smith saw horticulture along the coast only as far northeast as the Saco River, the lower portions of which were not occupied by the Eastern Abenaki. There is some evidence that horticulture was practiced upstream along the Kennebec, but it would have been a marginal effort at best. The territory of the Eastern Abenaki was covered by a mixed white pine, hemlock, and hardwood forest in coastal areas, changing to a spruce and fir forest in the interior. Neither the soil nor the climate was adequate for the available domesticates. A real economic commitment to horticulture was not possible until the fur trade made winter residence in large villages possible and provided the option of purchasing food in years of crop failure." (pg. 138).
- An excerpt from this text on Eastern Abenaki tribal names is in our Appendix.

Snow, Dean R. (1980). *The archaeology of New England*. Academic Press, NY. IS.

- Along with Bourque's *Diversity and Complexity in Prehistoric Maritime Societies: A Gulf of Maine Perspective* and *Twelve Thousand Years* and Sanger's *Discovering Maine's Archaeological Heritage*, this text provides a basic introduction to the archaeology of Maine. Snow applies his 1973 river drainage model to explain the prehistory of Maine (see pg. 4).
- "The river drainages into which I have subdivided the region are also archaeologically significant units. The only significant difficulty with the model is that small coastal drainages are not easily accommodated. For example, in Maine the major Kennebec and Penobscot drainages are in fact separated along the coast by minor drainages such as the Sheepscot, Damariscotta, and St. Georges." (pg. 5).
- See pages 20-23 for extensive comments on the myths of New England's past including Vikings, Celts, the Red Paint craze and the Spirit Pond at Cutler. Also see the quotes at the beginning of our bibliographic selections on pre-Columbian myths.
- "There are several sources relating to Eastern Abenaki ethnohistory before 1620, but one extraordinary source stands out among them. The origins of this source stem from the George Waymouth expedition to the Maine coast in 1605. Waymouth kidnapped five Indians, one of whom eventually made his way into the household of Ferdinando Gorges in England. This man and others were apparently interviewed by James Rosier, and Purchas (1625) subsequently published a very detailed accounting of the villages of the Eastern Abenaki. Each village is identified in terms of the river on which it was located, and in many cases it is possible to rediscover the exact locations of these villages (Snow 1976d) (Table 2.3). Purchas lists 21 villages and 23 leaders called *sagamores*." (pg. 36-37).
- Table 2.3, Population Data Derived from Purchas (1625), provides an important clue to the elimination of the Wawenoc Indians as an important regional tribe from recent Maine histories. (Why would the Wawenocs be less important than the Arosaguntacooks or the Pequakets?) In this list of villages, Snow lists at least 7 and possibly 8 Wawenoc villages as Kennebec. The last 3 villages, listed as Penobscot, also may have been Wawenoc in the late prehistoric period. (pg. 37).
- "Samuel Purchas published a description of what he called the country of 'Mawooshen.' Gorges (1890:76) calls the same place 'Moasham.' Both references are to the area later clearly identified as belonging to the Eastern Abenaki. The Purchas list in particular is quite explicit. He defines the area in terms of a series of river drainages extending from Mount Desert Island on the east to the upper portion of the Saco River on the west. Purchas gives us 10 terms that lead us to the modern names of 11 rivers (Table 2.3). These include the Union, Penobscot, Orland, Bagaduce, St. Georges (?), Damariscotta, Sheepscot, Kennebec, Androscoggin, Presumpscot, and Saco (Snow 1976d)." (pg. 55).
- "The ash splint basketry for which the Penobscot and others are well known today was introduced later in the colonial period by Swedes on the Delaware River and was therefore not part of the A.D. 1600 inventory (Brasser 1974). Smoking pipes were made of both clay and stone." (pg. 58).
- "The Indians of the Androscoggin River are known best to history as the Arosaguntacook. The river started out with the same name, but its name was later changed in honor of the colonial governor Edmund Andros (1637 - 1714). The Indians of the Kennebec are best thought of under that name even though the later importance of the village of Norridgewock led to the more frequent use of that name in late colonial documents. **Wawenoc Indians,**

who appear in many later documents, were simply residents of the coastal drainages between the Kennebec and Penobscot that I have chosen to lump with the Kennebec." (pg. 61).

- Chapter 4 (pg. 157-186) contains an important discussion of Rene Thom's catastrophe theory as applied to prehistoric and contact period population levels and dislocations. "...for the moment it is mainly a handy model for illustrating archaeological discontinuity graphically (Renfrew 1978). Figure 4.1 illustrates the collapse of a system using a simple cusp catastrophe as a model." (pg. 158).

- Commenting on the Damariscotta shell middens, Snow says "Coastal adaptations generally and the exploitation of shellfish in particular have been the focus of recent controversy in New England archaeology. I should say at the onset that I think that the abundance of prehistoric shellfish refuse and the controversy itself have combined to exaggerate the importance of this food resource to Indian populations. ... Clearly oysters, and shellfish generally, could not have been more than a supplementary part of the diet for most people most of the time." (pg. 178).

- The map on page 189, among others, provides graphic evidence for the lack of archaeological research in the Norumbega bioregion, which is between the Penobscot and Kennebec rivers. Almost all archaeological sites in Maine are east or north of the lower Penobscot River.

- Chapter 5 contains an interesting discussion of the "Rise and Fall of the Red Paint People." "The popular mythology that accumulated around the Late Archaic cemetery remains of northern New England has only recently been surpassed in bulk and absurdity by the currently popular Celtic craze." (pg. 201).

- Snow agrees with Bourque that at the end of the early horticultural period "...people were spending fall, winter, and spring in pit houses on coastal sites. They presumably spent the summer months taking salmon, alewife, shad, and eel at fishing stations on interior streams. Although smaller than Late Prehistoric settlements, the coastal sites were probably occupied for a longer period during the year and may have been more permanent than later coastal camps." (pg. 301).

- On the late prehistoric period Snow observes: "We have seen that the Eastern Abenaki had about 22 such main villages, most of which are now under modern towns and cities. The pattern of living at dual central places, coastal and interior, was replaced by a pattern of living at single intermediate central places on lower stream courses. Interior and coastal camps were by now not themselves central places, but temporary camps, and the criteria for their specific locations changed." (pg. 336).

- Snow agrees with Bourque that these settlement pattern changes occurred around 1100 AD in Maine and may be due to the peak of climatic warming that occurred at this time.

- "The rise of large central villages in northern New England after A.D. 1000 was accompanied by a decline in the importance of coastal camps. Coastal pit houses, and presumably winter residence on the coast, disappear after A.D. 1200 in the St. Croix and St. John drainages. None of Bourque's (1971:166-216) sites on the Maine coast show evidence of occupation after A.D. 1100. Indeed, Bourque had trouble finding any sites postdating A.D. 1100 along the coast." (pg. 336).

Soctomah, Donald. (2005). A Wabanaki perspective. In: *A symposium to celebrate one land - two worlds: Maine Mawooshen 1605 - 2005: The 400th anniversary of George Waymouth's voyage to New England.* Island Institute, Rockland, ME. IS.

- This chapter has been reproduced in .pdf format as an appendix in *Norumbega Reconsidered.*

Speck, Frank G. (1928). Wawenock myth texts from Maine. *43rd Annual Report of the Bureau of American Ethnology.* Bureau of American Ethnology, Washington, DC. pg. 180-181, 186. IS.

- Though Speck thought the Wawenocs "an unimportant" tribe (see his comments in *Penobscot Man,*) he took the trouble to visit the few remaining descendents of the Wawenocs residing at Becancour, Quebec in 1912, interviewing Francois Neptune, who is pictured in this report, and recorded surviving myth texts which are given at the end of the article.
- "It is one of the laments of ethnology that the smaller tribes of the northern coast of New England faded from the scene of history before we were able to grasp the content of their languages and culture. At this late day practically all have dwindled below the power of retaining the memory of their own institutions -- their link with the past. Nevertheless, some few groups along the coast have maintained existence in one form or another down to the present." (pg. 169).
- "On the western and southern boundaries of Maine the Wabanaki bands escaped extinction only by fleeing to Canada, where their descendants now live at the village of St. Francis. Of the tribal names included in this group, however, one in particular, the Wawenock, has long been reckoned among the obsolete." (pg. 169).

Speck, Frank G. (1940). *Penobscot man: The life history of a forest tribe in Maine.* University of Pennsylvania Press. Reprinted in 1998 by The University of Maine Press, Orono, ME. IS.

- One of Maine's most popular and frequently read commentaries on Native American history and the most important publication on Penobscot traditions, family hunting territories and origins, Speck gives voice to Native Americans who have been traditionally squelched or ignored, especially by his excellent and detailed descriptions of their material culture and their social life.
- Speck's anthropological study of the Penobscots is relevant to a study of any of the Abenaki communities in Maine. Speck makes this important comment in his postscript, written two decades after he did his anthropological research: "...the people we now designate as Penobscot are in reality an ethnic composite, the tribe itself a political unit, its culture a blending of native New England elements derived through a course of some centuries from perhaps wider horizons than we know of as yet." (pg. 301).
- "The Penobscot Indians refer to themselves as *Pa' nawampske' wi.ak,* 'People of the white rocks (country),' or 'People of where the river broadens out.' ...nearly all the Penobscot villages were on the Penobscot River, and their hunting grounds bordered it.." (pg. 7).

- "The loose tribal organization characterizing the people of the whole northeastern region, indeed, did not tend to develop very strict land distinctions outside of the family hunting territories. Close ethnic relationship, furthermore, made their contact easier and less liable to intertribal constraint." (pg. 7).
- "Some confusion exists in reference to the names of tribes and local subdivisions; unspecified inclusion under the names Tarratine and Etchemin of tribal bands which were later assigned proper names such as Norridgewock, Aroosagunticook, Kanibas, Sakoki, Wawenock, Sagadahock, Penobscot, Passamaquoddy, and Malecite." (pg. 12-13).
- "Weymouth, at about the same time (1605) encountered in Penobscot Bay people who if not Penobscot were Wawenock, and he left some few observations on the country." (pg. 13).
- "During 1615-16 a conflict is supposed to have arisen between the Penobscot (Etchemin or Tarratine) and the tribes (Abenaki) west of them, after which an epidemic of sickness occurred -- the historic 'plague' that nearly annihilated the natives of the northern New England coasts." (pg. 13).
- "With the Malecite, their neighbors on the northeast and east, the Penobscot are on most intimate terms, there being, as formerly, many intermarriages between the two tribes. The Penobscot, however, as a tribe, hold themselves somewhat above the latter." (pg. 16).
- "The Penobscot and the Passamaquoddy have always maintained a close relationship, and frequent intermarriages have taken place. The Penobscot are correctly aware of the dialectic similarity between Malecite and Passamaquoddy, attributing it to the fact that the latter are an offshoot from the former, their separation dating back several hundred years to a division of the Malecite at a breaking up of their main village *E'kpohak* near Spring Hill on St. John River. Those who migrated southward settled at Passamaquoddy Bay and founded the tribe." (pg. 17).
- "With the Passamaquoddy, the Malecite, and the Micmac, the Penobscot were joined in early times in a loose alliance for protection against the Iroquois." (pg. 17).
- "A small and unimportant tribe formerly dwelling on the coast, near Georges River, immediately west of Penobscot Bay, was known as *Walina' 'ki .a' k* (or *Wa' linak*) 'Cove (or little bay) people.' These people are recorded in the historical accounts as Wawenock. While supposed to be extinct or to be scattered among other tribes of the east, being remembered only by name among the Penobscot, some of their descendants are still to be found with the latter." (pg. 19).
- "The culture of the Penobscot is typical of the tribes east of the Piscataqua or the Saco River, and south of the St. Lawrence, which constitute the ethnic group known as the northeastern Algonkian or Wabanaki. Dependence upon hunting and fishing for subsistence amid extensive and well-watered tracts of forest, upon birch bark and wood for economic material characterize the area. Passing from west to east the tribes of this grouping include the present St. Francis Abenaki (formerly Norridgewock, Aroosaguntacook, Sokoki, and other remnants), the Wewenock, the Penobscot, the Malecite, the Passamaquoddy, and marginally the Micmac. Culturally these six tribes have many common attributes, though differences are numerous and marked when details are considered, and the same is true in regard to dialect. They are known among both Indians and Europeans as Wabanaki..." (pg. 21-22).
- "There is, furthermore, reason to believe that the tribes of the Wabanaki group came southward into New England, supposedly having crossed the St. Lawrence, and reached the coast where they settled, later branching off into bands which turned their faces farther

eastward. To support this it is also true that a break is found in the sequence of culture between the Wabanaki and the tribes south of them on the Massachusetts coast and that the two groups were in early colonial times politically quite disassociated." (pg. 23).

- "Said Captain Francis of the Penobscot some years ago, 'All the tribes between the Saco and River St. John were brothers: that the eldest lived on the Saco: that each tribe was younger as we passed eastward." (pg. 23).

- In his postscript, Speck makes another important point, probably because his text was criticized for constructing a romanticized concept of "Penobscot Man" as a single ethnic community. It was after this criticism that he added his postscript with the notation above about the Penobscot community as an ethnic composite. He also made one other point of particular importance for any attempt to reconstruct a Maine 16th century ethnic culture milieu: "The matter presented in the foregoing monograph is intended to draw a cultural picture in historic times of an Algonkian tribe of the northern New England forest -- the Canadian zone of the biologist. Its time-span is confined to horizons lying within the limits of the latter half of the nineteenth century." (pg. 301).

- By the late 19th century, there were only a few survivors of the Wawenoc community living in the St. Francis community in Quebec; by this time they were certainly an unimportant ethnic component of Maine's remaining indigenous population. Speck has avoided the thorny issue of attempting to reconstruct a description of or an analysis of the cultural significance of the Wawenoc community as it existed 350 years prior to his research on the Penobscots. At least, however, he acknowledges their previous existence.

- Also see Speck's publications in the Native Americans in Maine contemporary publications bibliography.

Spiess, Arthur E. and Cranmer, Leon. (Fall 2001). Native American occupations at Pemaquid: Review and results. *Maine Archaeological Society Bulletin.* 41(2). pg. 1 - 25). IS.

- "...analysis of the charred plant material from a late prehistoric (ca. 1420 to 1500 A.D.) feature confirmed corn and possibly bean horticulture on the site." (pg. 1).

- "The latest reanalysis indicates corn agriculture arriving in northern New England after 1100 A.D. (Heckenberger et al. 1992)." (pg. 22).

- "Conversion of the conventional radiocarbon age to calendar years ... places the date of harvest of that corn between 1430 and 1460 A.D. ...Thus, the corn is pre-European contact in age, and it documents a Native agricultural village on Colonial Pemaquid about 200 years before the European village." (pg. 22).

- *These identifications prove the agricultural nature of the Late Ceramic occupation at Colonial Pemaquid, and are a major addition to the understanding of central coastal Maine prehistory."* (pg. 22).

- "We suspect that the Native village at what was to become Colonial Pemaquid was a village mentioned in Purchas's 1625 census of the Maine coast." (pg. 24).

Sturtevant, William C., Ed. (1978). *Handbook of North American Indians.* Smithsonian Institution, Washington, DC.

- The largest and most comprehensive contemporary publication on Native Americans in North America, with egregiously inconsistent reporting on Maine's Native American communities in Volume 15.

Sullivan, James. (1804). The history of the Penobscot Indians. *Collections of the Massachusetts Historical Society.* 1st series, 9. pg. 207-232.

Swanton, John R. (1952). *The Indian tribes of north America.* Smithsonian Institution Bureau of MAerican Ethnology Bulletin 145. United States Printing Office, Washington, D.C.

Thayer, Henry O., Ed. (1892). *The Sagadahock colony, comprising the relation of a voyage into New England.* The Gorges Society, Portland, ME.

Thwaites, Reuben Gold, Ed. (1896-1901). *The Jesuit relations and allied documents: Travels and Explorations of the Jesuit missionaries in New France 1610-1791.* 73 vols. Burrows Brothers, Cleveland, OH. Reprinted in 1959 by Pagent Books, NY, NY. X.

- This text is frequently cited in our *Norumbega Reconsidered* publication.
- Many of the observations of Pierre Biard about the early history of French settlement in the maritime penninsula are located within these 73 volumes. See especially volume 2 page 223 pertaining to his visit to the ruins of the Popham Colony in 1611, where local Native Americans told Biard of the difficulties of trading with the English as well as of their hostility.
- Ruben Gold Thwaites has in his introduction this comment: "The rules of the church, prescribing a fish diet on certain holy days, led to a large use of salted fish throughout catholic Europe; and, by 1578, full a hundred and fifty French vessels alone, chiefly Breton, were employed in the Newfoundland fisheries, while a good trade with the mainland Indians, as far south as the Potomac, had now sprung up. The island colony proved valuable as a supply and repair station for traders and explorers, and thus served as a nucleus of both French and English settlement in America." (Vol I., pg. 7).
- Available on the web at: http://puffin.creighton.edu/jesuit/relations/relations_01.html.

Trigger, Bruce G., Volume Ed. (1978). *Volume 15, Northeast.* In: *Handbook of North American Indians.* Sturtevant, William C., Ed., Smithsonian Institution, Washington, DC.

- The definitive survey; excerpts from volume 15 are frequently referenced in this publication.
- See the Revisionist's Paradigm: Part I in *Norumbega Reconsidered* for Brasser's superficial comments on Maine's Native communities.

Trudel, Marcel. (1973). *The beginnings of New France, 1524-1663.* McClelland and Stewart, Ltd., Toronto, Canada.

Tuck, James A. (1971). An archaic cemetery at Port au Choix, Newfoundland. *American Antiquity*. 36(3). pg. 343-358.

- Among the first and most important publications on the maritime archaic culture of eastern Canada.
- "...'morphological variety, comprise the gouge; adze; plummet; ground slate points and knives, including the semi-lunar form of ulu which also occurs in chipped stone; simple forms of bannerstone; a variety of chipped-stone projectile points, mainly broad-bladed and side-notched forms; and the barbed bone point.' Further this tradition 'underwent regional specialization to various degrees' for 'better ecological adjustment'. (Ritchie 1965:79-80)." (pg. 354).
- "Two more concepts which bear on the Maritime Archaic are the Boreal Archaic (Byers 1959, 1962) and the Old Copper culture." (pg. 356).

Tuck, James A. (1975). The northeast maritime continuum: 8000 years of cultural development in the far northeast. *Arctic Anthropology*. 12(2). pg. 139-147.

- Tuck pioneered the formulation of the theory of a "maritime archaic" era in eastern coastal North America prehistory. This concept has been criticized and modified by Bourque in *Diversity and Complexity in Prehistoric Maritime Societies*. The alternative version of "maritime archaic" was the earlier myth of the Red Paint people (see Sanger, 2000) derived in part from Moorehead's 1920 excavation of Maine maritime sites in eastern Maine including at the Halls Falls Archaeologic site.
- The lifestyles and technology of the Maine maritime archaic population only differs slightly from that described by Turk for communities to the northeast.
- "The hypothesis that maritime adaptation on the Northeast coast (Maine and Atlantic Canada) began as early as 9000 years ago is suggested. ...rising sea levels have inundated evidence for this adaptation in Maine and the Maritimes. ... Rapid cultural change (associated with environmental change?) around 3500 years ago is suggested to have given the false impression of a population replacement at that time." (pg. 139).
- "This paper... takes as its basic tenet the explicit rejection of all migration hypotheses which cannot be absolutely documented." (pg. 139).
- "It has been pointed out by a number of workers from the time of Moorehead to the present that there is considerable difference between the 'Red Paint' people of Maine and the 'shellmound people' who appeared later and were the probable ancestors of the historically known natives of that area. Recently, Dean Snow (1972) proposed quite the opposite -- an *in situ* development from Archaic to shellmound peoples in the state of Maine." (pg. 141).
- "...a burial mound in southern Labrador dated at 7530±140 B.P. (I-8099) containing bifaces, gouges and red ochre suggests considerably earlier beginnings." (pg. 144).
- "...profound cultural changes undergone by coastal inhabitants of Maine and the Maritimes... [included] cessation of marine hunting, changes in terrestrial hunting patterns, adoption of bark rather than dugout boats, technological changes, etc." (pg. 145).

Watson, Lawrence W. (1907). The origins of the Melicities.*Journal of American Folk-Lore*. 20. pg. 160-162.

Wilbur, C. Keith. (1978). *The New England Indians: An illustrated sourcebook of authentic details of everyday Indian life*. Globe Pequot Press, Chester, CT. IS.

- The best introduction to the (southern) New England Indians for middle school and high school students, this text is lavishly illustrated, well organized and easy to peruse for a casual reader.
- Wilbur's listing of the tribes of New England is particularly telling commentary on the eradication of the tribal identity of the Wawenoc Indians as well as of the Kennebecs, Arosaguntacooks and Pequawkets from contemporary history texts. Wilbur provides the following definition of tribes living in northern New England: "Abnaki - New England's northernmost tribe were hunters, not farmers. Untouched by the epidemics, these dread and cruel Tarrantines (as they were called by the tribes to the south) warred on the disease-ridden tribe called the Massachusetts." (pg.73).
- Oversimplification of a very complex cultural milieu is the first step in ethnohistoric cleansing. A lot of misinformation in one sentence.

Willey, Gordon R. (1966). *An introduction to American archaeology, I: North and middle America*. Prentice-Hall, Englewood Cliffs, NJ. IS.

- A standard reference on North America's native inhabitants, this text contains important information about Native Americans living in Maine, especially with respect to archaic artifacts found at Ellsworth Falls. (Byers, etc.)

Williams, Roger. (1643). *A key into the language of America*. Reprinted in 2004, Dennis Cerrotti, Ed., Sea Venture Press, Brookline, MA. IS.

Williamson, William D. (1832). *The history of the state of Maine; from its first discovery, A. D. 1602, to the separation, A. D. 1820, inclusive, Volume I and II.* Glazier, Masters & Co., Hallowell, ME. Reprinted by The Cumberland Press, Inc., Freeport, ME. IS.

- The most detailed description of New England and Maine Indian tribes in any Maine history book. Williamson makes some mistakes such as misspelling Tarrantines and identifying Indians living on the Saco River as Sokoi (they were not - as Day makes clear, the Sokoi lived on the upper Connecticut River in Northfield). Nonetheless, this history, along with Sewall's *Ancient Dominions of Maine,* contains basic information on Native Americans in Maine, including the Wawenocs, that is no longer included in contemporary Maine and Native American history texts.
- "the latter [Tarratines] began the war. ...Gorges says, 'his [Sagamore's] chief abode was not far from Pemaquid.' His place of immediate residence was probably between that river and Penobscot bay. ...his political dominions included, at least, all the Indians upon the Kennebec, the Androscoggin, and probably the Saco. Capt. Smith further states... 'they hold the Bashaba to be chief, and the greatest among them.'" (pg. 214).

- "Samoset.....an inhabitant of the remote East, who, to the astonishment of the Pilgrim settlers at Plymouth, walking boldly and alone into their streets, greeted the forlorn colonists with 'Much welcome, Englishmen,' in a broken dialect of their own tongue."
- "these Taratine warriors....cut their way to the residence of the Bashaba; and when they had killed him and his adherents, they carried away his women and all his valuable effects, in triumph; laying waste his immediate territories. These were thought by some old writers, to have been the ruins of what the Europeans or natives have called the ancient *Arâmbeck*, or the remote parts of *Norombegua;* to which the victors, as far at least as to the western banks of Penobscot, or even to St Georges, might perhaps now have succeeded." (pg. 215).
- "To these distresses succeeded a pestilence, which spread far and wide, and was exceedingly fatal. It has been called the plague. It raged in the years 1617 and 1618, and its wasting effects extended from the borders of the Tarratines, through the whole country, to the Narragansetts." (pg. 216).
- "The people died suddenly, and in great numbers, through the whole intermediate coast. It is said, some native tribes became extinct; and their bones were seen years afterward by the English, bleeching above ground, at and around the places of their former habitations. The specific disease is not certainly known." (pg. 216).
- "The *Openangos* are supposed to have been the inhabitants upon the *Passamaquoddy-bay*." (pg. 458).
- "The *Tarratines* were the inhabitants of Penobscot river. They were one of the three *Etechemin* tribes. The *Wawenocks* lived about the Sheepscot, Pemaquid and St. George rivers in Maine, between the Kennebeck and Penobscot both exclusive." (pg. 459).
- "The aboriginal people of Maine belong to two great divisions, the Abenaques and the Etchemins. They are all, without doubt, the descendants of the same original stock. ...The two people have been by Historians, much confounded." (pg. 463).
- "All the older authors, Smith, Purchas, Winthrop, Prince and Hubbard agree, that the general name of the natives upon the Penobscot was '*Tarratines*'; and that they lived on terms of friendly intercourse with the Abenaques tribes until about A.D. 1615-16..." (pg. 464).
- "...the *Abenaques*, were the people who originaly inhabited the country between Mount Agamenticus and St. Georges river, both inclusive. This is confirmed by what we know of their general government, or common sovereign." (pg. 464).
- "'the *Bashaba* to be the chief and greatest among them,' ...His chief abode was not far from Pemaquid. ...His dominions, which were large, Gorges adds, were called by the general name of *Moasham*, or according to Belknap, *Mavooshen*; 'and he had under him many great Sagamores, some of whom had a thousand or fifteen hundred bowmen.' After his overthrow and death, he was never succeeded by another of equal rank or authority." (pg. 464-465).
- "The tribes of the *Abenaques* were four, 1. the *Sokokis*, or *Sockhigones*; 2. the *Anasagunticooks*; 3. the *Canibas*, or *Kenabes*; and 4. the *Wawenocks*." (pg. 465). Williamson has never been forgiven for misidentifing the Indians of the Saco River Valley, the Pequawkets as the Sokokis. This long standing error was corrected by Gordon Day (see above.)
- "The principal residence of *Kennebis*, the paramount lord, and his predecessors of the same titular name, was upon Swan Island, in a delightful situation..." (pg. 467).

- Of the domain of the Kennebis, Williamson notes: "The territories, which the tribe claimed, extended from the sources of the Kennebeck to this bay, and the Islands on the eastern side of the Sagadahock, probably to the sea." (pg. 467).
- "Old Norridgewock was a most pleasant site, opposite the mouth of Sandy river--the general and almost sole resorting place of the tribe, immediately after their numbers or ranks were thinned; and a spot consecrated to them by every sacred and endearing recollection." (pg. 467).
- "The Wawenocks inhabited the country eastward of Sagadahock, to the river St. George inclusive. They were the immediate subjects of the great Bashaba." (pg. 468).
- "The other division of the aboriginal people in Maine, were the Etechemins. They inhabited the country between the rivers Penobscot and St. John, both inclusive." (pg. 469).
- "There are three tribes of the Etechemins, --1. the *Tarratines; --2.* the *Openangos,* or '*Quoddy Indians; --*and 3. the *Marechites,* or *Armouchiquois.*" (pg. 470).
- "The *Tarratines* are particularly mentioned by Smith, Hubbard, Prince, Gorges and all the modern Historians of this country; and it is well established, that they were the native inhabitants of Penobscot, claiming dominion over the contiguous territories, from its sources to the sea. Smith, however, has represented the Penobscot mountains (in Camden) as a natural fortress, which separated them from their western borderers, or neighbors." (pg. 470).
- "After the conquests and glory achieved in their battles with the Bashaba and his allies; they [the Tarantines] were not, like their enemies wasted by disease and famine." (pg. 470).
- "The *Wawenocks* never made any figure after their ruinous war with the Tarratines."(pg. 482).
- "Charlevoix says, 'the Indians of the St. Francois, uniting the Anasagunticooks and Wawenocks, were a colony of the *Abenaques*, removed from the eastern parts of New-England, for the sake of French neighborhood.'" (pg. 482).
- Williamson notes that forty Wawenoc fighting men were noted as available in 1749 for service in the French and Indian Wars.
- "The Etechemins [Passamaquoddy], ... are still inhabitants of their native country, humbled, however in view of their decline and ultimate destiny. ... Their remaining population in 1820, amounted only to 1,235 souls, that is to say, 390 Tarratines [Penobscots], 379 Openangos, and 466 Marachites." (pg. 482).
- "The greatest aboriginal monarch of the east was entitled 'the *Bashaba*', previously mentioned, whose residence was with the Wawenock tribe. Besides his immediate dominions, extending probably from St. Georges to Kennebeck, the tribes westward to Agamenticus, and even farther, acknowledged him to be their paramount lord. His overthrow, in 1615 or 16, terminated the royal line and rank." (pg. 494).

Willoughby, Charles C. (1935). *Antiquities of the New England Indians with notes on the ancient cultures of the adjacent territory.* Peabody Museum of American Archaeology and Ethnology, Harvard University, Cambridge, MA. Reprinted in 1973 by AMS Press, Inc., NY, NY. IS.

- One of the most important and scholarly of the older publications on all Native Americans including those living in Maine.

Wilson, Margaret Jerram. (2007). *Norumbega navigators: Early English voyages to New England and the story of the Popham Colony*. Wilson Publications, Bath, England. IS.

Winship, George Parker, Ed. (1905). *Sailors' narratives of voyages along the New England coast, 1524-1624*. Houghton Mifflin, Boston, MA.

- See our information file reproduction of a section of this book by James Rosier, *A True Relation of Captain George Weymouth his Voyage. Made this Present Yeere 1605*.

Wiseman, Frederick M. (2001). *The voice of the dawn: An autohistory of the Abenaki Nation*. University Press of New England, Hanover, NH. IS.

Wood, William. (1634). *New England's prospect*. Thomas Cotes for John Bellamie. Reprinted in 1865, Deane, Charles Ed. *Publications of the Prince Society*, 1. Boston, MA. Reprinted in 1967, NY.

Appendix K

Native Americans in Maine
Other Contemporary Publications and Journal Articles

Abbe Museum. (1978). *The first fifty years of the Robert Abbe Museum of Stone Age Antiquities and a look ahead.* Bulletin XI. The Robert Abbe Museum, Bar Harbor, ME.

- Out of print.

Adams, Robert McC. (1974). Anthropological perspectives on ancient trade. *Current Anthropology.* 15(3). pg. 239-258.

Adams, William Y., VanGerven, Dennis P. and Levy, Richard S. (1978). The retreat from migrationism. *Annual Review of Anthropology.* 7. pg. 483-532. X.

Adney, E. Tappan, and Chapelle, Howard I. (1964). *The Bark Canoes and Skin Boats of North America.* Smithsonian Institution, Washington, D.C.

Adovasio, J.M. (1977) *Basketry Technology: A Guide to Identification and Analysis.* Aldine, Chicago, IL.

Andrews, J. Clinton. (1986). Indian fish and fishing off coastal Massachusetts. *Bulletin of the Massachusetts Archaeological Society.* 47(2). pg. 42-46.

Apess, William. (1836). *On our own ground: The complete writings of William Apess, a Pequot.* Reprinted in 1992, O'Connell, Barry, Ed. University of Massachusetts Press, Amherst, MA.

Appleton, Leroy H. (1950). *American Indian designs and decoration with over 700 illustrations.* Dover, NY, NY. IS.

Aubery, Father Joseph. (c. 1715). *French Abenaki dictionary.* From the manuscript of Father Joseph O'Brien which was hand copied from the translation by Stephen Laurent, Maine Historical Society, Portland, ME, 1995.

- This is the only printed version of this important dictionary. This work was originally compiled by Father Aubery at St. Francis in 1715, making it the earliest dictionary of the Abenaki dialect recorded. Fannie Hardy Eckstorm (1941) said of Aubery that he "knew perfectly the Abenaki dialect" and characterized this work (only in manuscript form at the time) as "the most scholarly Jesuit compilation the present writer [Eckstorm] knows" (Morey, 2005, pg. 127).

Axtell, James. (1979). Ethnohistory: An historian's viewpoint. *Ethnohistory*. 26(1). pg. 1-13.

Axtell, James. (1981). *The European and the Indian: Essays in the ethnohistory of colonial North America*. Oxford University Press, NY, NY.

Bailey, A.G. (1937). *The conflict of European and Eastern Algonkian cultures, 1504 - 1700*. New Brunswick Museum, St. John, Canada.

Barber, R.J. (1982). *The Wheeler's Site: A specialized shellfish processing station on the Merrimack River*. Peabody Museum Monograph. 7. Harvard University, Cambridge, MA.

Barbian, Lenore T. and Magennis, Ann L. (1994). Variability in late archaic human burials at Turner Farm, Maine. *Northeast Anthropology*. 47. pg. 1-19.

Barkham, Selma. (1978). The Basques: Filling a gap in our history between Jacques Cartier and Champlain. *Canadian Geographical Journal*. 96. pg. 8-19. X.

Bartone, Robert N., Quinn, Catherine A., Petersen, James B., and Cowie, Ellen R. (1992) *An Archaeological Phase I Survey of the Fort Halifax Project (FERC No. 2552) Kennebec County, Maine*. University of Maine at Farmington Archaeology Research Center. Submitted to Central Maine Power Company, Augusta. Farmington, ME.

Baxter, Rev. Joseph. (1867). *Journal of several visits to the Indians on the Kennebec River; 1717*. David Clapp & Son, Boston, MA.

Becker, Marshall J. (2002) A Wampum Belt Chronology: Origins to Modern Times. *Northeast Anthropology* 63. pg. 49-70.

Belcher, William R. (1989). The archaeology of the Knox Site, East Penobscot Bay, Maine. *Maine Archaeology Society Bulletin*. 29(1). pg. 33-46.

Belcher, William R. (Fall 1989). Prehistoric fish exploitation in East Penobscot Bay, Maine: The Knox site and sea-level rise. *Archaeology of Eastern North America*. 17. pg. 175-191.

Belcher, William R., Sanger, David and Cox, Bruce J. (1994). The Bradley Cemetery: A Moorehead burial tradition site in Maine. *Canadian Journal of Archaeology*. 18. pg. 3 - 38.

Bendremer, Jeffrey and Dewer, Robert. (1994) The Advent of Prehistoric Maize in New England. *Corn and Culture in the Prehistoric New World.* Edited by Johanessen and Hasforf, Christine. Westview Press, Minneapolis, MN.

Benes, Peter, Ed. (1991). Algonkians of New England: Past and present. *The Dublin Seminar for New England Folklife Annual Proceedings 1991.* Boston University, Boston, MA.

Bennett, M.K. (October 1955). The food economy of the New England Indians, 1605-1675. *Journal of Political Economy.* 63(5). pg. 369-397.

- Concludes that maize made up 65% of the diet of Native (southern?) New Englanders.

Bennett, Randall H. (Summer 1978). New England's last Indian raid. *The New-England Galaxy.* pg. 45-54.

Bierhorst, John, Ed. (1987). *In the trail of the wind: American Indian poems and ritual orations.* A Sunburst Book, Michael Di Capua Books, Farrar, Straus and Giroux. IS.

Binford, Lewis R. (1972). Willow smoke and dogs' tails: Hunter-gatherer settlement systems and archaeological site formation. *American Antiquity.* 45(1). pg. 4-20.

Bishop, Carl Whiting, Abbot, Charles Greeley and Hrdlicka, Ales. (1930). *Man from the farthest past.* In: Abbot, Charles Greeley, Ed. *Smithsonian Scientific Series: Volume 7.* Smithsonian Institution Series, Inc., NY, NY. IS.

Black, David W. and Whitehead, Ruth Holmes. (1988). Prehistoric shellfish preservation and storage on the northeast coast. *North American Archaeologist.* 9(1). pg. 17-30. X.

- "The building of substantial structures for drying and smoking shellfish would have been an unnecessary and therefore unlikely expenditure of energy unless other, bulkier types of meat or fish were to be preserved at the same time. Shellfish could have been sun-dried rapidly by shucking them and spreading the shucked meat on birch-bark sheets in the sun. For smoking, stringing small pieces of meat such as shellfish on spruce roots and hanging them over a fire, either outside our inside the wigwam, would have been the most efficient method of preservation and storage (see Willoughby, 1935:211-212 for a discussion and ethnographic substantiation of these points). None of these methods would necessarily leave discernible archaeological traces except for the deposits of shucked shells themselves." (pg. 24-25).

Blustain, Malinda S., Levesque, Margaret A., and Robinson, Brian S. (1999) Two Fossilized Late Archaic Textiles from Maine: Pyrite Pseudomorphs from the Hartford Cemetery Site. *Archaeology of Eastern North America.* 27, pg. 185-196.

Bond, C. Lawrence. (2004). *Native names of New England towns and villages: Translating 211 names derived from Native American words*. Third Edition. Alan B. Bond, PO Box 67, Rochester, VT 05767.

Borns, Harold W. Jr. (October 1972 and January 1973). Possible Paleo-Indian migration routes in northeastern North America - a geological approach. *Maine Archaeological Society Bulletin*. 34(1-2). pg. 55-59.

Borstel, Christopher. (1982). *Archaeological excavation at the Young Site, Alton, Maine*. Maine Historic Preservation Commission, Augusta, ME.

Bourque, Bruce J. (1971). Possible Paleo-Indian migration routes in northeast North America. *Maine Archaeological Society Bulletin*. 11(1). pg. 1-3.

Bourque, Bruce J. (1973). Aboriginal settlement and subsistence on the Maine Coast. *Man in the Northeast*. 6. pg. 3-20. IS.

- "Faunal samples from three multicomponent coastal sites, dating ca. A.D. 200-A.D. 1150, indicate that all components represent late winter-early spring occupations. There is no evidence for summer coastal occupation." (pg. 3).
- "Historic sources indicate that by ca. A.D. 1550 aboriginal populations exploited interior resources during late winter and early spring and coastal ones during late spring and summer. Possible explanations of this change in settlement systems include prehistoric climatic change and early European trade influences." (pg. 3).

Bourque, Bruce J. (1975). Comments on the late archaic populations of central Maine: The view from the Turner farm. *Arctic Anthropology*. XII(2). pg. 35-45. IS.

- "By 4500 B.P. a relatively large population exploiting marine and riverine resources, with special emphasis upon maritime hunting, was established. This population had close cognates as far north as Newfoundland." (pg. 35).
- "After c. 3700 B.P. a distinctly different archaeological pattern suddenly appears in western and central Maine. The technology and mortuary ceremonialism of this group are derived from the Susquehanna tradition and apparently replace earlier native patterns." (pg. 35).

Bourque, Bruce J. (1976). The Turner farm site: A preliminary report. *Man in the Northeast*. 11. pg. 21-30. IS.

Bourque, Bruce J. (1977). Fishing in the Gulf of Maine: A 5,000 Year History. In *The Gulf of Maine*. Ed. by G. Lawless. Blackberry Press, Brunswick, ME.

Bourque, Bruce J. (1992). Excavations at Cobbosseecontee Dam South. *Bulletin of the Maine Archaeological Society*. 32(2). pg. 15-29. IS.

Bourque, Bruce J. (1992). *Prehistory of the central Maine coast*. Garland Pub., NY. IS.

- A typographical catastrophe, this important report has been supplemented by Bourque's more important *Diversity and Complexity in Prehistoric Maritime Society: A Gulf of Maine Perspective* in 2001. Bourque remains, despite differences of opinion on the French versions of Maine's ethnohistory at the time of coastal settlement, the most important and comprehensive source of information about the ethnohistory of the maritime peninsula.
- Contains Bourque's initial description of the Susquehanna tradition as it applies to the archaeology of Maine; the Susquehanna being the non-maritime and anomalous culture which followed the maritime archaic.

Bourque, Bruce J. (1994). Evidence for Prehistoric Exchange on the Maritimes Peninsula. In *Prehistoric Exchange Systems in North America.* Plenum Press, NY.

Bourque, Bruce J. and Krueger, Harold W. (1991). *Dietary reconstruction of prehistoric maritime peoples of northeastern North America: Faunal vs. stable isotopic approaches.* Paper presented at the 24th annual meeting of the Canadian Archaeological Association, St. John's Newfoundland, Canada.

- This illustrates one of the ironies of the study of the history of Maine: the new technology of isotopic (bone, etc.) analyses for the evaluation of the diets of prehistoric Native Americans is enthusiastically embraced by Maine archaeologists while at the same time isotopic analysis of the radiological footprint of the Maine Yankee Atomic Power Company is strictly prohibited.

Bourque, Bruce J. and Krueger, Harold W. (1994). Dietary reconstruction from human bone isotopes for five coastal New England populations. In: *Paleonutrition: The diet and health of prehistoric Americans.* Sobolik, Kristen D., Ed., Southern Illinois University Center for Archaeological Investigations Occasional Paper No. 22. pg. 195-209.

Bourque, Bruce J., Morris, Kenneth, and Spiess, Arthur. (1978). Determining the season of death of teeth from archaeological sites: A new sectioning technique. *Science*. 199. pg. 530-531.

Boyd, Stephen G. (1885). *Indian local names with their interpretation.* Published by the author, York, PA.

- Defines the word "muskingum" as elk's eyes or deer eyes.
- Donahue, in *The Kingdom in Montville, Maine*, has this comment about the word muskingum: "town records as far back as 1807 refer to the area as Muskingum. Local legend has it that some of the early settlers were from Ireland (hence the name of the New Ireland Road) who had spent time along the Muskingum river in southeastern Ohio. Their

pronunciation of the name was interpreted by other locals as 'Moose Kingdom' - later shortened to the Kingdom" (pg. 2).

- It is unlikely that Irish immigrants first moved to Ohio in 1800 and then returned to settle Montville by 1807. Muskingum is instead one among many surviving Indian place names.

Bradley, James W. (1987). Native Exchange and European trade: Cross-cultural dynamics in the sixteenth century. *Man in the Northeast*. 33. pg. 31-46. X.

- "These 13 sites... fall into two rather amorphous clusters, one that includes the Taunton drainage and Buzzards Bay, the other on the outer Cape Cod. These clusters roughly coincide with the seventeenth-century Wampanoag and Nauset subgroups. Second, not only is there no pattern of village movement, virtually no village sites are known. Nearly half of these locations are burials. The rest are midden, or refuse deposits, in which small quantities of European material have been recovered. It should be noted that the quantities of European materials from most of these sites are very small. To sum up, the protohistoric period along the southern New England coast is, archaeologically speaking, almost invisible." (pg. 35).
- "Contrary to much of the existing literature (Willoughby 1935:273; Salwen 1978:166; Snow 1980:29-30), marine shell beads are a rare occurrence on Late Woodland and sixteenth-century Pokanoket sites. ...widespread usage does not occur until the intensification of contact and trade early in the seventeenth century. ...For the Pokanoket, the making an using of 'wampum' (in either discoidal or tubular form) was a seventeenth-century phenomenon." (pg. 41).
- "The one exception to this pattern of profound localism is that the Pokanoket may have been involved in an exchange network that brought native copper down the coast from Nova Scotia. This network appears to have operated during the Middle and Late Woodland periods and may have continued until the early seventeenth century." (pg. 41).
- "...the system of exchange and trade that operated in the Northeast was far more complex, dynamic, and interactive than is generally realized." (pg. 42).

Bradley, James W. (1998). *Origins and ancestors: Investigating New England's Paleo Indians*. Robert S. Peabody Museum of Archaeology, Andover, MA. IS.

Brain, Jeffrey P. (2003) The Popham Colony: An historical and archaeological brief. *Maine Archaeological Society Bulletin*. 43(1). pg. 1-28.

Brain, Jeffrey Phipps. (2007). *Fort St. George: Archaeological investigation of the 1607-1608 Popham Colony*. Occasional Publications in Maine Archaeology Number 12. The Maine State Museum, The Maine Historic Preservation Commission, and The Maine Archaeological Society, Augusta, ME. IS.

Brandon, William. (1973). *The last Americans: The Indian in American culture*. McGraw-Hill, NY, NY.

Brasser, T.J. (1974). Riding on the frontier's crest: Mahican Indian culture and culture change. *National Museum of Man Ethnology Division Mercury Series*. 13. Ottawa, Canada.

- This contains information pertinent to the study of Maine's Indian population.

Braun, David P. (1974). Explanatory models for the evolution of coastal adaptation in prehistoric eastern New England. *American Antiquity*. 39(4). pg. 582-596.

Brennan, Louis A. (January 1979). Coastal adaptation in prehistoric New England. *American Antiquity*. 41(1). pg. 112-113.

Brose, David S., Brown, James A. and Penney, David W. (1985). *Ancient art of the American Woodland Indians*. Harry N. Abrams, Inc., Publishers in association with the Detroit Institute of Arts. IS.

Bruce, Walter G. (1965). *Long Cove, a Maine shell-deposit site.* Massachusetts Archaeological Society Bulletin 27:1. pg. 8-12.

Burns, Robert L. (1971). *Mid-coast Washington county*. Maine Archaeological Society Bulletin 11. pg. 1-5.

Burrage, Henry S. (1899). *The Plymouth colonists of Maine*. Transcript. Maine Historical Society, ME.

- These quotes are from a transcript of a Nov. 16, 1899 Maine Historical Society meeting.
- "By the supplies received from the fishing vessels at and near Damariscove the Pilgrims were enabled to subsist, though most frugally, until the welcome time of harvest arrived. But the corn they then obtained did not furnish the colonists with a full year's supply, and there would have been hunger in their log-cabins, if they had not obtained subsistence from the neighboring Indians." (pg. 7).
- "The boat in which the corn was carried for this venture was one of two which the carpenter of the Pilgrims had built during the preceding year. 'They had a little deck over her midships to keepe ye corne drie,' says Bradford, 'but ye men were faine to stand it out all weathers without shelter; and ye time of ye year begins to growe tempestuous.' Mr. Edward Winslow was in charge of this Kennebec venture. Proceeding up the river, he found the Indians exceedingly well disposed, and had no difficulty in exchanging his store of corn for beaver, of which he obtained seven hundred pounds. When Winslow at length dropped down the river on his return homeward, he had laid the foundations of an exceedingly profitable trade, and he made his way back to Plymouth with high hopes that from this trade the colony would be able to discharge ere long its financial obligations in London. These hopes were not doomed to dissappointment. The sight of the beaver, as Winslow and his boat's crew landed

at Plymouth the proceeds of this Kennebec venture, was one with which the Pilgrims became more and more familiar as the years went by." (pg. 9).

- "After they had thus firmly established themselves on the Kennebec, Bradford and his associates came into possession of a trading house on the Penobscot. In 1629, some of the English merchant adventurers, who were interested in the Pilgrim enterprise, entered into business relations with one Edward Ashley and furnished him with goods for trading purposes." (pg. 17).
- "According to Bradford, between November, 1631, and June, 24, 1636, the Pilgrims sent to England 12,530 pounds of beaver, the most of which was obtained from the Indians on the Kennebec. It was from the sale of this beaver in a great measure that they were able at length to extricate themselves from the financial difficulties in which they had become involved through their London agents. But their troubles at Penobscot were not ended. At the trading house there they suffered a still greater loss from the French in 1635. Chevalier Charles de Menou, or as he is usually styled D'Aulnay Charnisay, appeared one day in the harbor... His orders were to expel the English as far as Pemaquid." (pg. 23).

Butler, Eva L. and Hadlock, Wendell S. (1957). *Uses of birch bark in the northeast*. Bulletin VII, The Robert Abbe Museum, Bar Harbor, ME. (out of print) IS. Butler, Eva L. and Hadlock, Wendell S. (1962). *A preliminary survey of the Munsungan-Allagash waterways*. Bulletin VIII, The Robert Abbe Museum, Bar Harbor, ME.

- Available for purchase from the Abbe museum.

Butler, Eva L. and Hadlock, Wendell S. (1994). *Dogs of the northeastern Woodland Indians*. Bulletin XIII, The Robert Abbe Museum, Bar Harbor, ME.

- Available for purchase from the Abbe museum.

Butler, Joyce. (1997). *Spirits in the wood*.

- Catalog of a 1997 exhibition on the traditional carving of ceremonial root clubs by the Wabanaki culture.

Byers, Douglas S. (1953). "Red paint tombs" in Maine. *Massachusetts Archaeological Society Bulletin*. 15(1). pg. 1-8.

Byers, Douglas S. (1962). New England and the Arctic. In: *Prehistoric cultural relations between the Arctic and temperate zones of North America*. Arctic Institute of North America, Technical Paper. 11. pg. 143-153.

Byers, Douglas S. (1979). The Nevin shellheap burials and observations. *Papers of the Robert S. Peabody Foundation for Archaeology*. 9. Andover, MA.

Cahill, Robert Ellis. (date unknown). *New Englands Viking and Indian Wars*. Old Saltbox Publishing, 20 Locust Street, #202, Danvers, MA.

Callum, Kathleen E. (1994). *The geoarcheology of the Nahanada site (16-90) Pemaquid Beach, Bristol, Maine*. Master's thesis, University of Maine, Orono, ME.

Camp, H. (1975). *Archaeological excavations at Pemaquid, Maine, 1965-1974*. Maine State Museum, Augusta, ME. W.

Carlson, Richard G., Ed. (1987). *Rooted like the ash trees: New England Indians and the land*. Eagle Wing Press, Inc., Naugatuck, CT. IS.

Cassedy, Daniel and Webb, Paul. (1999). New data on the chronology of maize horticulture in eastern New York and southern New England. In: Hart, John P., Ed. *Current northeast paleoethnobotany*. New York State Museum Bulletin No. 494, Albany, NY. pg. 85 - 100.

Catlin, George. (1844). *Letters and notes on the manners, customs, and condition of the North American Indians*. 2 vols. 3rd. ed. Wiley and Putnam, NY, NY. Reprinted 1913, Leary, Stuart, Philadelphia, PA under the title *North American Indians*.

Ceci, Lynn. (1975). Fish fertilizer: A Native North American practice? *Science*. 188. pg. 26-30.

Ceci, Lynn. (1979). Maize cultivation in coastal New York: The archaeological, agronomical and documentary evidence. *North American Archaeologist*. 1(1). pg. 45-74.

Ceci, Lynn. (Spring 1990). Radiocarbon dating 'village' sites in coastal New York: Settlement pattern changes in the middle to late woodland. *Man in the Northeast*. 39. pg. 1-28. X.

- "The findings suggest that: (1) shifts in settlement pattern to multicomponent central-base camps, originally called 'villages,' first developed in coastal New York during the Middle to Late Woodland period; and (2) the change process correlates with new intensified subsistence strategies before maize horticulture or European contact, new forms of burial ceremonialism, and new production of shell bead-blanks for long-distance trade. The project underscores the value of using old museum collections to address new theoretical questions." (pg. 1).
- "The traditional paradigm holds that sedentism increased in the Late Woodland (ca. A.D. 1000-1600) after maize or some maize-marine food combination improved subsistence so as to sustain large populations year round. Archaeological maize, however, is scarce." (pg. 2).
- "'Indian maize' was in fact scarce enough in local townships in the seventeenth century to serve as colonial barter; drawn from inland and southern sources it was commonly traded *to*

local Indians at *double* the price for colonists! Thus, the archaeological, documentary, and agronomical evidence collectively offer no support for the traditional 'maize' explanation for prehistoric 'village' development in coastal New York, an anomaly noted earlier by Kroeber (1963: 147-148)." (pg. 2).

- A particularly relevant study with respect to occupation of coastal Maine, where increasingly centralized, sedentary settlement patterns were based on the exploitation of rich coastal marine resources and not on extensive maize production.

Cell, Gillian T. (1969). *English enterprise in Newfoundland, 1577 - 1660*. University of Toronto Press, Toronto, Canada.

Chandler, E. J. (1997). *Ancient Sagadahoc: A narrative history*. Conservatory of American Letters, Thomaston, ME. W.

- A story of the Englishmen who welcomed the Pilgrims to the New World.

Chadwick, Joseph. (1889). An account of a journey from Fort Pownal -- now Fort Point -- up the Penobscot River to Quebec, in 1764. *Bangor Historical Magazine*. 4. pg. 141-148.

Chase, Henry E. (1885). Notes on the Wampanoag Indians. *Smithsonian Institution Annual Report (1883)*. Washington, DC. pg. 878-907.

Chase, Levi Badger. (1897). Early Indian trails. *Worcester Society of Antiquity Collections*. 14. pg. 105-126.

Christianson, D.J. (1979). The use of subsistence strategy descriptions in determining Wabanaki residence location. *The Journal of Anthropology at McMaster*. 5(1). pg. 81-124.

Church, Benjamin. (1865). *The history of King Philip's War*. Dexter, Henry M., Ed., Boston, MA.

Church, Benjamin. (1867). *The history of the eastern expeditions of 1689, 1690, 1692, 1696, and 1704 against the Indians and French*. B.K. Wiggin and W.P. Lunt, Boston, MA.

Cobblestone Publishing Inc. (November 1994). Indians of the northeast coast. *Cobblestone: The History Magazine for Young People*. 15(9). IS.

Coleman, Emma Lewis. (1925). *New England captives carried to Canada between 1677 and 1760 during the French and Indian Wars*. Southworth Press, 2 vols, Portland, ME.

Cole-Will, Rebecca, and Will, Richard (1996). *A probable middle archaic cemetery: the Richmond-Castle site in Surry, Maine.* Archaeology of Eastern North America, 24. pg. 95-148. W.

Congdon, Isabelle P. (1961). *Indian tribes of Maine.* The Brunswick Publishing Company, Brunswick, ME. W.

Conkling, P. (2005). Time capsules: The ecology of mid-coast Maine. In: *One land - two worlds: A symposium to celebrate the 400th anniversary of George Waymouth's voyage to New England.* Platt, D., Ed., Island Institue, Rockland, ME.

Coolidge, A.J. and Mansfield, J.B. (1860). *History and description of New England: Maine.* Austin J. Coolidge, 89 Court Street, Boston, MA.

- "Some of the old writers, as Charlevoix, Abbe Raynal, and La Hontan, as indeed some of the later ones, call all the natives east of the Piscataqua (except the Micmacs or Nova Scotia Indians) Abenaquies. Gallatin, Williamson, and some others, make two great divisions -- Abnakis, and Etchemins or Etetchemins, i.e. 'canoe-men.' Under the Abnakis are usually included the *Sokokis*, or Saco Indians; the *Anasagunticooks,* or Androscoggin tribe; the *Wawenocs*, who dwelt along the coast from Merry-meeting bay to the St. George's; and the *Canibas*, or Kenabes, who occupied the valley of the Kennebec, and who were again divided into the *Norridgewocks,* the *Taconnets*, about Waterville, and the *Cushnocs*, about Augusta." (pg. 20).
- "Under the Etchemins are generally reckoned the *Tarratines*, or *Penobscots* (which some writers are at a loss whether to class with the Abnakis or Etchemins), the *Passamaquoddys*, and the *Marachites* or *St. John's* tribe." (pg. 20-21).
- "Of all the tribes of Maine, the Penobscots and Passamaquoddys, who probably constitute half of the whole Indian population of New England, alone remain." (pg. 21).
- "...that the Anasagunticooks claimed dominion along the Androscoggin, from its sources to Merry-meeting bay -- that they took part in the ravages during Phillip's war at Pemaquid and along Casco bay -- that, in 1744, 160 warriors remained, in 1750, most of the tribe joined the St. Francis Indians, and, at the time of the Revolution, about forty might be found scattered among the islands and along the course of the river." (pg. 21).
- "...that the Wawenocs or Sheepscot Indians were the immediate subjects of the Great Bashaba, whose residence was near Pemaquid, and who was slain in the war with the Tarratines, the power of the tribe being then broken -- that, in 1747, but two or three families were left here, the remnant having gone to Canada." (pg. 21).
- "...that the Canibas, more usually called the Norridgewocks, because most of them resided here, were a brave, and yet docile people. They tell us of the great success of the Jesuit missionaries among them, and especially of Gabriel Druillettes, who first came in 1646, of James Bigot in 1688, and of Sebastian Rasles from 1685 to 1724 [when Norridgewock was destroyed by the English]." (pg. 21).

Cooper, John M. (1938). Land tenure among the Indians of eastern and northern North America. *Pennsylvania Archaeologist*. 8. pg. 58-59.

Cooper, John M. (1939). Is the Algonquian family hunting ground system Pre-Columbian? *American Anthropologist*. N.S. XLI. pg. 66-90.

Cowie, Ellen R. and Petersen, James B. (1999). Native American ceramic manufacture at the Tracy Farm Site in the central Kennebec River Valley, Maine. *Maine Archaeological Society Bulletin*. 39(2). pg. 1-42.

Cox, Steven L. (1987). Archaeological data recovery at site 61.20, Jonesport, Maine. *Maine Archaeological Society Bulletin*. 27(2). pg. 16-35. X.

Cox, Steven L. (1991). Site 95.20 and the Vergennes phase in Maine. *Archaeology of Eastern North America*. 17(1-2). pg. 133-136.

Cox, Steven L., and Kopec, Diane (1988). *An archaeological investigation of the Watson site, Frenchman Bay*. Maine Archaeological Society Bulletin 28(1). pg. 39-45. W.

Cox, Steven and Lawless, Gary. (1972). The Indian shell heap: Archaeology of the Ruth Moore site. *Time's Web*. William Morrow Co. Reprinted in 1994 by the Abbe Museum, Blackberry Books, Nobleboro, ME. IS.

Cox, Steven and Wilson, Deborah B. (1991). 4500 years on the lower Androscoggin: Archaeological investigation of the Rosie-Mugford site complex. *Maine Archaeological Society Bulletin*. 31(1). pg. 15-40.

D'Abate, R. (2005). A nation above all others. In: *One land - two worlds: A symposium to celebrate the 400th anniversary of George Waymouth's voyage to New England*. Platt, D., Ed., Island Institue, Rockland, ME.

Davis, Mary. (1996). *Encyclopedia of Native Americans in the Twentieth Century*. Garland Publishing, NY, NY.

Davis, Ronald B., Bradstreet, T.E., Stuckenrath, R. and Borns, Harold W. (1975). Vegetation and associated environments during the past 14,000 years near Moulton Pond, Maine. *Quaternary Research*. 5(3). pg. 435-466. X.

Day, Gordon M. (1963). The tree nomenclature of the Saint Francis Indians. *Contributions to Anthropology, 1960*. Part II. National Museum of Canada Bulletin 190, Ottawa, Canada. pg. 37-48.

Day, Gordon M. (1965). The identity of the Sokokis. *Ethnohistory*. 12. pg. 237-249. IS.

- In William Williamson's *History of the State of Maine,* the Sokokis are identified as that tribe inhabiting the Saco River valley. This error was perpetuated in Maine history books until Gordon Day correctly identified them as inhabitants of the Connecticut River Valley at Northfield, MA. The correct identification for the Indians of the Saco River is Pequawkets.

Descarte, Rene M. (1974). *The Cabot site: a Cermaic period occupation on North Haven Island.* Maine Archaeological Society Bulletin 14(2). pg. 6-19.

Diamond, Sigmund. (April 1951). Norumbega: New England xanadu. *The American Neptune*. 11. pg. 95-107. IS.

- "In 1542, Jean Allefonsce, a French pilot, reported that he had coasted south from Newfoundland and had discovered a great river. 'The river is more than 40 leagues wide at its entrance and retains its width some thirty or forty leagues. It is full of Islands, which stretch some ten or twelve leagues into the sea. ... Fifteen leagues within this river there is a town called Norombega, with clever inhabitants, who trade in furs of all sorts; the town folk are dressed in furs, wearing sable. ... The people use many words which sound like Latin. They worship the sun. They are tall and handsome in form. The land of Norombega lie high and is well situated.' (DeCosta, 1890)" (pg. 99).

Dincauze, Dena. (1968). *Cremation cemeteries in eastern Massachusetts*. Papers of the Peabody Museum of Archaeology and Ethnology. 59(1). Peabody Museum, Harvard University, Cambridge, MA.

Dincauze, Dena F. (1971). An archaic sequence for southern New England. *American Antiquity*. 36(2). pg. 194-198. Dincauze, Dena F. (1973). Prehistoric occupation of the Charles River estuary. *Archaeological Society of Connecticut Bulletin*. 38. pg. 25-39.

- This contains information pertinent to the study of Maine's Native Americans.
- The Davistown Museum has one interesting stone tool recovered from this estuary.

Dincauze, Dena F. (1975). The late archaic period in southern New England. *Arctic Anthropology*. XXI(2). pg. 23-34.

- "Comparisons are drawn within southern New England and, to the north, in Maine. Consideration is given to the social functions of the burial ceremonialism. The complexity of the social environments hypothesized for this period may partially explain the florescence of the cults." (pg. 23).
- "The Moorehead burial tradition contrasts strongly with the Susquehanna tradition burial modes. This distinctiveness was apparent half a century ago, when Moorehead himself recognized the uniqueness of the Susquehanna feature at Eddington Bend (Moorehead 1922:141)." (pg. 32).

Dincauze, Dena. (1976). *The Neville Site: 8,000 years at Amoskeag, Manchester, New Hampshire*. Peabody Museum Monograph No. 4. Peabody Museum, Harvard University, Cambridge, MA.

Dincauze, Dena Ferran and Meyer, Judith W. (1977). *Prehistoric resources of east-central New England: A preliminary predictive study*. National Park Service, U.S. Dept. of the Interior, Washington, DC.

Dincauze, Dena Ferran. (2000). *Environmental archaeology: Principles and practice*. Cambridge University Press, Cambridge. MA.

Dixon, R.B. (1914). The early migrations of the Indians of New England and the Maritime Provinces. *Proceedings of the American Antiquarian Society*. n.s. 24 pt. 1. Worcester, MA. pg. 65-76.

Dodge, Ernest S. (1957). Ethnology of northern New England and the Maritime Provinces. *Massachusetts Archaeological Society Bulletin*. 18. pg. 68-71.

Dow, Robert L. (1971). Some characteristics of Maine coastal kitchen middens. *Maine Archaeological Society Bulletin*. 1. pg 6-14. W.

Doyle, Richard, Hamilton, Nathan D., and Petersen, James. (1982). Early woodland ceramics and associated perishable industries from southwestern Maine. *Maine Archaeological Society Bulletin*. 22(2). pg. 4-21. W.

Dozier, Edward P. (1970). *The Pueblo Indians of North America*. Holt, Rinehart and Winston, Inc., New York, NY. IS.

Drake, Samuel G. (1865). *The history of the Indian Wars in New England from the first settlement to the termination of the war with King Philip in 1677*. 2 vols. Roxbury, MA.

Drake, Samuel G. (1880). *The aboriginal races of North America*. 15th ed. rev., NY.

Drooker, Penelope Ballard, Ed. (2004). *Perishables material culture in the northeast*. New York State Museum Bulletin 500, Albany, NY.

Eaton, Cyrus. (1851). *Annals of the town of Warren in Knox County, Maine with the early history of St. Georges, Broadbay and neighboring settlements on the Waldo Patent*. Masters, Smith and Co., Hallowell. Reprinted in 1887 by Masters & Livermore, Hallowell and in 1968.

- This book contains a large body of information about the history of Thomaston, St. George and Warren that is pertinent to the history of the early years of the Davistown Plantation, Montville and Liberty. It also describes the Wawenoc Indians. Most of the annotations are in our information file for Warren, but other annotations are in the Maine History: Antiquarian bibliography, Davistown Plantation bibliography and the information file Wreck of the Grand Design on Long Ledge, Mount Desert Island.
- **1744.** "As the St. John's Indians were concerned in the attack upon Annapolis, it was feared that the other eastern Indians would be disposed also to join their old allies in a new effort against the English ; especially as all the Etechemin tribes, whose country extended from the Penobscot to the St. Johns, formed, by their own account, one and the same people. War was therefore declared against all the Indians east of the Passamaquoddy ; and those to the west of that river were forbidden to hold any intercourse with them." (pg. 71-72).
- "In 1804, according to the treasurer's book, the town [of Warren] first began to derive a small revenue from the oyster fishery ; although a law for protecting such fisheries, and allowing selectmen to impose conditions upon the taking of them by people of other places, had been passed as early as 1796. In early times, oysters abounded in the lower part of the town, both in St. George's and Oyster rivers; and vessels from Portsmouth and other places, used to come, and carry off whole cargoes of them. After the passage of the above mentioned law, fewer vessels came for them. They were already on the decline, either from saw-dust washed down from the mills, as some suppose, or from other causes not ascertained ; and they have now become so scarce that few take the trouble to search for them. Small sums were occasionally paid into the treasury for these fish, till 1813." (pg. 279-280).

Eckstorm, Fannie Hardy. *The Indian routes of Maine*. Unpublished manuscript in the University of Maine Library, Orono, ME.

Eckstorm, Fannie Hardy. (1904). *The Penobscot man*. Houghton, Mifflin and Company, Boston, MA. Reprinted in 1924 by Jordan Frost Printing Co., Bangor, ME. IS.

Eckstorm, Fannie Hardy. (April 1913). Champlain's visit to Maine. *Sprague's Journal of Maine History*, 1(1). W.

Eckstorm, Fannie Hardy. (1919). The Indians of Maine. In: Hatch, Louis C., Ed. *Maine: A history*. 5 vols. Ameri. Hist. Soc., NY. pg. 43-64.

Eckstorm, Fannie Hardy. (1924). *The Indian legends of Mount Katahdin*. Appalachian Mountain Club, Boson, MA.

Eckstorm, Fannie Hardy. (1932). The handicrafts of the modern Indians of Maine. *Lafayette National Park Museum Bulletin III*. Jordan-Frost Printing Company, Bangor, ME. Reprinted 1980 and 1987 by The Robert Abbe Museum, Bar Harbor, ME. IS.

- Available for purchase from the Abbe museum.

Eckstorm, Fannie Hardy. (1934). The attack on Norridgewock, 1724. *New England Quarterly*. 7. pg. 541-578. IS.

Eckstorm, Fannie Hardy. (1939). *Maine maps of historical interest*. University Press, Orono, ME.

Eckstorm, Fannie Hardy. (June 1939). Who was Paugus? *New England Quarterly*. 12(2). pg. 203-226. IS.

Eckstorm, Fannie Hardy. (1941). *Indian place-names of the Penobscot Valley and the Maine coast*. Reprinted in 1960 and 1978 by University of Maine at Orono Press, Orono, ME. IS.

- No mention of Norumbega or Muskingum as place names in this text.

Eggan, Fred. (1967). Northern Woodland ethnology. In: *The Philadelphia Anthropological Society -- Papers presented on its golden anniversary*. Gruber, Jacob W., Ed. Columbia University Press, New York, NY.

Ewers, John C. (1957). Hair pipes in Plains indicant adornment, a study in Indian and White ingenuity. *Bureau of American Ethnology Bulletin*. 164. pg. 29-85.

Faulkner, Alaric. (1980). Identifying clay pipes from historic sites in Maine. *Maine Archaeological Society Bulletin*. 20(1). pg. 17-49.

Faulkner, Alaric and Faulkner, Gretchen. (1987) *The French at Pentagoet: An Archaeological Portrait of the Acadian Frontier*. Occasional Publications in Maine Archaeology 5. Maine Historic Preservation Commission, Augusta, ME.

Favour, Edith. (1974). *Indian games, toys, and pastimes of Maine and the Maritimes*. Bulletin X, The Robert Abbe Museum, Bar Harbor, ME.

Feder, Kenneth L. (1990). Late woodland occupation of the uplands of northwestern Connecticut. *Bulletin of the Massachusetts Archaeological Society*. 51(2). pg. 61-68.

Fernald, Peggy and Wellman, Alice N. (1970). *Brief description of birch bark canoe building*. Bulletin IX, The Robert Abbe Museum, Bar Harbor, ME.

- Out of print.

Fitzhugh, William W. (1975). Symposium on Moorehead and Maritime Archaic problems in northeastern North America. *Arctic Anthropology*. 12. pg. 1-147.
K-16

Flannery, Regina. (1939). *An analysis of coastal Algonquian culture*. Washington, DC.

Foster, Charles H., Ed. (1975). *Down East diary by Benjamin Browne Foster*. University of Maine Press, Orono, ME.

Foster, John W. (1881). *Pre-historic races of the United States of America*. S.C. Griggs and Company, Chicago, IL. IS.

Fowler, William S. (1947-48). Stone eating utensils of prehistoric New England. *American Antiquity*. 13. pg. 146-163.

Fowler, Wm. S. (1963). Classification of stone implements of New England. *Massachusetts Archaeological Society Bulletin*. 24(1).

Fowler, Wm. S. (1966). Ceremonial and domestic products of aboriginal New England. *Massachusetts Archaeological Society Bulletin*. 27(3,4).

Gage, Mary and Gage, James (2004). The Manana Island Petroglyph. *Maine Archaeology Society Bulletin*. 44 (1). pg. 15 - 20. IS.

Gallatin, Albert. (1836). *A synopsis of the Indian tribes within the United States east of the Rocky Mountains, and in the British and Russian possessions in North America*. American Antiquarian Society, Worcester, MA.

Ghere, David L. (1988). *Abenaki factionalism, emigration and social continuity in northern New England, 1725-1765*. Ph.D. dissertation. University of Maine, Orono, ME.

Ghere, David L. (1993). The "disappearance" of the Abenaki in western Maine: Political organization and ethnocentric assumptions. *American Indian Quarterly*. 17(2). pg. 193-207.

Ghere, David L. and Morrison, Alvin, H. (1996). Sanctions for slaughter: Peacetime violence on the Maine frontier, 1749-1772. *Papers of the 27th Algonquin Conference*. David H. Pentland, Ed. University of Manitoba, Winnipeg, Canada. pg. 105-116.

Giles (Gyles), John. (1736). *Memoirs of odd adventures, strange deliverances, etc. in the captivity of John Giles, Esq. written by himself*. Boston, MA.

Glidden, Charles H. (1893). *The legend of Wonalanset: A tale of the white hills*. Newtowne Publishing Co., Boston, MA. IS.

Godfrey, John F. (1881). Norumbega. *Collections of the Maine Historical Society.* VII. pg. 331-332. W.

Gookin, Daniel. (1806). Historical collections of the Indians in New England. *Massachusetts Historical Society Collections.* First series. Reprinted in 1970 by Towtaid.

Gramly, R. Michael (1981). Eleven thousand years in Maine. *Archaeology.* 34(6). pg. 32-39.

Gramly, Richard Michael. (1982). *The Vail site: A Paleo-Indian encampment in Maine.* Buffalo Society of Natural Sciences, Buffalo, NY.

Gramly, Richard Michael. (1988). *The Adkins site: A Paleo-Indian habitation and associated stone structure.* Persimmon Press, Buffalo, NY.

Gramly, Richard Michael. (1990). *Guide to the Paleo-Indian artifacts of North America.* Persimmon Press, Buffalo, NY.

Gramly, R. Michael. (1995). Perspective on Maine archaeology. *The Amateur Archaeologist.* 1(2). pg. 39-45.

Gramly, R. Michael. (1995). A quartz crystal fluted point from Maine. *The Amateur Archaeologist.* 1(2). pg. 65-69.

Gramly, R. Michael, and Rutledge, Kerry. (1981). A new Paleo-Indian site in the state of Maine. *American Antiquity.* 46. pg. 354-360. W.

Grant, Bruce. (1994). *Concise encyclopedia of the American Indian: Revised edition.* Wings Books, NY, NY. IS.

Griffin, J.B. (1967). Eastern North American archaeology: A summary. *Science.* 156(3772). pg. 175-191.

Grumet, Robert S., Ed. (1996). *Northeastern Indian lives, 1632 - 1816.* A volume in the series: *Native Americans of the Northeast: Culture, history, and the contemporary,* Calloway, Colin G. and O'Connell, Barry, Eds. University of Massachusetts Press, Amherst, MA.

Gyles, John. (1736). *Memoirs of odd adventures, strange deliverances, &c. in the captivity of John Gyles, Esq; commander of the garrison on St. George's River.* Written by himself. Printed and sold by S. Kneeland and T. Green, in Queen-Street, over against the prison., Boston, in N.E.

Gyles, John. (1875). Nine years a captive, or, John Gyles' experience among the Malicite Indians, from 1689 to 1698. With an introduction and historical notes by James Hannay, *Daily Telegraph*, Saint John, NB.

Hadlock, Wendell S. (1939). *The Taft's Point shell mound at West Gouldsboro, Maine.* Bulletin V, The Robert Abbe Museum, Bar Harbor, ME.

- Out of print.

Hadlock, Wendell S. (1941). Observations concerning the "red paint culture". *American Antiquity*. 7(2). pg. 156-161. IS.

Hadlock, Wendell S. (1941). *Three shell heaps on Frenchman's Bay*. Bulletin VI, The Robert Abbe Museum, Bar Harbor, ME. IS.

- Out of print.

Hadlock, Wendell S. (April 1943). Bone implements from shell heaps around Frenchman's Bay, Maine. *American Antiquity*. VII(4). Reprinted by Robert Abbe Museum, Bar Harbor, ME.

- See Hadlock's other publication on this topic (1941).

Hadlock, Wendell S. (1947). War among the northeastern Woodland Indians. *American Anthropologist*. 49(2). pg. 204-221.

- "The purpose of this paper is to present an account of the warfare of the period previous to the development of the fur trade and the struggle for supremacy between France and England." (pg. 204).
- "...the first Indians encountered on the St. Lawrence waterway [by Cartier] were agricultural people, later displaced by the hunting people who were in possession of the St. Lawrence at the time of Champlain." (pg. 208).

Hadlock, Wendell S. and Butler, Eva L. (1962). A preliminary survey of the Munsungan-Allegash waterways. *Robert Abbe Museum Bulletin*. 8. Bar Harbor, ME.

Hadlock, Wendell S. and Byers, Douglas S. (April 1956). Radio carbon dates from Ellsworth Falls, Maine. *American Antiquity*. 21(4). pg. 419-420.

Hadlock, Wendell S. and Stern, T. (1948). Passadumkeag, a red paint cemetery, thirty-five years after Moorehead. *American Antiquity*. 14. pg. 98-103. W.

Hamilton, Nathan D., Petersen, James B. and Doyle, Richard A., Jr. (1984). Aboriginal cultural resources of the greater Moosehead Lake region. *Maine Archaeological Society Bulletin.* 24(1). pg. 1-45.

Harp, Elmer, Jr. and Hughes, David. (1968). Five prehistoric burials from Port au Choix, Newfoundland. *Polar Notes.* 8.

- This gives information on the most important Canadian Maritime archaic burial site.

Harvey, D.C. (2000). *Asticou, sagamo of the Armouchiquois (Penobscots) on the frontiers of Acadia; fl. 1608–16.* Dictionary of Canadian Biography Online. http://www.biographi.ca/EN/ShowBio.asp?BioId=34150&query=panounias.

Heckenberger, Michael J., Petersen, James B. and Sidell, Nancy Asch. (1992). Early evidence of maize horticulture in the Connecticut River Valley of Vermont. *Archaeology of Eastern North America.* 20. pg. 125 - 149.

Hedden, Mark. (Spring 1987). Form of the cosmos in the body of the shaman. *Maine Archaeological Society Bulletin.* 27. pg. ii-iv.

- Also see Hedden's extensive publications on petroglyphs in the Norumbega Reconsidered bibliography.

Hodge, Frederick, W., Ed. (1907-10). *Handbook of American Indians north of Mexico.* Bureau of American Ethnology, Bulletin 30. 2 vols., Government Printing Office, Washington, DC.

Hoffman, B.G. (1955). The Souriquois, Etchemin and Kwedech: A lost chapter in American ethnography. *Ethnohistory.* 2(1). pg. 65-87.

Hoffman, Curtiss. (1989). Figure and ground: The late woodland village problem as seen from the uplands. *Bulletin of the Massachusetts Archaeological Society.* 50(1). pg. 24-28.

Holmes, G.K. (1907-1909). Aboriginal agriculture -- the American Indians. In: Bailey, L.H., Ed. *Cyclopedia of American agriculture: A popular survey of agricultural conditions, practices, and ideals in the United States and Canada.* NY, NY.

Horsford, Eben Norton. (1891). *The defences of Norumbega and a review of the reconnaissances of Col. T. W. Higginson, Professor Henry W. Haynes, Dr. Justin Winsor, Dr. Francis Parkman, and Rev. Dr. Edmund F. Slafter.* Houghton, Mifflin and Company, NY, NY.

Hough, Franklin Benjamin. (1856). *Papers relating to Pemaquid and parts adjacent in the present state of Maine, known as Cornwall county, when under the colony of New York. Compiled from official records in the office of the secretary of state at Albany, New York.* Weed and Parson, Albany, NY.

Howes, William J. (1943). Aboriginal New England pottery. *Massachusetts Archaeological Society Bulletin.* 5(1). pg. 1-5.

Hubbard, Lucius L. (1884). *Some Indian place-names in northern Maine.* James R. Osgood and Company, Boston, MA.

Hubbard, John. (1852). *Report of the Indian agent to the thirty-first legislature.* S. No. 45. Augusta, ME.

Hubbard, William. (1801). *A narrative of the Indian Wars in New England, ... 1607-1677.* Greenleaf, Worcester, MA.

Huden, John Charles. (1962). *Indian place names of New England.* Museum of the American Indian, Heye Foundation, NY, NY.

- "Sagadahoc = Abnaki the outflowing of a swift stream as it meets the sea."

Jack, Edward. (1895). Malecite legends. *Journal of American Folklore.* 8(20). pg. 200.

Jennings, Jessie D. (1989). *Prehistory of North America.* Mayfield Publishing Co., Mountain View, CA.

Johnson, Clifton. (1897). *An unredeemed captive.* Griffith, Axtell & Cady Co., Holyoke, MA. IS.

- "Being the story of Eunice Williams, who, at the age of seven years, was carried away from Deerfield by the indians in the year 1704, and who lived among the Indians in Canada as one of them the rest of her life..."

Johnson, Samuel. (1847). Some account of an ancient settlement on Sheepscot River. *Maine Historical Society Collections 2.* Series 1. William van Norden, NY, NY. pg. 229-237. W.

Johnson, Steven F. (1995). *Ninnuock [The People]: The Algonkian people of New England.* Bliss Publishing Company, Inc., Marlborough, MA. IS.

Josephy, Alvin M. Jr. (1994). *500 nations: An illustrated history of North American Indians.* Alfred A. Knopf, NY, NY.

- On the beginnings of the French and Indian Wars (1676): "From Massachusetts, the war spread to other parts of New England. Along the Maine coast, the Saco, Wawenoc, Kennebec, Pigwacket, and Arosaguntacook Indians joined in the attacks against the whites." (pg. 215).

Karr, Ronald Dale, Ed. (1999). *Indian New England 1524-1674: A compendium of eyewitness accounts of Native American life.* Branch Line Press, Pepperell, MA.

Kellogg, Douglas. (1987). Statistical relevance and site locational data. *American Antiquity.* 52. pg. 143-150.

Kellogg, Douglas. (1994). Why did they choose to live here? Ceramic period settlement in the Boothbay, Maine region. *Northeast Anthropology.* 48. pg. 25-60.

Kellogg, Douglas. (1995). How has coastal erosion affected the prehistoric settlement pattern of the Boothbay region of Maine? *Geoarchaeology.* 10. pg. 65-83.

Kenyon, V.B. (1979). A new approach to the analysis of New England prehistoric pottery. *Man in the Northeast.* 18. pg. 81-84.

Kidder, Frederic. (1859). The Abnaki Indians: Their treaties of 1713 and 1717, and a vocabulary. *Collections of the Maine Historical Society.* Vol. VI. pg. 203-228.

- "The Wawenocks were located on the sea-coast, and inhabited the country from the Sheepscot to the St. George; they are quite fully described by Capt. John Smith, who had much intercourse with them. From their situation on the rivers and harbors, they were much sooner disturbed by the settlements than any other of the tribes in Maine. In 1747 there were but a few families remaining. At the treaty at Falmouth, in 1749, they were associated with the Assagunticooks, among whom they were then settled, and with whom they soon after removed to Canada." (pg. 234).

Kingsbury, Isaac W. and Hadlock, Wendell S. (1951). An early occupation site, Eastport, Maine. *Massachusetts Archaeological Society Bulletin.* XII(2). pg. 22-26.

Kopec, Diane. (1985). The Eddie Brown collection of the West Grand Lake Area, Maine. *Maine Archaeological Society Bulletin.* 25(2). pg. 35-45.

Kopec, Diane. (1987). *The Abbe Museum's Frenchman Bay survey: A historic perspective.* The Robert Abbe Museum, Bar Harbor, ME. IS.

- Available for purchase from the Abbe Museum.

Kroeber, Alfred L. (1939). *Cultural and natural areas of Native North America.* University of California Press, Berkeley, CA.

Kupperman, Karen. (1980). Were the Indians alien? In: *Settling with the Indians: The meeting of English and Indian cultures in America, 1580-1640.* Rowman and Littlefield, Totowa, NJ.

Kupperman, Karen Ordahl. (2000). *Indians and English: Facing off in early America.* Cornell University Press, Ithaca, NY. IS.

Lahti, Eric et. al. (1981). Test excavations at the Hodgdon site. *Man in the Northeast.* 22. pg. 19-36.

- "Site is adjacent to the Embden petroglyphs on the Kennebec River, Maine." (Ray, *The Indians of Maine*, pg. 2).

Lafarge, Oliver. (1956). *A pictorial history of the American Indian.* Crown Publishers, Inc., NY, NY. IS.

Lauber, Almon Wheeler. (1913). Indian slavery in colonial times within the present limits of the United States. IN: *Studies in history, economics, and public law.* Vol. 54, no. 3, whole no. 134. Columbia University, NY, NY.

Laurent, Joseph. (1884). *New familiar Abenakis and English dialogues: The first ever published on the grammatical system.* Québec, Canada.

Leacock, Eleanor B. (1954). The Montagnais "hunting territory" and the fur trade. *Memoirs of the American Anthropological Association.* 56(5). Part 2. Memoir No. 78. X.

Leacock, Eleanor B. and Lurie, Nancy O., Eds. (1971). *North American Indians in historical perspective.* Random House, NY, NY.

Leadbeater, Helen M. (1978). Iriquoianesque pottery at Pequawket. *Maine Archaeological Society Bulletin.* 18(1). pg. 25-41.

Leger, Mary C. (1929). *The Catholic Indian missions of Maine, 1611-1820.* Studies in American Church History, Washington, DC.

Leland, Charles G. (1894). *The Algonquin legends of New England; or, myths and folklore of the Micmac, Passamaquoddy, and Penobscot tribes*. Houghton, Mifflin and Co., Boston, MA.

Lenhart, John. (1916). The Capuchins in Acadia and northern Maine (1632-1655). *Records of the American Catholic Historical Society*. 28(3). pg. 191-229, 300-327.

LeSourd, Philip S. (1986). *Kolusuwakonol: Peskotomuhkati-wolastoqewi naka Ikolisomani latuwewakon = Philip S. LeSourd's English and Passamaquoddy-Maliseet dictionary*. Robert M. Leavitt and David A. Francis Eds. Passamaquoddy-Maliseet Bilingual Program, Perry, ME.

LeSourd, Philip S. (2007). *Tales from Maliseet Country: The Maliseet texts of Karl V. Teeter (Studies in the Anthropology of North America)*. University of Nebraska Press, Lincoln, NE.

Levine, Mary Ann, Sassaman, Kenneth E. and Nassaney, Michael S. Eds. (1999). *The archaeological northeast*. Bergin & Garvey, Westport, CT.

Lore, Robert J. (Spring 2006). Adaptations in the edge environment: Faunal analysis of an Armouchiquois Indian village. *Maine Archaeological Society Bulletin*. 46(1). pg. 1-24. IS.

Loring, Donna M. (2008). *In the shadow of the eagle: A tribal representative in Maine*. Tilbury House Publishers, Gardiner, ME. IS.

Lorne Masta, Henry. (1932). *Abenaki Indian legends: Grammar and place names*. La Voiz des Bois-Francs, Victoriaville, PQ.

Luedtke, Barbara. (1988). Where are the late woodland villages in eastern Massachusetts? *Bulletin of the Massachusetts Archaeological Society*. 49(2). pg. 58-65. IS.

- "In the Midwest, as elsewhere in the New World, there seems to have been a long transition period during which cultigens slowly became incorporated into the diet, and then a radical transformation of diet and economy, after which people relied on cultigens for a significant proportion of their food. New Englanders, living in a region at the very northern limits of maize agriculture, should be expected to have been especially cautious in switching over to reliance on cultigens." (pg. 59).
- "...the earliest date for New England is still that associated with a corn kernel from the Hornblower II site on Martha's Vineyard: A.D. 1160+ 80 (Ritchie 1969:52)." (pg. 59).

- "On balance, I see no evidence for reliance on farming before the Late Woodland in eastern Massachusetts, but some evidence that it may have been established by A.D. 1300." (pg. 60).

Lyford, Carrie A. (1953). *Ojibwa crafts (Chippewa)*. Indian Handcrafts Series. Branch of Education, Bureau of Indian Affairs, Department of the Interior, US. IS.

MacDonald, George F. (1968). Debert: A Palaeo-Indian site in central Nova Scotia. *Anthropology Papers No. 16*. National Museums of Canada, Ottawa, Canada.

Maine Historical Society Library. (1969). *The Indians of Maine, preliminary inventory of material*. Maine Historical Society, Portland, ME.

Maine Writers Research Club. (1952). *Maine Indians in history and legend*. Severn-Wylie-Jewett Co., Portland, ME.

Malone, Patrick M. (1991). *The skulking way of war: Technology and tactics among the New England Indians*. Madison Books, MD.

Martin, Calvin. (1975). Four lives of a Micmac copper pot. *Ethnohistory*. 22(2). pg. 111-133. Martin, Calvin. (1978). *Keepers of the game: Indian-animal relationships and the fur trade*. University of California Press, Berkeley, CA.

- "Impact of European diseases, Christianity and technology (brass pots, guns, traps)... Martin's interpretations are highly controversial and have been challenged by other scholars." (Ray, *The Indians of Maine*, pg. 19).

Martin, Susan R. (1999).*Wonderful Power: The Story of Ancient Copper Working in the Lake Superior Basin.* Wayne State University Press, Detroit, MI.

McBride, Bunny. (1995). *Molly Spotted Elk: A Penobscot in Paris*. University of Oklahoma Press, Norman, OK.

McBride, Bunny. (1999). Princess Watahwaso: Bright star of the Penobscot. In: Kaufman, Polly, Ed. *Thriving beyond expectations: Women in Maine 1850 - 1969*. University of Maine.

McBride, Bunny and Prins, Harald. (1996). Walking the medicine line: Molly Ockett, a Pigwacket doctor. IN: Grumet, Robert S., Ed. (1996). *Northeastern Indian lives, 1632 - 1816*. University of Massachusetts Press, Amherst, MA.

McGuire, Joseph D. (1980). Ethnological and archaeological notes on Moosehead Lake. *American Anthropologist* n.s. 10. pg. 549-557.

McMullen, A. and Kopec, D. (n.d.) *An island in time: Three thousand years of cultural exchange on Mount Desert Island.* Bulletin XII, Sanger, David and Prins, Harald E. L., Eds., The Robert Abbe Museum, Bar Harbor, ME.

- Available for purchase from the Abbe museum.

McRae, Jill F. Kealey. (1995). *The Fannie Hardy Eckstorm collection : an ethnopoetic analysis Penobscot ways with story.* Thesis, Harvard Graduate School of Education, Cambridge, MA.

Milner, George R., Anderson, David G., and Smith, Marvin T. (2001). The Distribution of Eastern Woodlands Peoples at the Prehistoric and Historic Interface. In: *Societies in Eclipse: Archaeology of the Eastern Woodland Indians, A.D. 1400-1700.* David S. Brose, C. Wesley Cowan, and Robert Mainfort, Eds. Smithsonian Institution Press, Washington, D.C. pg. 9-18.

Mitchell, Harbour, III. (1992). A salvage effort on the coast of Maine: The Lehmann site(40-3). *Maine Archaeological Society Bulletin.* 32(2). pg. 1-14.

Mitchell, Harbour, III. (1993). The Carr site (41.66): A middle Ceramic period site in Northport, Maine. *Maine Archaeological Society Bulletin.* 33(2). pg. 33-?.

Mitchell, Harbour, III. (1995). Paleo-environmental reconstruction using early Holocene faunal assemblages and biological parameters of species therein. *Maine Archaeological Society Bulletin.* 35(1). pg. 1-12.

Mitchell, Harbour, III. (1997). 1000 B.P. in west Penobscot Bay: 41.68 & 41.68A. *Maine Archaeological Society Bulletin.* 37(1). pg. 23-?.

Mitchell, Lewis. (1990). *Wapapi akonutomakonol = The Wampun records: Wabanaki traditional laws.* Micmac-Maliseet Institute, University of New Brunswick, Fredericton, Canada.

Moorehead, Warren K. (1900). *Prehistoric implements: A reference book.* Robert Clark, Cincinnati, Ohio.

Moorehead, Warren K. (1913). Indian remains in Maine. *Science.* 38. pg. 326-327. W.

Moorehead, Warren K. (1913). Red paint people of Maine. *American Anthropologist.* 15. pg. 33-47.

Moorehead, Warren K. (1914). *The American Indian in the United States: Period 1850-1914*. The Andover Press, Andover, MA. IS.

Moorehead, Warren K. (1914). " ...a reply". *American Anthropologist*. 16. pg. 358-361.

Moorehead, Warren K. (1916). The problem of the Red Paint people. *Holmes Anniversary Volume*. pg. 359-365.

Moorehead, Warren K. (1917). Prehistoric cultures in the state of Maine. *Proceedings of the 19th International Congress of Americanists*. pg. 48-51.

Moorehead, Warren K. (1923). Primitive cultures in the state of Maine. *The Archaeological Report*. pg. 3-4.

Moorehead, Warren K. (1924). The ancient remains at Pemaquid, Maine. *Old-Time New England*. 14. pg. 132-141. W.

Moorehead, Warren K. (1928). Abbe Memorial Museum at Bar Harbor. *Science*. 68. pg. 396-397. W.

Moorehead, Warren K. (1929). Archaeological fieldwork in North America during 1928 Maine. *American Anthropologist*. pg. 348. Morgan, Lewis H. (1907). *Ancient society*. Henry Holt and Company, NY, NY.

- This text contains important information on early Abanaki band organization and identification. (See Snow, 1968, pg. 1147.)

Morrison, Alvin. (1973). Observations concerning an ethnohistorical taxonomy of the Wabenaki Algonquian Amerinds. *Maine Archaeological Society Bulletin*. 13(1). pg. 1-21. IS.

- "The ETCHEMIN either developed into, or at least were replaced by, today's MALISEET and PASSAMAQUODDY, ... But in the first decade and a half of the 1600's, the greatest ETCHEMIN overlord, Bashaba, lived on the Penobscot River, in what now is (and is shown on Kroeber's map) the heart of PENOBSCOT territory, while his authority spread to the Saco River and his influence extended far into ABNAKI and PENNACOOK lands. Later, Bashaba's successors (including Madockawando) continued the ETCHEMIN overlordship, but of ever-less-vast domains." pg. 14-15.
- One of the principle advocates of the Bashaba as a Etchemin.

Morrison, Alvin. (1974). *Dawnland decisions: Seventeenth-century Wabanaki leaders and their responses to the differential contact stimuli in the overlap area of New France and New England*. University Microfilms, State University of New York at Buffalo, NY.

Morrison, Alvin H. (1975). Membertou's Raid on the Chouacoet "Almouchiquois" - the Micmac Sack of Saco in 1607. *Papers of the Sixth Algonquian Conference, 1974.* William Cowan, Ed. Canadian Ethnology Service Paper 23.National Museums of Canada, Ottawa, Canada. pg. 141-179. W.

Morrison, Alvin H. (1976). Dawnland directors: status and role of seventeenth century Wabanaki Sagamores. *Papers of the Seventh Algonquian Conference, 1976.* William Cowan, Ed. Carleton University, Ottawa, Canada.

Morrison, Alvin H. (1991). Dawnland Directors' Decisions: Seventeenth-Century Encounter Dynamics on the Wabanaki Frontier. *Papers of the twenty-second Algonquian conference.* Carleton University, Ottawa, Canada. pg. 225-245.

Morrison, Alvin H. (2008). MawooshenResearch.
http://www.lakesregionofmaine.gen.me.us/sebago_anthro/index.html

Morrison, Kenneth M. (1978). *The people of the dawn: The Abnaki and their relations with New England and New France, 1600-1727.* University Microfilms, Ann Arbor, MI.

Morse, Dan F. (2006). Wampum manufacture in New Jersey. *The Chronicle.* 59(1). pg. 1. IS.

Mosher, John and Spiess, Arthur. (2004). An archaic site at Mattamiscontis on the Penobscot River. *The Maine Archaeological Society Bulletin.* 44(2). pg. 1-35. IS.

Muir, Diana. (2000). *Reflections in Bullough's Pond: Economy and ecosystem in New England.* University Press of New England, Hanover, NH. IS.

- While most of this text traces the evolution of the Industrial Revolution in New England to the current ecological crisis pertaining to chemical fallout issues, the first several chapters contain important observations pertaining to Native Americans in New England.
- Muir's primary observation is that hunting and gathering tribes maintained a viable equilibrium by limiting population growth and living within their resources. Muir notes that when the population outgrew the supply of game animals, there was a shift from hunting to harvesting shellfish. She also notes the large oyster shell heaps at Damariscotta and implies they may signify the impoverishment of the hunting and gathering tribes living north of the Kennebec. (pg. 9).
- Muir has this comment on the evolution of agricultural communities in southern New England "The change from hunting and gathering to depending on crops for half the annual food supply was made not suddenly or even in a single generation, but over the course of decades and centuries. It was a choice that redounded to enforce the original decision. A population growing too large to sustain itself by gathering the bounty of nature chooses to cultivate and store crops for the lean season. The surplus thus produced enables the

population to grow, which compels a more intensive agriculture, which results in population growth, which compels more intensive cultivation, which results in ..." (pg. 11-12).

- Frequently citing Dean Snow, Muir inadvertently perpetuates the anomalous deletion of the Wawenoc Indian from contemporary ethnohistoric writings. "North of the Kennebec, where corn was not grown, they lived as Europeans could live only in dreams: by plucking fruit and chasing the wild buck in the greenwood. It was that rare case of reality approaching idyll." (pg. 15).

- Not at all central to the purpose of Muir's important book, but still of interest to anyone concerned with the history of Native Americans in Maine is the question of the status of the Wawenoc Indians living *east* of the Kennebec River. The traditional practice by Native Americans of burning the under foliage of the coastal forests to open it for productive hunting as well as for agricultural use that both Muir and Cronon (*Changes in the Land*) describe also may apply to that small segment of the Maine coast that lies between the Kennebec and the Penobscot rivers. Muir, however, continues to rely on Dean Snow who in the *Archaeology of New England* designates the many Wawenoc villages between the Kennebec and Penobscot rivers as Kennebec and Penobscot Indian villages, effectively eliminating the Wawenocs from current history texts.

- For additional comments see the annotations on this book in the Industrial Revolution bibliography and in the Norumbega bioregion changes in the land bibliography.

Munson, Patrick. (1973) The Origins and Antiquity of Maize-Bean-Squash Agriculture in Eastern North America; Some Linguistic Evidence. *Variations in Anthropology*. Edited by Lathrap, D.W. and Douglas, Jody. Univeristy of Illinois Press, Urbana, IL.

Nash, R.J. Ed. (1983). *The evolution of Maritime cultures on the northeast and the northwest coasts of North America*. Department of Archaeology Publication 11, Simon Fraser University. W.

Newell, Catherine S. C. (1981). *Molly Ockett*. Bethel Historical Society, Bethel, ME.

Newman, Walter S. and Salwen, Bert, Eds. (1977). *Amerinds and their paleoenvironments in northeastern North America*. Vol. 288. New York Academy of Sciences, NY, NY.

- This text apparently contains a chapter titled: Early and Middle Archaic Site Distribution and Habitats in Southern New England by Dincauze and Mulholland.

Nickel, Harry G. (1965). The Cameron point excavation at Southport Island, Maine. *Maine Archaeological Society Bulletin*. 3. pg. 13-16. W.

Nies, Judith. (1996). *Native American history: A chronology of a culture's vast achievements and their links to world events*. Ballantine Books, NY, NY. IS.

Noel-Hume, Ivor. (1969). *Historical archaeology*. Alfred A. Knopf, New York, NY.

Norman, Craig. (1998). Controlled surface collection and artifact analysis of the Stevens Brook site, Presumpscot watershed. *Maine Archaeological Society Bulletin*. 38(2). pg 23-?. W.

Oldale, Robert N. (1985). Rapid postglacial shoreline changes in the western Gulf of Maine and the Paleo-Indian environment. *American Antiquity*. 50(2). pg. 145-150. W.

Oldale, Robert N., Whitmore, Frank C. and Grimes, John R. (1987). Elephant teeth from the western gulf of Maine, and their implications.*National Geographic Research*. 3(4). pg. 439-446.

Orchard, William C. (1975). *Beads and beadwork of the American Indians*. Museum of the American Indian. Heye Foundation, NY. IS.

Palmer, Rose A. (1929). *The North American Indians: An account of the American Indians north of Mexico, compiled from the original sources*. Smithsonian Scientific Series. Volume 4. Abbot, Charles Greeley, Ed. Smithsonian Institution Series, Inc., NY, NY. IS.

Parker, Arlita Dodge. (1925). *A History of Pemaquid with sketches of Monhegan, Popham, Castine*. Macdonald & Evans, Boston, MA.

- "The Pemaquid country was first known to Englishmen, so far as any written narrative relates, when it was visited by George Waymouth and his men, twenty-nine in number, June 3, 1605. Waymouth's ship was not the first that had skirted this rocky shore, but it was the first English ship that had come near enough to the Pemaquid peninsula to pass under the very eyes of that tribe of the 'Abenakis,' of eastern savages, know as 'Wawenocks.'" (pg. 7).
- "It was on the afternoon of May 30th [1605] that Waymouth's men first saw the savages. They were Wawenock braves who late in May had left their wigwams in Pemaquid to go 'fishing and fowling' down the shores of the St. George's region." (pg. 9).
- "Griffin returned to the ship to report that there were 'two hundred and eighty-three salvages, every one with his bowe and arrowes, with their dogges and wolves, which they keepe tame at command,' and 'not anything to exchange at all.' The English, somewhat staggered by the great number of savages as compared with their own company, became alarmed, and suspected treachery." (pg. 11).
- "'Wherefore, after good advice taken, we determined so soone as we could to take some of them, least (being suspitious we had discovered their plots) they should absent themselves from us.' On this pretext, they captured five savages." (pg. 11).
- "In July, 1605, ... Champlain sailed up the Sheepscot to the present Wiscasset Point, where he entered into an alliance with some friendly Indians, probably the Wawenocks, the same tribe with which Waymouth treated. By the back river he reached the Kennebec." (pg. 15).

- "Champlain makes one reference to the Waymouth ship. He says that Anasou, a native, told him while in the Kennebec, 'that there was a ship ten leagues off the harbor which was engaged in fishing, and that those on board her had killed five savages of this river, under cover of friendship." (pg. 15).
- "The captives told Gorges of the 'goodly rivers' and the stately harbors' of America, of the different savage tribes and where they were seated, and awakened in his soul an interest in the new world which did not perish with the years." (pg. 16).
- "Purchas makes the 'Pemaquid' one of the nine rivers that water the dominions of the Bashaba in a strange land called 'Mavooshen,' confusing the river perhaps with the Penobscot, while Strachey and Gorges apply the name 'Pemaquid' to the river explored by Waymouth. John Smith spoke of the whole coast as having formerly been called 'Norumbega, Musconkus, Penaquida, Canada, and such other names as those that ranged the coast pleased.'" (pg. 17).
- "...one cannot but regret that circumstances prevented Gilbert and Popham from appearing before the courts of that mysterious and challenging figure, the 'Bashaba.' About him much has been written, but little is really known. Purchas in his 'Pilgrims' makes him the chief lord of an extensive country called 'Mawooshen,' stretching from the Tarratines at the east to the River Piscataqua at the west. Purchas' whole description is too fanciful, however, to carry any weight. Rosier evidently believed that the savages with whom they treated used the word 'Bashaba' as a general term for ruler. 'They gave us some (tobacco),' he writes, 'to carry to our Bashaba.' Gorges says: 'That part of the country we first seated in seemed to be monarchical,' its ruler having the title of 'Bashaba.' 'The Bashaba,' he writes, 'and his people seemed to be of some eminence above the rest. ... His own chief abode was not far from Pemaquid.'" (pg. 27).
- "John Smith enumerated, under their several Indian names, the countries from the Penobscot to Massachusetts, and adds; 'Though most be lords of themselves, yet they hold the Bashabes of Penobscot the chiefe and greatest amongst them." (pg. 27).
- "Alliances were common, but there was no federation in the sense of one tribe's paying tribute to the people and rulers of another. The notion that the Bashaba as a sort of emperor was current with the early English, but not with the French who knew the savages more intimately. The 'Bashaba' was doubtless merely a prominent savage chief." (pg. 27).
- "The Indians fought stoutly to retain the lands east of Pemaquid and north of certain points on the Kennebec. At the conference with Gov. Shute in 1717 they said they were unwilling that the English should settle east of Pemaquid or north of certain mills on the Kennebec. In 1726, at a conference with Gov. Dummer at Falmouth, which ended the period of strife just described and which resulted in the ratification of a treaty, the savages took a similar stand, demanding the removal of the forts at St. George's and at Richmond." (pg. 195).

Pearo, Linda and Pelissier, Dorcus. (1997). *New dawn: The western Abenaki, a curricular framework for the middle level.* A joint publication of the Language and Cultural Affairs Program, University of Vermont Office of Rural Education and the Vermont State Department of Education, Burlington, VT.

Petersen, James B. (1991). Archaeological testing at the Sharrow site: A deeply stratified early to late Holocene cultural sequence in central Maine. *Occasional publications in*

Maine Archaeology 8. Maine Archaeological Society and Maine Historic Preservation Commission, Augusta, ME.

Petersen, James B. (1995). Preceramic archaeological manifestations in the far Northeast: A review of current research. *Archaeology of Eastern North America*. 23. pg. 207-229. W.

Petersen, James B. (1996). Fiber industries from northern New England: Ethnicity and technological traditions during the Woodland period. In: *A most indispensible art: Native fiber industries from Eastern North America*. University of Tennessee Press, Knoxville, TN.

Petersen, James B. and Blustain, Malinda. (2003). In the land of "Mawooshen:" Native American perishables from two contact period sites on the central Maine coast. *Perishables Material Culture in the Northeast*. Penelope Ballard Drooker, Ed. New York State Museum Bulletin 500, Albany, NY.

Petersen, James B. and Cowie, Ellen R, (2002). From hunter-gatherer camp to horitcultural village: Late prehistoric indigenous subsistence and settlement. *Northeast Subsistence-Settlement Change A.D. 700-1300*. John P. Hart and Christina B. Rieth, Eds. New York State Museum Bulletin 496. New York, NY. pg. 265-287. X.

Petersen, James B. and Hamilton, N.D. (1984). Early woodland ceramic and perishable fiber industries from the northeast: A summary and interpretations. *Annals of Carnegie Museum*. Carnegie Museum of Natural History. 53. pg. 423-445.

Petersen, James B., Hamilton, Nathan D. et. al. (1986). Late Paleoindian remains from Maine. *Current Research in the Pleistocene*. 3. pg. 19-21.

Petersen, James B. and Putnam, David E. (1992). Early Holocene occupation in the central Gulf of Maine region. In: *Early Holocene occupation in northern New England*. Robinson, Brian S., Petersen, James B. and Robinson, Ann K. Eds. Occasional Papers in Maine Archaeology no. 9., Augusta, ME. pg. 13-61.

Petersen, James B., Robinson, Brian S., Belknap, Daniel F., Stark, James and Kaplan, Lawrence K. (1994). An archaic and woodland period fish weir complex in central Maine. *Archaeology of Eastern North America*. 22. pg. 197-222. X.

Petersen, James B. and Sanger, David. (1991). An aboriginal ceramic sequence for Maine and the Maritime Provinces. In: *Prehistoric archaeology in the Maritimes: Past and present research*. Deal, Michael, Ed. The council of Maritime Premiers, Reports in Archeology No. 8. pg. 121-178.

Petersen, James B. and Wolford, Jack A. (2000). Spin and twist as cultural markers: A New England perspective on native fiber industries. In: *Beyond cloth and cordage: archaeological textile research in the Americas.* University of Utah Press, Salt Lake City, UT.

Prince, George. (1857). The voyage of Capt. Geo. Weymouth to the coast of Maine in 1605. *Maine Historical Society Collections*. VI. pg. 291-306.

Prince, J. Dyneley and Speck, Frank. (2005). *Volume 9: A vocabulary of Mohegan-Pequot.* American Language Reprint Series, Evolution Publishing, Bristol, PA.

Prins, Harald. (1984). Foul play on the Kennebec: The historical background of Fort Western and the demise of the Abenaki Nation. *Kennebec Proprietor.* 1(3). pg. 4-14. W.

Prins, Harald. (1987). The search for Cushnoc: A seventeenth century pilgrim trading post in the Kennebec Valley of Maine. *Kennebec Proprietor.* 4(1). pg. 8-13. W.

Prins, Harald. (1989). Natives and newcomers: Mount Desert in the age of exploration. In: An island in time: Three thousand years of cultural exchange on Mount Desert Island. *The Robert Abbe Museum Bulletin.* 12. pg. 21-36. W.

Prins, Harald. (1989). *Tribulations of a border tribe: A discourse on the political ecology of the Aroostook band of Micmacs (16th - 20th centuries).* Doctoral Dissertation, Ann Arbor, MI.

Prins, Harald. (1993). To the land of the Mistigoches: American Indian traveling to Europe in the age of exploration. *American Indian Culture and Research Journal.* 17(1). pg. 175-195.

Prins, Harald. (1996). Penobscot. In: Davis, Mary. *Encyclopedia of Native Americans in the Twentieth Century.* Garland Publishing, NY, NY. X.

Prins, Harald. (1997). Tribal network and migrant labor: Mi'kmaq Indians as seasonal workers in Aroostook's potato fields (1870-1980). In: *After King Philip's War: Presence and persistence in Indian New England.* Colin Calloway, Ed. University Press of New England, Hanover. pg. 231-255.

Prins, Harald. (1998). Chief Big Thunder (1827-1906): The life of a Penobscot trickster. *Maine History*. 37(3), pg. 140-158.

Prins, Harald. (2002). The crooked path of Dummer's Treaty: Anglo-Wabanaki diplomacy & the quest for Aboriginal rights. *Papers of the Algonquian Conference/Actes des Congres des Algonquinistes*. H.C. Wolfart Ed. U Manitoba Press, Winnipeg. pg. 84-106.

Prins, Harald. (2004 in press). Storm clouds over Wabanakiak: Confederacy diplomacy until Dummer s Treaty (1727). In: *Original Vermonters: Exploring New Directions in Abenaki Studies*. James Petersen, et.al. Eds. University Press of New England.

Prins, Harald and Bourque, Bruce. (1987). Norridgewock: Village translocation on the New England -- Acadian frontier. *Man in the Northeast*. 33. pg. 137 - 158.

Prins, Harald and McBride, B. (1989). A social history of Maine Indian basketry. *The Kennebec Proprietor*. 6(2). pg. 18-21. W.

Prins, Harald and McBride, B. (1996). Walking the medicine line: Molly Ockett, a Pigwacket doctor. In: *Northeastern Indian Lives, 1632-1816*. Robert Grumet, Ed. University of Massachusetts Press, Amherst. pg. 321-347.

Pryor, F.L. (1986). The adoption of agriculture: Some theoretical and empirical evidence. *American Anthropologist*. 88. pg. 879-897. X.

- The Micmacs are one of three societies that did not adopt agriculture (the others were Pomo and Paiute).

Quimby, George I. (1966). *Indian culture and European trade goods*. The University of Wisconsin Press, Madison, WI.

Ranbom, Sheppard. (2008). *King Philip's War: A poem*. Settlement House Books, Arlington, VA.

Ray, Roger B. (February 1970). The Norsemen and the Indians of Maine. *Maine Historical Society Newsletter*. 9(3).

Ray, Roger B. (1973). Maine Indians' concept of land tenure. *Maine Historical Society Quarterly*. 13(1). pg. 28-51.

Reid, John G. (1981). *Acadia, Maine, and New Scotland, marginal colonies in the seventeenth century*. University of Toronto Press, Toronto, Canada.
K-34

Riley, Thomas J., Edging, Richard and Rossen, Jack. (1990). Cultigens in prehistoric eastern North America: Changing paradigms. *Current Anthropology*. 31(5). pg. 525-541. X.

- "New data on archaeobotanical macromorphologies, the chemical and chromosomal composition of archaeobotanical specimens, and the geographical distribution of archaeobotanical remains challenge old paradigms. In particular, the diffusion of tropical cultigens across the Caribbean must now be seriously considered. This paper reports on current research suggesting alternatives to existing paradigms in relation to four plants (maize, tobacco, beans, and chenopods) and stresses prehistoric eastern North America's relationship to, instead of isolation from, Mesoamerica and South America." (pg. 525).

Ritchie, William A. (1965). The 'small stemmed point' in New England. *Pennsylvania Archaeologist*. 35(3-4). pg. 134-138. W.

Ritchie, William A. (1969). *The archaeology of Martha's Vineyard: A framework for the prehistory of southern New England*. Natural History Press, Garden City, NY.

- A primary information resource for the identification and classification of New England area projectile points.
- The Davistown Museum consultant, Jim Clark, utilized this text to catalog the Coffin Stream Assemblage installation from West Newbury, MA.

Ritchie, William A. and MacNeish, Richard S. (1949). The pre-Iroquoian pottery of New York state. *American Antiquity*. 15(2). pg. 97-124. IS.

- Excellent photographs help differentiate New York pottery from that made in Maine.

Robbins, Maurice. (1980). *Wapanucket: An archaeological report*. Trustees of the Massachusetts Archaeological Society, Attleboro, MA. IS.

- The following is the dedication page in the report:

Dedicated to
TUSPAQUIN
Last Sachem
of the
Wapanucket Area
and to
Monamie, His Wife
Daughter of Ousamequin (Massasoit)
and Sister of Metacomet (Philip)
****

Tuspaquin and Philip gave their lives in a vain attempt to preserve the Wampanoag nation. Monamie was captured by the English and her fate is unknown.

- The Davistown Museum has on exhibit (Wapanucket Hoard) some Native American artifacts that are from the WAP-8 excavation described in this report.

Robbins, Maurice and Agogino, George A. (1964) The Wapanucket No. 8 Site: A Clovis-Archaic Site in Massachusetts. *American Antiquity.* 29(4). pg. 509-513.

Robinson, Brian S. (1985). The Nelson Island and Seabrook Marsh site: Late archaic, marine oriented people on the central New England coast. *Occasional Publications in Northeastern Anthropology no. 9 (part 1).* Franklin Pierce College, Rindge, NH. pg. 1-107.

Robinson, Brian S. (1992). Early and middle archaic period occupation in the Gulf of Maine region: Mortuary and technological patterning. In: *Early Holocene occupation in northern New England.* Robinson, Brian S., Petersen, James B. and Robinson, Ann K., Eds. Occasional publications in Maine Archaeology 9. Maine Archaeological Society and Maine Historic Preservation Commission, Augusta, ME. pg. 63-116.

Robinson, Reuel. (1907). *History of Camden and Rockport, Maine.* Camden Publishing Co., Camden, ME. IS.

- Robinson is yet another Maine historian who rewrote the entrenched oral tradition that the Wawenoc Indians were an important, if not the foremost Abenaki community on the west side of the Penobscot River, in opposition to the Etchemins on the east side.
- For a complete rendition of Robinson's comments on the Wawenocs in Maine pre- and proto-history, see the Davistown Museum's information file from this text, The Aboriginals.

Rosier, James. (1605). *A Vocabulary of Etchemin.* American Language Reprint series, Volume 39. Evolution Publishing, Bristol, PA.

- "In 1605, James Rosier obtained 86 words of an unnamed language along the coast of Maine, first printed in Samuel Purchas's 'Pilgrimes' (1625). Rosier's vocabulary has mixed Maliseet/Eastern Abenaki characteristics and possibly represents the Etchemin language. Also included in this volume is a more certain list of the Etchemin numbers from 1 to 10 recorded by Marc Lescarbot in 1607."

Rostlund, E. (1952). Freshwater fish and fishing in native North America. *Publications in Geography.* 9. University of California, Berkeley, CA.

Rowe, John H. (1940). Excavations in the waterside shell heap, Frenchman's Bay, Maine. *Excavators Club Papers.* 1(3). Harvard University, Cambridge, MA. Rowe, John H.

(1941). Archaeology and history in Eastern Maine. *Massachusetts Archaeological Society Bulletin.* 2(11). pg. 7-13. W.

Rumsey, Barbara. (Summer 2000). Waldron vs. Smith: Shipwreck at the eastward, 1671. *Maine History.* 39(2). pg. 69.

Sabine, Lorenzo. (1857). *Indian tribes of New Jersey.* Sanger, David. (1971). Passamaquoddy Bay prehistory: A summary. *Bulletin of the Maine Archaeological Society.* 11(2). pg. 14-19. W.

Sanger, David. (1973). Cow Point: An archaic cemetery in New Brunswick. *Mercury Series Paper.* No 12. National Museum of Man, Ottawa, Canada. Sanger, David. (1975). Culture change as an adaptive process in the Maine-Maritimes region. *Arctic Anthropology.* 12(2). pg. 60-75. W.

Sanger, David. (1976). The earliest settlements. In: *Maine forms of American architecture.* Deborah Thompson, Ed. Downeast Magazine, Camden, ME. pg. 3-14.

Sanger, David. (1977). Some thoughts on the scarcity of archaeological sites in Maine between 10,000 and 5,000 years ago. *Maine Archaeological Society Bulletin.* 17(1). pg. 18-25.

Sanger, David. (1981). Unscrambling messages in the midden. *Archaeology of eastern North America.* 9. pg. 37-42. W.

Sanger, David. (1982). Changing views of aboriginal seasonality and settlement in the Gulf of Maine. *Canadian Journal of Anthropology.* 2. pg. 195-204.

Sanger, David. (1985). Cultural ecology in Passamaquoddy Bay, New Brunswick. *Maine Archaeological Society Bulletin.* 25(1). pg. 10-16.

Sanger, David. (1985). Seashore archaeology in New England. *The Quarterly Review of Archaeology.* 6(2). pg. 3-4. W.

Sanger, David. (1986). An introduction to the prehistory of the Passamaquoddy Bay region. *The American Review of Canadian Studies.* 16(2). pg. 139-159.

Sanger, David. (1987). *The Carson site and the late ceramic period in Passamaquoddy Bay, New Brunswick.* Mercury Series Paper No. 135., Canadian Museum of Civilization.

- This text contains a "detailed construction of the Quoddy tradition" (Bourque, 1995).

Sanger, David. (1988). Maritime adaptation in the Gulf of Maine. *Archaeology of Eastern North America*. 16. pg. 81-100.

Sanger, David. (1989). Insights into Native American life at Fernald Point. In: *An Island in Time*. Robert Abbe Museum Bulletin 12. Robert Abbe Museum, Bar Harbor, ME. W.

Sanger, David. (1991). Cow Point revisited. In: *Prehistoric archaeology in the Maritime Provinces: Past and present research*. Deal, Michael and Blair, Susan, Eds. The Council of Maritime Premiers, Fredericton, New Brunswick, Canada. pg. 73-83. W.

Sanger, David. (1991). Five thousand years of contact between Maine and Nova Scotia. *Bulletin of the Maine Archaeological Society*. 32(2). pg. 55-61.

Sanger, David. (1996). An analysis of seasonal transhumance models for pre-european State of Maine. *The Review of Archaeology*. 17(1). pg 54-58 {published Fall 1997}.

Sanger, David and Belknap, Daniel F. (1987). Human responses to changing marine environments in the Gulf of Maine. In: *Man and the mid-holocene climatic optimum*. McCinnon, Neal A. and Steward, Glenn S.L., Eds. Proceedings of the 17th Annual Chacmool Conference, Calgary, Department of Archaeology, University of Calgary, pg. 245-261.

Sanger, David, Davis, Ronald B., MacKay, Robert G. and Borns, Harold W. (1977). The Hirundo Archaeological Project -- An interdisciplinary approach to central Maine prehistory. In: *Amerinds and their paleoenvironments in northeastern North America*. Newman, Walter S. and Salwen, Bert, Eds. Annals of the New York Academy of Sciences, vol. 288, NY, NY. pg. 457-471.

Sanger, David and MacKay, Robert. (1973). The Hirundo archaeological project -- preliminary report. *Man in the Northeast*. 6. pg. 21-29.

Saunders, Charles Francis. (1912). *The Indians of the terraced houses*. G.P. Putnam's Sons, NY, NY. Schoolcraft, Henry R. (1851). *The American Indians: Their history, condition and prospects*. Rev. ed. Rochester, NY.

- Schoolcraft makes no mention of the Wawenoc, Sheepscot, Abenaki or Wabanaki Indians. Also, there are no listings in the index for Penobscot or Samoset.

Schoolcraft, Henry R. (1857). *History of the Indian tribes of the United States: Section 6: Synopsis of the history of the New England tribes*. Philadelphia, PA.

Sewall, Rufus King. (January 23, 1896). Mavooshen: Land of a lost race. *Lincoln County News*. pg. 123-126.

- "A minute description of the Wawenocks, the native race of Lincoln County; their connection with the Damariscotta shell-heaps; their origin and their extinction." (pg. 123).
- See the essay on the Confederancy of Mawooshen in the Davistown Museum's *Norumbega Reconsidered* publication for a discussion and see our information file on Mavooshen for excerpts from this article.

Shaw, Leslie C. (1988). A biocultural evaluation of the skeletal population from the Nevin site, Blue Hill, Maine. *Archaeology of Eastern North America*. 16. pg. 55-77.

Sibley, John Langdon. (1851). *A history of the town of Union, Maine, to the middle of the nineteenth century*. Benjamin B. Mussey and Co., Boston, MA. Reprinted 1970, 1987 by New England History Press, Somersworth, NH.

- "There is no evidence that this was a place much resorted to by Indians, though the Wawenocks inhabited the country from Sagadahock to St. George's River. It is obvious, however, that they were here occasionally. It is said that during the French war several lived along Crawford's River, and between Seven-tree Pond and Round Pond, near the latter. Stone hatchets, chisels, and other Indian implements, have been found near the Upper Bridge, in the vicinity of which was a good place for fishing at the waterfall. About half-way between Nye's Corner and Sunnybec Pond, very near the spot where the school-house now stands, two Indian skeletons were ploughed up in repairing the road some twenty-five years since. Hatches, arrow-heads, &c. were found by the early settlers near the mouth of Crawford's River. A brass kettle, as large as a pail, was also found there." (pg. 23).
- "Not any Indians were living here when the first settlers came. They often visited the town afterwards, 'hunted along almost every year,' and were on friendly terms with the inhabitants." (pg. 25).
- See the other annotations for this citation in the Davistown Plantation bibliography.
- Also see a quote from this text about Vaughan & Pardoe, a tool manufacturer located in Union, in the Registry of Maine Toolmakers.
- An excerpt from Chapter 9 on manufactures can be found in the Davistown History Project's information files section.

Sidell, Nancy. (1999). Prehistoric plant use in Maine: Paleoindian to contact period. In: Hart, John P., Ed. *Current northeast paleoethnobotany*. New York State Museum Bulletin No. 494, Albany, NY. pg. 191 - 224.

Simmons, William S. (1986). *Spirit of the New England tribes: Indian history and folklore*. University Press of New England, London. IS.

Sleeper, Myron O. (1949). Indian place names in New England. *Bulletin of the Massachusetts Archaeological Society*. 10(4). pg. 89-93.

Smith, B.L. (1948). An analysis of the Maine cemetery complex. *Massachusetts Archaeological Society Bulletin*. 9. pg. 17-72.

Smith, Bruce. (1989). Origins of agriculture in eastern North America. *Science*. 246. pg. 1566-1571. W.

Smith, Nicolas N. (1955). The survival of the Red Paint complex in Maine. *Massachusetts Archaeological Society*. Bulletin 17. pg. 4-6.

Smith, Walter B. (1930). *The lost Red Paint People of Maine*. Bulletin II, The Robert Abbe Museum, Bar Harbor, ME.

  • Out of print.

Smith, Walter B. (1930). *The lost Red Paint People of Maine*. Bulletin III. Lafayette National Park,{Robert Abbe Museum?} Bar Harbor, ME.

Snow, Dean R. (1968). A century of Maine archaeology. *Maine Archaeological Society Bulletin*. 8. pg. 8-25.

Snow, Dean R. (1969). *A summary of excavations at the Hathaway site in Passadumkeag, Maine, 1902, 1947, and 1968*. Department of Anthropology, University of Maine, Orono, ME.

Snow, Dean R. (1969). *A summary of prehistoric sites in the state of Maine*. Department of Anthropology, University of Maine, Orono, ME.

Snow, Dean R. (January 1970). The Penobscot Indians in Thoreau's time. *Thoreau Journal Quarterly*. 2(1). pg. 7-11. W.

Snow, Dean R. (1970). A middle woodland site on the coast of Maine. *Maine Archaeological Society Bulletin*. 10(1,2). pg. 1-10.

Snow, Dean R. (1973). *The evolution of maritime adaptation in aboriginal Maine*. Paper read at the 72nd Annual Meeting of the American Anthropological Association, New Orleans, LA.

Snow, Dean R. (1973). A model for the reconstruction of late eastern Algonquian prehistory. *Studies in Linguistics*. 23. pg. 77-85.

Snow, Dean R. (1975). The Passadumkeag sequence. *Arctic Anthropology*. 12(2). pg. 46-59. W.

Snow, Dean R. (1978). Shaking down the new paradigm. *Archaeology of Eastern North America*. 6. pg. 87-91.

Sockabasin, Allen J. (2007). *An upriver Passamaquoddy*. Tilbury House Publishers, Gardiner, ME. IS.

Soctomah, Donald. (2002). *Passamaquoddy at the turn of the century, 1890-1920: Tribal life and times in Maine and New Brunswick*. Passamaquoddy Tribe of Indian Township, ME.

Soctomah, Donald. (2003). *Hard times at Passamaquoddy, 1921-1950: Tribal life and times in Maine and New Brunswick*. Passamaquoddy Tribe of Indian Township, ME.

Soctomah, Donald. (2005). *Let me live as my ancestors had 1850-1890: Tribal life and times in Maine and New Brunswick*. Passamaquoddy Tribe of Indian Township, ME.

Soctomah, Donald. (2005). *Meddybemps cultural study: N'tolonapemk Village - a visit to our ancestors' place*. Passamaquoddy Tribal Historic Preservation Office, ME.

Speck, Frank G. (1915). Basis of American Indian ownership of the land. In: *University lectures delivered by members of the faculty in the free public lecture course 1914-1915*. University of Pennsylvania, Philadelphia, PA. pg. 181-196.

Speck, Frank G. (1915). The eastern Algonkian Wabanaki confederacy. *American Anthropologist*. 17. pg. 492-508. IS.

Speck, Frank G. (1915). The family hunting band as the basis of Algonkian social organization. *American Anthropologist*. 17. pg. 289-305. W.

Speck, Frank G. (1919). The functions of wampum among the Eastern Algonkian. *American Anthropological Association Memoirs*. 6. pg. 3-71. W.

Speck, Frank G. (1919). Penobscot shamanism. *American Anthropological Association. Memoirs*. No. 28. pg. 239-298. W.

Speck, Frank G. (1926). Culture problems in northeastern North America. *Proceedings of the American Philosophical Society*. 65(4). pg. 272-311. W.

Speck, Frank G. (1935). "Abenaki clans" -- Never! *American Anthropologist*. 37. pg. 528-530. X.

- "There is, in short, no reason to perpetuate any longer the illusion that any of the Wabanaki peoples possessed a clan organization." (pg. 530).

Speck, Frank G. (1935). Penobscot tales and religious beliefs. *Journal of American Folklore*. 48(4). pg. 18-19.

- "The Penobscot and other Wabanaki units have these characteristic traits of Northeastern America: limited nomadism centering around the reindeer or caribou and the moose, absence of agriculture, similarities in hunting and fishing devices, skin and birch-bark canoes, skin and bark covered conical wigwams, skin leggings, tailored coats with hoods for protection in winter, skin moccasins of a fairly uniform type, birch-bark vessels and baskets, cedar or basswood fibre bags and thongs, characteristic decorative motives in birch-bark etching and in various later forms of embroidery, the absence of stratification in social organization, the family-unit with exclusive hunting districts, weakness of government, abandonment of the aged and of orphans, occasional economic anthropophagy, certain games and contests, the absence of religious ceremonial gatherings, characteristic conjuring shamanism, and general tendencies toward individualism in society and religion." (pg. 2).
- Also see Speck, 1940, *Penobscot Man* in the Native Americans: Principal Sources bibliography.

Speck, Frank G. (1941?). Art processes in birchbark of the River Desert Algonquin : A circumboreal trait. *Anthropological papers*. Bureau of American Ethnology, Smithsonian Institution, Washington, DC. No. 17, pg. 229-274.

Speck, F.G. and Dexter, R.W. (1948). Utilization of marine life by the Wampanoag Indians of Massachusetts. *Journal of the Washington Academy of Sciences*. 38. pg. 257-265. W.

Speck, Frank G. and Eiseley, Loren C. (1939). Significance of hunting territory systems of the Algonkian in social theory. *American Anthropologist*. N.S., XLI. pg. 269-280. W.

Spiess, Arthur E. (1979). *Reindeer and caribou hunters: An archaeological study*. Studies in Archaeologiy Series. Academic Press, NY.

Spiess, Arthur E. (Fall 1980). The Maine archaeological survey for prehistoric sites. *Maine Archaeological Society Bulletin*. 20(2). pg. 19-22. X.

Spiess, Arthur E. (1982). A skeleton in armor: An unknown chapter in Maine archaeology. *Maine Archaeological Society Bulletin*. 22(1). pg. 17-24. W.

Spiess, Arthur E. (1985). Wild Maine and the rusticating scientist: A history of anthropological archaeology in Maine. *Man in the Northeast*. 30. pg. 101-129.

Spiess, Arthur E. (1990). Deer tooth sectioning, eruption, and seasonality of deer hunting in prehistoric Maine. *Man in the Northeast.*39. pg. 29-44.

Spiess, Arthur E. (2004) The Hassen Collection, Otter Creek Points, and the Archaic on the Kennebec River near Augusta. *Maine Archaeology Society Bulletin.* 44(1). pg. 1-14. IS.

Spiess, Arthur E. (September 1983). The evergreens: 5000 years in interior northwest Maine. *Maine Archaeology Society Bulletin.* 23(1). pg. 9-26.

Spiess, Arthur E., Bourque, B. and Cox, S. (1983). Cultural complexity in Maritime cultures: Evidence from Penobscot Bay, Maine. In: *The evolution of Maritime cultures on the northeast and the northwest coasts of North America.* Nash, R.J. Ed., Department of Archaeology Publication 11, Simon Fraser University. pg. 91-108.

Spiess, Arthur E. and Hedden, Mark. (1983). *Kidder Point and Sears Island in prehistory.* Occasional Publications in Maine Archaeology 3. Maine Historic Preservation Commission, Augusta, ME.

Spiess, Arthur E. and Lewis, Robert A. (2001). *The Turner farm fauna: five thousand years of hunting and fishing in Penobscot bay, Maine.* Occasional Publications in Maine Archaeology No. 11. Maine Archaeological Society and Historic Preservation Commission, Augusta, ME.

Spiess, Arthur E. and Wilson, Deborah B. (1987). Michaud: A Paleoindian site in the New England - Maritimes region. *Occasional Publications in Maine Archaeology.* 6. Maine Historical Preservation Commission and the Maine Archaeological Society, Augusta, ME.

Spotted Elk, Molly. (2002). *Katahdin: Wigwam's tales of the Abnaki tribe.* Maine Folklife Center, Orono, ME. IS.

- Molly Spotted Elk's real name was Mary Alice Nelson. This text was edited by Pauleena MacDougall. In addition to tales and legends, it contains a Penobscot language dictionary.

Starbird, Charles M. (1928). *The Indians of the Androscoggin Valley.* Lewiston Journal Printshop, Lewiston, ME.

Steele, Ian K. (1990) *Betrayals: Fort William Henry and the massacre.* Oxford University Press, New York, NY.

Stirling, Matthew W. (1955). *Indians of the Americas: A color-illustrated record.* National Geographic Society, Washington, DC. IS.

Stoutenburgh, John, Jr. (1960). *Dictionary of the American Indian.* Philosophical Library, New York, NY. IS.

Sullivan, James. (1804). The history of the Penobscot Indians. *Massachusetts Historical Society Collections.* 9. pg. 207-232.

Sullivan, Lawrence E., Ed. (1987). *Native American religions: North America.* Macmillan Publishing Company, NY, NY. IS.

Swanton, John R. (1952). *The Indian tribes of North America.* Bureau of American Ethnology, Bulletin 145, Government Printing Office, Washington, DC.

- "In the 17th century their chief, known to the whites as Bashaba, seems to have extended his authority, probably his moral authority only, over the tribes to the westward as far as the Merrimac. ...Bashaba, or Bessebas, became the center of a myth among the whites in which he was elevated to the dignity of a local King or emperor." (pg. 16-17).

Sylvester, Herbert Milton. (1910). *Indian Wars of New England.* W.B. Clarke Company, Boston, MA.

Thayer, Henry O. (1899). A page of Indian history. *Maine Historical Society Collections 10.* Series 2. The Thurston Print, Portland, ME. pg. 81-103.

Thomas, Peter A. (Fall 1981). The fur trade, Indian land and the need to define adequate environmental parameters. *Ethnohistory.* 28(4). pg. 359-378. IS.

Thornton, J. Wingate. (1857). Ancient Pemaquid. *Maine Historical Society Collections 5.* Series 1. Brown Thurston, Printer, Portland. pg. 139-305.

Trigger, Bruce G. (1987). Introduction to papers on the beginnings of the fur trade. *Man in the Northeast.* 33. pg. 27-30.

Trumbull, James Hammond. (1880). The Indian tongue and its literature. In: Winsor, Justin, Ed. *Memorial history of Boston, 1630-1880.* 4 vols. Boston. MA. IS.

Tuck, James A. (1976). *Ancient people of Port au Choix.* Institute of Social and Economic Research, Memorial University, St. John's, NFLD.

Underhill, Ruth M. (1971). *Red Man's America*. University of Chicago Press, Chicago, IL.

Vaughan, Alden T. (1965). *New England frontier: Puritans and Indians 1620-1675*. Little, Brown, and Co., Boston, MA. IS.

Venables, Robert W. (2004). *American Indian history: Conquest of a continent, 1492-1783*. Volume 1. Clear Light Publishing, Santa Fe, NM.

Venables, Robert W. (2004). *American Indian history: Confrontation, adaptation & assimilation, 1783 - present*. Volume 2. Clear Light Publishing, Santa Fe, NM.

Vetromile, Eugene. (1859). The Abnaki Indians. *Collections of the Maine Historical Society*. Vol. VI. pg. 203-228.

Vetromile, Eugene. (1866). *The Abnakis and their history, or, Historical notices on the aborigines of Acadia*. J.B. Kirker, New York, NY.

Von Lonkhuyzen, Harold W. (1989). A reappraisal of the praying Indians: Acculturation, conversion, and identity at Natick, Massachusetts, 1646-1730. *New England Quarterly*. 62. pg. 396-428.

Voorhis, P. (1982). Grammatical notes on the Wawenock language. *Kansas Working Papers in Linguistics Volume 7 Studies in Native American Languages*. University of Kansas, Lawrence, KS. W.

Warhus, Mark. (1997). *Another America: Native American maps and the history of our land*. St. Martin's Press, New York, NY.

Waters, Joseph H. (1962). Animals used as food by Late Archaic and Woodland cultural groups in New England. *Science*. 137(3526). pg. 283-284. X.

- "Failure of Late Archaic people at sites studied to use mollusks in quantity as food may have been determined by cultural barriers, and not by lack of availability." (pg. 283).

Westervelt, Francis A. (1916). The final century of the wampum industry in Bergen County, New Jersey. *Papers and proceedings*. Bergen County Historical Society, NJ. Reprinted in 1924.

Whipple, Chandler. 1972). *First encounter: The Indian and the white man in New England*. The Berkshire Traveller Press, Stockbridge, MA. IS.

Whitehead, Ruth Holmes. (1980). *Elitekey: Micmac material culture from 1600 A.D. to the present.* The Nova Scotia Museum, Halifax, Canada. IS.

Whitney, Seth Harding. (1887). *The Kennebec Valley: This work is devoted to the early history of the valley; also relating many incidents and adventures of the early settlers; including a brief sketch of the Kennebec Indian.* Sprague, Burleigh & Flynt, printers to the state, Augusta, ME. Reprinted in 1989 by the Upper Kennebec Valley Chamber of Commerce.

- Whitney notes a Bashebas as living at the south end of Swan Island in the Kennebec River at Dresden. Swan Island was an ancient Canibas village site and is noted by various historians as the ancestral homeland of the Canibas.

Wiggins, John H. (September 27, 1967). Norumbega, the lost empire of New England. *Ellsworth American*, Ellsworth, ME.

Willey, G. and Sabloff, J. (1974). *A history of American archaeology.* Thames and Hudson, London, England.

Williams, Lorraine E. and Flinn, Karen A. (1990). *Trade wampum, New Jersey to the Plains.* New Jersey State Museum, Trenton, NJ. IS.

Willoughby, Charles C. (1890-92). *Indian antiquities of the Kennebec Valley.* Reprinted in 1980 by the Maine Historic Preservation Commission, Augusta, ME. IS.

- Introduction and text notes by Arthur E. Spiess. A reproduction of the original handwritten text with Willoughby's exquisite hand colored drawings of prehistoric tools and artifacts, which were collected at sites near Fort Popham as well as at Riverside on the east bank of the Kennebec River just north of Augusta. This obscure text, which wasn't published until 1980, played a major role in advancing Willoughby's career in archaeology.

Willoughby, Charles C. (1898). Prehistoric burial places in Maine. *Archaeological and Ethnological Papers of the Peabody Museum.* 1(6). pg. 388-436. Reprinted in 1971.

Willoughby, Charles C. (1901). Prehistoric workshops at Mt. Kineo, Maine. *American Naturalist.* 35. pg. 213-219. Willoughby, Charles C. (1906). Homes and gardens of New England Indians. *American Anthropologist.* 8. pg. 116.

- Champlain "...describes Nauset Harbor as three or four leagues in circuit, 'entirely surrounded by little houses around each one of which there was as much land as the occupant needed for his support.'" (pg. 129).
- "The habitations of the New England Indians were of three general types -- the round house, the long house, and the conical house. The first two forms occurred throughout this area.

The conical house seems to have been more common in Maine than in other sections of New England, where if used at all it was probably employed as a temporary shelter only." (pg. 115).

- A nifty description of the gardens and homes of coastal New England, as observed by the early commentators.

Willoughby, Charles B. The adze and the ungrooved axe of the New England Indians. *American Anthropologist.* 9. pg. 296-306.

Wilson, Deborah B. (1998). *The Indiantown Island archaeological project report.* Boothbay Region Land Trust, Inc., Boothbay Harbor, ME.

Wilson, Charles B. (1883). Indian relics and encampments in Maine. *American Antiquarian and Oriental Journal.* 5. pg. 181-183.

Wilson, Richard G., Ed. (1987). *Rooted like the ash trees: New England Indians and the land.* Eagle Wing Press, Inc., Naugatuck, CT.

Winthrop, John. (1734). *Selections from an ancient catalogue of objects of natural history.* Reprinted in 1844, New Haven, CT.

Woodward, Grace Steele. (1963). *The Cherokees.* University of Oklahoma Press, Norman, OK. IS.

Woolfolk, John. (December 2001). Corn: The plant that made America possible. *Muzzleblasts.* 63(4). pg. 33-35.

Yesner, David. (1980). Archaeology of Casco Bay: A preliminary report. *Maine Archaeological Society Bulletin.* 20. pg. 60-74. W.

Young, Arthur H. (1965). The Pemaquid dig. *Maine Archaeological Society Bulletin.* 4. pg. 1-6.

Youngken, Heber H. (1925). The drugs of the North American Indians. *American Journal of Pharmacy.* 97(3). pg. 158-185.

Appendix L

Native American Special Topics

Damariscotta Shell Middens

The Damariscotta oyster shell heaps as well as the hundreds of other clam shell heaps located in the estuaries between the Kennebec and Penobscot rivers document the existence of thriving communities of Native Americans in coastal Maine. While this area was the dominion of the Wawenoc Indians, the numerous trails leading from the Norumbega back country to these coastal sites indicate that these were shared resources used on a seasonal basis by other tribes such as the Kennebecs and Penobscots, who in turn would share their resources such as the Kenduskeag alewife run with the Wawenocs and other tribes. The following list represents a compilation of all the articles and annotations in the Museum files on this subject. Additional citations are welcomed.

Allison, Roland. (1964). Shell heaps around Deer Island. *Maine Archaeological Society Bulletin*. 2. pg. 3-5.

Backman, Dave. (1996). The Lady Slipper Midden Site (14.31). *Maine Archaeological Society Bulletin*. 36(1). pg. 1-16.

Berry, George S. (1898). The great shell mounds of Damariscotta. *New England Magazine*. 19. pg. 178-188.

Castner, Harold W. (1948). *The prehistoric oyster shell heaps of the Damariscotta River*. Damariscotta, ME.

Ceci, L. (1984). Shell midden deposits as coastal resources. *World Archaeology*. 16. pg. 62-74.

Chadbourne, H.P. (1859). Oyster shell deposit in Damariscotta. *Maine Historical Society Collections*. 6(1). pg. 345-351.

Cushman, David. (January 27, 1864). *Clam shell deposits*. col. 110, box 3c/35, manuscripts collection, Maine Historical Society, Portland, ME.

Cushman, David Quimby. (1882). *The history of ancient Sheepscot and Newcastle, including early Pemaquid, Damariscotta, and other contiguous places, from the earliest discovery to the present time; together with the genealogy of more than four hundred families*. E. Upton & Son, Printers, Bath, ME.

- A most elegant history of the ancient Sheepscot.
- On clam shell deposits, Cushman notes "There is one of them on what is called the Hawthorne farm in the town of Cushing, once owned by Mr. Isaac Burton. It is a peninsula extending Southward into the St. George's river about ten miles... Here the Indians had their encampment, raised their corn, and continued to live through untold generations. The clam shell deposit was near the bank, helped to form the bank, and was from one to eight or ten feet deep. The whole deposit was about three rods wide and fourteen rods long. It is the accumulation of ages. ...It makes capital soil; and the seed which is cast there, whether it be corn, oats, potatoes or turnips, is sure to produce a plentiful crop. I have never seen better. It is the richest, surest, best part of the farm, by far. The river fogs moisten the crops in summer, and the influence of the salt water keeps back the frosts in autumn. The crop is as certain as anything can be." (pg. 310-311).
- "Here they spent their winters, and when the cod and whale fishery could not be pursued, they resorted to the clam banks for food. These never failed them. In the spring they went up river and caught salmon and shad, and at other seasons of the year they pursued the game..." (pg. 311).
- "In the town of Bremen, on a farm owned by Mr. Jacob Keene is another of these clam shell deposits. It is not so extensive as that in Cushing, yet it is near the water, in a fine, sunny, warm place, at the edge of the river looking Southward, near a spring of water, and defended in the rear by rising grounds and dense forests. ...Excellent corn grew there in the summer of 1863." (pg. 312).
- "On the upper end of Loud's Island, formerly Muscongus Island, is found another of these beds of clam shells. It was once undoubtedly quite extensive; but the most of the bank containing it, has been washed away by the heavy seas that roll in, during Southeasterly storms, from the broad Atlantic." (pg. 321).
- "The spot chosen for encampment was similar to the others described;--on the bank, and near the mouth, of a river; never in the interior; with fresh water at hand, and an easy water communication in different directions. The spot was level and sunny, looking Southward, and defended from the cold raw winds which swept down from the interior. The clam banks were near." (pg. 313).
- "Oyster shell deposit in Newcastle. ...On that rich and beautiful peninsula, was their encampment. Here they lived, and died, and were buried. All the marks of savage life found at clam shell deposits are found here. In this place they cooked and eat their oysters; and the shells were carried out and deposited in a precisely similar manner that the Indians did the clam shells at the mouths of the various rivers. But where did they get their oysters? In the stream that ran by their place of settlement in the large bay above and in Oyster Creek which enters into this bay on the eastern side. Here they used to be found in abundance, but when the mills were put upon the river, which was done at an early period of the settlement, they were killed out. An occasional one is now found; and Captain Samuel Glidden who was born upon this point, and till within a short time (1852, when this was written) owned and resided here, has told me that within the period of his remembrance a bushel of oysters have been taken out of this creek in a single tide. ...The chief deposit is at the Eastern point on the bank of the river and opening into the bay above, and on the Northern point upon the bay, and opposite to the island where was their place of interment." (pg. 313-314).

- "It is supposed by many that in this vicinity was the lost 'city of New England' called Norumbega, or the ancient city of Arumpeag which is thought to mean the place of men. And on an island in the beautiful bay above, traditions says, was the place where they used to bury their dead." (pg. 315).
- "When the settlers first came to these parts, vessels used to come from the Westward to dig for oysters and carry them away and they found it a profitable business. But as soon as the thick deposit of saw dust which constantly came down from the mills situated above that the English erected there, began to accumulate on the bottom, and sunken slabs and other lumber increased, the breathing holes of the oysters were stopped, their sustenance was cut off and they perished." (pg. 315).
- There is extensive commentary on the Indian cemetery at the northern tip of Loud's Island, now washed away. "The specimens carried away have been almost endless, and some are found there at the present time. The sea has also done its part in carrying away these relics of the dead. About twenty acres have been washed away within the memory of man, and with it the entire cemetery of these sons of the forest." (pg. 317).
- See the other annotations for this text in the Ancient Pemaquid bibliography.

Goldthwait, Richard P. (1935). The Damariscotta shell heaps and coastal stability. *American Journal of Science*. Series 5. 30. pg. 1-13.

Johnson, F. (1935). *Excavations in the Glidden shell heap on the Damariscotta River, Newcastle, Maine*. Unpublished manuscript. R. S. Peabody Foundation, Andover, MA.

Loomis, G.F. and Young, D.B. (1912). On the shell heaps of Maine. *American Journal of Science*. 34. pg. 17-42.

- "*...it must be then deduced that the original object, of coming to the sea shore, was not clams but rather fishing,* and possibly hunting, but especially fishing." (pg. 20).
- "...Sawyer's Island is characterized by the tremendous abundance of deer remains, so that it would appear that the hunting must have rivalled the fishing, as doubtless this island was then a part of the mainland." (pg. 20).
- "...and staple food, on this Island [Sawyer] was the great auk, the bones of which occurred in large numbers, as did those also of many other birds, many of which we have not been able to identify." (pg. 21).
- "That they were spring camps is also confirmed by the condition of the horns on the crania of the male deer, which were found in the heap." (pg. 22).
- "Lastly these heaps are also testimony to the sinking land, for the camps were beyond doubt originally well above the tide's reach." (pg. 22).
- Large numbers of deer jaw bones were recovered from Sawyer's Island. (Table, pg. 24).
- "The absence of individuals with partly developed or perfect antlers indicates, further, that the camps were simply spring camps, which also coincides with the best fishing season, and is the evidence that these heaps were made during periodic visits to the sites." (pg. 25).

Mercer, Henry C. (1897). An exploration of aboriginal shell heaps revealing traces of cannibalism on the York River, Maine. *Publications of the University of Pennsylvania, Series in Philology, Literature and Archaeology.* 6. pg. 111-137.

Morse, Edward Sylvester. (1868). Evidence of great antiquity in the shell heaps at Goose Island. *Boston Society of Natural History Proceedings.* 11. pg. 301-302. W.

Moses, T.F. (1878). Shell heaps of Maine. *Proceedings, Central Ohio Scientific Association.* 1. Urbana, OH. pg. 70-76.

Myers, A.C. (1965). *The Damariscotta oyster shell heaps: Some further considerations.* Unpublished senior thesis. Department of Anthropology, Princeton University.

Prentiss, D.W. (1903). Descriptions of an extinct mink from the shell-heaps of the Maine coast. *Proceedings of the U.S. National Museum.* 26. pg. 887-888.

Putnam, Frederick Ward. (1883). Shell heaps on the coast of Maine. *Science.* 1. pg. 319.

Sanger, David and Kellogg, Douglas E. (1983). Preliminary report on sea-level rise in the Damariscotta Estuary, central Maine coast. In: *New England seismotectonic study activities in Maine during fiscal year 1982.* Thompson, Woodrow S. and Kelley, Joseph T. Eds. Maine Geological Survey, Augusta, ME. pg. 137-145.

Sanger, David and Sanger, Mary Jo (Elson). (1986). Boom and bust on the river: The story of the Damariscotta oyster shell heaps. *Archaeology of Eastern North America.* 14. pg. 65-78.

- "As sea-levels rose throughout the Holocene, head of tide pushed upstream and over bedrock sills in the Damariscotta River. Oysters followed, and found a fertile niche that was basically predator free. Some time around 2400 B.P. Native Americans discovered the oysters, and by 1500 B.P. had built shell middens up to 30 ft (9 m) high. Increasing sea-level rise resulted in higher salinity levels, and eventually predators such as oyster drills joined forces with the Native Americans. Shortly thereafter the oysters were annihilated and the humans moved on, seeking more fertile ecosystems." (pg. 65).
- "We construct a series of events that attests to a heavy dependency on a single species, such that when the species was eliminated, the Native Americans abandoned the area." (pg. 65).
- "In the nineteenth century, few archeological sites in northeastern North America attracted as much attention as did two large oyster shell heaps and numerous lesser ones along the Damariscotta River in Maine." (pg. l65).
- "Native American oysters no longer flourish in the Damariscotta River, and likely did not in numbers for several centuries." (pg. 67).
- "All of these discussions related to the cultural significance of the oyster shell middens were severely limited by the poorly developed state of knowledge of regional prehistory. Even in

1965, Myers had to refer to outdated concepts in place since the 1930s, especially as reviewed by Willoughby (1935)." (pg. 69).

- "Local folklore also claimed that the sites were major Native American settlements occupied in the 17th century (Castner 1954), despite the total absence of any evidence to support the assertion." (pg. 69).
- "Gamage's notes and sections, ...led to speculation about the length of time that the site was used, and the presence of three distinct periods of occupation. A recent analysis of the Whaleback collection at the Peabody Museum indicated a rather different interpretation." (pg. 70).
- "The ceramics constitute the bulk of the diagnostic artifacts." (pg. 70).
- "The analysis of the two largest middens, Glidden and Whaleback, suggests that the middens began to accumulate somewhere around 2400 B.P. and were probably abandoned before 1000 B.P., or long before Europeans colonized the area in the 17th century. The period of greatest utilization, based on the ceramics, would be from about 2200 to 1500 B.P. It should be noted that some later occupation along the banks of the Damariscotta is indicated by the presence in a local collection of very late prehistoric to Contact period artifacts from a small midden downstream of the Glidden site. Significantly, the collector told Sanger that he found the artifacts in a clam midden context overlying an oyster midden." (pg. 72).
- "Downstream of the study area, recent surveys by the University of Maine have documented nearly 200 clam shell middens in the estuaries of the Damariscotta and the adjacent Sheepscot rivers, many of them with Late Ceramic period (post-1200 B.P.) occupations." (pg. 76).

Sewall, Rufus King. (1895). *Ancient voyages to the western continent: Three phases of history on the coast of Maine*. The Knickerbocker Press, NY, NY. IS.

- More quotations and annotations on this text can be found in the Ancient Pemaquid information file: The First Colonial Dominion of Maine and in the essay on Sylvanus Davis.
- The following quotation is taken from pages 24 - 28:

SITE.

Damariscotta river is an inlet of the sea, inland off Monhegan Island, in the County of Lincoln ; an effluent of the tide-waters of Pemaquid, expanded into a shallow bay or basin above the flow of the Salt-water Falls, at the foot of a fifty-foot fresh-water cascade, over which a great lake above, embracing the waters of Muscongus and Damariscotta Lakes rush to reach the salt sea below. The Indians called the site, with its environment, 'Ped-auk-go-wack,' 'place of thunder.'

Popham colonists wrote of this river. They called it 'Ta-mes-cot,' embodying native sounds, descriptive of the food resources of its waters.

The Indian said of it : 'Na-mas-coota' : 'fish water place.' The Penobscots still call it 'Ma-damas-couta,' as Sabattis interprets it : 'Many fish (alewices) water.'

Father Rasle, in *Jesuit Relations,* records 'that during a month fish ascend in such numbers, one could fill fifty thousand barrels a day, could the labor be endured -- the fish crowding one upon another, a foot deep.'

DEPOSIT OF SHELLS

They are heaped chiefly in marginal aggregation, along the shores of the outlet of the basin described, near the 'Salt-water Falls,' so called at the meeting of the bay above, with the tide waters below, on both shores.

The shells are chiefly of the oyster in mature condition, and of very large size. Gilbert of the Popham Colony wrote home in 1607, 'their men found oysters there, nine inches long, and heard of others twice as big.' The nine-inch oyster was a shell-fish of the river, 'Ta-mes-cot,' and the bigger ones in a river near on the other side, *i.e.*, the Sheepscott, where big fat fellows still grow.

The shells are horizontally disposed, shell on shell, ends to the shore. They are seldom found in pairs, but laying on the side instead of on edge, shell within shell.

There is a central heap on the east shore, back of high-water mark, left as if rolled in a mighty wave, thirty odd feet deep, oval shaped, terraced with smaller heaps, from five to fifteen feet diameter, as seen in 1859. This ridge has since been dug over for grinding up the shells into hen-food. High-water mark was found to be the base-line of the shell heaps on both shores of the outlet. On the west, the shells are piled from the water-line at a sharp angle, twenty-five to thirty feet, showing nearly a vertical fall, the shells horizontally disposed, shell lying in shell, layer on layer, no shells mated, quite perfect in condition.

This deposit is interleaved with dark, rich vegetable mould, indicating lapse of periods of time intervening, sufficient to make a few inches of soil.

An arched tunnel for twenty-five feet by three feet in diameter had been cut into the deposit on the west shore side, and disclosed only shells in different stages of decay, bleached on the surface, cream colored and friable beneath. Many shell mounds are distributed over the entire shell-covered area of the peninsula of the west shore of the outlet of the bay or basin, at the foot of the great falls of 'Ped-auk-go-wack.'

'The great heaps are made up of the oyster, exclusively. The shells are of extraordinary size, and belong to a variety not much found on this coast, the long-necked species. The heaps are immense in size, covering acres.'

GEOLOGICAL MEASURE.

These shell deposits were measured by Dr. Jackson in 1838 for his geological survey of Maine, and his official report makes them 'one hundred and eight rods long by eighty to one hundred wide, and twenty-five or six feet deep ; making not less than forty-four million, nine hundred and six thousand cubic feet.'

RELICS, INDUSTRIAL AND KITCHEN.

In and throughout these deposits are bits of charcoal, bones of fish and animals, and of the human frame ; stone hatchets, chisels, and deep-sea sinkers ; bone stilettos, and tools of art and the chase ; pottery, sometimes ornamented ; and even lumps of clay...

Smith, Walter B. (1929). *The Jones Cove shell-heap at West Gouldsboro, Maine.* Bulletin I, The Robert Abbe Museum, Bar Harbor, ME.

- Out of print.

Snow, D.R. (1972). Rising sea level and prehistoric cultural ecology in northern New England. *American Antiquity.* 37(2). pg. 211-222.

- This article contains extensive discussion of the shell middens along the Maine coast including those at the Damariscotta estuary.
- "The earliest date from the Damariscotta midden indicates that a shift toward the exploitation of shellfish along the Maine coast was underway by 1900±250 radiocarbon years: A.D. 50 (Snow 1969:3). Bourque (1971) infers a similar beginning date for midden accumulation at his sites on Deer Isle on the basis of ceramic attributes cross-dated with sherds of known age from New Brunswick and New York. It is convenient for the present to use A.D. 1 as the probable beginning of shellfish exploitation." (pg. 212).
- "Most middens are made up almost exclusively of the common clam; in a few instances, they are composed almost entirely of quahog shells. It is not clear which of these represent early 'pre-clam' middens, and which (if any) are early historic accumulations that resulted from the florescence of wampum manufacture from quahog shells. Finally, there are huge middens in 1 locality that are made up almost entirely of oyster shells." (pg. 214).
- "The largest heap, Whaleback, was removed for commercial purposes in the 1880's. Whaleback was originally 347 ft long, 123 ft wide, and 16 ft thick at the center." (pg. 214).

Varney, Lloyd H. (1971). A Blue Hill Bay coastal midden site. *Maine Archaeology Society Bulletin.* 2(1). pg. 14-32.

Wyman, Jeffries. (1867). An account of some of the kjœkkenmœddings, or shell-heaps, in Maine and Massachusetts. Essex Institute Press, Salem, MA.

The Indian Pandemic of 1617-1619

Ashburn, Percy M. (1947). *The ranks of death: A medical history of the conquest of America.* Ashburn, Frank D., Ed. NY, NY.

Cook, Sherburne F. (1973). Interracial warfare and population decline among the New England Indians. *Ethnohistory*. 20(1). pg. 1-24. X.

- "The tremendous decline in numbers suffered by the North American Indians in the early days of European colonization may be ascribed to a number of factors. Among these is disease introduced by the whites, which accounted certainly for more than half the population loss. Also of outstanding significance was warfare." (pg. 1).
- "There were three periods of intense military effort, the Pequot War, 1634, the Dutch War, 1643, and King Philip's War, 1675-1676. The number of Indians killed on the field of battle is estimated as 2,950, or close to eight percent of the total population loss suffered by the tribes concerned during the period from 1620 to 1750." (pg. 1).
- "The second serious conflict involved the inhabitants of the central Maine coast, an Algonkian group known as the Etechemin. Gorges (1837) places a great war just prior to 1616-1618: '...for that war had consumed the Bashaba and most of the great sagamores ... and those that remained were sore afflicted with the plague (of 1617) so that the country was in a manner left void of inhabitants.'" (pg. 2).
- "Nevertheless, as Williamson (1839) pointed out, the great Sagamore, or Bashaba, held in dominion the valleys of the Penobscot, Pemaquid, Kennebec, and Saco. He was undoubtedly killed, together with most of his subordinate chiefs, the villages were destroyed, and the survivors subject to famine. All this happened, according to Gorges, prior to the plague which finished them off, and indicates extraordinary devastation. It will be noted that we have here no exact estimates of the number of lives lost. On the other hand, the evidence is strong that there was almost total destruction." (pg. 3).

Cook, S.F. (1973). The significance of disease in the extinction of the New England Indians. *Human Biology*. 45. pg. 485-508.

Crosby, Alfred W., Jr. (1972). *The Columbian exchange: Biological and cultural consequences of 1492*. Greenwood Press, Westport, CT. IS.

Crosby, A.W. (April 1976). Virgin soil epidemics as a factor in the aboriginal depopulation in America. *William and Mary Quarterly*. 23(2). pg. 289-299. IS.

- "Virgin soil epidemics are those in which the populations at risk have had no previous contact with the diseases that strike them and are therefore immunologically almost defenseless." (pg. 289).
- "...many of the most important events of aboriginal history in British America occurred beyond the range of direct observation by literate witnesses." (pg. 290).

Dobyns, Henry F. (1966). Estimating aboriginal American population: An appraisal of techniques with a new hemispheric estimate. *Current Anthropology*. VII. pg. 395-449.

Dobyns, Henry F. (1983). *Their number became thinned*. University of Tennessee Press, Knoxville, TN.

L-8

Hoornbeek, Billee. (1976-1977). An investigation into the cause or causes of the epidemic which decimated the Indian population of New England 1616-1619. *New Hampshire Archaeologist*. 19(7). pg. 35-46.

Jacobs, Wilbur R. (1974). The tip of an iceberg: Pre-Columbian Indian demography and some implications for revisionism. *William and Mary Quarterly*. 3rd ser. XXXI. pg. 123-132.

Malone, Patrick M. (1991). *The skulking way of war: Technology and tactics among the Indians of southern New England, 160 - 1677*. Madison Books, Lanham, MD.

Massachusetts Historical Society. (1837). Gorges' brief narration. *Massachusetts Historical Society Collections 6*. Third Series. American Stationers' Company, Boston, MA.

- "See Chapter 10, pg. 57, for information on the plague of 1616-1620." (Ray, *The Indians of Maine*, pg. 41).

Miller, Virginia P. (Spring 1976). Aboriginal Micmac population: A review of the evidence. *Ethnohistory*. 23(2). pg. 117-127. IS.

- See the annotations in the Native Americans Principal bibliography.

Snow, Dean R. and Lanphear, Kim M. (1988). European contact and Indian depopulation in the northeast: The timing of the first epidemics. *Ethnohistory*. 35(1). pg. 15-33. X.

- "The efforts of Dobyns (1966, 1983) notwithstanding, there is still little certain knowledge about pre-1500 population levels." (pg. 15).
- "While the 1616 epidemic was the first to appear in the Northeast, the sources clearly indicate that it did not spread far into the interior. The first epidemic to reach the interior was probably the 1633 smallpox epidemic." (pg. 23).
- "We conclude that it was the introduction of susceptible and possibly infected children along with the shortened transatlantic crossing that determined the timing of the first smallpox epidemics in the Northeast." (pg. 28).
- "It is unnecessary to assume a series of pandemics in the Eastern Woodlands during the sixteenth century. Indeed, given the known effects of the epidemics in the Northeast, the assumption of earlier equally severe epidemics would necessarily entail the projection of unrealistically high population levels for 1520." (pg. 28).

Spiess, Arthur E. and Spiess, Bruce D. (1987). New England pandemic of 1616-1622: Cause and archaeological implication. *Man in the Northeast*. 34. pg. 71-83. IS.

- "Between 1616 and 1622 a virulent pandemic spread through coastal Massachusetts, New Hampshire, and southern Maine. Local mortality ranged close to 100%, causing dramatic social change. Symptoms of the diseases reported by European explorers implicate hepatic failure. The causative agent may have been a hepatitis virus. ...The current lack of archaeological visibility of the catastrophe should be considered by research archaeologists." (pg. 71).

Starna, William A. (1992). The biological encounter: Disease and the ideological domain. *The American Indian Quarterly*. 16(4). pg. 511-519. X.

Williams, H.V. (1909). The epidemic of the Indians of New England 1616-1620, with remarks on Native American infections. *Johns Hopkins Hospital Bulletin*. 20. pg. 340-349.

Pathways and Canoe Routes of Native Americans in New England

Cook, David S. (1985). *Indian canoe routes of Maine*. Covered Bridge Press, North Attleborough, MA. IS.

- Cook, a Maine archaeologist and teacher, has spent a lifetime canoeing through the back woods of northern Maine. Cook uses Fannie Eckstrom's research, many of them unpublished papers from the Folger Library in Orono, including her unpublished *Indian Trails of Maine* (ca. 1920) as a jumping off point for his description of the canoe routes of Maine.
- "All rivers have places where the fishing is still excellent. On the major canoe routes such a spot is most assuredly an ancient campsite. These places are particularly evident when ascending a river in a canoe. The rapids that today require a portage are the same as they have been for the last few thousand years. Most towns have their old mill dams built over falls where Indians fished. The falls made the fish easy to catch for the Indian, and provided power for the mill wheels of pioneer industry, nuclei for many small towns." (pg. 26).
- "The Indians first burned one side of the log and then dug out the charred wood with stone tools until they had a depression suitable for cooking. Cold water and the meat were put into the hollowed log and red hot rocks were dropped in until the meat was cooked to the broth they loved." (pg. 28).
- "Old beaver ponds were free of obstructions for canoes because the dead wood and stumps had been rotted away by years of flooding. In the old days canoe travelers would break open small dams allow the water to run for an hour or so to fill up a small brook so that their canoes would float. The industrious beavers would repair the hole during the night to save the precious water for their own purposes." (pg. 40).
- "The prehistoric canoe routes of Maine fall into four general categories: major routes, short routes, cut-offs, and neighborhood routes. The major routes were along the great north-south rivers; the Saco, Androscoggin, Kennebec, Penobscot, St. John, and their major tributaries. These routes ended in some important place, such as a large town or tribal center, ...The short routes went over the interconnecting tributaries and allowed direct travel between *watersheds when water levels permitted*. ...The cut-offs were used for safety and convenience and are

characterized by the numerous portage points that have been found on the coastal peninsulas. The ocean is very dangerous for canoes and the carry paths across the long and narrow capes saved the paddlers many miles of dangerous paddling in cold waters and high waves. ...neighborhood routes, were byways through hunting and trapping regions but had poor connections as canoe routes to any other place." (pg. 42-44).

- "The mid-coastal region from the Kennebec to the Penobscot, like the rest of the Maine coast, has many excellent canoe routes. The Eastern, Sheepscot, Damariscotta, Medomac, and St. George Rivers all rise in the area south of Soudabscook Stream, a Sebasticook/Penobscot canoe route. These rivers roughly parallel each other and outlet in the ragged coastal region so popular with tourists today. Many tourists would be surprised to know just how long people have been going there for clams, lobsters, and cool sea breezes." (pg. 55).

- "Coastal canoeing is very dangerous. The rocky shores, strong tides, and sudden storms make canoe travel difficult at best. The Indian canoe travelers sought the safest way and took advantage of the numerous options offered by the various rivers and lakes. These are situated in such a way as to afford interior canoe routes paralleling the coast and traversing good hunting terrain with no exposure to the sea. The many islands of the coast provide protected inside passages for canoe travelers while sheltering them from the rough conditions in the Gulf of Maine." (pg. 56).

- "At places like Pemaquid Point, open for miles to the sea, the coast was impossible for canoes. To avoid this dangerous stretch the Indians had a cut-off from the Damariscotta River to New Harbor, and another to Round Pond and no doubt another higher up to Broad Sound." (pg. 56).

- "The Indians had an inside route from the blue hills of Camden east to Belfast. On the east side of Penobscot Bay the coastal rivers provided interior canoe routes all the way to Lubec in extreme eastern Maine." (pg. 56).

- "The Aroostook River, important for its many canoe routes, also runs very close to important outcroppings of 'Munsungun cherts,' that the native people valued for making stone tools." (pg. 93).

- "These Munsungun cherts, like the felsite of Mount Kineo, have acted as a magnet drawing people into the Munsungun Lake region since the end of the last Ice Age. At some point in the distant past, they began coming by canoe. A careful study of the canoe routes and the distribution of Munsungun chert in archaeological collections may yield important insights about canoes and ancient trade in this material." (pg. 93).

- For more comments on this book see the essay on pathways and canoe routes of Native Americans in the Norumbega Reconsidered and the Wawenoc Diaspora Section.

Groening, Tom. (September 23, 2000) Augusta road less traveled. *Bangor Daily News*. pg. B3.

Hallett, Leaman F. (April 1956). Indian trails and their importance to the early colonists. *Bulletin of Massachusetts Archaeological Society*. XVI. pg. 41-46. X.

- "Thomas Purchas came to Maine from England about the year 1626, landing at Saco. From the eastern part of Casco Bay there was an Indian thoroughfare that led to the falls of the

Penobscot in what is now the town of Brunswick. Skirting the shores of Casco Bay and journeying by this route, Purchas reached the falls and found a very favorable location for trade with the Indians as they descended the river in passing from their villages to the mouth of the Sagadahoc, or to the camping grounds on the shores or islands of Casco Bay. In establishing himself at the falls he secured the Indian trade of the Androscoggin in the same way as the Pilgrims of Plymouth, in erecting their trading house at Cushenoc, now Augusta, secured the Indian trade of the Kennebec." (pg. 41-42).

- "The Connecticut path from Boston to Windsor, Hartford and Weathersfield saw generations of colonists pass along the way before it widened for cart or coach travel. For a long period the ancient Indian trail remained a path, although it admitted the passage of footmen, horsemen and driven cattle. It played a major part in the establishment of the postal system in this country. The first colonial post route was started in 1672 between New York and Boston by way of Hartford, and the post rider of that day traveled over the old Indian trails between these points. The many lakes and ponds along its course were bountifully supplied with fish, and an occasional Indian village offered its crude hospitality to the early settlers. Wilderness homes sprang up at favored places long before towns were settled. Then, as now, the ninety-five miles to Windsor and the one hundred and two miles to Hartford pay tribute to the Indian facility in choice of terrain." (pg. 44).

Haviland, William A. (2005). A safe passage to the sea: An ancient canoe route at Deer Isle, Maine. *Maine Archaeological Society Bulletin*. 45(1). pg. 25-30. IS.

Marlowe, George Francis. (1942). *The old bay paths: Their villages and byways and their stories*. Hastings House, Publishers, NY, NY. IS.

Stark, William. (1988). *Indian trails and superhighways*. American Canal and Transportation Center, York, PA.

Wallace, Paul A. W. (1965). *Indian paths of Pennsylvania*. Harrisburg, PA.

Williamson, Joseph. (1859). Castine and the old coins found there. *Collections of the Maine Historical Society*. Volume VI. pg. 105-126.

- "It was not on the peninsula that these coins were found, nor within the limits of the town of Castine, but on the banks or shore of the Bagaduce River, about six miles from the site of Castin's fort, in the town of Penobscot. This river, at its mouth, forms the harbor of Castine, and is navigable for small vessels for several miles above the village. At about six miles above, is a point called 'Johnson's Narrows,' or 'Second Narrows,' ...A path leads across the point, and from the adaptation of the shore as a landing place, it is probable that the usual passage from Biguatus to Mt. Desert, was up this river as far as the narrows. Near the narrows the coins were discovered. ...some twenty-five yards from the shore, and in the direct line of a beaten track through the bushes, which has been used as a path across the point for a time beyond the remembrance of the oldest inhabitants. At the termination of this path on the shore, is an indentation or landing place, well adapted for canoes, and the natural features and facilities of the spot are confirmatory of a tradition that one of the Indian routes from the peninsula to Mount Desert and Frenchman's Bay was up the Bagaduce river, and from thence across to Bluehill Bay." (pg. 114-115).

Petroglyphs in Maine

The petroglyphs of Maine constitute one of the most interesting archaeological fragments that remain as testament to the thriving Native American communities who once inhabited the shores and rivers of coastal and inland Maine. This section of The Davistown Museum bibliography is dedicated to the memory of Joan Haskell Brack (1939-1999), a distant descendant of Native Americans, who was interested in and helped facilitate the documentation of the petroglyphs on her property at Holmes Point in Machias Bay. The Native American displays in The Davistown Museum are also dedicated to the memory of Joan. We hope to expand this special topic bibliography as time allows and provide a complete listing of all the citations on this topic. The following is a preliminary listing.

Hedden, Mark H. (1983-1987). *Maine Archaeological Society Bulletin.*

- The following articles in the *Maine Archaeological Society Bulletin* are all on petroglyphs. References courtesy of Ray and Faulkner.
    - Vol. 23, no. 1 (Spring 1983)
    - Vol. 23, no. 2 (Fall 1983)
    - Vol. 24, no. 1 (Spring 1984) "Sexuality in Maine Petroglyphs"
    - Vol. 24, no. 2 (Fall 1984) "The Form of the Cosmos in the Body of the Shaman"
    - Vol. 25, no. 1 (Spring 1985) "Petroglyphs on Hog Island, Machias Bay"
    - Vol. 27, no. 1 (Spring 1987)
    - Vol. 27, no. 2 (Fall 1987) "Canoe Figures at Embden and Machiasport."
    - Vol. 31, no. 1 (Spring 1991) "A winged figure incised on a slate pebble."

Hedden, Mark. H. (Spring 1989). Petroglyph evidence for a possible 19th century survival of Algonkian (Passamaquoddy) shamanism in eastern Maine. *Maine Archaeological Society Bulletin.* 29(1). pg. 21-28.

- The article deals with the Elliott site, Grand Lake Stream, Maine. Reference courtesy of Ray and Faulkner.

Hedden, Mark. H. (2002). Contact period petroglyphs in Machias Bay, Maine. *Archaeology of Eastern North America.* 30. pg. 1-20. IS.

Lahti, Eric. (1976). *Oil rubbings of petroglyphs.* Maine Archaeological Society Bulletin 16(1). pg. 30-31.

Lahti, Eric. (1976). *The Machias petroglyphs.* Maine Archaeological Society Bulletin 16(2). pg. 3-6.

Lahti, Eric. (2001). *Goodwill-Hinckley archaeological survey 1996.* Maine Archaeological Society Bulletin 41:1. pg. 25-34.

Mallery, Garrick. (1893). Picture-writing of the American Indians. *Tenth Annual Report of the Bureau of Ethnology to the Secretary of the Smithsonian Institution, 1888-1889 by J. W. Powell, Director.* Government Printing Office, Washington, D.C. Reprinted in 1972 in 2 vols. by Dover Publications, Inc., New York, NY. IS.

Ray, Roger B. (1985). The Machiasport petroglyphs. *Maine Historical Society Quarterly.* 25(1). pg. 22-39.

Ray, Roger B. (1987). The Embden, Maine petroglyphs. *Maine Historical Society Quarterly.* 27(1). pg. 14-23.

Ray, Roger B. (1991). The petroglyphs at Grand Lake Stream, Maine. *North American Archaeologist.* 12(3). pg. 257-268.

Snow, Dean R. (1976). The Solon petroglyphs and eastern Abenaki shamanism. In: *Papers of the Seventh Algonquian Conference.* Cowan, William, Ed., Carleton University Press, Ottawa, Canada. pg. 281-288.

Whitehead, Ruth Holmes. (1992). A new Micmac petroglyph site. *The Occasional.* 13(1). pg. 7-12.

Index

www.ingramcontent.com/pod-product-compliance
Lightning Source LLC
Chambersburg PA
CBHW080509090426
42734CB00015B/3007